One-Track Mind

CW01500537

The song remains the most basic unit of modern pop music. Shaped into being by historical forces—cultural, aesthetic, and technical—the song provides both performer and audience with a world marked off by a short, discrete, and temporally demarcated experience. *One-Track Mind: Capitalism, Technology, and the Art of the Pop Song* brings together 16 writers to weigh in on 16 iconic tracks from the history of modern popular music. Arranged chronologically in order of release of the tracks, and spanning nearly five decades, these essays zigzag across the cultural landscape to present one possible history of pop music. There are detours through psychedelic rock, Afro-pop, Latin pop, glam rock, heavy metal, punk, postpunk, adult contemporary rock, techno, hip-hop, and electro-pop here. More than just deep histories of individual songs, these essays all expand far beyond the track itself to offer exciting and often counterintuitive histories of transformative moments in popular culture. Collectively, they show the undiminished power of the individual pop song, both as distillations of important flashpoints and, in their afterlives, as ghostly echoes that persist undiminished but transform for succeeding generations. Capitalism and its principal good, capital, help us frame these stories, a fact that should surprise no one given the inextricable relationship between art and capitalism established in the twentieth century. At the root, readers will find here a history of pop with unexpected plot twists, colorful protagonists, and fitting denouements.

Asif Siddiqi is Professor of History at Fordham University in New York and specializes in the history of technology, Soviet history, and global histories of science. He has held visiting positions at Harvard University, MIT, Caltech, and the Smithsonian Institution. He received a Guggenheim Fellowship in 2016 and was a visiting scholar at Princeton University's Davis Center for Historical Studies in 2021–22.

Ashgate Popular and Folk Music Series
Series Editors:
Lori Burns, Professor, University of Ottawa, Canada
Justin Williams, Associate Professor of Music, University of Bristol, UK

Popular musicology embraces the field of musicological study that engages with popular forms of music, especially music associated with commerce, entertainment, and leisure activities. The Ashgate Popular and Folk Music Series aims to present the best research in this field. Authors are concerned with criticism and analysis of the music itself, as well as locating musical practices, values, and meanings in cultural context. The focus of the series is on popular music of the twentieth and twenty-first centuries, with a remit to encompass the entirety of the world's popular music.

Critical and analytical tools employed in the study of popular music are being continually developed and refined in the twenty-first century. Perspectives on the transcultural and intercultural uses of popular music have enriched understanding of social context, reception, and subject position. Popular genres as distinct as reggae, township, bhangra, and flamenco are features of a shrinking, transnational world. The series recognizes and addresses the emergence of mixed genres and new global fusions, and utilizes a wide range of theoretical models drawn from anthropology, sociology, psychoanalysis, media studies, semiotics, postcolonial studies, feminism, gender studies, and queer studies.

Studies in Maltese Popular Music
Philip Ciantar

The Music and Noise of the Stooges, 1967–71: Lost in the Future
Michael S. Begnal

The Genesis and Structure of the Hungarian Jazz Diaspora
Ádám Havas

One-Track Mind: Capitalism, Technology, and the Art of the Pop Song
Edited by Asif Siddiqi

For more information about this series, please visit: www.routledge.com/music/series/APFM

One-Track Mind

Capitalism, Technology, and the Art of the Pop Song

Edited by Asif Siddiqi

Routledge
Taylor & Francis Group

LONDON AND NEW YORK

Cover credit: © Getty images

First published 2023
by Routledge
4 Park Square, Milton Park, Abingdon, Oxon OX14 4RN

and by Routledge
605 Third Avenue, New York, NY 10158

Routledge is an imprint of the Taylor & Francis Group, an informa business

British Library Cataloguing-in-Publication Data
A catalogue record for this book is available from the British Library

Library of Congress Cataloging-in-Publication Data
A catalog record has been requested for this book

ISBN: 978-0-367-55372-2 (hbk)
ISBN: 978-0-367-55373-9 (pbk)
ISBN: 978-1-003-09320-6 (ebk)

DOI: 10.4324/9781003093206

Typeset in Times New Roman
by Newgen Publishing UK

Contents

Figures

Contributors

Gina Arnold is a former rock critic. She holds a PhD from Stanford University in Modern Thought and Literature, and teaches rhetoric and writing at the University of San Francisco. She is the author of four books on music and is the co-editor of the *The Oxford Handbook of Punk*.

Christine Caccipuoti has served as a producer and host of the podcast *Footnoting History* since its creation in 2013. Her primary research interests, as showcased through *Footnoting History*, center on the families of France's Emperor Napoleon I and England's King Henry II. Christine coedited *Independent Scholars Meet the World: Expanding Academia beyond the Academy* (University Press of Kansas, 2020) and has contributed entries on Blanche Caldwell Barrow and Jane Manning James to Oxford University Press's *American National Biography*. More information about her can be found at ChristineCaccipuoti.com.

Amy Coddington is an assistant professor of music at Amherst College, where she teaches classes on American popular music. She is working on a book titled *How Hip Hop Became Hit Pop: Rap, Race, and Commercial Radio*, under contract with University of California Press, which explores how rap broke through to a mainstream audience in the 1980s and 1990s through programming on commercial radio stations. She has published related essays in *the Journal of the Society for American Music* and *The Oxford Handbook of Hip Hop Music*.

Gabrielle Cornish is Assistant Professor of Musicology at the University of Miami's Frost School of Music. Her research broadly considers music and everyday life in the Soviet Union. In particular, her monograph-in-progress, *Socialist Noise: Sound and Soviet Modernity after Stalin*, traces the intersections between music, technology, and the politics of socialist modernity during the Cold War. Her research has been supported by the Fulbright Program, the Association for Slavic, East European, and Eurasian Studies, and the American Council for Learned Societies. Her writing has appeared in *the Journal of Musicology* and the *Slavic and East European Journal*, and she has bylines in *Slate*, *The Washington Post*, and *The New York Times*.

Esther Liberman Cuenca is Assistant Professor of History at the University of Houston-Victoria, where she teaches courses on European, American, and world history, as well as classes on the history of popular culture. She has published widely on the topic of medievalism, and most recently on the music of *Game of Thrones* in the journal *Popular Music*. She received her PhD in 2019.

Glenn Hendler is Professor of English and American Studies at Fordham University, where he teaches courses in US literature and culture, sound studies, and cultural theory. He writes on popular and unpopular literature in the nineteenth century, film, television, and contemporary cultural politics. He is author or editor of several books, including the 33 1/3 volume on David Bowie's *Diamond Dogs* (2020), *Public Sentiments: Structures of Feeling in Nineteenth-Century American Literature* (2001), and *Keywords for American Cultural Studies* (third edn., 2020).

Austin McCoy is an assistant professor of history at West Virginia University. His research interests focus on social movements and activism, the carceral state, and hip-hop culture.

George Plasketes is Professor of Media Studies in the School of Communication and Journalism at Auburn University in Alabama. His body of published work includes six books, and essays, journal articles, and book chapters on a variety of music, media, and popular culture subjects: late, great songwriter Warren Zevon; B sides; cover songs; debut albums; Elvis and Presleyterian Culture; *Saturday Night Live* creator Lorne Michaels; baseball pitcher Bill "Spaceman" Lee; the failed television musical drama *Cop Rock*; TaB diet soft drink; the underexposed music of the television series *Northern Exposure*; and the Band's sainthood song "The Weight." A native of Chicago, he is currently chronicling the mid-1960s Chicagoland music scene in *How the Midwest Was Won*, to be published by McFarland Press. He has been married to Julie Grace Plasketes, an artist, since 1982. Their daughter, Anaïs, and son, Rivers, reside in New Orleans and in Brooklyn.

Scott Poulson-Bryant is an assistant professor of African American Studies at the University of Michigan. A cultural historian and critic with areas of specialization in African American popular culture and performance studies, his research has appeared in the *Journal of Popular Music Studies*, *American Studies*, *Palimpsest: A Journal on Women, Gender, and the Black International*, and *Biography: An Interdisciplinary Quarterly*. His journalism has appeared in *The New York Times*, *Rolling Stone*, *The Village Voice*, and other publications, and he was one of the founding editors of *VIBE Magazine*. His books include *HUNG: A Meditation on the Measure of Black Men in America* and *The VIPs: A Novel*, and he is currently finishing a monograph, *Everybody is a Star: Cultural Citizenships and the Glamour of Blackness in 1970s US Popular Culture*.

Helen Reddington is a senior lecturer in music production at the University of East London. Originally a fine art printmaking graduate, she joined a punk band while at Brighton Art College. In the 1980s her bands the Chefs and Helen and the Horns were regulars on BBC's *John Peel Show*. She has been writing on both punk and women musicians and producers since 2007, while continuing as an active songwriter and performer under the moniker Helen McCookerybook. Her book on women instrumentalists in British punk bands, *The Lost Women of Rock Music: Female musicians of the punk era*, was published by Equinox in 2012. *She's at the Controls: Sound engineering, production and gender ventriloquism in the 21st century* was published by Equinox in 2021, further developing her research on unheard women's voices in the popular music industry. Learn more at her website: www.mccookerybook.com

Simon Reynolds is the author of eight books about pop culture, including *Shock and Awe: Glam Rock and its Legacy* (2016), *Retromania: Pop Culture's Addiction to Its Own Past* (2011), *Rip It Up and Start Again: Postpunk 1978– 84* (2005), *Energy Flash: A Journey Through Rave Music and Dance Culture* (1998), *The Sex Revolts: Gender, Rebellion and Rock 'n' Roll* (co-written with Joy Press, 1995), and *Blissed Out: The Raptures of Rock* (1990). He started his career as a music critic at *Melody Maker*, where he was a staff writer during the late '80s. Since then he has freelanced for magazines including the *New York Times*, *Village Voice*, *The Guardian*, *Pitchfork*, *Artforum*, *The Face*, and *The Wire*. He operates a number of blogs centred around the hub Blissblog: http://blissout.blogspot.com/. Born in London, a resident of New York during much of the 1990s and 2000s, he currently lives in Los Angeles.

Susan Schmidt Horning is Associate Professor of History at St. John's University in Queens, New York. She is the author of *Chasing Sound: Technology, Culture, and the Art of Studio Recording from Edison to the LP* (Johns Hopkins University Press, 2013; 2015), and essays in *Music and Technology in the Twentieth Century* (Johns Hopkins, 2002), *The Electric Guitar: A History of an American Icon* (Johns Hopkins, 2004), and *The Bloomsbury Handbook of Music Production* (Bloomsbury Academic, 2020). Her interest in music technology dates back to her earlier life as a rock musician and first experience in a 1960s recording studio.

Asif Siddiqi is a professor of history at Fordham University in New York and specializes in the history of technology and Soviet history (as well as the intersection between the two). He has written many books and articles on space exploration, and more recently on popular music. His essay on Brian Eno and David Byrne's *My Life in the Bush of Ghosts* was published in *Creativity: Technology and Music* (2016). He has held visiting positions at Harvard University, MIT, Caltech, and the Smithsonian. He received a

Guggenheim Fellowship in 2016 and was a visiting scholar at Princeton University's Davis Center for Historical Studies in 2021–22.

Louie Dean Valencia is an associate professor of digital history at Texas State University. His books include *Antiauthoritarian Youth Culture in Francoist Spain: Clashing with Fascism* (Bloomsbury, 2018) and *Far-Right Revisionism and the End of History* (Routledge, 2020). His research focuses on popular culture, urban studies, historical memory, everyday life, identity, and youth. He has taught on the faculty at Harvard University and earned his PhD from Fordham University.

Oliver Wang is a professor of sociology at California State University-Long Beach and the author of *Legions of Boom: Filipino American Mobile DJ Crews of the San Francisco Bay Area* (Duke University Press, 2015). Since 1994, he has written regularly on music, food, and pop culture for outlets including NPR's *All Things Considered, The Los Angeles Review of Books, Los Angeles Times*, and KCET's *Artbound*. In the mid-2000s, he created the audioblog, Soul-Sides.com, and since 2017, he has been the co-host of the weekly music interview podcast, *Heat Rocks*.

Simon Zagorski-Thomas is Professor at the London College of Music (University of West London) and is chair of the UK and Ireland branch of IASPM, as well as founder and chair of the 21st Century Music Practice research network with over 250 members in 30 countries. He was the co-founder of the Art of Record Production conference in 2005 and, until 2017, was also co-chair of the Association for the Study of the Art of Record Production. He worked for 25 years as a composer, sound engineer, and producer, and is, at present, conducting research into twenty-first century musical practice. His books include *The Art of Record Production*, which he co-edited with Simon Frith, *The Musicology of Record Production* (winner of the 2015 IASPM Book Prize), the second *Art of Record Production* book on creative practice (edited with Katia Isakoff, Serrge Lacasse, and Sophie Stévance) and *The Bloomsbury Handbook of Music Production* (edited with Andrew Bourbon). He is Series Editor of the CUP Elements series on 21st Century Music Practice, and is currently writing a monograph on practical musicology for Bloomsbury Academic Press to be published in 2022.

Acknowledgments

Like most edited books, this has been a long journey and there are many people to thank. First and foremost, I want to thank Simon Reynolds for support and encouragement. Simon and I came up with the project over dinner in October 2016, and without his ideas, this project would have undoubtedly remained dormant. I also want to thank all those at the original dinner, including Glenn Hendler, Susan Schmidt Horning, Trevor Pinch, and mostly Nicholas Paul, who had the idea for the brilliant title. Tragically, Trevor Pinch passed away and was not able to participate in the project but his spirit definitely lives on in all of these essays. And I must thank especially Esther Cuenca whose support was crucial to the project. Obviously, thanks goes out to the 15 other contributors in the volume—some of whom were part of the original workshop and some who joined later, but all of whom put up with my incessant emails for the past several years. I am so grateful and honored that they contributed such wonderful essays to this volume. Through a global pandemic (and much more), we persevered in our shared love of pop music with words that opened up worlds.

Much gratitude to the O'Connell Initiative for the Global History of Capitalism for its generous funding and support, which allowed us to organize a very successful workshop at Fordham University's Lincoln Center campus in New York in June 2019. This book exists because of that sponsorship. At Fordham, I want to thank Dave Hamlin and especially Audra Croke, whose efforts ensured a successful workshop.

At Routledge, I want to thank Heidi Bishop for taking on this book and also Kaushikee Sharma for her invaluable help in taking care of all the logistics.

One-Track Mind

An Introduction

Asif Siddiqi

The song remains the most basic unit of modern pop music. Shaped into being by historical forces—cultural, aesthetic, and technical—the song provides both performer and audience with a world marked off by a short, discrete, and temporally demarcated experience. Of course, the song has a history that long predates late-twentieth-century pop, but its arrival as a metric of popular music was manifest in the intersection of postwar youth culture, mass media, and capitalism.[1] One obvious referent here is, of course, the 7" 45-RPM "single," first introduced commercially in 1949, bringing into popular lexicon the idea of a "hit," the word itself functioning as an attack on cultural complacency, a sonic shock, and a dose of a drug.[2] The more widely known a song, the more likely its being conflated with "hit." To signifiers such as "song," "hit," and "single" we can add the generic "track," a noun whose roots date back to the late fifteenth-century French word *trac*, alluding to imprints on the ground left by animals. The recorded track, too, left imprints, aural raids into our daily experience of sound, a small serving of "wanted sound" in negative contrast to the "unwanted sound" that Hillel Schwartz describes in *Making Noise*.[3] The word "track" eventually came into ubiquitous use as a metonym for "song" in the 1950s, when recording engineers spoke of multi-track recording. Later, in the early 1980s, the rise of the 12" remix single wrested the lexicon of "track" from its technical origins into the world of DJs and eventually into rave culture as both a comment on the inadequacy of "song" and a critique of it.

But long before then, the song and the track had undergone transformations. With the birth of mainstream rock 'n' roll as a self-conscious idiom in the 1950s—stripped of Blackness, steeped in suburbia, and stoked by rebellion—the imaginations set free within the (now, usually) three-minute aural experience were no longer simply aesthetic. The song was a new *political* avatar, both a mirror and an instrument of cultural politics. Music and politics, of course, have always been intertwined in both personal pain (think Bessie Smith) and the grand historical narrative (think Mozart), but by the 1950s, technologically enabled by the 7" single and commercially promoted by the capitalist imperative, the song marked off a newer territory, one where the song was both commercial *and* political, a peculiar marriage of two often

DOI: 10.4324/9781003093206-1

antithetical forces that frequently mitigated the power of each. This territory, where the commercial met the political, where an individual song came to embody, subvert, and reinforce the cultural status quo, is the principal setting for the essays in this proposed volume. As such, each of the 16 essays presented here are interventions, through a single song, into the history of irruptions, eruptions, and disruptions in the cultural politics of the late-twentieth and early twenty-first centuries.

There have been previous attempts to use discrete musical formats—the album, the song, the performance—to open up larger questions of cultural politics.[4] There are literally hundreds of books now on individual albums.[5] The implicit assumption in these texts is that, in some way, these albums represent important moments in the history of pop, either as saltation or as subversion. Albums are imbued with gravitas. There are also any number of popular tracts—think of the many books on the discographies of Dylan and the Beatles—that take a kind of forensic approach to a group of older songs, representing genre or performer, coercing readers into thinking of the slightly cadaverous notion of "a body of work." Some, like Marc Myers' *Anatomy of a Song: The Oral History of 45 Iconic Hits that Changed Rock, R&B and Pop* (2016), operate in the liminal space between archive (through details of recordings) and fetish (through pictures of sleeves).[6] Others, such as Greil Marcus's *The History of Rock 'n' Roll in Ten Songs* (2014) claim universalism, that these songs themselves represent, embody, and distill the meter, the rhyme, and rhythm of rock 'n' roll in their DNA.[7]

The current volume pays a debt to these works as well as to broader-conceived scholarship on the idea of the song in the *longue durée*, such as Nicholas E. Tawa's *Supremely American: Popular Song in the 20th Century* (2005) and Denis Stevens's *A History of Song* (1971, revised and updated many times), but our approach is also more eclectic and less comprehensive.[8] In fact, the 16 songs represented here make no claim to universalism or comprehensiveness. In other words, this is not a history of pop through 16 songs—although one could certainly read it as such. Having come to this project as both scholars and fans, the songs presented here are ones that resonate with each of us. But although the precise selection of songs here is determined primarily by the choice of authors and, in turn, by what the authors themselves found interesting, all these songs are examples of what we consider important milestones in the history of pop. Some of them were massive international hits, while others remain hardly known even today; but *all of them* lay claim to be open doors in the architecture of pop music through which we can pass to begin important conversations about its history.

Given our explicit goal of elucidating the cultural politics of the pop song, we are self-conscious that any selective process that collects 16 authors and the songs chosen somewhat arbitrarily conveys its own set of politics. Did we represent women singers? People of color? The marginalized? Are we hostage to reactionary and rockist worldviews usually dominated by the straight white male demographic? We acknowledge that these are important questions.

But instead of confronting them in overwrought justifications, we deal with questions of race, gender, class directly within each essay, and not as any kind of universal political position that the authors agree on. In fact, part of the value of this project is that the selection of the authors and the songs was a result of serendipity, accident, and deliberation. As such, we probably don't agree on much besides what we ourselves write about.

Yet, there are some consistent motifs running through the book, threads that emerged not by force but organically as the book came together. A brief account of the birth of this project illuminates some of these themes. The idea for the book originated when one of its contributors, Simon Reynolds, was visiting New York in October 2016 to give a talk at Fordham University's Manhattan campus. Simon was visiting at my invitation to weigh in on his recently published book *Shock and Awe* (2016).[9] After the talk, a group of Fordham faculty convened with Simon at a Mexican restaurant near Columbus Circle where, over margaritas and tacos, we began thinking of a book project that could bring together writers and scholars who each could explore in depth individual songs that, for one reason or another, resonated deeply with them. A scholar of medieval political culture and a fan (and fanatic) of turn-of-the-century electronic dance music, Nicholas Paul provided the perfect rubric for the project—"One-Track Mind"—although he regrettably decided not to participate on account of more pressing obligations. From that conversation, the project acquired wings when Fordham's O'Connell Initiative for the Global History of Capitalism funded a workshop in New York in June 2019 to discuss each paper individually and to find common threads in our work. The addition of a sponsor's theme could have easily been a pretext to coerce arguments into contrived shapes, but as it turned out, capital's long shadow proved to be a persistent and common point of reference for many if not all the papers. As more contributors joined the project, other overarching themes were rendered visible amid these histories, ones that illuminate the rich, exciting, and oftentimes strange history of modern popular music.

As will be evident from a cursory read, the business of pop music—corporations, labels, marketing—loom large over these narratives. Capitalism and its principal good, capital, help us frame these stories, a fact that should surprise no one given the inextricable relationship between art and capitalism established in the twentieth century. The moment an artist shares her music with the masses, the track becomes entrapped within structures designed to profit off it. The profit-making motive, in turn, shapes, to a large degree, what we find "popular." Many of the songs presented here fell victim to misbegotten intentions of faceless corporate managers who reduced art to supply and demand and thus fell afoot of actual human preferences. Glenn Hendler, in his essay on David Bowie's 1974 single "Rebel Rebel," revisits how the US single version of the track, a kind of "Latinized" version of the original song reflecting Bowie's emerging interest in Black and Latin music, was marketed aggressively by his record company to album-oriented radio (catering largely to white audiences invested in "rock"), thereby ensuring its commercial

4 *Asif Siddiqi*

failure. Hendler's in-depth archaeology of a particularly transitional period for Bowie—an artist always in transition—showcases the racial politics of American radio of the '70s, when slight deviations from white, blues-oriented classic rock could land a song in purgatory. Misplaced marketing also characterized the career of Moby Grape, one of the most buzzed-about bands of high psychedelia in the late '60s. In her essay on Moby Grape's "Omaha," Susan Schmidt Horning shows how, in marketing the band's debut album in 1967, their label, Columbia Records, released *five* singles off the album simultaneously for radio play. Sabotaged by this highly clumsy marketing blitz, "Omaha" all but disappeared from the pop charts, although as Schmidt Horning shows, the group's very limited canon accrued a different kind of capital—cult(ural) capital. Through the decades, influential musicians and artists invoked Moby Grape as a key touchstone of late-60s psychedelia. Obscurity granted Skip Spence, the author of "Omaha," a kind of legendary cult status that mainstream popularity would have impeded.

In some cases, corporate behavior provoked sharp discontent. In Louie Dean Valencia's essay on Hanson's "MMMBop," we discover how the band essentially left their label, Island Def Jam, as a way to escape the unneeded interference of corporate shills over the content, promotion, and distribution of their music, mirroring the path of many independent "college rock" bands from the 1980s. Valencia shows that Hanson was one of the first bands to make use of the burgeoning fan community on the internet, a practice that enabled direct contact between artist and audience but also freed the trolls to paroxysms of homophobia and toxic masculinity. Much later, the direct expression made possible by social media also revealed a somewhat unsavory side to the band members themselves that has complicated the band's relationship to their fans. Sometimes the relationship between corporation and artist was adversarial and even destructive. In his history of the Neil Young's "Transformer Man," George Plasketes shows how the Geffen record company sued Neil Young in court on the charge of releasing music that didn't sound sufficiently "like Neil Young." As Young's artistic muse took him through many different genre albums in the 1980s, including excursions into electronic new wave, rockabilly, country & western, and heavy metal, Geffen's suit became a bellwether mark for the battle between art and commerce in both the boardroom and the courtroom. What many missed at the time was the deeply personal nature of Young's engagement with electronic music (and his use of the vocoder on "Transformer Man"), which was a desperate avenue allowing Young to communicate with his son Ben, diagnosed with severe cerebral palsy.

If capitalism's all-encompassing presence in these stories highlights the cold, calculating, and cynical face of pop music, there are also narratives here of uplift and hope, especially in the registers in which pop has been able to produce hybrids of seemingly antagonistic sensibilities, offering meta-narratives of co-production and even co-existence. Oliver Wang, in his essay on Gerald Wilson's "Viva Tirado," tracks the incredible and often strange journey of a song, originally released in 1960, that mirrored the contentious history of Black/Brown politics in Southern California through multiple iterations by different artists in the '60s, '70s, and '90s. He writes:

> Here was a song, originally written by an African American in praise of a Mexican bullfighter, remade by a Chicano jazz/rock group...given the name "El Chicano" by a White manager...then sampled by a Chicano MC, mentored by an African American rap icon, as a way to instill pride in young Chicana/os through an Afro-diasporic artform whose fans include Black, Brown, White, and Asian youth across the world, only to be remade twenty years later by a pair of first-generation Mexican American brothers who merged hip-hop with banda and penned an updated anthem celebrating Mexican migrant communities.

In the biography of this single track, we see expectations continually subverted as the song, unmoored from its distant origins, found new hybrid iterations in the urban geography of greater Los Angeles. Here, we find the song's ability to produce occasional moments of hybridity and harmony in a history otherwise marked by separation and discordance. In a similar vein, Simon Zagorski-Thomas's piece on le Grand Kallé and African Jazz's 1960 African hit "Indépendance Cha Cha" offers a story of different communities, separated by history, class, power, and culture—the Bills and the *évolué*—meeting for three minutes to produce a joyous ode to independent Congo as millions made the uncertain leap from the colonial to the postcolonial eras. In offering a new way to think of this widely known paean to decolonization, Zagorski-Thomas invites us to consider its "musicological frame" and how power is played out in the history and legacy of this particular song. The history of this track, he notes,

> reminds us of the complex and divisive social structures that these musicians embody, and foreshadows the tragic events that followed-on almost immediately from this jubilant expression of hope and confidence and led to a long, violent, and painful narrative in which all these themes of power, inequality, and resentment were played out.

Pop music has been a powerful vehicle, reflecting and in turn shaping our expectations of gender and sexuality. All the authors featured here, in one way or another, confront this question in their essays, some more explicitly than others. Amy Coddington offers a story of empowerment through the transcending of genre expectations in her essay on Salt-N-Pepa's "Shoop." A track written and performed by Salt, Pepa, and DJ Spinderalla, "Shoop" struck a nerve in the early '90s, seamlessly inverting the conventions of the pop format whereby men were expected to ogle at women. Instead, here was a song "where women look freely at the men around them, make their own decisions about who to talk to, and call the shots once they have made contact." In reminding us of the power of this track, Coddington highlights the incredible skill and talent that Salt (Cheryl James) and Pepa (Sandra Denton)—as women and as African American writers and producers of their own music—brought to the table in "usher[ing] in the era of hip-hop becoming hit pop." We find a similar sensibility in Helen Reddington's essay on "Oh Bondage! Up Yours!" the 1977 single from the punk band X-Ray Spex, which foregrounds Poly Styrene's explosive energy while also offering a corrective to the received history of punk about the "Black women who were pioneering presences within punk rock." As a feminist broadside in a culture dominated by white males, "Oh Bondage! Up Yours!" generated a plethora of condescending, patronizing, and sexist responses in the male-dominated music media in late 1970s. In personalizing her recovery of this contentious attack on Poly Styrene, Reddington shows how the track distilled a powerful sense of agency for young girls, who could now be seen and heard: "[The song] was our battle hymn, an articulation of punk that spoke to us and included us." There is a similarly personal investment at play in Scott Poulson-Bryant's essay on Prince's "When You Were Mine," which reveals the individual, private, and intimate ways a single song can speak to a listener. Recalling the rush of listening to the song in the mid-80s as a young man, Poulson-Bryant sees the track less as Prince's stab at the genre of new wave than as something entirely different and private, a queer manifesto. In "When You Were Mine," Prince made sense "through the intimate parameters of my own Black, queer ear," Poulson-Bryant writes, the song embodying "a desire to imagine him outside of the confines of critical taste and gatekeeping." Here, in the intimacy of the solitary listening experience, the song embodies "one of the quintessentially queer aspects of Prince."

As deeply personalized is Gina Arnold's take on the Replacements' "Unsatisfied," a powerful distillation of youthful ennui and frustration from the heyday of '80s college rock. In the sweet spot between unadulterated entropy and disarming charm characteristic of so much of the Replacements' oeuvre, Arnold finds a powerful antidote to the Reaganite '80s. Principal songwriter Paul Westerberg rarely, if ever, made any explicit comment on the politics of the day, but the emotive chaos that he tapped into stood in direct opposition to the reactionary, watered-down, and homogenized culture that pervaded, it seemed, every single nook and cranny of television, radio, and print media in the 1980s. If the Replacements' refusal to partake of the political rhetoric of the day was itself a political act, there were others who took truth to power without any equivocation or ambiguity. Austin McCoy's essay on NWA.'s "F- tha Police" (the "fuck" in the title was censored in the original vinyl and CD releases) recovers a particularly fraught moment in race relations in Los Angeles in the 1980s, when an unapologetically racist, lawless, and authoritarian police force brutalized a generation of young African Americans. McCoy situates the history of the incendiary track within the heavily militarized LAPD's so-called "thin blue line" policy, which saw social disorder as just a moment away if not kept in check. McCoy shows how, in offering a powerful critique of the lawlessness of the LAPD, "F- tha Police" also functioned as journalism. In fact, the power of the track—as with many of the best pop songs—was that, despite its local concerns, it held universal appeal. As McCoy notes:

> MC Ren, Ice Cube, and Eazy-E recording a song as 'underground street reporters' underscores the notion that they were not just speaking about their experiences, or for themselves, but expressing a view about law enforcement that other Black Americans shared but were afraid to say publicly.

As with the NWA track, many of the songs presented here left a record of the times, representing a form of history writing. Esther Liberman Cuenca's essay on Led Zeppelin's "Immigrant Song" traverses one such history, focusing on the Viking invasions of the British Isles in the centuries prior to the Norman Conquest. But as Cuenca shows, this was as much an imagined history as it was real, one that tapped into a deep strand of medievalism— the representation of the Middle Ages in popular culture—that had seen its flowering in the nineteenth century. This particularly masculine vision saw its full-bodied manifestation in the howling "Immigrant Song," a song that Led Zeppelin saw as a metaphor for its first triumphant tour of Iceland in 1970, but which then became "portable" in wildly different contexts in the 40 years since its creation, including in several Hollywood movies in the twenty-first century. Cuenca's astute analysis suggests the ways in which contemporary pop songs serve to reify imagined histories even as they themselves leave lasting legacies. In a similar fashion, the recording of history was very much encoded into "Candle in the Wind 1997," Elton John's soliloquy for the tragically extinguished Royal casualty, Lady Diana Spencer. In disentangling the strange and long history of this song, Christine Caccipuoti expertly tracks its transformation from a lament for the brief and anguished life of Marilyn Monroe to, more than two decades later, the best-selling British single of all time. As Caccipuoti shows, having tapped into a moment of unified and public grief fed by emerging 24-hour mass media outlets, "Candle in the Wind 1997" completely eclipsed its original incarnation in the British collective memory. Due in no small part to John's own efforts, who has "refused to allow it to be used anywhere [else], by anyone, since the funeral [of Diana]," the song has remained frozen in time, like a history book that itself has now become part of history.

If "Candle in the Wind 1997" was a literal form of historical memorialization, other pop songs encoded history into their words and music through more material techniques, such as digital sampling. In my essay on MIA's 2007 single "Paper Planes," I unwind the complicated threads of this global hit song that eluded easy categories. MIA's ambivalent lyrics point to the illegal market for immigrant visas in the post-9/11 world, suffused as it was, with anxieties about terrorism and globalization. But as a global hit by a woman of color from the postcolonial South, the song also subverted the expectations of capital. Notably, the song incorporated a digitized sample from a Clash song that itself critiqued American empire. In producing a musical genealogy, MIA was, I argue, using her song as "a tool for writing and rewriting history for those for whom history has always been written by others." As the song shows so effectively, digital sampling in the hands of postcolonial artists can be as much about crafting a future as about rewriting the colonial past. Five months before "Paper Planes" appeared on the album *Kala*, the New York-based DJ, musician, and record producer James Murphy, under the name LCD Soundsystem, issued his second studio album, *Sound of Silver*, featuring the track "All My Friends." Like "Paper Planes," the LCD Soundsystem song appeared to capture the zeitgeist of the moment, a torch song for the waning years of the first decade of the twenty-first century. Gabrielle Cornish's essay on "All My Friends" confronts Murphy's fundamental conundrum: the fool-hardy quest to be "cool" in the face of the relentless and infinite pressure of obsolescence. Pop music has always had a rocky relationship with notions of "cool"—which often resides in the image of the outsider and the still-to-be-profited-from—which clashes with the imperative to appeal to popular if not populist trends.[10] Yet this song, Cornish argues, was able to sidestep these questions in a setting (New York City) where "ideas of 'cool' and 'uncool,'" were paramount. "Positioned within the 'retromania' of the first decade of the new millennium," she writes, "[the song] plays with notions of aging, fashion, and nostalgia to compelling—and very cool—ends."

Pop songs are not always about the past, about history, or steeped in retromania. Some of the best and most thrilling ones unlock possible futures. This was undoubtedly true for perhaps the most influential track in this volume, Donna Summer's "I Feel Love." Like LCD Soundsystem's "All My Friends," "I Feel Love" builds on repetition, but where the former essentially repurposes a post-punk dance sound, the latter invents sounds never heard before. Revisiting the history of this track through interviews with the principals involved, Simon Reynolds positions "I Feel Love" as a "single whose status as a world-historical pop event is incontestable." In disassembling the machinery of the track, Reynolds provides glimpses into the factory at the heart of its creation, a studio environment wherein the creative visions of Donna Summer, Giorgio Moroder, and Pete Bellotte were fitted into each other in perfect consonance, producing the rippling "sound from tomorrow." Eschewing guitars completely, they centered the track around a Moog synthesizer figure, delayed bass pulses, and a metronomic kick drum that collectively sounded like a transmission from a disorienting future, an envelope of sound and attack that still, more than 40 years later, sounds like it is from another world. Reynolds traces the aftershocks of "I Feel Love" through a dizzying array of genres in subsequent decades—disco, post-punk, house, techno, and trance—a javelin thrown in the direction of "brutal futurism," branded with "mechanistic repetition, icy electronics, [and] a blank-eyed fixated feel of posthuman propulsion."

In their final versions, these meditations illuminate, analyze, and deconstruct; hopefully they also entertain, delight, and inform. At their root, readers will find here brief histories of 16 important tracks from the history of pop, with unexpected plot twists, colorful protagonists, and fitting denouements. Arranged chronologically in order of release of the tracks, these essays zigzag across the pop landscape of the last six decades to present one possible history of pop music. There are detours through psychedelic rock, Afro-pop, Latin pop, glam rock, heavy metal, punk, post-punk, adult contemporary rock, techno, hip-hop, and electro-pop.

From le Grand Kallé and African Jazz's "Indepéndence Cha Cha" in 1960 to M.I.A.'s "Paper Planes" in 2007, these 16 tracks represent one canon in the history of modern pop. Put together by a combination of serendipity, deliberation, and fandom, the essays themselves constitute a mixtape of text as diverse as the tracks themselves. Some of the authors seek answers in the world that bridges popular culture with theory. Others find meaning in more personal meditations on how a single song could change the world of an individual. Still others occupy a middle ground between the personal and theoretical, between thought and expression, as Lou Reed once noted. But our hope is that, as with a mixtape, read from beginning to end, the reader will find resonance with the rhythms and aesthetics of some essays over others, returning (more than once) to some more than others. Ultimately, we hope that readers will find answers as to how and why songs have the power to inscribe themselves into our private worlds, orient us to new directions, and sometimes, dislodge our comfortable foundations and lift us towards uncertain futures. Enjoy.

Notes

1 David Fowler, *Youth Culture in Modern Britain, c. 1920-c. 1970: From Ivory Tower to Global Movement—A New History* (Houndmills: Palgrave McMillan, 2008); Dan Laughey, *Music and Youth Culture* (Edinburgh: Edinburgh University Press, 2006); Grace Palladino, *Teenagers: An American History* (New York: Basic Books, 1999); Mitchell K. Hall, *The Emergence of Rock and Roll: Music and the Rise of American Youth Culture* (New York: Routledge, 2014).

2 Spencer Drate, ed., *45 RPM: A Visual History of the Seven-Inch Record* (New York: Princeton Architectural Press, 2002); Richard Osborne, *Vinyl: A History of the Analogue Record* (London: Routledge, 2016), 117–42.

3 Hillel Schwartz, *Making Noise: From Babel to the Big Bang & Beyond* (New York: Zone Books, 2016).

4 For representative books on single songs, see Greil Marcus, *Like a Rolling Stone: Bob Dylan at the Crossroads* (New York: Public Affairs, 2005); Jody Rosen, *White Christmas* (London: Fourth Estate, 2003). For the transcendental gig, see David Nolan, *I Swear I Was There: Sex Pistols, Manchester, and the Gig that Changed the World* (Ramsbottom, Milo, 2001); Clinton Heylin, *Judas! From Forest Hills to the Free Trade Hall: A Historical View of the Big Boo* (New York: Lesser Gods, 2017).

5 Bloomsbury publishes a series dedicated solely to explorations of individual albums, under the title "33 1/3." As of August 2021, there have been 154 books in the series, the last one dedicated to Pearl Jam's *Vs.*

6 See for example Marc Myers, *Anatomy of a Song: The Oral History of 45 Iconic Hits that Changed Rock, R&B and Pop* (New York: Grove Press, 2016).

7 Greil Marcus, *The History of Rock'n'Roll in Ten Songs* (New Haven: Yale University Press, 2014).

8 Nicholas Tawa, *Supremely American: Popular Song in the 20th Century: Styles and Singers and What They Said About America* (Lanham, MD: Scarecrow Press, 2005); Denis Stevens, *A History of Song* (London: Hutchinson, 1971).

9 Simon Reynolds, *Shock and Awe: Glam Rock and Its Legacy, from the Seventies to the Twenty-First Century* (New York: Dey Street, 2016).

10 For notions of "cool" before the advent of rock 'n' roll, see Joel Dinerstein, *The Origins of Cool in Postwar America* (Chicago: University of Chicago Press, 2017). See also Dick Hebdige, *Subculture: The Meaning of Style* (London: Routledge, 1979).

Bibliography

Dinerstein, Joel. *The Origins of Cool in Postwar America*. Chicago: University of Chicago Press, 2017.

Drate, Spencer, ed. *45 RPM: A Visual History of the Seven-Inch Record*. New York: Princeton Architectural Press, 2002.

Fowler, David. *Youth Culture in Modern Britain, c. 1920-c. 1970: From Ivory Tower to Global Movement—A New History*. Houndmills: Palgrave McMillan, 2008.

Hall, Michael K. *The Emergence of Rock and Roll: Music and the Rise of American Youth Culture*. New York: Routledge, 2014.

Hebdige, Dick. *Subculture: The Meaning of Style*. London: Routledge, 1979.

Heylin, Clinton. *Judas! From Forest Hills to the Free Trade Hall: A Historical View of the Big Boo*. New York: Lesser Gods, 2017.

Laughey, Dan. *Music and Youth Culture*. Edinburgh: Edinburgh University Press, 2006.

Marcus, Greil. *The History of Rock'n'Roll in Ten Songs*. New Haven: Yale University Press, 2014.

Marcus, Greil. *Like a Rolling Stone: Bob Dylan at the Crossroads*. New York: PublicAffairs, 2005.

Myers, Marc. *Anatomy of a Song: The Oral History of 45 Iconic Hits that Changed Rock, R&B and Pop*. New York: Grove Press, 2016.

Nolan, David. *I Swear I Was There: Sex Pistols, Manchester, and the Gig that Changed the World*. Ramsbottom, Milo, 2001.

Osborne, Richard. *Vinyl: A History of the Analogue Record*. London: Routledge, 2016.

Palladino, Grace. *Teenagers: An American History*. New York: Basic Books, 1999.

Reynolds, Simon. *Shock and Awe: Glam Rock and Its Legacy, from the Seventies to the Twenty-First Century*. New York: Dey Street, 2016.

Rosen, Jody. *White Christmas*. London: Fourth Estate, 2003.

Schwartz, Hillel. *Making Noise: From Babel to the Big Bang & Beyond*. New York: Zone Books, 2016.

Stevens, Denis. *A History of Song*. London: Hutchinson, 1971.

Tawa, Nicholas. *Supremely American: Popular Song in the 20th Century: Styles and Singers and What They Said About America*. Lanham, MD: Scarecrow Press, 2005.

1 Le Grand Kallé and African Jazz—"Indépendance Cha Cha" (1960)

Simon Zagorski-Thomas

Introduction

Although it could be told in many ways, I'm going to tell the story of this song as a story about power. The story of the "Indépendance Cha Cha" provides a lens through which I want to explore some of the nuanced ways in which music can reflect different manifestations of power. Obviously it is a song about gaining independence from colonial masters. It also tells a story of how Congolese musicians sought out a musical language that was both cosmopolitan and modern and yet avoided ceding power to the normalized European colonial tropes of "cosmopolitan" and "modern." It also embodies some of the tensions within the Democratic Republic of Congo in the middle of the twentieth century: of class, gender, and education, and of the urban/rural divide.

The "Indépendance Cha Cha" was written in 1960 by Joseph Kabasele, also known as le Grand Kallé, during the round table discussions in Brussels at which it was announced that the Belgian Congo, a colony for over 75 years, would become an independent state later that year. As such, it is clearly a song about indigenous citizens exerting power and taking back control of their country. Kabasele and Vicky Longomba had been invited by Thomas Kanza, who had been the first African citizen of the Belgian Congo to graduate from the Louvain University near Brussels and was, in 1959, working for the European Economic Community. This gesture harked back to the tradition of praise songs and the importance of music in the social mechanisms of Congolese cultures. Indeed, the lyrics in the verses of the song are a list of the organizations and people involved in the Congolese delegation at the round table. This tradition of "important" people being immortalized in song is an important trope in folk music and this way embodiment of power in musical practice was crystallized even further from the 1970s onwards with the action of *mabanga*, of paying a musician to mention your name in a performance as an indication of your prestige. And so it was that le Grand Kallé and African Jazz played each night at the Plaza Hotel in Brussels for the edification of the delegates and the entertainment (mixed with surprise) of the Belgians. They wrote and recorded the "Indépendance Cha Cha" to celebrate this momentous

DOI: 10.4324/9781003093206-2

event. The beginning of the 1960s was a point at which many ex-colonies in Africa were gaining independence from their European masters, and the record became a pan-African hit that boosted Kabasele's status from that of a Congolese star to an international one. Immediately after the release of the single (See Figure 1.1), le Grand Kallé and Africa Jazz toured in both France and West Africa,[1] and the song was played extensively on radio stations in these ex-colonies.[2] As Alain Mabanckou wrote in *Libération*, in an article relating to both its importance and poignance, "Qu'est-ce qu'une révolution si elle ne se fait pas en chantant?" (What is a revolution if it is not done by singing?)[3]

But the story of this record and the events that led up to it are not simply about a reversal of the power structures in the Belgian Congo. As the events that played out before and after the round table exemplify, the gaining independence is seldom as simple as one group of people taking power away from another. While the relatively (for the time) liberal Belgian government may have been motivated on ideological grounds to solve the developing crisis in the Belgian Congo by granting independence, the Belgian economy was still highly reliant on its ownership of Congolese industries and resources. The owners of those interests and the many other international companies, particularly US ones, that had invested heavily in the region were not about

Figure 1.1 The 7" release of "Indépendence Cha Cha." Credit: Public Domain.

to cede those interests and profits to the new national government and the Congolese people. At the same time, the Congolese delegation, as the long list of organizations mentioned in the song testifies, was far from being a homogenous group. They were divided on regional, religious, ethnic, and ideological grounds, and as soon as the round table was over their bitter disputes and unholy alliances bubbled over into violent disputes, fueled by foreign interests including both the Soviet Union and the CIA. This was the moment when Patrice Lumumba, the first elected prime minister of the new Democratic Republic of Congo, was imprisoned and then murdered. As with many of the discussions on this subject, Gary Stewart's *Rumba on the River*[4] is a key text about the development of Congolese popular music in the second half of the twentieth century.

Power

If I am going to tell the story of this song as a story about power then I had better start by clarifying exactly what I mean by power. The perhaps slightly arcane definition I am going to start with is "the perception of the potential for an action or behaviour." A lot of the metaphors we use for power relate to a position or a state of being, but they are fundamentally concerned with the ability to do something. However, we do not need to exercise a power in order to have it. If you or I perceive that I have the power to behave in a particular way, then whether or not I exert the power you are still likely to alter your behavior based on the perception that it is a possibility.

While theories of power such as that offered by Bourdieu[5] are mostly concerned with the circumstances and mechanisms through which some affordance is granted—money, knowledge, connections, superstition, and so forth—they tend to think of these things as sociological black boxes rather than exploring the psychological mechanisms involved. In this chapter I want to discuss how some of these cognitive processes work and how they are reflected in the musical culture behind this song.

It may seem a bit of a leap from Congolese music practice to the idea of social class but one of the enduring divisions in the story of Congolese rhumba as well as more modern musical forms is the distinction between musicians from a more rural village background and those from Léopoldville/Kinshasa, where the recording industry emerged. In most parts of the world the distinction between those brought up in an agricultural tradition and those who live in towns and cities creates cultural and behavioral distinctions that emerge from ones based on working practices and economics. The process of learning through doing as an apprentice participant rather than through formal education separated from the professional practice you are learning about is one such distinction. Learning as a participant encourages nonverbal or tacit knowledge which is less likely to be questioned or changed than "book learning" or even practical training that is based on verbal explanation. This tendency to preserve traditional ways of working often extends into ways of behaving and believing as well. The musical traditions of the villages tended to be more conservative, and being embedded in the daily life of a small community, they were more part of everyday culture. In the city, music was a business of entertainment, and as such, musicians in the city lived on the edge of respectability and were also always looking for new trends to mark them out as different from the rest of the crowd. Of course, not everyone who moved to the city had the resources or the drive to ensure that their children could participate in the processes of formal education. While urban conglomerations provided better opportunities for social mobility, they also created concentrations of competition, and those who didn't succeed in those circumstances faced not only similar privations as those in the rural areas but also a lack of the social infrastructure and sense of community which those smaller groupings could provide and which had built up over generations.

Évolués and Bills

Joseph Athanase Tchamala Kabasele was born in 1930 in Matadi, the main seaport for the Belgian Congo, around 150 kilometers inland from the mouth of the Congo River just before it becomes unnavigable to larger vessels. When he was still a baby his parents moved to Léopoldville, and his family can be seen as an example of what both the Belgians and the Congolese called *évolués*, a disturbingly eugenics-related term for the more educated, lower-middle-class Black Congolese. Although the term relates to them being more "evolved" than the rest of the native population, the Belgians restricted the education of their colonial population. They provided a limited amount of secondary schooling and technical education to create a class of clerks, railway workers, and nurses who spoke French, but it wasn't until 1954 that the Congolese were allowed to go to university. Kabasele's uncle, Joseph Malula, had taken another route to being an évolué by entering the Catholic priesthood and, much later, becoming a cardinal. The évolués of the city certainly looked down upon the less educated citizens of the villages and the urban working class, but it was also true that being a musician was not a suitable profession for a respectable évolué.

Victor Longomba Besange Lokuli, commonly known as Vicky Longomba, was the other vocalist on "Indépendance Cha Cha" and was born in Kinshasa in 1932. At that time Kinshasa was the name of a Blacks-only suburb of Léopoldville and only after independence became the name of the whole city. Vicky also went through enough school to get a job as a clerk before he started to make a living as a musician. Charles Mwamba, also known as "Dechaud," (born in 1935) and Nicolas Kasanda, or Docteur Nico, (born in 1939), the two guitarists on the recording, were brothers and were born in a village near Luluaborg (now Kanaga) in the central province of Kasai. They followed a rural tradition of taking their surnames from other relatives, and so Charles was named after his uncle and Nico after his grandfather. Both of their parents were musical, but they also aspired to get away from the rural life and give their sons an education in Kinshasa. Against their parents' wishes, the two boys took up the guitar and started to hang out at Opika Studios near the zoo and the river in Kinshasa. Charles ran away from home for two years when he was 14 and lived and worked with a well-known singer called Jhimmy, who was successfully making records for Opika at the time. Nico was better behaved, and although he too started to work at the studio in 1952 and played on some of Kabasele's early recordings, he graduated as a technical teacher from the Leopold II Institute in 1957 before he became a full-time musician. So all of these musicians, as well as Roger Iziedi, one of the percussionists on the record, had come from aspirational families in which they were being brought up to be évolués before they rebelled. Despite this rebellious streak and their rejection of their families' life choices, there was still a strong sense of difference and class distinction when they mixed with musicians who came from backgrounds that were more avowedly rural or working class and who were therefore usually less educated.

One of the most famous Congolese musicians in international terms in the later part of the twentieth century was François Luambo, also known as Franco. He was born in 1939, 80 kilometers south of Léopoldville. Franco's father died when he was ten, leaving his family in poverty, and his mother took the family to Kinshasa. His older friend Paul "Dewayon" Ebengo taught him guitar and Franco played his homemade guitar in the Bayaka market in the city to encourage customers to buy his mother's fried cakes. Dewayon worked in a textile factory at night and neither of them went to school. In 1950, when Franco was 12 and Dewayon was 16, they formed a band and spent the next three years scratching a living until Henri Bowane signed them up to the house band at Loningisa Studios. By the late 1950s the two most popular groups in Léopoldville were le Grand Kallé's (Kabasele's) African Jazz and Vicky Longomba and Franco's group, OK Jazz.

Although it is too simplistic to characterize African Jazz as évolué and OK Jazz as the more 'village' or working-class band, there is an element of truth to this. In the late 1950s a subculture started to emerge that reflected the values of this working-class sector of urban society. They were disaffected youths who drew on the imagery of populist international cinema, particularly American cowboy films but also Indian Bollywood films. They were known as "Bills" (after Buffalo Bill) or Hindoubills (to combine the Indian and western imagery), dressed in checkered shirts, jeans, neck scarfs, and cowboy boots, and often had a penchant for marijuana. Franco, as the main song writer and guitarist for OK Jazz, was a young man who fitted this demographic, and some of the photographs of the band from this period show them in neck scarves and checkered shirts in contrast to the famous photographs of African Jazz in suits and ties.

We should recognize all the complexities and ambiguities that make this narrative something that needs to be treated with caution, but Vincent Luttman, a UK guitarist who works with Congolese musicians in London, says, "Musically Kabasele's African Jazz appealed to the sophisticated or educated Congolese, whereas Franco's OK Jazz appealed to the masses on the street."[6] It is also true, though, that these individual musicians didn't define their identity through the lens of a single category such as évolué or Bill, and neither did these social categories come from a single homogenous group of people. In both instances, for example, there would be people who would consider themselves members of a given group because it accorded with who they already thought they were, and others who were there because they aspired to be that kind of person. This might include those who were enculturated as évolué but who aspired to the "coolness" of the rebellious insouciance of a Bill, or a working-class kid who aspired to the sophistication of the évolué. We can see these types of complexity in musical subcultures from punks and second-wave mods/new wave in 1970s UK to gangsta and progressive lyrics in hip hop in 1980s USA as well as 'slack' versus 'conscious' lyrics in 1990s Jamaican ragga.

It may seem that at this moment, at the start of the 1960s in Congolese rhumba, the sophistication and education of the évolués was riding the crest of the cultural wave, and indeed, le Grand Kallé and African Jazz were closely associated with Patrice Lumumba, who was seen as an intellectual and someone who could lead the évolué beyond their past role as the servants of the colonists. However, in a few short months Lumumba would be dead, and as Luttman puts it: "After the assassination of Lumumba on September 7, 1960, Kabasele's career declined markedly over the next few years. Whether that's a coincidence or otherwise is not for me to say."[7] Franco and OK Jazz, who maintained a populist stance during the elections, managed to increase their national and international popularity under the one-party Mobutu regime.

When Thomas Kanza invited Kabasele and Vicky Longomba to go to Brussels for the round table, Longombe also invited Franco, but he turned the offer down, saying he was busy with OK Jazz. However, Vicky and Antoine "Brazzos" Armando (guitarist with OK Jazz) did go, which raises the question whether Franco had a different reason for declining. Kabasele, Nico, Dechaud, Iziedi, Vicky, and Brazzos, along with a conga drummer called Pierre "Petit Pierre" Tantula, formed the band who went to Brussels under the title of le Grand Kallé and African Jazz and recorded "Indépendance Cha Cha." If we consider Congolese musical society in the simplified and schematic form of évolués and Bills for a moment, then moving into the world of the colonial masters would represent a clear tipping of the scales of power in favor of the évolués. Those who chose to go to Brussels would have had to be confident that they would be perceived as behaving in the right way on the international stage, and that would be much more likely if you had an évolué background.

Didier Gondola[8] has argued that the development of the Bill subculture was as much about gender politics as it was about class. He suggests that the notion of masculinity that was embodied in the évolué culture was perceived by Bills as an emasculation of the Congolese man. The masculinity portrayed in Hollywood's Wild West and Bollywood's Wild East was much more attractive to the young men in the townships of Léopoldville than the European-style, catholic, monogamous, and obsequious role of the évolué— especially given that the rewards of the latter were restricted and not open to everyone who "applied." As we have introduced gender politics to this discussion, an important part of this song's story and its relationship to the narratives of power is the total absence of any female characters.

In Léopoldville immediately after the Second World War, there were twice as many men as women, as it was much more difficult for women to find work in the city. And if music was not considered a respectable profession for a man in this environment, this was doubly true for women. Once the extended sexual rituals of music were removed from the strict social control of a tight-knit community and made into a commercial activity, the parallels with prostitution also came to the fore. Of course, male participation in the transactions of heterosexual prostitution has seldom met with the same social disapprobation or ostracism faced by female participants, and the same has been true in many cultures, with its metaphorical counterpart in music. Léopoldville in the 1950s is only one in a huge list of places and times in which a woman's being a professional singer was considered a sign of promiscuity and low morals. The two most famous female singers—there is no evidence of professional women instrumentalists to be found in Congolese popular music until the 1970s— were Pauline Lisanga and Lucie Eyenga, although both Gary Stewart[9] and Vincent Luttman[10] list several others.

The inequalities of power between the sexes had prompted women in Léopoldville to organize themselves into associations called *moziki*—mutual self-help groupings with names like Violette, the Rose, and Elegance—and these were active in the music industry as much as everywhere else. Gondola points to what he calls "the Janus-head"[11] of the Bills' attitude to women in that they were often both protective and predatory, embodying the all-too-familiar notion of women as property. The place where women did feature prominently and frequently in Congolese rhumba of this period was, of course, in the song titles and lyrics—from "Marie-Louise" by Wendo Kolosoyi and "Para Fifi" by Kabasele to the phenomenon of Negro Jazz winning over the audience at the club *Chez Faignond* by "shouting out" to the Violette moziki who used the club as their unofficial headquarters. However, "Indépendance Cha Cha" has a clear message about gender and power in that, for a song about the serious business of politics, all the "shout outs" are to male politicians and male-run political organizations. The chorus lyric in Lingala, which says "Indépendance (cha cha), we've won it," is sung by male voices, and the "we" that gets named in the verses is entirely male.

Networks of Power

So far I have focused on examples of power that exist between two individuals or groups, but of course, life is always more complicated than that. The relationship between the évolués and the Bills (or other rural and working-class Congolese) was always constructed and negotiated in relation to the third party: the Belgians. The economic clout of the colonial power and the tight social control they exercised over all Congolese created as much tension between the évolués and the Bills as it did between either of those groups and the Belgians. As Renton, Seddon, and Zellig point out,[12] even the act of granting independence was performed as a kind of passive-aggressive exercise of power. The Belgians announced at the round table in February 1960 that the Congolese would become independent on June 30 of that year— an astonishingly short timescale given that they had made little attempt to prepare for this eventuality previously. Both Patrice Lumumba, leader of the Mouvement National Congolais, and Joseph Kasavubu, leader of ABAKO (a party promoting the interests of an ethnic subgroup, the Kongo people), asked the Belgians privately to delay independence and install an interim government. The Belgians refused, a power play that in retrospect seems designed to cause trouble for the new regime before it even began. Of course, the way the history of oppression had played out meant that none of the Congolese leaders could be seen to be begging favors of the former colonial power, and especially not to be seen to be admitting that they weren't ready for power and needed help. Given that Congolese people had spent the previous year or more in both active and passive revolt against the colonial rulers, there was no way for this story to be told other than through the lyrics of the chorus of this song: "Indépendance Cha-cha to zuwi ye!" (Independence Cha-cha, we've won it!). It is hard to believe that the Belgian government was not deliberately sowing the seeds of discord between the évolués, who were set up to be the obvious inheritors of the government, and the majority of the rural and working-class population. The only other possible explanation seems to be an astonishing level of incompetence or naïveté in the Belgian ruling class.

Another network of power that is important in regard to the creation and distribution of this track is the recording industry. Although all the musicians who wrote and recorded this song were Congolese, and it is their names which will remain associated with it for as long as it is listened to, the power behind the industrial process was European. It is a strange quirk of history that all of the studio and recording companies that helped to establish the Congolese music industry—and there were around half a dozen important ones—were all Greek owned. Greek entrepreneurs owned a lot of the independent small-trading companies in the Belgian Congo, and once the recording of local music was proven to be profitable by one of them, Nicolas Jeronimidis and the Ngoma Studio, it set a precedent that others followed. However, the recording was only one step in the industrial process. American, Dutch, German, and Swiss companies produced the recording technologies—initially microphones and either a disc-cutting lathe or, later, a tape recorder. Most of the record pressing was done in Europe at pressing plants in Belgium, France, or Holland. In addition, the Belgian-owned radio stations in the Congo and Greek- and Belgian-owned record shops constituted yet another layer of ownership of the fruits of this musical enterprise.

The question of how those fruits were distributed between the various participants in this network is, on the one hand, a simple matter of capitalism, and on the other, is dependent on the distribution of power between those participants. While economics thinks of price as being determined by the costs of supply and the level of demand, it is perhaps less common to think of the distribution of profits in an economic enterprise being determined in the same way. The musicians are more in need of money than anyone else in the supply chain, and their demand for that profit means that they are prepared to "pay" more for it, that is, to receive lower profits. In the case of each of the suppliers, the less the individual transaction contributes to their overall well-being—that is, the smaller a part it is of their turnover—the lower will be their demand (they will want to "pay" less for it by receiving higher profits in return for their outlay). In basic terms, if I need the money for my survival or comfort more than the person I am bargaining with, then they will have the power to negotiate a disproportionate share of the profits in any transaction.

"Indépendance Cha Cha" was recorded in a Brussels studio associated with the Gramophone Company, but they were not interested in the recording and let Kabasele sell the rights to the Belgian company Fonior, who owned a studio in Léopoldville and had been releasing Congolese music already. No details of the profit split are available, but it was normal practice for the performers to receive a small one-off payment and for the composer and/ or owner of the recording to split the profits with the label. Of course, the distributors and the retailers would also be taking a substantial cut of the wholesale and retail prices. Although it was a hit across Africa in the early 1960s as many former colonies achieved independence, I can find no reliable figures about its number of sales.

The final network that I want to discuss is a more global musical and technological one. Much has been written about the transfer of African musical practices to the Americas and the Caribbean as part of the slave trade. Sara McGuinness[13] has written about how Victor and the Gramophone Company went into partnership after the Wall Street Crash of 1929 to market Latin American music in Africa, including several discs of Cuban son labeled as foxtrot/rhumba, and how these GV series records sparked a trend for Cuban music in the Belgian Congo[14]—with Kabasele being one of the principal players. Interestingly, the sales of the GV series must have been relatively insignificant in the early 1930s when they were first released because of the tiny number of record players in Africa at the time. Even radio didn't come to Léopoldville until 1937, and radios were pretty scarce. In 1939 Radio Congolia was launched, which like the early bantu radio stations in South Africa involved broadcasting the station through permanent outdoor public address systems as well as wirelessly.[15] While this didn't increase record sales for the labels, it did produce advertising revenue for the radio stations, and the demand for Latin music increased. As prosperity increased, so did the ownership of radios and record players among the Black population, and the interest in new Cuban music was sustained.

In 1957 Kabasele recorded "Baila," a version of the new Cuban *chachachá* dance craze that was sweeping Latin and North America, and other groups followed the trend. While the power or influence of other musical styles on Congolese musicians was in part driven by the levels of exposure that companies such as Congolia and the Gramophone Company could create, the economics of taste were (and remain) an unpredictable business. While it has been said many times that the popularity of Cuban music in the Congo flows from the recognition of the influence of African slaves on its development, it is much harder to explain why Cuban son, Jamaican reggae, and US jazz, gospel, blues, and funk have all had different levels of influence in different African countries. How much these influences are a matter of taste and how much they are affected by levels of exposure is beyond the scope of this discussion, but both of those forces are expressions of power, either on the individual micro-level of taste or on the macro-level of international company policies. Bob White has proposed another factor in the adoption of what were, after all, the relatively sanitized Afro-Cuban rhythms of songs such as "The Peanut Vendor" on the GV Series. He says:

> Listening to this music was pleasurable in part because it represented the possibility of being cosmopolitan on terms that made intuitive and aesthetic sense to Congolese audiences…many Congolese comment on the fact that Afro-Cuban popular music was seen as thoroughly "modern"… perhaps it was simply because only people from a certain social category in Leopoldville had access to the phonographs required to play such music.[16]

> Afro-Cuban music was so attractive to Congolese musicians and audiences not only because of the way that it sounded, but also because of what it stood for. It provided urban Congolese with an alternative to a particular form of cosmopolitanism—Belgian colonialism—that was strict and stiff, if not cruel.[17]

This way of adopting a form of cosmopolitanism that carried the cache of Western approval and modernism and yet also sidestepped the problem of valorizing the culture of one's colonial masters was a means of not ceding power to the Belgians. An inverted form of this phenomenon can also be found in the ways in which "village" Congolese music, which suffered from the colonial stigma of being primitive or not évolué, was assimilated into Congolese popular music like "Indépendance Cha Cha." As we noted previously, both Dechaud and Nico came from this "village" background, with these traditional and folk resonances in their musical language. The sound of the guitar may have been modern to Congolese because of the frequently heard tres (a Cuban guitar-like instrument) on the GV series records, but it also had traditional resonances with lute-like instruments that were part of Congolese musical heritage. The patterns that were used on these instruments and, perhaps even more tellingly, on the likembe (or thumb piano) form the basis of the Congolese guitar techniques that early users of the guitar, like Wendo Kolosoyi, developed and later masters such as Franco and Docteur Nico honed to perfection.[18] Creating a modern and cosmopolitan musical style that incorporates these tropes from traditional African forms is another way of taking some control and power. The muted rhythm guitar lines that Dechaud is playing behind Nico's more melodic and ringing tres-like (and in some places jazz-inflected) lines provide a direct connection between the sound of "Indépendance Cha Cha" and the traditional music of the likembe.

In much the same way, the popular singing style of Tino Rossi, a French-Corsican with a tremulous light countertenor voice who gained fame in the 1930s and 1940s, was both popular and influential in Léopoldville, and both le Grand Kallé and Vicky Longomba adopted some of those mannerisms. Importantly, though, they were also a way of inflecting traditional Congolese singing styles with a recognizable modernity that was decidedly un-Belgian. So while the more Cuban two-part harmony of the chorus, which is sung in a combination of French and Lingala, has a semi-military precision in the way that it follows the slightly march-like chachachá rhythm, the verses, with their references to Congolese *griot* praise singing, are like a sinuous African vocal melody with the tone of Tino Rossi.

Conclusion

Going back to my definition of power as "the perception of the potential for an action or behavior," I have looked at the kinds of individuals and groupings of individuals involved in the making of "Indépendance Cha Cha" who were engaged in this type of "perception of potential," that is, who either had or did not have, and either exercised or did not exercise, power. I have also looked at the circumstances in which those decisions about actions and behavior were made.[19]

Even when discussing individuals, our brains are busy categorizing them—village or urban, évolué or Bill, Black or white, male or female, rich or poor. Indeed, categorizing is a fundamental characteristic of human intelligence: we wouldn't fall into the category of human if we didn't have a highly developed capability for creating categories. There's a great deal of interesting writing on the theory of categorization,[20] and my whole thesis hinges on whether you agree with the implicit definitions I have employed to select and propose my categories and the ways in which those definitions contain implicit assumptions about causality.

Within science and technology studies, one of the vital concepts in theories of the social construction of technology is the *technological frame*, and with it the associated concept of *interpretative flexibility*. Put crudely, these ideas outline the fact that technological innovation is influenced by the subjective interpretations of participants: their thoughts on what the pressing problems are, what the function of existing technology is, and how those problems might be solved. Of course, these ideas apply both to the participants in the development of particular innovations and to the participants in the analysis themselves. The sociologists and historians who developed these theories, such as Wiebe Bijker, Trevor Pinch, and Thomas Hughes,[21] were also challenging themselves to exercise interpretative flexibility and not to restrict themselves to a particular frame. It is a formalization of the age-old problem of avoiding getting stuck in a way of thinking or manner of interpretation.

Returning to the making of "Indépendance Cha Cha," my analysis constitutes what we might call a *musicological frame*: a set of decisions that serve to define the questions I am asking about the piece. As I have mentioned, I am using the notion of affordances for action or behavior as a way of defining power, and I have also chosen to categorize the participants and causality in a variety of ways listed above. I could have chosen a different tack—perhaps foregrounding creativity and authenticity and categorizing participants using more conventional musical divisions (instrument played, type of musical education, and so forth). This particular musicological frame is, therefore, an ideological choice. It is ideological in terms of the questions it chooses to ask rather than in terms of whether the internal logic of the answers is skewed by subjective bias (although others may judge that it is skewed in that way as well). Given that this chapter was set in motion by a study day funded by the O'Connell Initiative for the Global History of Capitalism at Fordham University, it perhaps makes sense that the ideological slant of my research question leans towards the power relationships that set this particular moment of musical activity in motion. It also, perhaps, makes sense that the thrust of my argument is about social forces rather than individual creativity—although, of course, that is not to deny there is an equally powerful narrative about those individuals as unique musical identities.

In that spirit of exploring musicality through the lens of social forces, what better way could there be of using music to express the taking back of control of your nation after over 75 years of colonial rule than through a series of musical metaphors and symbols that simultaneously express a new form of cosmopolitanism and modernity while also harking back to your ancient musical roots? Of course, this lovely, infectious tune also references the gender inequalities of the time through the total absence of females in it. It reminds us of the complex and divisive social structures that these musicians embody, and foreshadows the tragic events that followed on almost immediately from this jubilant expression of hope and confidence and led to a long, violent, and painful narrative in which all these themes of power, inequality, and resentment were played out. As Alain Mabanckou point out,[22] the joy of this song foreshadows the disillusionment that the post-colonial period was going to bring to many African states:

> Independence in this song by Grand Kallé celebrated first and foremost the departure of the white man, the right of Africans to manage their continent themselves. The dances and the joy had made us forget that disillusionment would come very quickly.[23]

However, its resilience as an optimistic symbol can seen in its use by Congolese B-One TV in their celebration of the fiftieth anniversary of independence in 2010,[24] and by Afro Fiesta/Playing for Change on the sixtieth anniversary.[25] Le Grand Kallé's career as a performer was not so resilient, and after Rochereau and Doctor Nico left the band in 1965 to pursue their own careers, he retired from singing and moved into management and promotion.

Notes

1 Tshonga Onyumbe, "KALLE Jeef Ou Joseph Kabasele Tshamala Biographie et Œuvre d'un Chanteur Congolais," *Annales Aequatoria* 20 (1999): 323–53.
2 Florent Mazzoleni, "The Music of African Independence," *Africultures* 83, no. 1 (2011): 30–6.
3 Alain Mabanckou, "Indépendance Cha-Cha." *Libération*, July 8, 2000.
4 Bob White, "Congolese Rumba and Other Cosmopilitanisms," *Cahiers d'études Africaines*, no. 168 (2002): 19.
5 White, "Congolese Rumba and Other Cosmopilitanisms," 29.
6 For example, George Lakoff, *Women, Fire, and Dangerous Things: What Categories Reveal about the Mind*, Chicago: University of Chicago Press, 1990.
7 David Garbin and Wa Gamoka Pambu, *Roots and Routes: Congolese Diaspora in Multicultural Britain*, London: Roehampton University/CORECOG, 2009.
8 Ch. Didier Gondola, *Tropical Cowboys: Westerns, Violence, and Masculinity in Kinshasa*, Bloomington: Indiana University Press, 2016.
9 Gary Stewart, *Rumba on the River: A History of the Popular Music of the Two Congos*, London: Verso Books, 2003.
10 Garbin and Pambu, *Roots and Routes: Congolese Diaspora in Multicultural Britain*.
11 Gondola, *Tropical Cowboys: Westerns, Violence, and Masculinity in Kinshasa*, 116–48.
12 David Renton, David Seddon, and Leo Zeilig, *The Congo: Plunder and Resistance*, London: Zed Books, 2007.
13 Sara McGuinness, "Grupo Lokito: A Practice-Based Investigation into Contemporary Links between Congolese and Cuban Popular Music," PhD, SOAS, University of London, 2012.
14 Elina Djebbari, "Cultural Diplomacy in the Cold War: Musical Dialogues between Cuba and West Africa, 1960–1970," edited by Giulia Bonacci, Adrien Delmas, and KaliArgriadis, 183–205. Johannesburg: Wits University Press, 2020.
15 Wiederroth, "Radio Broadcasting for Blacks during the Second World War: 'It Could Be Dangerous,'" *Historia* 57 (2012): 104–49.
16 White, "Congolese Rumba and Other Cosmopilitanisms," 19.
17 Ibid., 29.
18 Damien Mondondo Pwono, *Institutionalization of Popular Music in Zaire*, Pittsburgh: University of Pittsburgh, 1992.
19 Clearly, these participants range from named individuals to national groupings such as "the Belgians," and the affordances that define these various forms of power range from economics and education to race and gender. And within those definitions of power and affordance there are implicit and explicit assumptions about causality. When I assert something such as that "the inequalities of power

between the sexes had prompted women in Léopoldville to organize themselves into associations called *moziki*," I am ascribing that organizational activity to what seems like a single cause. Of course, the "inequalities of power between the sexes" are not a single cause, they are a categorical grouping of phenomena which I am choosing to enlist and which would be difficult to delineate in an uncontroversial and detailed manner. There may also have been other more positive and communal causes of the women in Léopoldville's organizational proclivities, and statements like these throughout my essay should be seen as general and pragmatic rather than absolutist. They construct a simplified and schematic representation of reality rather than a description and, as such, invite the reader to consider whether it is useful to interpret this phenomenon "as if" this schematic representation were "true."

20 Mabanckou, "Indépendance Cha-Cha."
21 See for example Trevor Pinch, Wieber Bijker, and Thomas Hughes, *The Social Construction of Technological Systems: New Directions in the Sociology and History of Technology*. Cambridge: MIT Press, 2012.
22 Mabanckou, "Indépendance Cha-Cha."
23 "L'indépendance dans cette chanson de Grand Kallé célébrait d'abord et avant tout le départ du Blanc, le droit des Africains de gérer eux-mêmes leur continent. Les danses et la joie nous avaient fait oublier que la désillusion arriverait très vite" Mabanckou "Indépendance Cha Cha."
24 A YouTube video of the 2010 B-One TV special can be seen at: www.youtube.com/watch?v=qrNXD5qhSZI
25 A YouTube of the 2020 Playing For Change performance in South Africa can be seen at: www.youtube.com/watch?v=2bhM2IY7FM4

Bibliography

Djebbari, Elina. "Cultural Diplomacy in the Cold War: Musical Dialogues between Cuba and West Africa, 1960–1970." In *Cuba and Africa, 1959–1994: Writing an Alternative Atlantic History*, edited by Giulia Bonacci, Adrien Delmas, and Kali Argriadis, 183–205. Johannesburg: Wits University Press, 2020.

Garbin, David and Wa Gamoka Pambu, eds. *Roots and Routes: Congolese Diaspora in Multicultural Britain*. London: Roehampton University/CORECOG, 2009.

Gondola, Ch. Didier. *Tropical Cowboys: Westerns, Violence and Masculinity in Kinshasa*. Bloomington: Indiana University Press, 2016.

Lakoff, George. *Women, Fire, and Dangerous Things: What Categories Reveal about the Mind*. Chicago: University of Chicago Press, 1990.

Mabanckou, Alain. "Indépendance Cha-Cha." *Libération*, July 8, 2000, www.liberation.fr/planete/2010/07/08/independance-cha-cha_664583

Mazzoleni, Florent. "The Music of African Independence." *Africultures* 83, no. 1 (2011): 30–6.

McGuinness, Sara. "Grupo Lokito: A Practice-Based Investigation into Contemporary Links between Congolese and Cuban Popular Music." PhD, SOAS, University of London, 2012, https://eprints.soas.ac.uk/14703/1/Mcguinness_3420.pdf

Onyumbe, Tshonga. "KALLE Jeef Ou Joseph Kabasele Tshamala Biographie et Œuvre d'un Chanteur Congolais." *Annales Aequatoria* 20 (1999): 323–53.

Pwono, Damien Mandondo. *Institutionalization of Popular Music in Zaire.* Pittsburgh: University of Pittsburgh, 1992.

Renton, David, Seddon, David, and Zeilig, Leo. *The Congo: Plunder and Resistance.* London: Zed Books, 2007.

Stewart, Gary. *Rumba on the River: A History of the Popular Music of the Two Congos.* London: Verso Books, 2003.

White, Bob W. "Congolese Rumba and Other Cosmopilitanisms." *Cahiers d'études Africaines*, no. 168 (2002): 663–86. https://journals.openedition.org/etudesafricai nes/161

Wiederroth, Nicole. "Radio Broadcasting for Blacks during the Second World War: 'It Could Be Dangerous'" *Historia* 57 (2012): 104–49.

2 Gerald Wilson—"Viva Tirado" (1962)

Oliver Wang

At some point in the early 1960s, Los Angeles bandleader Gerald Wilson and his wife, Josefina Villasenor, took a trip down to Tijuana's famed Monumental Plaza de Toros—the "Bullring by the Sea"—located just hundreds of feet from the US–Mexico border. There, they witnessed the greatness of matador José Ramón Tirado, a legend on the Mexican torero circuit. As Wilson told me in a 2002 interview, "I was at a bullfight one day and I saw this young man. It was so very exciting, I tried to get this excitement down in his number." He was referring to the song that Tirado's performance inspired, arguably Wilson's most famous composition: "Viva Tirado."

Originally recorded in 1962, "Viva Tirado" would enjoy an intergenerational and cross-community lifespan that Wilson could never have predicted. In the years since its original release, "Viva Tirado" has become a quintessential song about Los Angeles and its people, even if few seem to recognize it as such. It was never intended to be civic anthem, but thanks to the song's unlikely journey via various cover versions and samplings, "Viva Tirado" has sustained a decades-long conversation that encompasses what Josh Kun has described as "the congealed histories of black and brown dialogue" between the city's African American and Latinx communities.[1] The song's now signature keyboard melodies and bass riffs have come to herald a spirit of intercultural exchange that has spanned eras and continents yet always seems to wind its way home to Los Angeles.

Wilson's own personal journey to Los Angeles first came in the winter of 1940 when he boarded a train in Chicago, bound for LA, as part of Jimmie Lunceford's big band. By the time the San Bernardino Mountains came into view, Wilson decided the Southland would be his future home, telling interviewers Steve Isoardi and Buddy Collette, "As I looked out the window of my bunk in the sleeper, I see this beautiful sunshine…I made up my mind that day I was going to live in Los Angeles."[2] World War II would postpone his relocation when Wilson was, ironically, sent back to Chicago to lead a segregated US Navy band. However, upon discharge in 1944, Wilson returned to Los Angeles and remained there until he passed away at age 96 in 2014.

DOI: 10.4324/9781003093206-3

Figure 2.1 Gerald Wilson (on right) in the late 1960s. Credit: Michael Ochs Archives/ Getty Images.

Wilson became a leader in the vibrant Central Avenue jazz scene, then the heart of Black cultural life in the city, just south of downtown (see Figure 2.1). During the 1940s and '50s, Wilson went from player to bandleader to recording artist. His personal life flourished as well; in the late 1950s, he met and married Villasenor, a Mexican American from LA. Their 1960 marriage came during an era of shifting legal and social tides, barely a dozen years after the landmark *Perez vs. Sharp* decision made California the first state to strike down anti-miscegenation laws.[3]

Wilson and Villasenor's marriage left a deep cultural impact on Wilson. "She, of course, influenced me and exposed me to her culture in the many years we've been married. I've been to many places in Mexico and Spain," Wilson told me. Trips to Tijuana were frequent, not least of all to the Bullring by the Sea, where Wilson first saw José Ramón Tirado in action.

The song Wilson composed in homage to the torero is infused with the "coolness" West Coast jazz was known for, especially with guitarist Joe Pass playing in a breezy style reminiscent of mentors Wes Montgomery and Django

Reinhardt. However, it would be pianist Jack Wilson who provided "Viva Tirado's" most memorable motif: a syncopated, seven-note, two-measure riff that can be heard on practically every version of the song recorded since.

Wilson first included "Viva Tirado" on *Moment of Truth* (Pacific Jazz, 1962). It arrived amid a complicated era for race relations in Los Angeles. Josh Sides chronicles how segregation between the region's communities of color increased in the postwar period, especially in South Central, where long-standing Mexican American residents reacted to the influx of Black migrants via a form of "Brown flight" by moving out to inner-ring suburbs such as East Los Angeles and Huntington Park as well as more outlying neighborhoods in the San Gabriel Valley.[4] Yet, if Black and Chicana/o youth were moving apart residentially, the city's music scenes were a counterforce to reunite them.

John Dolphin's Central Ave. record store, Dolphin's of Hollywood, housed the radio station KRKD. Its DJs, such as Dick "Huggy Boy" Hugg and Hunter Hancock, broadcast to local youth of all stripes, inviting them to "get on down here to Vernon and Central, Central and Vernon."[5] In response, racist city officials tried to limit the area's popularity, using alcohol bans and other legislation to dissuade visitors. Against this push, Gaye Theresa Johnson suggests that

> radio broadcasts from Dolphin's of Hollywood transmitted an invitation to a multi-racial, *discursive* space of listenership as well as a physical space of interracial congregation.... These spaces and places, physical and discursive, were mutually constitutive. Hugg and Hancock later recalled watching the "crawl of cruisers"— white and Black—that maintained Central Avenue as a predominately Black but thriving interracial space, even when the city mobilized against it.[6]

This is part of the history congealed within a "Viva Tirado," reflecting both Wilson's relationship to his Mexican American wife as well as his willingness to cross literal and figurative borders. While other forces conspired to separate the city's communities, Wilson's homage exemplified cross-cultural contact and exchange, a theme found in many of the song's future iterations. However, though "Viva Tirado" became one of Wilson's most covered compositions, he was not primarily responsible for the song's long-term success. For that, the Black jazz composer, so enamored with Mexican culture, would need an assist from a band of young Mexican American musicians seeped in African American R&B and jazz traditions.

Of the thousands who heeded Huggy Boy's call to "get on down here to Vernon and Central," many were Mexican American teenagers whose families had settled on LA's Eastside. These teens came of age before rock 'n' roll and R&B were racially segregated into artificially separate genres, when local artists like Edmundo "Don Totsi" Tostado could score hits like 1948 "Pachuco Boogie," a catchy dance number that originated from Tostado's Central Ave. jazz gigs and featured Cab Calloway–style scatting but en español.[7]

As the LAPD and other city officials cracked down on Central Ave. venues during the 1950s, intrepid DJs/promoters such as Huggy Boy and Johnny Otis—Greek by heritage but "Black by persuasion"—headed east, especially to El Monte, where Otis's Legion Stadium concerts drew multiracial crowds by the thousands every week.[8] By decade's end, a cohort of Mexican American rock 'n' roll musicians arose, including the Armenta Brothers, Bobby "Rey" Reyes, and most famously, Richie "Valens" Valenzuela, whose late '50s hits like "My Donna" and "La Bamba" would become synonymous with the Southland's emergent Chicana/o communities.

In their study of the Southland's Mexican American music scenes, David Reyes and Tom Waldman suggested that these youths dealt with fraught race relations yet their status as neither white nor Black had unintended benefits: "Being on the margin of American pop culture creates its own kind of freedom. Chicanos listen to what they want, without having to satisfy their own or others' race-based expectations."[9] This liminal freedom from the iron cage of racial categories is what George Lipsitz described as Chicana/o music's "bifocality" that allowed it to be "accessible from both inside and outside of their community" while simultaneously engaging with an "intuitive postmodernism—delighting in difference, undermining univocal master narratives and celebrating the decentered and polyglot nature of popular culture."[10]

One rising Eastside band embedded within these flows of cultural fluidity and hybridity was the VIPs. Formed in the mid 1960s, The VIPs aspired to follow in the footsteps of Eastside hitmakers such as Thee Midniters and Cannibal and the Headhunters. By the late '60s, the VIPs had landed a gig as a house band at Kabuki Sukiyaki, located on Crenshaw Blvd. by Coliseum St., then the heart of what the Japanese American community called Seinan (meaning "southwest"). The VIPs had a rotating membership in the band's early years, but its core included keyboardist Bobby Espinoza, guitarist Mickey Lespron, trumpeter Bobby Loya, bassist Freddie Sanchez, and drummer John De Luna. The band played a mix of rock 'n' roll, jazz, pop, and R&B. De Luna recalled some of their répertoire:

> Freddie sang James Brown's "I Feel Good" and I did "Funny How Time Slips Away" by Willie Nelson, an uptempo R&B song called "Get Down With It," and a famous East L.A. ballad called "For Your Love," [by doo-wop singer Ed Townsend]. "Hideaway" by Freddie King and "Bumpin' On Sunset" by Wes Montgomery were showcases for Mickey, and Bobby Espinosa showed his stuff on Jimmy Smith's "Got My MoJo Workin.'"[11]

However, they also shared an interest in Latin jazz, and it was while attending gigs at the famed Lighthouse Club in Hermosa Beach that the members first heard Gerald Wilson performing "Viva Tirado."[12]

The VIPs created their own version of "Viva Tirado" that they used as an instrumental interlude between sets. By 1970, the group came to the attention of producer/manager Eddie "Gordo" Davis, one of the city's main music impresarios.[13] Davis was white, but he saw tremendous potential in the region's Mexican American musical talent, and beginning in the early '60s he teamed with a Chicano talent scout, Billy Cardenas, to sign acts to a variety of independent labels including Rampart, Faro, and Gordo.[14] The pair signed and/or managed such Chicano artists as the Premiers, the Romancers, and most significantly, Cannibal and the Headhunters, who enjoyed a 1965 chart-topper with their cover of "Land of 1,000 Dances."[15]

As part of their demo session, the VIPs included their version of "Viva Tirado." Whereas Wilson's original was a slicker, flowing composition, the VIPs' cover was tighter, anchored by a catchy four-note bass line, set to a tresillo rhythm. This bass line was the VIPs' addition—it was not in Wilson's arrangement—and it helped make their version of "Viva Tirado" irresistibly funky.

Davis was taken with this new spin on "Viva Tirado" and wanted to release it on his Gordo imprint but, according to De Luna, the manager insisted on renaming the band El Chicano. This was no random act; Davis had paid close attention to the burgeoning Chicano Movement, which by 1970 had swept over Los Angeles. Heavily influenced by the Black Power Movement and similar social movements of the era, organizations such as the Brown Berets and United Mexican American Students (UMAS) helped make LA a central site for "Brown Power" consciousness-raising and mobilizing, culminating in both the 1968 "blowouts" in local high schools as well as the anti-war Chicano Moratorium demonstrations that peaked by the late summer of 1970.

At least one other local band was already in dialogue with these movements. In 1968, East LA's Thee Midniters—managed by Davis's main rival, Eddie Torres—cut "The Ballad of Cesar Chavez" to celebrate the famed labor organizer, and Torres also released another Midniters' single entitled "Chicano Power" on his newly formed label La Raza.[16] Davis wanted to capitalize on the moment by rebranding the VIPs as El Chicano.

The problem was that the VIPs still associated the term "Chicano" with its negative, pre-Movement connotations, that is, with "images of a half-breed, cultural nomad who did not fit in, either in Anglo society or in Mexican society."[17] According to De Luna, when the band balked at the name change, Davis threatened to form a "fake El Chicano band" and attribute the single to them instead.[18]

In the end, Davis opted to release the single—credited to El Chicano—and it became a sensation.[19] According to Steven Loza, the song was a number-one hit on local charts for 13 consecutive weeks, and nationally it became one of the first singles to chart in every major genre except for country/western, including jazz, pop, and R&B.[20] "Viva Tirado" became a crossover hit in every sense of the term, and its success quickly converted the once-reluctant VIPs' members to embrace their new identity as El Chicano.

El Chicano's "Viva Tirado" became the song's definitive version, far more so than Wilson's original. By the mid-70s, covers of their version—identifiable by that four-note bass line—cropped up across the world, from Belgium's El Chicles to Italy's Duke of Burlington, Panama's Los Mozambiques to Jamaica's Augustus Pablo, as well as versions by Los Angeles' rock/soul band the 5th Dimension and New York's salsa powerhouse the Fania All-Stars. In most instances, the bands that covered it were also steeped in a cross-cultural aesthetic all their own. For example, Los Mozambiques were part of a wave of Panamanian groups drawing from any number of Afro-Antillean styles— jazz, cumbia, reggae, soul—circulating through the migrant crossroads of Panama's docks. Likewise, El Chicles were created by the Dutch-born com-poser Nico Gomez, whose mix of Brazilian, Latin, African, and American musical influences made it difficult to pin down where in the world the band hailed from. These parallels may be coincidental, but I would like to think that the song's popularity was partially based in how different artists resonated with the song's evocation of porous cultural borders and blended identities.[21]

Davis seemingly predicted all of this. His liner notes for El Chicano's 1970 *Viva Tirado* LP are worth quoting at length:

All the music in this album was performed by personally qualified Mexican-American musicians on the premises of a club owned by Japanese. It was produced by two cats, one of which is half English and half Mexican and the other of which is half French and half Jew. It was engineered by the cat who is half English and half Mexican, a New Zealander and a Scotchman. It will be merchandised by an Italian who works for a company that is operated by many people of many racial extractions, headquartered in the United States of America, that can be owned by anyone anywhere in the world that wants to buy a piece of the action. Brother, to my way of thinking, that's where it's at! There are no language barriers in instrumental music and music in the international language.

Davis's celebration of hybridity was facile; after all, he was writing his liner notes only five years after the Watts Riots and in the midst of rising ethnic nationalism that accentuated identity politics rather than minimizing them. However, there is something to be said for how "Viva Tirado," begin-ning with Gerald Wilson's trans-border inspiration, managed to capture—in spirit and sound—a cross-cultural sentiment that was as much about unifying differences as it was about celebrating them. This all happened within an idealized space brought forth through musical imagination; what Josh Kun has described as an "audiotopia," that is:

identificatory "contact zones," [that are] both sonic and social spaces where disparate identity-formations, cultures *and* geographies historically kept and mapped separately are allowed to interact with each other as well as enter into relationships whose consequences for cultural identification are never predetermined.[22]

This notion—of separated communities encountering one another through sonic-scapes—reverberates throughout "Viva Tirado's" genealogy, especially during its El Chicano iteration. Think of Loya first hearing the song performed at the Lighthouse or the VIPs performing it during their set breaks at the Kabuki and the strange collision/collusion of forces that allowed a white producer to brand a band "El Chicano" without their initial permission.

Most of all, "Viva Tirado," like many hit songs, was an accident of history, never as self-consciously political as Thee Midniters' "Chicano Power," yet it was "Viva Tirado" that became a definitive anthem of the Chicano Movement. Its success highlighted the idea of music as congealed history, with the song encapsulating years of interaction between LA's Black and Brown communities in mixed musical venues as well as the symbolic exchange of musical influences, with R&B-inspired hits by Chicana/o artists (for example, "Land of a Thousand Dances") and Latin-influenced hits by Black artists (think of Richard Berry's "Louie Louie").[23] Regardless of the VIPs' original intentions, their hit embodied decades of sociocultural alignments, and 20 years later, those exchanges continued with "Viva Tirado" once again at the center.

By the late 1980s, the social landscape of LA had shifted dramatically. If the postwar migration of African Americans changed the demographic complexion of South Central, by the 1980s it was newly arriving Mexican and Central American immigrants who became the new face of South LA, drawn to low-wage industrial and service work that replaced the previously high-wage manufacturing sector left gutted by the deindustrialization of the 1970s.[24] The old Central Avenue corridor, once the center of Black cultural life in Los Angeles, was now overwhelmingly Brown; if any DJ exhorted youth to "get on down" to Vernon and Central, odds were they were shouting, "¡Andale!"

Meanwhile, working-class communities had to contend with double-digit unemployment, the collapse of the Southland's industrial sector, and rampant abuses by the LAPD. In describing the South Central of the 1980s, Jeff Chang suggests the area was

> the epitome of a growing number of inner-city nexuses where deindustrialization, devolution, Cold War adventurism, the drug trade, gang structures and rivalries, arms profiteering, and police brutality were combining to destabilize poor communities and alienate massive numbers of youth.[25]

For Black and Brown youth subjected to that alienation, destabilization (and police interrogation), one of the few sources of pleasure could still be found through music, especially with the rise of an LA hip-hop scene. As Pancho McFarland describes in his history of Chicana/o hip-hop,

> Youth who looked a certain way, listened to rap music, or had certain types of tattoos were criminalized through informal (police and private citizens singling them out and labeling them as criminal) and formal means (legislation that did not allow them to congregate or be out at certain hours).... In the face of such denigration of their identities, young people created a subculture with a new set of values, morals, aesthetics, and identities.[26]

In the midst of this, a new single gained airplay during the spring and summer of 1990, almost exactly 20 years after El Chicano's "Viva Tirado" had risen: Kid Frost's "La Raza." With its mix of English, Spanish, and Caló street slang, "La Raza" stood out from previous rap-en-español hits by foregrounding not just linguistic difference but a specific message of ethnic pride: the term "la raza" itself translates into "the people," or literally, "the race." For example, Frost raps,

> It's in my blood to be an Aztec Warrior
> Go to any extreme and hold no barriers
> Chicano, and I'm Brown and proud
> Want some chingazos [punches]?
> Simón ese [ok, friend], let's get down.

There are overlapping audiences addressed here. The most obvious are other Mexican Americans, especially those who are familiar with pachuco slang: cholos, vatos, esés, etc. However, when Frost spoke to listeners, the "you" of "some of *you* don't know what's happening, que pasa? / I's not for *you* anyway / this is for la raza," (italics added) he was clearly addressing a *non*-Chicana/o audience. His song was an invitation as much as it was an anthem. Moreover, if he flew his Aztlán banners within the song, the cultural vernacular of "La Raza" was also rooted in hip-hop, a growing lingua franca for youth around the world by the early 1990s. As a Chicano rapper, Frost's decision to channel a Brown Power anthem through an ostensibly Black/Afro-diasporic musical form suggests that he was making a self-conscious move towards a cross-cultural dialogue.

"La Raza," with its blend of linguistic and musical styles, exemplifies George Lipsitz's concept of "strategic antiessentialism" whereby artists deliberately adopt/appropriate elements from other cultures as a way to resist or contest dominant identity formations.[27] Paradoxically, Frost's use of hip-hop as a vehicle to deliver his Chicana/o pride manifesto affirms an ethnic nationalist identity while simultaneously bridging communities. The most obvious gesture lies in Frost's deft working of Caló into hip-hop rhyme patterns and a gangsta rap rhetoric of violent, masculine brio: "My cuete's [gun's] loaded, it's

full of balas [bullets] / I put it in your face, and you won't say nada [nothing]."
However, while the blend of Chicana/o and Black vernacular traditions was
important, it was not the only cross-cultural meeting point signified within
"La Raza."

The song begins with a simple, syncopated, four-note bass line which, after
two bars, is joined by a nimble drum break. The bass line already hints towards
its source, and four bars in the original sample becomes more recognizable as
a blend of jazz keyboards, guitar, and drums float underneath, abetted by a
sprinkling of Latin percussion: here was the return of El Chicano's "Viva
Tirado."[28]

On one hand, the choice of sample by producer Tony G. was obvious and
appropriate; both El Chicano and Kid Frost hailed from LA's Eastside, and
"Viva Tirado" would almost certainly have been part of the soundtrack of
Frost's childhood. Moreover, just as "Viva Tirado" became a key song during
the youth-led Chicano Movement of the '70s, "La Raza" aspired to serve a
similar function for Frost's generation of Chicana/o youth.

As seen in its previous iterations, the use of "Viva Tirado" in "La Raza"
also tapped into a deeper history of Black/Brown encounters and fusions,
homages and adoptions. Frost himself was a product of an intercultural
Los Angeles hip-hop scene, having come up in the early 1980s as a protégé
of the African American rapper Ice-T as well as a participant in the famed
Uncle Jamm's Army rap parties that drew youth of all colors from across
the Southland.[29] Frost's 1990 debut album, *Hispanic Causing Panic*, was
a Chicano corollary to the gangsta rap of Black artists such as Ice-T and
NWA. It was also a groundbreaking affirmation of a Chicana/o community on the margins of mainstream recognition. As journalist Mandalit del
Barco described, "Frost's raps gave voice to the modern-day pachuco, driving
souped-up, lowriding cars, cruising with their homeboys."[30]

That Frost should "give voice" via hip-hop elicited initial skepticism from
some in the Chicana/o community. As he told interviewer Brian Cross, "You
play rap for some of the hardcore Chicanos, even some of my homeboys,
and they say why you wanna rap ése, about fuckin' blacks, homes, fuckin'
mietas?"[31] The use of "Viva Tirado" within "La Raza" was a useful strategy
to bridge the gap. Rafael Pérez-Torres examined "La Raza" as an example
of what he called "mestizaje" or a hybridity inherent in many Latina/o cultural works.[32] It is through musical mestizaje that artists are able to "articulate a cultural strategy for agency and change while at the same time evoking
a sense of historical place and connection."[33] Pérez-Torres argued that even
though the sampling of "Viva Tirado" may have seemed like an example of
decentered, postmodern pastiche, within a mestizaje perspective it was also an
attempt at sustaining Chicana/o traditions:

> Kid Frost's use of "Viva Tirado" evokes that moment of great political
> and social activism among Chicano communities in the late '60s and early
> '70s. From the affirmation of Brown Power to the Blowouts, the Chicano

Movement formed a high-water mark of the struggle by Chicanos for civil rights and political engagement. The musical incorporation of El Chicano suggests a recollection of subaltern resistance.[34]

In other words, Kid Frost's use of "Viva Tirado" linked traditions within the Chicana/o community while also recalling the intercultural history that birthed Wilson's original and El Chicano's cover. In his own words, Frost suggested "oldies"—the rock 'n' roll and R&B canon that El Chicano's "Viva Tirado" exists within—evoked a mnemonic audiotopia for its listeners. "Chicanos are really fond of memories, los recuerdos," Frost claimed, adding:

> They want to listen to music and think of memories and drink and think about the old days when they were with their parents.... So I incorporated the oldies into my sound cause I know how deep the oldies are. People like "Thin Line [Between Love and Hate]" and "Smiling Faces," Bill Withers—we used them 'cause I knew it would be a lot easier for them to listen to the stories.[35]

By sampling oldies, Frost could make hip-hop legible to skeptical Chicana/o peers, and this would become a defining feature of similar rap music of the era. Many of the most popular samples used by Chicana/o rappers in the early 1990s were drawn from so-called lowrider classics, that is, 1960s and '70s soul tunes popular in Eastside barrios.[36] For example, in 1991, Tony G., Frost, and Will Roc produced a major hit for Latin Alliance—a "supergroup" made up of different Latino rappers—called "Lowrider," named after the 1975 hit by the Long Beach band WAR, who, like Gerald Wilson and his orchestra, were an African American–led ensemble playing in a Latin-inspired groove.

Tony G. also helped produce the Riverside rap group Lighter Shade of Brown, whose 1991 album, *Brown and Proud*, directly sampled or referenced oldies including "Spill the Wine" (named after the 1970 Eric Burdon/WAR song) and "Poquito Soul" (named after the 1969 "Poquito Soul," another Eddie Davis–produced single, by One G Plus Three). In Frost's repertoire, other songs sampled the likes of Bill Withers' "Ain't No Sunshine" and Sly and the Family Stone's "It's a Family Affair."[37] His and Tony G.'s use of "Viva Tirado" was just one of many examples of deploying oldies to evoke idealized memories of family and community through a strategically cross-cultural playlist.

Remarkably, 20 years after "La Raza," the "Viva Tirado" chain would gain a new link, one that wrapped its way back to Whittier Boulevard and Legion Stadium, Crenshaw Boulevard and Kabuki Sukiyaki, to Central Avenue and Vernon, even back to Mexico itself in a wondrous completion of a full circle, separated by nearly 50 years.

In another lifetime, brothers Sergio and Francisco Gómez might have answered Huggy Boy's call to come on down to Vernon and Central. Born in the central Mexican state of Michoacán, the Gómez brothers came to South Central as children, at one point living barely a mile from the former store-front for Dolphin's of Hollywood. The brothers came of age in yet another different era of Los Angeles, where new migrant settlements had shifted the locus of the city's Latina/o communities from the older Eastside toward densely populated Southeast neighborhoods such as Bell, Huntington Park, and South Gate.

Though younger than Kid Frost, the Gómez brothers would become the veteran rapper's contemporaries by 1993, when the sibling duo, then known as Juvenile Style, released their first hip-hop album, *Time 2 Expand*. Sonically, their debut shared more in common with the gangsta rap beats of Dr. Dre and DJ Quik than with the oldies-influenced sound of Frost or Lighter Shade of Brown, but lyrically Juvenile Style followed their elder brethren in mixing Caló slang with English.

Juvenile Style dropped *Brewed in South Central* two years later, but their rap career foundered. Sergio Gómez admitted, "We truly didn't have an iden-tity of our own because we were trying to do what somebody had already done a long time ago."[38] Over the course of the mid-to-late 1990s, the brothers tinkered with a mesh of styles reminiscent of a childhood that *Los Angeles Times* reporter Agustin Gurza described as follows:

> At home, their family played strictly Mexican pop music, the cumbias, nortenas and banda tracks that compose the running soundtrack for blue-collar Latino life in L.A. But at school and at parties, the boys switched to the soundtrack of urban youth everywhere, dominated by rap and hip-hop in English.[39]

In particular, the Gómez brothers began merging banda with hip-hop, a fusion that caught the ear of former record executive Guillermo Santiso, who began to manage the pair by the early 2000s. Santiso explained that this new "banda rap" style made the siblings among "the first ones able to combine both things, Mexican music and the street culture, in a way that had mass appeal."[40] Meanwhile, the brothers began calling themselves Akwid, a port-manteau of their Juvenile Style nicknames, AK and Wikid.

As Akwid, their debut album, *Proyecto Akwid*, went platinum and garnered them the Latin Grammy award for Best Latin Rock/Alternative Album.[41] By 2010, after the group had already racked up five best-selling albums, they released *Clasificado R*, which included the song "Esto Es Pa Mis Paisas," an homage to Kid Frost's "La Raza" that included the rapper as a featured cameo.

"Esto Es Pa Mis Paisas" could be described as a cover of "La Raza" as it opens with both an interpolation of El Chicano's four-note "Viva Tirado" bass line plus Frost/Tony G.'s drum track. However, where one expects the signature keyboard riff from "Viva Tirado," Akwid replaces it with the same melody now played with fat puffs from a banda tuba. It was an inspired makeover, nodding to the previous iterations of "Viva Tirado" yet putting an unmistakably new stamp on it.

More than just the musical echoes however, "Esto Es Pa Mis Paisas" also continued "Viva Tirado's" traditions of intercultural exchange. The song's title, which translates into "This is for my countrymen," was a riff on Frost's "La Raza" hook—"This is for la raza"—except that while Frost was primarily shouting out fellow Chicana/os, Akwid dedicated their tribute to Latina/o migrants like themselves who grew up with a transnational confluence of cultural markers. As Francisco Gómez told interviewer Josh Kun in 2010, "I remember going to parties and seeing all these Mexican gangsters wearing sombreros. They got in their rides and bumped Dr. Dre and Eazy-E, but at the party they were dancing to banda."[42] With "Esto Es Pa Mis Paisas," Sergio Gómez explained, "we are not diminishing Chicanos. We're just talking about it from the other side—the way L.A. looks through the eyes of a paisa."[43] Frost chimed in, "Their idea made sense, to make it a celebration of a new generation of Mexicans. We're all the same big pot of *menudo*, and every now and then you need to add some new flavor."[44]

As I've stressed, these iterations of "Viva Tirado" help capture snapshots of Los Angeles in different eras. By the time Akwid's contribution arose, the symbolic distance between Gerald Wilson's Los Angeles and José Ramón Tirado's Tijuana of the early 1960s had now collapsed into "Bajalta California," a concept championed by Michael Dear and Gustavo Leclerc to describe how both Los Angeles/San Diego and Tijuana/Mexicali metropoles had blended into a single, massive economic and cultural region "that just happens to be dissected by an international border."[45] Kun, in a 2004 essay entitled "What Is an MC if He Can't Rap to Banda," suggests that "by placing Akwid's South Los Angeles on the map of Bajalta California, the region's cultural products begin to be heard within new geopolitical contexts," and that Akwid's banda rap could be heard as "the soundtrack not to the formation of new national identities, but to the formation of new transnational, mobile ones."[46]

Moreover, by interpolating the "Viva Tirado" melody with a banda brass section, Akwid made a sonic move no less weighted with cross-cultural significance than those of their predecessors. The song could reach fans of both hip-hop and regional Mexican music, and as such, Kun argues that Akwid's twist on banda should be understood less as a regional style *from* Mexico than as "the music of Mexicans *in* the US, a music that refused to choose between assimilation and ethnic isolation."[47]

If I can briefly channel the spirit of Eddie "Gordo" Davis from his *Viva Tirado* liner notes: here was a song, originally written by an African American in praise of a Mexican bullfighter, remade by a Chicano jazz/rock group—given the name "El Chicano" by a white manager, no less—then sampled by a Chicano MC, mentored by an African American rap icon, as a way to instill pride in young Chicana/os through an Afro-diasporic art form whose fans include Black, Brown, white, and Asian youth across the world, only to be remade twenty years later by a pair of first-generation Mexican American brothers who merged hip-hop with banda and penned an updated anthem celebrating Mexican migrant communities.

In contemplating this serendipity within "Viva Tirado's" journey, what comes to mind is Gaye Theresa Johnson's discussion of how Black/Brown coalitional politics in LA have followed similarly unpredictable paths. She writes:

> Black-Brown antagonisms in present-day Los Angeles are real. But there are also powerful forces at work that have great stakes in generating discourse intended to obscure the richer and more enduring history of coalitional politics that these same groups have forged, time and again. These struggles remain enduring models to be *rediscovered and reinvented by others, in other spaces, at other times, for other purposes.*
>
> (emphasis mine)[48]

As I have tried to highlight, "Viva Tirado" has transcended and bridged "other spaces" and "other times" throughout its serendipitous lifespan. From its moment of inception within a Tijuana plaza de toros, the song has resonated with and inspired desires to forge ties across borders, across identities, across peoples. So long as the memory of the song hasn't completely faded, "Viva Tirado" still continues to circulate out in the world, no doubt awaiting its next opportunity to be rediscovered and reinvented by others, in other spaces, for other purposes.[49]

Notes

1   Josh Kun, *Audiotopia: Music, Race and America* (Los Angeles: University of California Press 2005), 222. The idea of a "congealed history" comes from Tia DeNora (via inspiration from Theodor Adorno), who saw music as a manifestation of a "socio-musical landscape" of "social forces, musical materials, composers and listeners," whose actions and interactions are captured [that is, congealed] within resulting compositions. Tia DeNora, *After Adorno: Rethinking Music Sociology* (Cambridge: Cambridge University Press, 2003), 30.
2   Clora Bryant, *Central Avenue Sounds: Jazz in Los Angeles* (Los Angeles: University of California Press, 1998), 238
3   Dara Orenstein, "Void for Vagueness: Mexicans and the Collapse of Miscegenation Law in California." *Pacific Historical Review* 74, no. 3 (2005): 367–407.
4   Josh Sides, *L. A. City Limits: African American Los Angeles From the Great Depression to the Present* (Los Angeles: University of California Press, 2003): 109–110
5   Gaye Therese Johnson, "Spatial Entitlement: Race, Displacement, and Reclamation in Post-war Los Angeles," in *Black and Brown Los Angeles: A Contemporary Reader*, ed. Josh Kun and Laura Pulido (Los Angeles: University of California Press, 2010): 11
6   Ibid.
7   Ruben Molina, *Chicano Soul: Recordings and History of an American Culture* (Mictlan, 2007): 9.

8 Johnny Otis, *Upside Your Head!: Rhythm and Blues on Central Avenue* (Connecticut: Wesleyan University Press, 1993): xxvi.

9 David Reyes and Tom Waldman, *Land of a Thousand Dances: Chicano Rock 'n' Roll from Southern California* (Albaquerque: University of New Mexico Press, 1998): xiv.

10 George Lipsitz, "Cruising around the historical bloc: postmodernism and popular music in East Los Angeles." *Cultural Critique* 5 (1986): 161–2.

11 Jose Sierra, "A Conversation with John E. De Luna, Part 1." MoonFlowerCafe. com, 2008.

12 Molina, *Chicano Soul*, 77. As a quick aside: Venues play a crucial role in this history. Sites like Legion Stadium, the Lighthouse and Kabuki Sukiyaki (and later on, the rotating Uncle Jamm's Army rap parties of the '80s) drew audiences from across the Southland and became important points of contact between segregated communities. Hermosa Beach, for example, was and is an affluent, predominantly White beach community, 25 miles southwest of East LA, but at the Lighthouse, many of the Southland's experimentations with Latin jazz first came to life, especially after Howard Rumsey's Lighthouse All-Stars became a resident band there in the early 1950s.

13 According to the liner notes of El Chicano's debut album, *Viva Tirado*, Davis was such a fixture in the Chicano scene that his Mexican American friends renamed him "Gordo Enamorado Simpatico Pelon," (which loosely translates into "fat, charming man.")

14 Reyes and Waldman, *Land of a Thousand Dances*, 55.

15 John Mortland, "California Dreaming." *Phoenix New Times*. September 2, 1999.

16 Reyes and Waldman, *Land of a Thousand Dances*, 95.

17 Eric Zolov, "La Onda Chicana: Mexico's Forgotten Rock Counterculture," in *Rockin' Las Américas: The Global Politics of Rock in Latin/o America*, edited by Deborah Pacini Hernandez, Héctor D. Fernández l'Hoeste, and Eric Zolov (Pittsburgh: University of Pittsburgh Press, 2004), 35.

18 Sierra, "A Conversation with John E. De Luna, Part 1." Reyes and Waldman offer an interesting discussion regarding the "post-1967 alignment between Chicano groups and Chicano politics," much of which would end up influencing LA groups like El Chicano and Tierra. As they write, "[Chicano bands] did not want to be considered disloyal to the race, but they also derived their creativity and style from a range of American and Anglo-American sources. ...In the end the bands were willing to acknowledge their Mexican heritage, but unwilling to renounce their American influences." Reyes and Waldman, *Land of a Thousand Dances*, 105.

19 Gerald Wilson told me he didn't even discover that El Chicano had covered his song until he heard it being played on the radio during a trip to Chicago.

20 Steven Loza, *Barrio Rhythm: Mexican American Music in Los Angeles* (Chicago: Illinois University Press, 1993), 103.

21 One of my favorite examples of how "Viva Tirado" attracted artists with a cross-cultural/ethnic bent would be the *Viva Tirado* album recorded in 1971 for GNP by Jack "Mr. Bongo" Costanzo, in collaboration with singer Gerri Woo. Costanzo, an Italian American from Chicago, was a well-known *bonguero* in Latin music circles, while San Diego's Woo was of half-Black/half-Chinese descent.

22 Josh Kun, *Audiotopia: Music, Race and America* (Los Angeles: University of California Press, 2005), 23.

23 Reyes and Waldman, *Land of a Thousand Dances*, 16.

24 Victor Viesca, "The Battle of Los Angeles: The Cultural Politics of Chicana/o Music in the Greater Eastside." *American Quarterly* 56, no. 3 (2004): 722.
25 Jeff Chang, *Can't Stop, Won't Stop: A History of the Hip-Hop Generation* (New York: MacMillan, 2006), 315.
26 Pancho McFarland "Chicano Rap Roots: Black-Brown Cultural Exchange and the Making of a Genre," *Callaloo* 29, no. 3 (2006): 941.
27 Lipsitz, "Cruising around the historical bloc," 205.
28 The bass line is an interpolation of El Chicano's version, but the keys and guitar sound directly sampled from the El Chicano record.
29 Brian Cross, *It's Not About a Salary…Rap, Race and Resistance in Los Angeles* (London: Verso, 1993): 190.
30 Mandalit Del Barco, "Rap's Latino Sabor," in *Droppin' Science: Critical Essays On Rap Music and Hip Hop Culture*, ed. William E. Perkins (Pennsylvania: Temple University Press, 1996): 73
31 Cross, *It's Not About a Salary*: 95. Cross writes the word "mietas" in the book, but my assumption is that he probably meant "mayate," a caló slang term for African Americans.
32 Deborah Pacini Hernandez offers a well-measured discussion of the complexities in trying to apply the concept of mestizaje to Latina/o cultural and musical practices (Deborah Pacini Hernandez, *Oye Como Va!: Hybridity and Identity in Latino Popular Music* (Pennsylvania: Temple University Press, 2010): 3.
33 Rafael Pérez-Torres, "Chicano Hip Hop and Postmodern Mestizaje," in *The Chicana/o Cultural Studies Reader*, ed. Angie Chabram-Dernersesian (Oxfordshire: Routledge Press, 2006): 325.
34 Ibid, 212.
35 Cross, *It's Not About a Salary*, 195.
36 Lowrider culture is itself a long-standing tradition in which young Chicana/os use car customization, street cruising—and oldies music—as a way to connect to cultural legacies and community-solidarity within the Chicana/o community (Amy Best, *Fast Cars, Cool Rides: The accelerating world of youth and their cars* (New York: New York University Press, 2006): 31). "Lowrider music" is, like so much of music connected to the Chicana/o community, racially mixed and/or ambiguous—including everything from the early R&B ballads that Huggy Boy might have played out of his Central Avenue DJ booth, to the dance tunes enjoyed by patrons of Johnny Otis's Legion Stadiums shows, to radio hits like El Chicano's "Viva Tirado." What links them aren't necessarily obvious musical (or cultural) signifiers as much as a shared history of enjoyment and consumption by multiple generations of youth, Black and Brown alike. Notably too, lowrider culture, may have had its roots in Chicana/o communities, but by the 1980s and especially 1990s, African American rappers such as Dr. Dre, DJ Quik, and Snoop Dogg had heavily borrowed from its iconography for music videos and album art. Like "Viva Tirado," lowrider culture has become a symbol for LA's unique, polyglot traditions.
37 See The-breaks.com.
38 Agustin Gurza, "Two brothers, two cultures, one sound," *Los Angeles Times*. November 28, 2003.
39 Ibid.
40 Ibid.

41 Josh Kun, "Hecho In El Lay: How Akwid Raps for a Changing City." *Los Angeles Magazine*. September 1, 2010.
42 Ibid.
43 Ibid.
44 Ibid.
45 Michael Dear and Gustavo Leclerc, eds. *Postborder City* (New York: Routledge, 2013): xii.
46 Josh Kun, "What Is an MC If He Can't Rap to Banda? Making Music in Nuevo L.A." *American Quarterly* 56, no. 3 (2004): 745. Kun also is very clear in stating that "Akwid's music should not be heard solely as producing a 'new' US multicultural or postethnic national identity, and therefore enabling the typically reactionary state and federal 'investments' in cultural diversity that so often result" (ibid). In other words, rather than seeing Akwid's music as somehow transcending ethnic identities, Kun argues that they are creating new ones, rooted in such globalized concepts as Bajalta California.
47 Kun, "Hecho In El Lay," 749.
48 Johnson, "Spatial Entitlement," 22.
49 This was a substantially updated version of an earlier essay (Oliver Wang, "The Journey of 'Viva Tirado': A Musical Conversation within Afro-Chicano Los Angeles," *Journal of Popular Music Studies* 22, no. 4 (2010): 348–66). Special thanks to Josh Kun, who originally helped set me down this song's path. Thanks also to Gaye Theresa Johnson, Karen Tongson, Gus Stadler, Eothen Alapatt, Loren Kajikawa, R. J. Smith, and the late Gerald Wilson.

References

Best, Amy. *Fast cars, cool rides: the accelerating world of youth and their cars.* New York: New York University Press, 2006.

Bryant, Clora ed., *Central Avenue Sounds: Jazz in Los Angeles*. Los Angeles: University of California Press, 1998.

Chang, Jeff. *Can't Stop, Won't Stop: A History of the Hip-Hop Generation.* New York: MacMillan, 2006.

Cross, Brian. *It's Not About a Salary…Rap, Race and Resistance in Los Angeles.* London: Verso, 1993.

Dear, Michael, and Gustavo Leclerc, eds. Postborder City, New York: Routledge, 2013.

Del Barco, Mandalit. "Rap's Latino Sabor." In *Droppin' Science: Critical Essays On Rap Music and Hip Hop Culture*, edited by William E. Perkins, 63–84. Pennsylvania: Temple University Press, 1996.

DeNora, Tia. *After Adorno: Rethinking Music Sociology*. Cambridge: Cambridge University Press, 2003

El Chicano. *Viva Tirado. Kapp Records*, 1970.

Gurza, Agustin. "Two brothers, two cultures, one sound." *Los Angeles Times*. November 28, 2003. http://articles.latimes.com/2003/nov/28/entertainment/et-gurza28

Hernandez, Deborah Pacini. *Oye Como Va!: Hybridity and Identity in Latino Popular Music*. Pennsylvania: Temple University Press, 2010.

Johnson, Gaye Theresa. "Spatial Entitlement: Race, Displacement, and Reclamation in Post-war Los Angeles." In *Black and Brown Los Angeles: A Contemporary*

Reader, edited by Josh Kun and Laura Pulido, 316–40. Los Angeles: University of California Press, 2010.

Kid Frost. "La Raza." (12" single). Virgin Records, 1990.

Kun, Josh. "What Is an MC If He Can't Rap to Banda? Making Music in Nuevo L.A." *American Quarterly* 56, no. 3 (2004): 741–58.

Kun, Josh. *Audiotopia: Music, Race and America.* Los Angeles: University of California Press, 2005.

Kun, Josh. "Hecho In El Lay: How Akwid Raps for a Changing City." *Los Angeles Magazine.* September 1, 2010. www.lamag.com/laculture/hecho-in-el-lay/

Lipsitz, George. "Cruising around the historical bloc: postmodernism and popular music in East Los Angeles." *Cultural Critique* 5 (1986): 157–77.

Lipsitz, George. *Footsteps in the Dark: The Hidden Histories of Popular Music.* Minneapolis: University of Minnesota Press, 2007.

Loza, Steven. *Barrio Rhythm: Mexican American Music in Los Angeles.* Chicago: Illinois University Press, 1993.

McFarland, Pancho. "Chicano Rap Roots: Black-Brown Cultural Exchange and the Making of a Genre." *Callaloo* 29, no. 3 (2006): 939–55.

Molina, Ruben. *Chicano Soul: Recordings and History of an American Culture.* Los Angeles: Mictlan, 2007.

Mortland, John. "California Dreaming." *Phoenix New Times.* September 2, 1999. www.phoenixnewtimes.com/music/california-dreaming-6420475

Orenstein, Dara. "Void for Vagueness: Mexicans and the Collapse of Miscegenation Law in California." *Pacific Historical Review* 74, no. 3 (2005): 367–407.

Otis, Johnny. *Upside Your Head!: Rhythm and Blues on Central Avenue.* Connecticut: Wesleyan University Press, 1993.

Pérez-Torres, Rafael. "Chicano Hip Hop and Postmodern Mestizaje." In *The Chicana/ o Cultural Studies Reader*, edited by Angie Chabram-Dernersesian, 324–39. Oxfordshire: Routledge Press, 2006.

Reyes, David, and Waldman, Tom. *Land of a Thousand Dances: Chicano Rock 'n' Roll from Southern California.* Albuquerque: University of New Mexico Press, 1998.

Roberts, John Storm. *Latin Jazz: The First of Fusion, 1880's to Today.* New York: Schirmer Trade, 1999.

Sides, Josh. *L.A. City Limits: African American Los Angeles From the Great Depression to the Present.* Los Angeles: University of California Press, 2003.

Sierra, Jose. "A Conversation with John E. De Luna, Part 1." MoonFlowerCafe, 2008.

Viesca, Victor. "The Battle of Los Angeles: The Cultural Politics of Chicana/o Music in the Greater Eastside." *American Quarterly* 56, no. 3 (2004): 719–39.

Wang, Oliver. "The Journey of 'Viva Tirado': A Musical Conversation within Afro-Chicano Los Angeles." *Journal of Popular Music Studies* 22, no. 4 (2010): 348–66.

Wilson, Gerald. "Viva Tirado." *Moment of Truth.* Pacific Jazz, 1962. LP.-Personal Interview. July 2002.

Zolov, Eric. "La Onda Chicana: Mexico's Forgotten Rock Counterculture." In *Rockin' Las Américas: The Global Politics of Rock in Latin/o America*, edited by Deborah Pacini Hernandez, Héctor D. Fernández l'Hoeste, and Eric Zolov, 22–42. Pittsburgh: University of Pittsburgh Press, 2004.

3   Moby Grape—"Omaha" (1967)

Susan Schmidt Horning

The Cut

If you listen to Moby Grape's "Omaha" through headphones, you hear a gradually building harmonic drone, sounding at first like a stuck car horn, or is it bagpipes? *What is* this sound? It seems to come out of the left—no, center—and it keeps getting louder. Just as it reaches a crescendo, it moves right and FWACK! snaps left. FWACK! FWACK! It snaps left and right again, then wiggles to the center before careening off to the right to make way for the first guitar riff out of the left channel. Dadada-da-da-dada-da-daaaa, the last note ascending, the riff repeats, this time descending as a second, more trebly sounding guitar plays the same riff an octave higher out of the right speaker and the two continue the riff in unison. The drummer keeps time, fast polka-style on the upbeat, then suddenly shifts the tempo into a charging rock beat interspersed with regimental drum rolls, and you hear the vocal command, "Listen my friends!" repeated over and over in a call and response, interspersed with sparse, almost haiku-like lyrics. "You thought never, but... listen my friends!...I'm yours forever." The introduction makes you want to listen to it again and again. It has *power* and sounds like nothing you have ever heard. Something similar returns in the middle section with a round of vocal "Ahhhhh"s that sound as if they were routed through an Echoplex cranked all the way, shimmering into an intense crescendo culminating in the sound of a swarm of locusts that abruptly cuts to a drum roll. Both stunning and subtle, the track just moves like a freight train from beginning to end, stopping and starting but never losing momentum. The psychedelic flourishes never overpower the solid rock beat or the soulful vocal, and as the last guitar riffs begin to fade, a drum roll is joined by what sounds like a joyful "Ahh-ha-ha!" from deep in the studio, and you just know this band was as excited playing this song as you have been listening to it. Again!

Moby Grape's "Omaha" opens with psychedelic fanfare, but ultimately it is a song about friendship and community ("Listen my friends!"), about commitment ("Won't leave you ever!"), and about the joy of love ("So outta sight, bein' in love!"). In short, it conveys the sounds and spirit of the year 1967, arguably the *annus mirabilis* of rock. So much happened that year with lasting

DOI: 10.4324/9781003093206-4

consequences. Larry Miller and Tom "Big Daddy" Donahue introduced progressive radio on KMPX, the beginning of DJ-centered, album-oriented FM
rock programing that swept the nation and forever changed radio.[1] Albums by
the Doors, Jefferson Airplane, Love, Pink Floyd, the Jimi Hendrix Experience,
the Byrds, Cream, and Buffalo Springfield appeared that year; all considered
classics in the psychedelic rock canon.[2] In April, CBS News aired a prime-time
television special, *Inside Pop: The Rock Revolution*, hosted by esteemed con-
ductor and composer Leonard Bernstein, thus bringing rock to the attention
of audiences of all ages nationwide while elevating it to the status of art.[3] *The
San Francisco Chronicle* heralded "the Summer of Love," a term that to this
day symbolizes the promise of the counterculture.[4] For three days in June,
the Monterey International Pop Festival spread "music, love and flowers,"
and D. A. Pennebaker's film of the event, released nationwide the following
year as *Monterey Pop*, propelled the careers of Jimi Hendrix and Janis Joplin,
among others.[5] The Beatles' *Sgt. Pepper's Lonely Hearts Club Band*, released
just two weeks before Moby Grape's self-titled debut album, revolutionized
rock recording and introduced the "concept album." By year's end, the first
rock musical, *Hair*, opened off Broadway and the first issue of *Rolling Stone*
rolled off the presses.[6] When on January 9, 1968, *Look* magazine published a
special issue with a posterized cover photo of Beatle John Lennon by Richard
Avedon and "California's Incredibles from Hippies to Hell's Angels" inside—
by noted fashion photographer Irving Penn—West Coast psychedelic rock
had officially transmogrified from a bohemian underground music scene into
high art and moved into the wider public consciousness.[7]

Origins

In 1966, Moby Grape came together in the San Francisco Bay area, the epi-
center of this musical and cultural transformation, although none of the
members hailed from there. They came out of the Pacific Northwest, Southern
California, and Canada, playing in teen surf bands and club bands, backing
up artists like Etta James, Bobby "I Fought the Law" Fuller, and at one point,
San Francisco's first topless dancer, Carol Doda. Drummer Don Stevenson
from Seattle and guitarist Jerry Miller from Tacoma played in the Frantics,
a neatly coiffed cover band that sported matching suits and choreographed
steps.[8] Bob Mosley from San Diego played bass and sang with the Misfits,
the Joel Scott Hill Trio, and for a time, with the Frantics. Peter Lewis came
from Hollywood royalty, his mother being the film and television star Loretta
Young, and played with the Cornells, a surf band composed of other off-
spring of Hollywood celebrities, before discovering Bob Dylan and the Byrds,
whereupon he took up fingerpicking and formed Peter and the Wolves, an
LA-based folk-rock group.[9] Canadian Skip Spence moved to California as a
teenager and played guitar in the Topsiders in the early 1960s, then in an early
iteration of Quicksilver Messenger Service. When Jefferson Airplane's Marty
Balin saw Spence at the San Francisco club the Matrix, he was so impressed

with Spence's "beautiful aura" that he convinced him to learn drums and join the Airplane.[10] In two weeks, he managed to become a more than capable drummer, and he played and co-wrote songs on the Airplane's first album. Although his song "My Best Friend" appeared on the Airplane's *Surrealistic Pillow*, Spence did not. After he took off to Mexico with a girl instead of showing up for a gig one night, Balin fired him.[11] By then, the Airplane had also fired their manager, Matthew Katz, who proceeded to convince the very charismatic Spence to allow him to form a band around him.

In August, Katz held auditions at his California Avenue office in San Francisco. He invited Lewis, who had begun working with Mosley. In turn, Mosley, remembering his time with the Frantics, brought in Miller and Stevenson. Their first rehearsal felt like an alchemical reaction, "Like that scene in *Raiders of the Lost Ark* with all the beams of light flying around," remembered Miller.[12] "The five of us started playing and it was just plain old magic."[13] Everyone sang, everyone wrote music, and collectively the five made beautiful harmonies, vocally and instrumentally. Each of the three killer guitarists—a novel lineup at the time—played in a different style, complementing each other and giving the band a unique and diverse sound. Moby Grape, named after a running joke of the time (What's big and purple and swims in the ocean?), practiced eight hours a day on an old paddleboat in Sausalito Harbor called the Ark, a club that paid musicians with free huevos rancheros breakfasts after the sets ran into the early morning hours. Other up-and-coming musicians rehearsing at the nearby heliport, Janis Joplin, Lee Michaels, and Buffalo Springfield, came to hear Moby Grape, and word got around that they were "an outstanding band [playing] some of the greatest rock and roll to emerge yet from San Francisco."[14] Katz convinced them to sign a contract giving him legal rights to the name Moby Grape, ostensibly in order to book them, but that turned out to be nothing more than a jive hustle, and by early 1967 the relationship with Katz was unraveling. The band soon learned the hard way what Jefferson Airplane had already concluded, that Katz was a terrible manager.[15] Moby Grape fired Katz in 1967 and it took the band nearly four decades of litigation to regain the rights to their name.

The Signing

During the months of long rehearsals at the Ark, Moby Grape developed their repertoire, refined their vocal harmonies, and drew a following. By the end of 1966, they were playing sold-out shows at the Matrix, the Avalon Ballroom, and Bill Graham's Fillmore, and had attracted the attention of record labels, all seeking the next big thing, America's answer to the Beatles. Ralph J. Gleason described the San Francisco scene as

> the Liverpool of America...a giant pool of talent for the new music world of rock. The number of recording company executives casing the

scene at the Fillmore and the Avalon is equaled only by the number of anthropologists and sociologists studying the Haight-Ashbury hippy culture.[16]

Drawing the respect of audiences and fellow musicians alike—Sam Andrew of Big Brother and the Holding Company declared them "better than the Beatles"—Moby Grape became the most sought-after of the San Francisco bands by late 1966.[17] Columbia staff producer David Rubinson flew out from New York, and after hearing them at the Ark, he rented an apartment in San Francisco, determined to stay close and sign the band. "The three-guitar orchestrations were phenomenal," remembered Rubinson, "the songs were great and they had these four-part harmonies, sometimes five. They were the best American band I'd seen."[18] Moby Grape were sensational live performers, particularly Skip Spence and Bob Mosley, "both murderously intense."[19]

Seven record companies tried to sign them, but the serious bidding came down to just three: the prestigious, long-standing Columbia Records, Jac Holzman's ultra-hip Elektra Records, and the jazz and rhythm-and-blues indie powerhouse Atlantic Records. Clive Davis was about to be named Columbia Records' president by the head of CBS Records, Goddard Lieberson, and Davis would soon bring the staid Columbia Records into the rock world by signing Janis Joplin.[20] In the film *Clive Davis: The Soundtrack of our Lives* (2017), Atlantic Records co-founder Ahmet Ertegun reflected on the label rivalry as rock became big business in the late '60s: "On more than one occasion," recalled Ertegun, "we found ourselves in competition for a great new act. And both Clive and I were after a group called Moby Grape." Ahmet recalled that the group told him, "Look, we're going to sign with you but we promised Clive one last meeting." Trusting that the band would keep their word, Ahmet told them, "Don't sign anything. And call me!" At 10 o'clock that evening, he got the call. "'We got great news for you. We signed with Clive'. I said, what do you mean you signed with Clive?! You promised me!" The band assured Ahmet "'Naw, man, you're gonna be very happy. You know how you really dig our music? Well, Clive has agreed that you can come and listen in the studio while we make the album'. I said, 'Oh, shit!'"[21] Was the band really that naïve or just having fun with the "straights," so to speak?

The cultural gulf and generation gap that existed between label executives and artists was far greater in the 1960s. Record label executives of the World War II generation were just beginning to recognize the need to hire the "house hippie" or "company freak" to be able to mediate between the "turtle-necked titans of the record industry and the unpunctual, crazy monsters called musicians."[22] With so many labels vying to sign them, Moby Grape had incentive to be brash and full of themselves; as Peter Lewis recalled, "We were maniacs... . We just thought we were so good, that we could do what we wanted to."[23] Indeed, the band had also developed a reputation for unpunctuality. Bill Graham introduced Moby Grape at their first Fillmore gig as "a great bunch of juvenile delinquents," and they lived up to it by repeatedly showing up late for gigs, to the point where Graham once installed a time clock on the stage of the Fillmore and gave band members cards to punch in.[24]

The Recording

By March 1967, the band was in Los Angeles to begin recording their first album at Columbia Studios. They did intensive pre-production rehearsals at a CBS radio studio in Hollywood, rehearsing, cutting, and changing arrangements, recalled David Rubinson, then the producer.[25] Live recordings of their gigs at the Matrix and the Fillmore from late 1966 reveal that the band had already achieved tight and powerful arrangements of short, catchy pop gems, but listening to these early live shows in comparison to the final recording reveals how much they refined the songs for the album.[26] The producer had a hand in some of these changes, like the rhythm Don Stevenson plays in the Peter Lewis composition "Fall on You." On the November 1966 Fillmore live recording, Stevenson plays the staccato beat on the toms in unison with the opening guitar riff. In the studio, Rubinson urged Stevenson to make a change.

> Don, would you do me one favor just for me? Play that rhythm that you play in the bridge all the way through… . Because it lifts right off the ground in the bridge, man, and there's a reason for it. You get into a groove and it drives like a motherfucker and that's where it's at.[27]

After some disagreement about the introduction, the band followed the producer's suggestion, and "Fall on You" is one of the most driving songs on the album.

With no similar production notes on "Omaha," I wondered if that opening reverse-tape ping-pong was Rubinson's idea, or perhaps that of Columbia engineer Roy Halee, who Miller said worked with them on some of the songs. Halee had been experimenting with unorthodox recording methods at Columbia. He linked four or five tape machines running with echoes and reverbs in the studio hallway in the days before digital delay, and he placed a mic in a studio garbage can and banged on it to get the sound of an explosion on the Lovin' Spoonful's "Summer in the City."[28] Jerry Miller claims, however, that the opening of "Omaha" was Skip's idea, involving "a Theremin and a backward guitar."[29] Although it is difficult to detect the sound of a theremin, the "backward guitar" created by reversing the tape in playback had been popularized by the Beatles with John Lennon's backward vocal at the end of "Rain" (1966). Whatever went into recording "Omaha," when Moby Grape performed it live, they did not have the technological support available to bands today; no "psychedelic fanfaring" of reverse-tape as on the record, just five voices, drums, bass, three guitars, and the truth, to paraphrase Harlan Howard's description of country music.[30] One reviewer described their live sound in 1967 as a physical assault, "You did not so much hear as feel [it] in your thorax and sternum and spleen, as vital organic functions became disrupted."[31] *Crawdaddy's* Paul Williams called their music "violent," not in the sense of being hurtful but rather because "every song is attacked with great force and abandon, Moby Grape assault their audience, bathing them in almost unavoidable joy."[32]

They cut 14 songs in March and April, with the sessions spread apart because they had to return to the Bay Area for gigs. The band had to work efficiently. Total recording costs were just $11,000 as they cut nearly all the songs live with only vocals overdubbed. Along with "Ain't No Use," "Naked, if I Want To," and "Indifference," "Omaha" was recorded on April 23, 1967.[33] How the song got its name remains a mystery. Jerry Miller recalled hearing Skip work on the song upstairs in his house in San Francisco, when he called it simply "Listen, My Friends." "He didn't know what to call it," remembered Miller, "so he just said 'Omaha',"[34]—an interesting choice, since the name appears nowhere in the lyrics. In fact, Nebraska's largest city could not be further from the two coastal centers of the music industry, New York and Los Angeles. Maybe that was the point. Skip Spence had a uniquely creative mind, boundless energy, and his songwriting followed few conventions.

Capitalism

In "The Vinyl Crap Game," a sociological study of the pop record industry in the 1960s and early 1970s, R. Serge Denisoff analyzed the perspectives of music business insiders after interviewing various industry veterans for insight into the way the business operated. Record companies made records, distributed them, and attempted to convince the public "to buy the product." But one industry veteran revealed that company employees "are no more informed or enlightened in their tastes than is the general public."[35] Hence, as in a crap-shoot, luck and timing are important. But record companies are "not the innocent victims of the caprices of Adam Smith's 'invisible hand',," Denisoff found. "The companies' business orientation and philosophies greatly color their performance at the vinyl crap table."[36] Large companies like Columbia could afford to adopt the "throw it up against the wall and see if it sticks" philosophy, otherwise known as "the Buckshot System. Throw them all out there, hopefully some of them will hit."[37] This could explain Columbia's ill-considered decision to release five singles *simultaneously* from *Moby Grape*. Literally all but three of the album's 13 songs were released on 45-RPM singles for radio play, leading to confusion and choice paralysis among DJs (see Figure 3.1). As all these strong, three-minute tracks landed on the market, in competition with each other, only "Omaha" became a chart hit, spending just three weeks on *Billboard's* Hot 100 and peaking at #88 on July 15, 1967.[38] On August 8, Radio London's John Peel named it "climber of the week."[39] The album peaked on the *Billboard* "200" at #24 in September. "In a just world," one reviewer noted in 2003, "'Omaha' would have been a massive hit. In the Summer of Love, it should have been, had Columbia not—in a disastrous

Figure 3.1 The "45-RPM covers 1967" was part of the Columbia Records press kit
distributed at the ill-fated album launch party at the Avalon Ballroom, July
1967. Credit: Jeff Gold.

web of over-hype—released it simultaneously with four other singles from the
album."[40] Yet another label blunder in marketing Moby Grape came next.

Failing to plug heavily just one single was a disastrous idea, but the
company's over-the-top marketing blitz and album release party made things
worse. In the era of "Don't trust anyone over thirty" and "Hype is unhip,"
the company did more damage than good with ads in the trades that ran, for
example, "The week the country went Grape. Moby Grape. In one fell swoop.
Just as we planned it.... . Airplay and sales have been the grapest [sic] ever, all
over the map."[41] (See Figure 3.2) In *The Conquest of Cool*, Thomas Frank
cited Columbia Record's famous 1968 print ad, "But the Man Can't Bust Our
Music," as an example of business co-optation of the counterculture, but the
company had already launched that strategy with Moby Grape.[42] On June 6,
1967, Columbia Records hosted an over-the-top album release party at the
Avalon Ballroom. They invited press, distributed lavish velveteen-covered
press kits with all five 45 RPM singles in picture sleeves with photos of the
band, a Moby Grape button, a full-size poster, and promo sheets declaring
the label's intent to "make the entire country Moby Grape conscious."[43] The
event also involved 700 bottles of wine with vintage Moby Grape labels but no
corkscrews, and purple orchids floating from the ceiling creating a dangerously
slippery floor covered in dropped petals. When humorist Cynthia Heimel saw

the press kit, she thought "it looked psychedelic, yet it was done by ad people. I believe the word 'hype' was coined that very day."[44] One of the hippest new bands in the Bay Area was suddenly deemed decidedly unhip because of all the industry hype. Later that evening, three members of the band were arrested in Marin County with weed and underage girls. Although authorities later dropped the charges, the damage was done; as Miller said, "The mud stuck."[45] In addition to the corporate hubris and marketing fiasco, the band contributed to some of their problems. According to Don Stevenson, "The hype did us in, in a way, along with our behavior."[46] But the next bad decision was made by their manager, Matthew Katz, with repercussions far into the future.

Monterey Pop, Skip's Magnetism, and Bad Behavior

Ten days after the release party for *Moby Grape*, the band played their biggest venue yet, on the Monterey Fairgrounds at the first major outdoor rock festival. Organized by musician John Phillips and producer Lou Adler, the Monterey International Pop Festival featured dozens of rock, pop, soul, jazz, and folk artists. If you have seen Jimi Hendrix kneeling on stage, suggestively squirting lighter fluid on his Stratocaster, and then setting it afire, you have seen his performance at Monterey, thanks to D. A. Pennebaker's documentary of the festival. Janis Joplin's raw vocal on "Ball and Chain," the Who's creative destruction of their gear as they ended "My Generation," and Otis Redding's powerful "Try a Little Tenderness" are among the other performances in *Monterey Pop* that have achieved iconic status through inclusion in numerous subsequent documentaries. Moby Grape's electrifying and brisk five-song set is unfortunately absent from the film because Matthew Katz reportedly demanded a cool million in order to sign the release for filming. The organizers balked and rescheduled Moby Grape for the awkward opening spot on Saturday. Although their tour manager explained that the band was more than willing to sign the release, Phillips told him, "Matthew holds the paper on these guys, so we can't do that."[47] Thus the opportunity for Moby Grape to appear in a film that has since been canonized as essential documentary cinema was lost.

Although Moby Grape never made the final cut of *Monterey Pop*, cameras did roll during their set, and along with other audiovisual records of their live performances, at Monterey and elsewhere, we get a glimpse into the band's magnetic stage presence. A single outtake of their performance of "Hey Grandma" and various audio recordings of the other songs they played at Monterey are available online.[48] Watching Moby Grape open the Saturday evening concert, you see and hear the excitement and joy in their performance. Before launching into "Mr. Blues," Bob Mosley greets the audience, "Welcome majestic crowd! You can't believe what it's like up here seeing all of you!"[49] Counting off "Hey Grandma," Skip Spence was the spark plug full of energy, driving the band, all teeth, big smile, and you can understand why some thought he literally levitated off the ground during performances.

Jim Mazzeo, who did lighting for Grape's shows, recalled: "When Skippy would play at the Ark, or sometimes at the Avalon or the Fillmore, he would get a smile on his face that would literally lift his feet about seven inches off of the floor."[50] Jerry Miller recalled a performance at the Roostertail club in Detroit: "Skippy twisted himself up so tight that he flew off the stage right into the middle of somebody's table... . like a rocket."[51] Stevenson remembered it as well: "He didn't get hurt. He just bounced back up and started playing again."[52]

During a TV appearance in New York City on *The Steve Paul Scene*, the camera focused on Spence wearing a dark suit jacket over a white T-shirt, with a lavender necktie swept over his right shoulder. When he sings, "You're sure lookin' good, you're lookin' so good, you're lookin' so...OH!" he flips his head away from the mic, shaking rapidly as if in an epileptic fit, or like a shimmying Tina Turner. This kind of energy was unusual for the Bay Area bands, and for that matter, most rock bands of this period, who were

Figure 3.2 Advertisement from *Record World* from July 1, 1967, promoting the *Moby Grape* debut album. Credit: Cash Box/Record World, Sandy Graham.

more concerned with appearing cool than crazy. His demeanor was more akin to the rock 'n' roll pioneers—Elvis, Jerry Lee Lewis, Little Richard—and Spence has been a source of fascination and awe for musicians and writers for decades. After one memorable meeting in early 1970, science fiction author William Gibson wrote an essay describing in detail Skip's appearance, specifically the cut of his jeans, finding him "an astonishing figure," and while never having heard Moby Grape, Gibson surmised, "I knew I was experiencing star quality."[53]

After Monterey, Moby Grape went on a brief tour with the Mamas and the Papas and the Buckinghams, a confused and improbable bill if there ever was one, but typical of the multiple-act rock and pop revues that were a holdover from the early days of rock 'n' roll. Moby Grape was supposed to be the flip act, but as Stevenson recalled, "It wasn't the best way to bring [the Mamas and the Papas] on. We'd end with Omaha and it sounded like a buzzsaw going off. Then they'd come on and do something super-soft like 'Monday Monday'." Peter Lewis remembered the audience filing out after their set:

> The next day at breakfast Mama Cass came up to us and said: "You guys are a bunch of punks. You should be grateful to tour with the biggest band in America." We survived one more date, then the Mamas And the Papas kicked us off the tour.[54]

Their behavior, more than the power of their music, was increasingly getting Moby Grape into trouble—they showed up late for dates, called out to the audience during the Buckinghams' set, and generally acted like punks years before punk was fashionable in rock 'n' roll.

There is a hint of this in the *Moby Grape* album cover. There are no liner notes, but the album jacket sent a clear message while keeping a sense of mystery. On the cover, five unsmiling, ruggedly handsome young men look straight into the camera, two standing and three seated in front of a second-hand store holding various items. The names of the band members appear in the black border surrounding the Jim Marshall photograph, so we know that the suede-jacketed man seated center with his left hand holding a serving spoon and his right resting on a washboard, middle finger extended in the "fuck you" position, is drummer Don Stevenson. To the right, behind Skip Spence, is an American flag, but tinted orange because "in some kind of conservative political panic" during the height of Vietnam War protests, someone strongly objected to this scruffy bunch representing America, a concern at least one member found highly insulting.[55] That photo, as in-your-face as the intro of "Omaha," intimidating as well as alluring, caused quite a stir in 1967, with some record stores refusing to stock it, let alone put it on display. Consequently, Columbia eventually airbrushed the offending finger and altered the flag.

Wow and the Beginning of the End

Bucking the trend toward lengthy improvisation among psychedelic bands like the Grateful Dead, *Moby Grape* included only short, radio-ready songs, all but one at three and a half minutes or less. In concert, the band did some extended improvisatory work on Skip Spence's "Dark Magic," but Rubinson steered them away from that on the album in an attempt to "crystallize what they had," a decision he later regretted.[56] He made up for that in the production of the second album, a two-disc package, *Wow/Grape Jam* (1968), which included more experimental effects, such as the coda on "Bitter Wind," orchestral embellishments, and a cut featuring Lou Waxman and his Orchestra with Arthur Godfrey on banjo and ukulele that required listeners to shift their turntable speed to 78 RPM. Several lengthy instrumentals with guest artists Al Kooper and Mike Bloomfield made up the bonus album, *Grape Jam*. The brief liner notes explain how the music "just happened—at various odd hours all through the session for the 'real' album [*Wow*].... Just laying down some music when the mood struck…finding out again that music can be fun."[57]

By the time *Wow/Grape Jam* appeared in April 1968, the fun was on the wane. Their new manager, Michael Gruber, had booked them on a grueling schedule of dates crisscrossing the country during the previous summer, leaving them no time to write and rehearse new material to match the perfect gem of a debut album that was *Moby Grape*. They began recording *Wow* in Los Angeles, living in a house in Malibu, but when they partied harder than they worked, Columbia insisted they move the recording to New York. *Wow* offered an eclectic mix of songs, with more post-production than the first album and less live ensemble studio recording, much to Stevenson's regret. "At least in California we were a band. In New York, we'd work with only one, two, maybe three guys at a time."[58] In New York, the band began to fall apart. As Mosley saw it, "Going to New York just brought trouble to New York."[59] Skip got involved with a self-proclaimed witch named Joanna, consumed a great deal of LSD, and became increasingly unhinged. Early in June, he took a fire axe to his drummer's hotel room door, the last in a number of hotels from which the band had been evicted. Finding no Stevenson, he headed to the studio, where Rubinson eventually talked Spence into dropping the axe before the police carted him off to the Tombs, and eventually to Bellevue Psychiatric where he spent the next six months, diagnosed as paranoid schizophrenic. The remaining members of Moby Grape regrouped in California to work on the third album, *Moby Grape '69* (1969), praised by some as an "unrecognized forerunner of the nascent West Coast country rock movement" of the early 1970s, and full of beautiful harmonies, rich guitar lines, and sharp songwriting.[60] It also included Skip's haunting "Seeing," a surreal ballad recorded just weeks before his breakdown and clearly portending his mental state with its chorus of "Save me, save me." Meanwhile, after his release from Bellevue, Skip went to Nashville to record a solo album, *Oar*, a somewhat cracked masterpiece, unrecognized in its time but since then not only widely praised but emulated by an album titled *More Oar: A Tribute to the Skip Spence Album* (1999), featuring covers by Robert Plant, Tom Waits, Beck, and Alejandro Escovedo, among others.

The remaining Moby Grape did a month-long tour of Europe in early 1969, after which Bob Mosley quit the band to join the Marines. By the time they recorded the last contractual obligation to Columbia, *Truly Fine Citizen*, in May 1969, the band was down to just three of the original members: Stevenson, Miller, and Lewis. Discharged from the Marines after just nine months, Mosley, also diagnosed as schizophrenic, lived for a time under bridges in the San Diego area.[61] The original band reunited for one final album in 1971, *20 Granite Creek* (1971), with Rubinson as producer once again. Over the years, Moby Grape periodically reunited, but was unable to play under that name because of the 1966 contract with Matthew Katz, instead using various pseudonyms like the Melvilles and the Legendary Grape.[62] Katz repeatedly sought restraining orders, but a judgment in 2005 finally restored the band's right to perform as Moby Grape.[63] These days, Don Stevenson busks in Toronto subway stations, playing for the joy of it, and plays occasional club dates. Bob Mosley and Jerry Miller both gig regularly. Peter Lewis plays solo and with his daughter, Arwen, who recently covered the entire *Moby Grape* album. After years of homelessness and institution-alization, Skip Spence died in 1999. Various members of Moby Grape have reunited from time to time with Skip's son, Omar, "cut from the same cloth," channeling both his father's energy and Bob Mosley's powerful vocals on "Seeing" and "Omaha" at SXSW 2010.

Covers

"Omaha" made a difference. Even though it was never a top hit, and was covered infrequently, that song and the first Moby Grape album awoke in countless youth and future rock stars an excitement for the new sounds of psychedelic energetic rock. Robert Plant, Chrissie Hynde, and other artists have cited Moby Grape's influence, and have covered some of their songs in concert.[64] On her brief tour as JP, Chrissie, and the Fairground Boys, Hynde covered *Wow*'s "Murder in my Heart for the Judge" and vowed, "If we have anything to do with it, by the end of this tour every 30-year-old in America will know who Moby Grape is."[65] Bruce Springsteen covered "Omaha" with his first band, the Castiles, in 1967, and he has played it in concert with the E Street Band.[66] In 2008, an East Coast basement band called the Patron Saints released a double CD set of live recordings they made of cover tunes between 1966 and 1968.[67] Their "Omaha," recorded in 1967 or '68, sizzles with garage rock energy and enthusiasm. The liner notes by Patron Saints' guitarist Eric Bergman call it "arguably one of the best songs by one of the best groups ever to strap on guitars, Moby Grape.... . 'Omaha' is still one of my favorite songs from that era."[68] The British glam rock band Slade covered "Omaha" in a live BBC studio session around 1969, although the track was not released commercially until 2009.[69] Perhaps the best-known cover of "Omaha," by the '80s-era experimental alternative rock band the Golden Palominos, came out on 7" single and on their 1985 album *Visions of Excess*. The arrangement pays tribute to the original but almost deconstructs it, turning it into "a truly incisive piece of '80s psychedelia…that sounds like a pop hit."[70] REM lead singer Michael Stipe, the guest vocalist, handles all of the call-and-response duties. Jack Rabid noted in his *AllMusic* review that Stipe's guest appearance would likely turn on new audiences—especially those not attuned to '60s psychedelia—to Moby Grape.

> If the multitudes of Stipe fans…seek Moby Grape records (or Spence's interesting solo work, *Oar*) from days gone by, this 7" will have served any purpose it was designed to. And it's just plain a good record to spin on your turntable, regardless of what you do or don't know about where the tune came from.[71]

Coda

Moby Grape became both a beneficiary and a victim of the new rock industry and those who controlled the levers of commerce and power. They benefitted from being in the right place at the right time, a manager who supported their formation, and a record company and producer who helped them create a masterpiece. But the manager took advantage of their trust and through repeated litigation prevented them from future opportunities. The record company's overhyped promotional campaign soured some fans, and the release of five singles diluted what could have been a clear radio and chart hit with "Omaha." Getting busted after the launch party became one more strike against them, then came the missed opportunity to appear in *Monterey Pop*, their bad behavior, and Columbia's decision to send them to New York to finish *Wow*, a move which led to Skip's involvement with hard drugs, his psychotic break, and the band's demise.

Moby Grape the group and *Moby Grape* the album, revered by musicians and fans ever since the 1967 debut, are first a lesson in "unrealized potential" and an album among the best first albums ever recorded. I do not remember the first time I heard Moby Grape, or "Omaha." That summer of 1967, I was 15, playing guitar in an all-girl rock band, hip to the latest releases, making regular pilgrimages to the local Disc Records at Summit Mall. I do not recall the day I bought the *Moby Grape* LP, but my well-worn copy still sounds great, with the full-size poster neatly folded in the album jacket, waiting for the right time to be framed and hung, a moment that no doubt passed when I left my teens. But the moment for Moby Grape's music never passed. All of it, and especially "Omaha," is as fresh today as it was in 1967.

Notes

1 Susan J. Douglas, *Listening In: Radio and the American Imagination* (Minneapolis: University of Minnesota Press, 2004): 256–9.
2 Michael Gallucci, "Top 25 Psychedelic Rock Albums," *Ultimate Classic Rock*, February 23, 2021. https://ultimateclassicrock.com/psychedelic-rock-albums/
3 CBS News Special, *Inside Pop—The Rock Revolution*, CBS, April 25,1967.
4 Mike Mahoney, "Good Hippies' Summer Plans," *The San Francisco Chronicle*, April 6, 1967, 3.
5 D. A. Pennebaker, T*he Complete Monterey Pop Festival*. The Criterion Channel, 1968a; Harvey Kubernick and Kenneth Kubernick. *A Perfect Haze: The Illustrated History of the Monterey International Pop Festival* (Solana Beach, CA: Santa Monica Press, 2011).
6 *Hair: The American Tribal Love-Rock Musical* opened at New York's Public Theater October 17, 1967, later moving to Broadway in April 1968; *Rolling Stone*, 1:1, November 9, 1967.
7 "A Special Issue on Sound and Fury in the Arts," *Look*, January 9, 1968.
8 Cam Cobb, *What's Big and Purple and Lives in the Ocean? The Moby Grape Story*. (London: Jawbone Press, 2018), picture facing p. 160; Jerry Miller, "Interview with Jerry Miller of Moby Grape (Part #2)," uploaded by Garret K. Woodward, July 4, 2017.; Don Stevenson, "#15: Don Stevenson of Moby Grape." Jaymz Bee Podcast, March 15, 2019.
9 Cobb, *What's Big and Purple and Lives in the Ocean?* 107.
10 Rob Hughes, "Dark Magic: Skip Spence," *Uncut*, June 2020, 84.
11 Hughes, "Dark Magic," 84–5.
12 Rob Hughes, "Great albums that fell off the critical radar: *Moby Grape*." *Uncut*, December 2003.
13 Miller, "Interview with Jerry Miller."
14 Jeff Tamarkin, *Got a Revolution* (New York: Atria Books, 2003), 120.
15 Stevenson, "#15: Don Stevenson of Moby Grape."; David Fricke, "The Grape." Liner notes to *Vintage: The Very Best of Moby Grape* 2-CD set, Columbia/ Legacy, 1993.
16 Ralph J. Gleason, "Dead Like Live Thunder." *San Francisco Chronicle*, March 19, 1967, iv–v.
17 Rob Hughes, "The Story of Moby Grape: Chaos and Courtrooms, Acid and White Witches." *Louder Sound*, 2016.
18 Hughes, "Dark Magic," 85.
19 Rob Hughes, "Dark Star: The Tragic Genius of Skip Spence." *Louder Sound*, 2015.
20 Frederic Dannen, *Hit Men: Power Brokers and Fast Money Inside the Music Business* (New York: Times Books, 1990), ch. 4.
21 Chris Perkel, dir. *Clive Davis: The Soundtrack of Our Lives*. Netflix, 2017, 18:29–19:42.
22 Danny Fields described himself as a "kept hippie," quoted in Serge R. Denisoff, "The Vinyl Crap Game: The Pop Record Industry." *Journal of Jazz Studies* 1 (2) (January, 1974): 18.
23 Richard Morton Jack, *Psychedelia: 101 Iconic Underground Rock Albums 1966-1970*. New York: Sterling, 2017.
24 Moby Grape, "Live at Matrix (1966-xx-xx) us Electric Blues/Jazz Rock/Acid," uploaded by Veteran of the Psych Wars. www.youtube.com/watch?v=bbPo VziNtLM, 37:04; Cobb, *What's Big and Purple and Lives in the Ocean?* 142.

25 Fricke, "The Grape," liner notes.
26 Moby Grape, "Live at Matrix (1966-xx-xx) us Electric Blues/Jazz Rock/Acid,";
 Moby Grape, "Fillmore Auditorium San Francisco 1966-11-25," posted by High
 Deaf, www.youtube.com/watch?v=vb5UGDXk66c.
27 Moby Grape, *Vintage: The Very Best of Moby Grape*, COL 483958 2, Compact
 Discs. Columbia Legacy, 1993, disc 1, cut 3.
28 Blair Jackson, "The Mix Interview: Roy Halee." *Mix*, October 2001, 30–42.
29 Cobb, *What's Big and Purple and Lives in the Ocean?* 158.
30 Michael Hicks, *Sixties Rock: Garage, Psychedelic, and Other Satisfactions*
 (Urbana, IL: University of Illinois Press, 1999), 72.
31 Quoted in Sculatti, *Moby Grape* liner notes, Sundazed release.
32 Paul Williams, "The Golden Road: A Report on San Francisco," in *The Crawdaddy!
 Book*, ed. Paul Williams (New York: Hal Leonard, 2002), 181.
33 Recording dates on track listings in Moby Grape, *Vintage: The Very Best of
 Moby Grape*.
34 Cobb, *What's Big and Purple and Lives in the Ocean?* 130.
35 Denisoff, "The Vinyl Crap Game," 4.
36 Ibid, 4.
37 Ibid, 7.
38 "Moby Grape Chart History," www.billboard.com/music/moby-grape.
39 John Peel, "#05" *John Peel Show Radio London*, November 8, 1967, https://arch
 ive.org/details/05-john-peel-show-radio-london-11-08-67, 23:24–25:45.
40 Hughes, "Great Albums that Fell off the Radar."
41 *Record World*, July 1, 1967.
42 Thomas Frank, *The Conquest of Cool: Business Culture, Counterculture, and the
 Rise of Hip Consumerism* (Chicago: University of Chicago Press, 1997), 7.
43 Record Mecca, "Moby Grape—Ultra Rare 1967 Promotional Box Set," *Record
 Mecca*, https://recordmecca.com/item-archives/26319-2/
44 Cited in Alice Echols, *Scars of Sweet Paradise: The Life and Times of Janis Joplin*
 (New York: Henry Holt, 1999), 186.
45 Hughes, "The Story of Moby Grape: Chaos and Courtrooms, Acid and White
 Witches."
46 Don Stevenson, "#15, Don Stevenson."
47 Quoted in Cobb, *What's Big and Purple and Lives in the Ocean?* 193.
48 D. A. Pennebaker, *Monterey Pop Outtakes: Moby Grape*, Criterion Channel,
 1968b—includes "Hey Grandma"; Moby Grape, "Monterey Pop Festival (1967)
 'Indifference', 'Sitting by the Window' & 'Omaha'" uploaded by HotRockin
 Johnny. A brief clip of one other song, "Lazy Me," plays during Ahmet Ertegun's
 speech in Chris Perkel, dir. *Clive Davis: The Soundtrack of Our Lives*, Netflix,
 2017. segment at 18:29–19:42.
49 Mosley's greeting can be heard at the end of track 9 on Moby Grape, *Moby Grape
 Live*, Sundazed SC1121.
50 Quoted in Cobb, *What's Big and Purple and Lives in the Ocean?* 158.
51 Hughes, "Dark Magic," 84.
52 Quoted in Cobb, *What's Big and Purple and Lives in the Ocean?* 198.
53 William Gibson, "Skip Spence's Jeans," in *Distrust That Particular Flavor*
 (New York: G. P. Putnam's Sons, 2012), 176–7.
54 Hughes, "The Story of Moby Grape."
55 Fricke, "The Grape," 15.

56 Ibid., 12.
57 Moby Grape, *Grape Jam* (Columbia MGS 1), 1968.
58 Fricke, "The Grape," 16.
59 Quoted in Hughes, "The Story of Moby Grape."
60 Jim Allen, "Moby Grape: Still Shining in the Shadows," *PleaseKillMe*, June 26, 2019.
61 Jamie Reno, "Moby Grape's Bob Mosley Homeless in San Diego: Living Under Bridges in Rose Canyon Area," *San Diego Reader*, February 10, 1994.
62 Lee Zimmerman, "Explore the Bitter Vintage of Moby Grape," *Goldmine: The Music Collector's Magazine*, October 1, 2012.
63 Read the full 30-page Statement of Decision: www.bluoz.com/StatementofDecision.072005.pdf.
64 Plant's appreciation of Moby Grape is well known, and he has covered "8:05" and "Seeing": https://forums.ledzeppelin.com/topic/14495-moby-grape/
65 George Varga, "Pretender's Chrissie Hynde Branches Out With New Band," *The San Diego Union-Tribune*, August 26, 2010.
66 www.coveredbybrucespringsteen.com/viewcover.aspx?recordID=515 and Bruce Springsteen, "'Let's Roadhouse!' #9 - 'Omaha' - Omaha, NE - 11/15/12," posted by roulette909, www.youtube.com/watch?v=0eX6cRpqDaM&feature=youtu.be.
67 The Patron Saints. *Before Bohob, Vol. 1*, 2008.
68 Bergman liner notes, *Before Bohob*.
69 Slade, *Live at the BBC*. SALVODCD211 compact disc, 2009.
70 Trouser Press, "Golden Palominos," *Trouser Press*, https://trouserpress.com/reviews/golden-palominos/
71 Jack Rabid, "Omaha Review," *AllMusic*, www.allmusic.com/album/omaha-mw0000938566.

References

Allen, Jim. "Moby Grape: Still Shining in the Shadows." *PleaseKillMe*, June 26, 2019. https://pleasekillme.com/moby-grape/

Bell, Max. "Moby Grape: *Great Grape*." *New Musical Express*, 1974. www.rocksbackpages.com/Library/Article/moby-grape-igreat-grapei

Burke, Ted. "A Moby Grape Survivor: Two Related Incidents to Begin With." *San Diego Reader*, January 29, 1976. www.sandiegoreader.com/news/1976/jan/29/cover-a-moby-grape-survivor/

CBS News Special. *Inside Pop—The Rock Revolution*. CBS News, April 25, 1967. www.youtube.com/watch?v=afU76JJcquI

Cobb, Cam. *What's Big and Purple and Lives in the Ocean? The Moby Grape Story*. London: Jawbone Press, 2018.

Conley, Paul. "Moby Grape Just Can't Catch a Break." National Public Radio *All Things Considered*, December 21, 2007. www.npr.org/templates/story/story.php?storyId=17498799

Dannen, Frederic. *Hit Men: Power Brokers and Fast Money Inside the Music Business*. New York: Times Books, 1990.

Denisoff, R. Serge. "The Vinyl Crap Game: The Pop Record Industry." *Journal of Jazz Studies* 1 (2) (January, 1974): 3–26.

Douglas, Susan J. *Listening In: Radio and the American Imagination*. Minneapolis: University of Minnesota Press, 2004.

Echols, Alice. *Scars of Sweet Paradise: The Life and Times of Janis Joplin*. New York: Henry Holt, 1999.

Frank, Thomas. *The Conquest of Cool: Business Culture, Counterculture, and the Rise of Hip Consumerism*. Chicago: University of Chicago Press, 1997.

Fricke, David. "The Grape." Liner notes to *Vintage: The Very Best of Moby Grape* 2-CD set, Columbia/Legacy, 1993.

Gibson, William. "Skip Spence's Jeans," in *Distrust That Particular Flavor*. New York: G. P. Putnam's Sons, 2012.

Gleason, Ralph J. "Dead Like Live Thunder." *San Francisco Chronicle*, March 19, 1967.

Hicks, Michael. *Sixties Rock: Garage, Psychedelic, and Other Satisfactions*. Urbana, IL: University of Illinois Press, 1999.

Hughes, Rob. "Great albums that fell off the critical radar: *Moby Grape*." *Uncut*, December 2003. www.rocksbackpages.com/Library/Article/great-albums-that-fell-off-the-critical-radar-imoby-grapei

Hughes, Rob. "Dark Star: The Tragic Genius of Skip Spence." *Louder Sound*, 2015. www.loudersound.com/features/dark-star-the-tragic-genius-of-skip-spence

Hughes, Rob. "The Story of Moby Grape: Chaos and Courtrooms, Acid and White Witches." *Louder Sound*, 2016. www.loudersound.com/features/the-story-of-moby-grape-chaos-and-courtrooms-acid-and-white-witches

Hughes, Rob. "Dark Magic: Skip Spence." *Uncut*, June, 2020.

Jack, Richard Morton. *Psychedelia: 101 Iconic Underground Rock Albums 1966–1970*. New York: Sterling, 2017.

Jackson, Blair. "The Mix Interview: Roy Halee." *Mix*, October 2001, 30–42.

Kopp, Bill. "Moby Grape's Peter Lewis: A rock and roll survivor, now on 'The Road to Zion'." *Goldmine: The Music Collector's Magazine*, November 18, 2019. www.goldminemag.com/articles/moby-grapes-peter-lewis-a-rock-and-roll-survivor-now-on-the-road-to-zion

Kubernick, Harvey. *1967: A Complete Rock Music History of the Summer of Love*. New York: Sterling, 2017.

Kubernick, Harvey and Kenneth Kubernick. *A Perfect Haze: The Illustrated History of the Monterey International Pop Festival*. Solana Beach, CA: Santa Monica Press, 2011.

Mahoney, Mike. "Good Hippies' Summer Plans." *The San Francisco Chronicle*, April 6, 1967.

Oppenheim, David, dir. *Inside Pop—The Rock Revolution* CBS News SpecialTV, April 25, 1967. www.youtube.com/watch?v=afU76JJcquI

Peel, John. "#05." *John Peel Radio Show*, November 8, 1967. https://archive.org/details/05-john-peel-show-radio-london-11-08-67

Pennebaker, D. A., dir. *The Complete Monterey Pop Festival*. The Criterion Channel, 1968a. www.criterionchannel.com/the-complete-monterey-pop-festival

Pennebaker, D. A. *Monterey Pop Outtakes: Moby Grape*. The Criterion Channel, 1968b.www.criterionchannel.com/videos/outtakes-moby-grape

Perkel, Chris, dir. *Clive Davis: The Soundtrack of Our Lives*. Netflix, 2017.

Rabid, Jack. "Omaha Review," *AllMusic*, www.allmusic.com/album/omaha-mw0000938566

Record Mecca. "Moby Grape—Ultra Rare 1967 Promotional Box Set," *Record Mecca*. https://recordmecca.com/item-archives/26319-2/

Reno, Jamie. "Moby Grape's Bob Mosley Homeless in San Diego: Living Under Bridges in Rose Canyon Area." *San Diego Reader*, February 10,1994. www.sandiegoreader.com/news/1994/feb/10/city-lights-moby-grapes-mosley-homel ess-san-diego/

Savage, Jon. "Moby Grape: *Vintage: The Very Best Of Moby Grape*." *MOJO*, 1993. www.rocksbackpages.com/Library/Article/moby-grape-vintage-the-very-best-of-moby-grape

Sculatti, Gene. "Moby Grape: *Moby Grape*." Sundazed re-release sleeve and pro-gramme notes, 2007. www.rocksbackpages.com/Library/Article/moby-grape-imoby-grapei

Tamarkin, Jeff. *Got a Revolution*. New York: Atria Books, 2003.

Tamarkin, Jeff. "Moby Grape: When Bad Things Happen to Good Bands." *Best Classic Bands*, 2017. https://bestclassicbands.com/moby-grape-6-9-17/

Trouser Press. "Golden Palominos," *Trouser Press*, https://trouserpress.com/reviews/golden-palominos/

Varga, George. "Pretender's Chrissie Hynde Branches Out With New Band," The San Diego Union-Tribune, August 26, 2010. www.sandiegouniontribune.com/sdut-no-pretending-2010aug26-htmlstory.html.

Williams, Paul. "The Golden Road: A Report on San Francisco." In *The Crawdaddy! Book*, edited by Paul Williams, 171–83. New York: Hal Leonard, 2002.

Willis, Ellen. "The Ordeal of Moby Grape, June 1968." In *Out of the Vinyl Deeps: Ellen Willis on Rock Music*, edited by Nona Willis Aronowitz, 196–98. Minneapolis: University of Minnesota Press, 2011.

Zimmerman, Lee. "Explore the Bitter Vintage of Moby Grape." *Goldmine: The Music Collector's Magazine*, October 1, 2012. www.goldminemag.com/articles/explore-the-bitter-vintage-of-moby-grape

Discography

Moby Grape. *Moby Grape*. Columbia CL2698, 33 1/3 RPM, 1967.

Moby Grape. *Wow/Grape Jam*. Columbia CS9613/MGS1, 33 1/3 RPM, 1968.

Moby Grape. *Moby Grape '69*. Columbia CS9696, 33 1/3 RPM, 1969.

Moby Grape. *20 Granite Creek*. Warner/Reprise WPCR-17752, Compact Disc, 1971.

Moby Grape. *Vintage: The Very Best of Moby Grape*. COL 483958 2, Compact Discs. Columbia Legacy, 1993.

Moby Grape. *Moby Grape Live*. Sundazed SC11210, Compact Disc, 2010.

Slade. *Live at the BBC*. SALVODCD211. Compact Disc, 2009.

Spence, Alexander. *Oar*. Sundazed SC11075, Compact Disc, 1999.

The Golden Palominos. *Visions of Excess*. CELL 6118, 33 1/3 RPM. Celluloid, 1985.

The Patron Saints. *Before Bohob, Vol. 1 1966–68*. PSCD-111/112. Compact Disc, 2008.

Various. *More Oar: A Tribute to the Skip Spence Album*. Birdman BMR023, Compact Disc, 1999.

You Tube

Miller, Jerry. "Jerry Miller Talks About Moby Grape Debut." Uploaded by Saint Bryan, May 9, 2016. www.youtube.com/watch?v=WJ8jMVQaT0g

Miller, Jerry. "Interview with Jerry Miller of Moby Grape (Part #1)," uploaded by Garret K. Woodward, July 4, 2017. www.youtube.com/watch?v=mMtAmIfVqEI&t

Miller Jerry. "Interview with Jerry Miller of Moby Grape (Part #2)," uploaded by Garret K. Woodward, July 4, 2017. www.youtube.com/watch?v=6IcgEpxZrkA

Moby Grape. "Fillmore Auditorium San Francisco 1966-11-25," uploaded by High Deaf. www.youtube.com/watch?v=vb5UGDXk66c

Moby Grape. "Live at Matrix (1966-xx-xx) us Electric Blues/Jazz Rock/Acid," uploaded by Veteran of the Psych Wars. www.youtube.com/watch?v=bbPoVziNtLM

Moby Grape. "Monterey Pop Festival (1967) 'Indifference', 'Sitting by the Window' & 'Omaha'" uploaded by HotRockin Johnny. www.youtube.com/watch?v=hm8Wj4keXH4

Springsteen, Bruce. "'Let's Roadhouse!' #9 - 'Omaha' - Omaha, NE - 11/15/12," posted by roulette909. www.youtube.com/watch?v=0eX6cRpqDaM&feature=youtu.be

Stevenson, Don. "#15: Don Stevenson of Moby Grape." Jaymz Bee Podcast, March 15, 2019. www.youtube.com/watch?v=AOiooAo9do0&feature=emb_rel_end

4 Led Zeppelin—"Immigrant Song" (1970)

Esther Liberman Cuenca

Viking Medievalisms and the Afterlife of Classic Rock

Much of the humor in the rock mockumentary *This Is Spinal Tap* (1984)—such as, for example, when a pathetic miniature of Stone Henge descends onto Spinal Tap's stage—depends on director Rob Reiner and his star and co-writer Christopher Guest's assumption of the audience's familiarity with the music of the British band Led Zeppelin and, particularly, their fetishization of age-old Britannia. The members of Led Zeppelin were not the only rockers who mythologized Britain's ancient and medieval past in song, but they were likely the most well known, as well as one of the most iconic rock groups to do it. Much of the scholarly explorations of the medieval world as represented in Led Zeppelin's music has focused on guitarist Jimmy Page and frontman Robert Plant's enthusiasm for J. R. R. Tolkien's trilogy of novels *The Lord of the Rings* (1954–55), the imagery from which was featured heavily in their iconic album *Led Zeppelin IV* (1971) with the songs "Misty Mountain Hop" and "The Battle of Evermore."[1] "Ramble On," another ode to Tolkien's classic, appeared on an earlier album, *Led Zeppelin II* (1969). Yet, Tolkien was not the only medieval touchstone for the band. Sandwiched between these homages to *The Lord of the Rings* was "Immigrant Song," the first track on *Led Zeppelin III* (1970), a short, punchy rock masterpiece featuring Plant's primal screams, which conjured images of Viking invaders in search of greener pastures and docile people to conquer.

In examining the history of "Immigrant Song," as well as its significance to the medievalisms (or the representations of the Middle Ages in popular culture) in it, I draw on "medieval" tropes that remain underexamined in scholarship on Led Zeppelin—the Vikings and their literary legacy in both medieval and modern England. I also explore here the afterlife of this song in other media, which underscores how its medievalisms were easily integrated into other contexts. Over 40 years after the original, Trent Reznor and Atticus Ross's cover of "Immigrant Song," with vocals by the Yeah Yeah Yeah's frontwoman Karen O and specially commissioned by director David Fincher for his feature film adaptation of *The Girl with the Dragon Tattoo* (2011), was used in a story that featured a neo-Gothic setting—a violent, icy,

DOI: 10.4324/9781003093206-5

and dark Scandinavian landscape. Later, director Taika Waititi used the original version of the song effectively in his entry for the Marvel Cinematic Universe's *Thor: Ragnarok* (2017), the third film in a series that leaned heavily on modern representations of Norse mythology. I argue that the medievalisms of "Immigrant Song" made it an ideal conduit through which ideas about the medieval world of the Vikings were communicated in popular culture and which also served as part of a larger tradition of Viking medievalisms that first gained currency in the nineteenth century and became prevalent in the twentieth century. In other words, the song's biography is indicative of the lasting impression that Vikings, as violent marauders and able sailors, have made on music and cinema that represent medieval Scandinavia, effectively bridging the medieval past and modern present through a rock song that has become portable to other media.

Background

The first time Led Zeppelin played "Immigrant Song" in public was at the two-day Bath Festival of Blues and Progressive Music on June 28, 1970. Though Zeppelin had only received fourth billing and £500 in 1969 when Fleetwood Mac was the billed headliner, in 1970, the band, under the management of the ambitious Peter Grant, made considerably larger demands. This time, Zeppelin wanted to be the headliners. The band's name on the program could attract up to 30,000 attendees, and as such, they demanded their names be doubled in size on posters advertising the event. Most importantly, Zeppelin's gig fee went up to a whopping £20,000, which was, according to one of the festival's promoters, "the equivalent of the price of a house in Knightsbridge."[2] The live debut of "Immigrant Song" also happened to coincide with a period of transition for the band, the Bath Festival itself being a turning point for Zeppelin's critical reception in the press. The band played for about three hours, coming out to perform five encores to an adoring crowd of 30,000 fans. Never one to receive accolades from the press, the critics deemed it to be one of the most important shows of the band's career.[3]

Already well established with American audiences, and having toured the United States extensively, Zeppelin had turned down an offer of $250,000 to play at a football stadium in New Haven, Connecticut, to appear at the Bath Festival in 1969, the first time they played at the event. But it was credibility more than largesse that the band lacked in those early years. As music journalist Dave Schulps put it, Zeppelin's "first real, major acceptance [was in the United States]. That tends to piss the English critics off. Anything that gets discovered in America English critics have a problem with."[4] The 1970 headlining event seemed to cement their successful appearance from the year before and brought Zeppelin more critical praise. Chris Charlesworth and Chris Welch, writing for the July 4, 1970, edition of *Melody Maker*, described the show glowingly, saying that Zeppelin had kicked off with a new riff from their next album called "Immigration Song" [sic]. They actually took some time to warm up the crowd, but this may have been intentional as they built up to a fantastic climax with an act lasting over three hours[5]

The band garnered respect in their homeland at last.

The inception of "Immigrant Song," however, began before the Bath Festival, mainly during the band's stint in Reykjavík, Iceland, a week earlier on June 22. Though the basis of the song was conceived before the band landed in Reykjavík, Plant had been inspired enough by his Icelandic experience to write new lyrics, recounting the event to music journalist Chris Welch:

It was always like that with Led Zeppelin, like, "Who do they think they are? To be so pompous?" And we weren't being pompous, we did come

Figure 4.1 Led Zeppelin at Chateau Marmont in 1969. From left: Jimmy Page, Robert Plant, John Paul Jones, and John Bonham. Credit: ZUMA Press, Inc./ Alamy Stock Photo.

from the land of ice and snow. We were guests of the Icelandic government on a cultural mission representing the musicians of Britain. We
were invited to Reykjavik to play a concert and the day before we arrived
all the civil servants went on strike, the blue-collar workers, and the gig
was going to be canceled.[6]

According to Plant, the local university scrambled for two days to prepare a space for the band's performance, which was part of the Reykjavík Art
Festival. The band's warm reception at the airport prefaced an enthusiastic
turnout for the sold-out gig they played at Laugardalshöll, an indoor sporting
arena that accommodated the thousands in attendance that day. That the gig
took place during a time of social unrest did not seem particularly noticeable
to the band. Throughout the 1970s, labor and women's strikes were common-
place in Iceland, the most famous of them, Kvennafrídagurinn (Women's Day
Off) in October 1975, led to the promotion of unprecedented gender equity
laws. Though such civil agitation became less common in the decades that
followed, it provided the backdrop for a performance in a country on the cusp
of radical social change.[7] Iceland's youth had turned out for the band in full
force, packing the concert hall and airport arrivals area to greet their intrepid
guests. Plant, who was 21 years old at the time, reminisced that it was "the
kind of response and confederacy between us and the kids, the people our
own age, in a little country of 200,000 people," that allowed all of them to
have "the most remarkable time."[8] In this respect, the members of Zeppelin
were not mere rockers but genuine talents—cultural ambassadors who were
also connected to the highly lucrative youth market of rock 'n' roll music (see
Figure 4.1).

Zeppelin's Influences

Led Zeppelin was, fundamentally, a pop band that happened to play heavy
rock music. The foundation of their popularity was rooted in the almost
tireless energy with which Plant, Page, John Paul Jones (the bassist), and
John Bonham (the drummer, also known as Bonzo) embarked on multi-city
tours for months on end. Their fame was first made in the United States, and
they became accustomed to playing large festivals and concert arenas for tens
of thousands of fans. Driving their ships to new lands, fighting hordes of
promoters, and singing and crying and wailing as they did onstage for much
of the year (to echo the lyrics in "Immigrant Song") in their early touring days
were all part of the master battle plan to achieve worldwide popularity. Their
pit stop in Iceland on their way to the Bath Festival left such a long-lasting
impression on Plant that, despite all their successes up to that point, he was
inspired to write a song that celebrated the band's scaling the most important
summit of all: cultural relevancy. As Plant remarked, "'Immigrant Song' was
about that [Reykjavík] trip and it was the opening track on the album that
was intended to be incredibly different."[9] According to Baldvin Baldvinss,

who reviewed the show for the Icelandic daily newspaper *Tíminn*, "[The band] played one song from the next album [*Led Zeppelin III*], they worked on the last two months and should be released in late July."[10] The song Baldvinss was referencing was likely "Bron-yr-Aur Stomp," which Zeppelin played along with at least three songs from *Led Zeppelin II*, including "Whole Lotta Love," and songs from their debut album, *Led Zeppelin* (1969), including "Dazed and Confused" and "Communication Breakdown."[11] Bron-yr-Aur was the name of the Welsh cottage where the band recorded *Led Zeppelin III* and later *Led Zeppelin IV*, though the band was also fond of working and recording in Headley Grange in Hampshire. The hard rock "Immigrant Song" notwithstanding, the band had been consciously moving towards a more folk-heavy sound on their upcoming album, *Led Zeppelin III*, which was released in October 1970 with "Immigrant Song" as its first track.

The tonal shift to folksiness reflected popular music trends of the early 1970s. Plant and Page were fans of Sandy Denny (and her band Fairport Convention) as well as singer Joni Mitchell. Undoubtedly, the band's bucolic surroundings during the recording of *Led Zeppelin III* and *Led Zeppelin IV* also invoked images of a pre-modern Britain, a place and age associated with English folk music.[12] Looking back to the early 1970s, Simon Kirke, the drummer of Bad Company (which was later signed to Zeppelin's label Swan Song), said, "There was a lot of folk in Zeppelin, believe it or not. Probably the heaviest folk band that has ever existed."[13] The connection between medievalism and Zeppelin's reimagining of English folk music was most prominent on the first track from the B side of *Led Zeppelin III*. "Gallows Pole" was a musical take on the old ballad "The Maid Freed from the Gallows," first popularized in the nineteenth century.[14] Both the ballad and the Zeppelin song conjured certain gender and social dynamics traditionally associated with a bygone medieval world.

Even though it relies heavily on medievalist imagery, "Immigrant Song" is not a folk song but, rather, a hard-rock blast of primal energy and cocksure swagger. It has none of the relative English gentleness of "Stairway to Heaven" or "Gallows Pole," or the literary homages to *The Lord of the Rings* exemplified by "Ramble On," "Battle of Evermore," and "Misty Mountain Hop." But much like these neo-medievalist interpretations of folk music and literature, "Immigrant Song" is broadly representative of the type of arrogation of a medieval past that was common in Zeppelin's music. A musical appropriation that was more overt, however, was Page and Plant's heavy borrowing of traditional rhythm and blues music associated with Black singers in the Southern United States. Though Page lent a type of hard-rock virtuosity to his reinterpretation of Black music, there simply would not be a Led Zeppelin as we know them today without the influence of Black musicians.[15] Zeppelin was not unique in their practice of copying Black blues guitarists, particularly in South London's late 1960s rock scene. Eric Clapton, Jeff Beck, and, of course, the Rolling Stones commandeered the sounds and lyrical stylings of Black musicians.

Eventually, the two influences—medievalism and Black American blues—melded into one. Although the lyrics to "Gallows Pole" had indefinite origins in the balladry of a pre-modern past, Page's music for the song was ultimately adapted from Black folk blues singer Huddie William Ledbetter, also known as Lead Belly, who recorded "The Gallis Pole" in 1939. The B side of the US single of "Immigrant Song," the acoustic ditty "Hey, Hey, What Can I Do," which became a staple of classic rock radio in later years, is also indicative of Zeppelin's enormous debt to Black blues music—with its down-on-his-luck longing for an unfaithful woman against a backdrop of southern churches and honky-tonk bars. This song is also reminiscent of the music of the Faces (fronted by Rod Stewart), who were also captivated by honky-tonk music and were Zeppelin's contemporaries in the same London music scene.

Zeppelin and the Legacy of Masculinist and Viking Medievalisms

From Zeppelin's view in England, the "western" shore, as sung about in "Immigrant Song," was both America and Iceland, and these lands fell to the Led Zeppelin invasion before Britain did. The Viking imagery of a single-minded drive for domination echoed Plant's sentiments that Iceland had been served up to the band on a platter, their gig in Reykjavík cementing Anglo-Icelandic relations—in more ways than one.[16] When Plant looked back fondly on that trip in one of his interviews, he said "Anglo-Icelandic relations" with a wink and a nod in his tone, gesturing toward sexual conquest as well. The song itself, with Plant's warlike wails and the thunderous riffs of Page's guitar mimicking a battle cry, was an aural representation of the band's hypermasculine image, predicated as it was on raucous stories of their concert after-parties, liaisons with groupies, and (in Page's case particularly) underage girlfriends.[17]

Though Zeppelin's reputation as a "party band" may have been largely an exaggeration circulated by their hard-bargaining and protective manager, Peter Grant, stories of their wrecking hotel rooms, late-night drinking, interest in the occult, and sexual adventures played up their image as preternaturally gifted wild men who harnessed the power of the rock gods to make deeply melodic, heartfelt music. In this sense, the band was appealing to a young, white male audience, foreshadowing the popularity of bands with similar reputations and fan bases in the following decade (such as Def Leppard, Mötley Crüe, and Guns N' Roses). "Immigrant Song" was indeed one of many songs in the Led Zeppelin catalogue that reinforced their status as a cock-rock band—music for boys and "dudes," and, nowadays, the biggest star in the constellation of "dad rock."[18]

Nirvana's Kurt Cobain had trouble reconciling his admiration for Zeppelin's artistry with his feminist politics. "Stairway to Heaven," after all, had been one of the first songs he learned to play on guitar. "Although I listened to Aerosmith and Led Zeppelin," he admitted, "and I really did enjoy some of the melodies they'd written, it took me so many years to realize that a lot of it had to do with sexism. The way that they just wrote about their dicks and having sex."[19] Zeppelin's phallic song catalogue, however, did not fully alienate women from seeking out their music, though scholars noted that the band may have had limited appeal to women. One of the foremost scholars on Zeppelin, Susan Fast, systematically analyzed the band's appeal to female fans in an attempt to understand her own deeply felt admiration for the music:

> Listening to the energy and strength of "Immigrant Song" was an incredibly empowering experience. I had no idea what the lyrics were—I could understand only snatches of them—but that riff, with its crisp octave snap that repeated at about the same rhythm as an energized heartbeat, its timbre so insistent and confident, the bass guitar pounding that rhythm into every part of my body, and Plant's majestic if incomprehensible proclamations: that song was where I wanted to live.[20]

For Fast, "Immigrant Song" was the gateway drug to an "empowering experience," one that she believed women could have while listening to the music. Though she acknowledged that male fans most likely outnumbered female ones, she argued that an overidentification of Zeppelin's appeal to men has come at the expense of erasing women from the band's larger fandom. The women Fast surveyed loved the music because they found the sexual energy of the band intoxicating but also, at the same time, they were drawn to the technical mastery and the emotionality of the music.[21] It was for the latter two reasons that Fast became a fan and, later, a scholar of Zeppelin's music.

Even though Fast thought the lyrics were incomprehensible when she first listened to it, "Immigrant Song" is a song cloaked in medievalist imagery of conquest and triumph, and a modern song that holds very old ideas about history. Plant's understanding of this medieval past was almost quaint, saying in a radio interview that Led Zeppelin had "never played this far north [in Reykjavík] before,"[22] and that when the band had gone to Iceland, "it made you think of Vikings and big ships."[23] As Caitlin Carlos has argued, Led Zeppelin's particular brand of medievalism, much of it influenced by Tolkien's works, banked on a type of nostalgia for an idyllic, rural Britain reflecting the postwar, post-industrial anxieties that many British youth in the 1960s and 1970s experienced.[24] *The Lord of the Rings*, though published in the 1950s, only found its popularity with baby boomers in the following decade. "Immigrant Song" may not have been necessarily the same type of medievalist throwback as Tolkien's fantasy of the calmer, greener times of a pre-Conquest "Shire" (standing in for England), but it nevertheless looked backward to that era as a darker, icier version of medieval history, one in which English rural life, as fetishized by Tolkien, was violently disrupted.

The Viking era, especially as it relates to English history in the pre-Conquest period, is one that has marked the collective imagination with certain medieval stereotypes, to which Plant alluded in both the song itself and in interviews about it: invasions from the north, expert sailors in big ships, tales of gore involving pillaging and, eventually, complete domination over peoples inhabiting the soft green fields of yore. These images were not very far off from the literary ones popularized by medieval chroniclers themselves. Although accounts of Viking atrocities ranged from the mundane to hair raising, they were plentiful in the history writing of the time. Asser's biography of King Alfred the Great (848–99), who has been cast in the nineteenth- and twentieth-century British nationalistic tradition as England's great defender against the Viking horde, related in a matter-of-fact way that in one year "the Viking army, which had settled in East Anglia, broke in the most insolent manner the peace which they had established with King Alfred."[25] This insolent manner was left to the medieval reader's imagination. A British film based on Asser's work, *Alfred the Great*, was released (a year before "Immigrant Song") in 1969, and its depiction of Viking warfare was fairly representative of the type of Norse medievalisms current in British media at the time.[26]

The Anglo-Saxon Chronicle, which monastic chroniclers began during the reign of Alfred the Great as a chronological account of important events in English history, was replete with "tales of gore" that focused on Viking warfare and the Norsemen's attacks on the English. In 866, the Viking "raiding-army went from East Anglia over the mouth of the Humber to York city in Northumbria; and...an immense slaughter was made of the Northumbrians there...and both the kings were killed, and the survivors made peace with the raiding-army."[27] The particular violence visited on Northumbria was expounded on in Abbo of Fleury's hagiography of St. Edmund from the late ninth century, in which Abbo had written that the Viking chieftain Ivar "suddenly invaded the country, just like a wolf, and slew the people, men and women and innocent children, and ignominiously harassed innocent Christians."[28]

These Christian sources, though written by clerical authors within the elite ranks of the Church over a millennium before Zeppelin recorded "Immigrant Song," show the enormous debt that modern popular culture owes to relatively obscure medieval chronicles and biographies, however distantly removed they might have been. "Immigrant Song" demonstrates how Viking medievalisms can echo down through the ages from the original medieval source material written many centuries ago and, additionally, from translations of Norse sagas into English that were published for both American and British audiences in the nineteenth and twentieth centuries. These translations were critical to making Norse literature—and its images of Vikings as a whole—accessible to much of the English-speaking world. As Geraldine Barnes has noted, the newly summarized or translated versions of the Vinland sagas and other Norse tales in the nineteenth and twentieth centuries allowed American readers to imagine moments of adventure and discovery, especially as Vinland itself was geographically closer to the New World than the Old. For the British, the failed colony of Vinland represented their fears of how carefully calibrated imperial projects could fail.[29] It is difficult to disentangle this reading from "Immigrant Song," a product of Britain's Commonwealth years, as a postmodern (and possibly ironic) celebration of British imperialism. "We are your overlords," indeed.

Viking Metal and the Cinematic Afterlife of "Immigrant Song"

Led Zeppelin's "Immigrant Song" predates Viking metal, which emerged in Scandinavia in the late 1980s and 1990s and was characterized by loud, distorted electric guitars and thundering drumbeats. Viking metal has nothing to do with traditional Viking music given that no such music, as it was played or performed in the medieval era, has survived into the present day. As a subgenre of heavy metal, and much like the parent genre that gave birth to it, Viking metal reflects hypermasculine sensibilities that exaggerate a love of warfare, chaos, and adventure and reject social norms that may soothe warlike men into domesticity or submission.[30] Ashley Walsh has argued that an integral component to Viking metal is its fixation on Old Norse religion and the gods that populate that pantheon, as well as its utter rejection of Christianity in favor of a musical aesthetic that promotes ethnic and nationalist symbols based in pagan medievalism.[31]

"Immigrant Song" fits squarely into the classic rock genre, rather than that of heavy metal, but its construction of an "exotic netherworld ruled by heathen deities whose power over nature is equal to their power over man," makes it an important forerunner of Viking metal classics such as King of Asgard's "Up on the Mountain," Heavy Load's "Heathens from the North," and Black Sabbath's "Valhalla."[32] This nostalgic longing for a pre-Christian past in Viking metal has also cultivated a White nationalist strain in some of the music that is, unfortunately, not out of place in the wider fetishization of Viking culture, as some medieval scholars have recently examined.[33] White ethnic nationalism had always been part of the text, rather than subtext, of the nineteenth and early twentieth-century recovery of the medieval past, especially among German scholars searching for the foundations of a "pure" Teutonic heritage. This reframing of the past had come to define Nazi and other White fascist reconstructions of history in the middle of the twentieth century.[34]

The Millennium trilogy novels of Stieg Larsson, especially his first and most famous one, *The Girl with the Dragon Tattoo* (2005), is about misogyny but also contends with Sweden's complicity in Nazism during World War II. The villain of *Dragon Tattoo* is revealed, after all, to be a Nazi. What is less discussed, however, is the integration of medievalist tropes in the novel (and in its two feature film adaptations). Director David Fincher's 2011 adaptation of *Dragon Tattoo* used a version of "Immigrant Song" that renders the medievalisms of both the song and film with more complexity. In their essay about the corporatism of the *Dragon Tattoo* novel, Kevin Moberly and Brent Moberly explicitly drew comparisons between it and Tolkien's *Lord of the Rings* novels, drawing attention to the medievalist imagery of Lisbeth Salander's dragon tattoo and the Arthurian-like roles that Salander and

Mikael Blomkvist occupy in their quest to solve the central mystery of the novel.[35]

Given Fincher's background in directing music videos, and perhaps because the female protagonist of the story is a battle-hardened hacker with a punk aesthetic, "Immigrant Song" is heard in a highly stylized music video that serves as the title sequence of the film. The opening credits show the melding of dark, malleable figures (stars Rooney Mara and Daniel Craig) with a flurry of images that best can be described as sentient computer detritus: wires, keyboards, and CPU hard drives. Trent Reznor, whom Fincher had asked to score the film and adapt pop songs for the soundtrack, was at first mystified about the proposition of covering "Immigrant Song," saying:

> I like Zeppelin, I like that song, and I really like Karen O, but that's not particularly where I think my trajectory is headed. I've learned with [Fincher] to say, "Um, let's see." What I didn't understand at the beginning of that was he was hearing that as the teaser trailer for the film. Ultimately, and as you've just seen, [it's in] the title crawl, and I think it works great.[36]

The use of "Immigrant Song" in Fincher's film allowed the English-speaking film, which had a cast of American and British actors, to better connect to its Scandinavian setting. The film's beautiful but barren and dark vistas, huge mansions, the villain's torture lair, and the grotesque imagery involving missing or murdered women enhanced the film's neo-Gothic themes. The feminization of the song, achieved with Karen O's playful vocals, shifted it away from masculine conquest to female vengeance, exemplified in Salander's mission to make men face justice for their crimes against women.

A more recent and perhaps equally memorable use of "Immigrant Song" was in the 2017 Marvel blockbuster *Thor: Ragnarok*, directed by Taika Waititi. The original version of the song not only played over the climactic battle scene in Asgard but it was also the song that helped secure Waititi the directing gig for the tentpole film. Zeppelin's oblique reference to Thor in "Immigrant Song" is not the only one in their discography; they also mention Thor in "No Quarter," a song on the album *Houses of the Holy* (1973), in which "the winds of Thor are blowing cold." Even so, it is "Immigrant Song" that is most associated with the pop-Norse mythology that Waititi wanted to explore for his vision of the Thor character (played by Chris Hemsworth). Waititi, who began to have meetings with Marvel Studios in 2015, included "Immigrant Song" in a sizzle reel for studio head Kevin Feige when Waititi pitched an idea on how to reinvent the Thor character for the franchise. "I remember Kevin being really excited about the song right from the early meetings," Waititi said. "He was like, 'We should explore that song because it could be perfect for the film.'"[37] Zeppelin seemed to agree and let Marvel Studios use the song once the film was completed and the band had seen the teaser trailer, which had been cut to "Immigrant Song."

"Immigrant Song"—with its rock 'n' roll glamour and references to Norse mythology—complemented the new direction that the *Thor* film and character were taking under Waititi's direction. The aesthetics of *Thor: Ragnarok*, which centers on fantastical images such as Valkyrie (Tessa Thompson) riding the mythological Pegasus as she descends upon Asgard, mimicked the types of album covers used by progressive rock and metal bands of the 1970s and 1980s. Prior to *Thor: Ragnarok*, the last time "Immigrant Song" was used in a big Hollywood film was in the 2003 Jack Black–starring comedy *The School of Rock*, a warm and kid-friendly ode to classic rock music. "Immigrant Song" was one of many songs that Black's character used to educate his young pupils about the magic of rock music, but the song's use in that movie did not have much meaning beyond that. The song's use in *Thor: Ragnarok*, however, has layered meanings. As Dina AlAwadhi and Jason Dittmer have argued, a song that started out its popular culture imprint celebrating conquest and colonization had been turned on its head by director Waititi and the way he subtly critiques the imperialistic mythology that undergirds Thor's existence. The first two *Thor* films uncritically accepted a colonialist status quo in which Odin (Anthony Hopkins), Thor's father, is cast as the benevolent king over the nine realms that constitute his empire. As AlAwadhi and Dittmer point out, it is only when Odin's oldest daughter, Hela (Cate Blanchett), is unleashed that Asgard's true and bloody history is revealed: before Thor's birth, Hela served as Odin's right hand in subjugating other realms to their power, and she has come to revive the legacy of Asgard's imperialist ambitions.[38]

The insertion of "Immigrant Song," which celebrates conquest and colonization, into wildly popular entertainment like *Thor: Ragnarok*, which undermines colonialist narratives, acts as a vehicle to reject white supremacy and reimagine the *Thor* movie as an anti-racist "text." The song is played twice in the film, at critical junctures in Thor's journey to self-discovery; the final time we hear it is when Thor has been stripped of his hammer, hair, and eye, and has come to stop Hela from renewing Asgard's wars of conquest. As AlAwadhi and Dittmer put it:

> Ultimately, Hela is only defeated through the destruction of Asgard, and the system it once represented, and the Asgardian refugees turn to Earth to find a new home, echoing Immigrant Song's final words: "You'd better stop and rebuild all your ruins / For peace and trust can win the day despite of all your losing."[39]

Waititi's casting of background performers of all ethnicities in Asgard, as well as of Black American actor Thompson as queer-coded Valkyrie, was also a way in which he amplified the film's anti-racist and anti-colonialist themes. (Black British actor Idris Elba, who played Heimdall, had been originally cast in Kenneth Branagh's first *Thor* film to some controversy). For the *Thor* film and franchise as a whole, casting decisions and the thematic rejection of imperialism are not insignificant gestures given the history of Viking medievalisms in popular culture. Viking metal music and media either imagine Norse culture as ethnically white or reify whiteness as naturally dominant. Very rarely do these pop medievalisms engage with the actual history of Viking migrations, which involved not only raiding but also trade in North Africa, the Mediterranean, and the Middle East. To strip away the white nationalism from the pop-Norse mythology in *Thor: Ragnarok*, a film with a global reach and audience, is to transform its Viking medievalisms to better reflect the cultural and religious diversity of the Vikings as they actually existed in history.

Conclusion

"Immigrant Song" tells not a story of peaceful immigration but one of conquest—of rock music, critics, and legions of fans. It was, despite Robert Plant's protests to the contrary, Led Zeppelin at their cockiest, but it is also a track that demonstrates how far the band had to travel from the land of ice and snow to garner the respect they craved. Written in Iceland while there as cultural emissaries of the British government, and performed in England at the Bath Festival—all in one heady month in the summer of 1970—"Immigrant Song" represents a critical transition in Zeppelin's artistry on the album *Led Zeppelin III* (1970). Though "Immigrant Song" itself is not considered one of the many Zeppelin folk tunes in their extensive discography, it is the opening track on an album that signaled a new direction for the band, one that tapped into the folk music trends of the late 1960s and early 1970s. For Zeppelin especially, their appropriation of medievalist images and sounds—with the hard-rock "Immigrant Song" but also the folksier "Gallows Pole" and later "Stairway to Heaven"—was a practice that underscored their adoption of different musical and literary traditions, including African American blues. For "Immigrant Song," it was its Viking medievalisms, first popularized in the nineteenth century, that at their core reflected a medieval Christian literary tradition that whispered (and shouted) tales of gore.

"Immigrant Song" itself was also an inspiration and point of reference for musicians and artists working in other genres. One may see, for example, similar historical themes of masculine conquest in 1980s and 1990s Viking metal music, some of which traffic in white supremacist imagery. The connection between Viking medievalisms and white, masculinist ethnonationalism has been ruptured in two recent films that use "Immigrant Song" in compelling ways. In David Fincher's adaptation of *The Girl with the Dragon Tattoo* (2011), the song—as reconceptualized by Trent Reznor, Atticus Ross, and Karen O— plays as a music video at the start of a film that reframes it as a woman's quest for vengeance against Nazis and misogynists. In *Thor: Ragnarok* (2017), the song plays twice in crucial moments of character development for Thor, who at the end of the film realizes his mission to stop imperialist wars that seek to subjugate and colonize.

The afterlife of "Immigrant Song" has been proven to be a fruitful for artists to explore and even question how Norse medievalisms can be communicated in popular entertainment. In this sense, the flexibility with which "Immigrant Song" can be interpreted reflects Led Zeppelin's trajectory in the decade they dominated the rock music scene. As virtuosos of rock, they reinterpreted and refined their style to suit different genres, adding their own twist on a variety of musical traditions that included classical music, folk, blues, and reggae. Their engagement with medievalist tropes was but one facet of a wildly inventive aesthetic that mined often-imagined pasts to produce some of the most vital rock music of the 1970s.

Notes

1   Karl Spracklen, "Leisure, Popular Culture and Memory: The Invention of Dark Age Britain, Wales, England, and Middle-Earth in the Songs of Led Zeppelin," *International Journal of the Sociology of Leisure*, 1 (2018): 139–52.

2   Mick Wall, "Collapsing stages, Hell's Angels, and a band called Led Zeppelin," *Louder*, September 2, 2019, www.loudersound.com/features/collapsing-stages-hells-angels-and-a-band-called-led-zeppelin

3   Lee Marlow, "Getting the inside story behind Led Zeppelin's 'lost' film," *Louder*, July 19, 2017, www.loudersound.com/features/getting-the-inside-story-behind-led-zeppelins-lost-film

4   As quoted from *The Led Zeppelin Story*, directed by Mark McLaughlin (Port Washington, NY: Koch Vision, 2004), DVD, at 22:40.

5   Chris Charlesworth, "Led Zeppelin at the Bath Festival, June 28, 1970," *Just Backdated: A Blog by Chris Charlesworth*, June 27, 2018, http://justbackdated.blogspot.com/2018/06/led-zeppelin-at-bath-festival-june-28.html

6   Robert Plant, "Led Zeppelin—Robert Plant Interview (Iceland 1970)," YouTube video, 2:57, posted by Led Zeppelin, April 16, 2008, www.youtube.com/watch?v=Qpij-eSKIBk

7   Eirikur Bergmann, *Iceland and the International Financial Crisis: Boom, Bust and Recovery* (London: Palgrave Macmillan, 2014), 40; Gunnar Karlsson, "Iceland: Finance," *Encyclopedia Britannica*, last updated Sept. 14, 2020, www.britannica.com/place/Iceland/Finance#ref752815

8   Plant, "Led Zeppelin—Robert Plant Interview (Iceland 1970)."

9   Gregg Akkerman, *Experiencing Led Zeppelin: A Listener's Companion* (Lanham, MD: Rowman and Littlefield, 2014), 39; Plant, "Led Zeppelin—Robert Plant Interview (Iceland 1970)."

10   Led Zeppelin, "June 22, 1970—Laugardalsholl Hall," *Led* Zeppelin, www.ledzeppelin.com/show/june-22-1970

11   Ibid.

12   Erin Sweeney Smith, "Post-Imperialism, Imaginary Geography and the Women of Led Zeppelin's IV," *Popular Music* 36, no. 3 (2017): 413.

13   As quoted from *The Led Zeppelin Story*, dir. Mark McLaughlin, at 31:50.

14   Francis James Child and George Lyman Kittredge, eds., *The English and Scottish Popular Ballads*, vol. 2, part 2 (New York: Houghton, Mifflin, 1886), 346–55.

15   Susan Fast, *In the Houses of the Holy: Led Zeppelin and the Power of Rock Music* (Oxford: Oxford University Press, 2001), 86–7.

16   Plant, "Led Zeppelin—Robert Plant Interview (Iceland 1970)."

17   Fast, *In the Houses of the Holy*, 4.

18 Simon Frith and Angela McRobbie, "Rock and Sexuality," in *On Record: Rock, Pop and the Written Word*, ed. Frith and Andrew Goodwin (New York: Routledge, 1990), 372–5.

19 Brittany Spanos, "The Tao of Kurt Cobain: 12 Great Quotes from the Nirvana Frontman," *Rolling Stone*, February 20, 2017, www.rollingstone.com/music/ music-news/the-tao-of-kurt-cobain-12-great-quotes-from-the-nirvana-frontman-112939/

20 Susan Fast, "Rethinking Issues of Gender and Sexuality in Led Zeppelin: A Woman's View of Pleasure
      and Power in Hard Rock," *American Music* 17, no. 3 (1999): 257–8.

21 Fast, "Appendix: Fan Questionnaire," in *Houses of the Holy*, 203–4.

22 Reykjavik Arts Festival, "Led Zeppelin at the Reykjavik Arts Festival 1970," Vimeo video posted by Reykjavik Arts Festival, April 24, 2014, 4:12, https:// vimeo.com/92853792

23 Dave Lewis, "Immigrant Song," *Led Zeppelin: The Complete Guide to Their Music* (London: Omnibus Press, 2010).

24 Caitlin Vaughn Carlos, "'Ramble On': Medievalism as Nostalgic Practice in Led Zeppelin's Use of J.R.R. Tolkien," *The Oxford Handbook of Music and Medievalism*, ed. Stephen C. Meyer and Kirsten Yri (Oxford: Oxford University Press, 2020), 530–43.

25 Simon Keynes and Michael Lapidge, eds., *Asser's Life of King Alfred the Great* (New York: Penguin Books,1983), 88.

26 Christopher A. Snyder, "'To be or not to be'—King: Clive Donner's *Alfred the Great (1969)*," in *The Vikings on Film: Essays on Depictions of the Nordic Middle Ages*, ed. Kevin J. Harty (Jefferson: McFarland, 2011), 43. See also Carl Olof Cederlund, "The Modern Myth of the Viking," *Journal of Maritime Archaeology* 6, no. 1 (2011): 53–5.

27 Michael J. Swanton, ed., *The Anglo-Saxon Chronicle* (New York: Routledge, 1998), 68.

28 Paul Halsall, "Medieval Sourcebook: Abbo of Fleury: The Martyrdom of St. Edmund, King of East Anglia, 870," Internet History Sourcebooks Project, Fordham, 1998, https://sourcebooks.fordham.edu/source/870abbo-edmund. asp?fbclid=IwAR0kF4rIo_cwgvywuU-C_Bmjbb6Lwti2qHD5nLTqeJpes5bL 7cofJCt-JoQ

29 Geraldine Barnes, "Nostalgia, Medievalism and the Vinland Voyages," *Postmedieval: A journal of medieval cultural studies* 2 (2011): 141–54.

30 Simon Trafford, "Viking Metal," in *The Oxford Handbook of Music and Medievalism*, eds. Stephen C. Meyer and Kirsten Yri (Oxford: Oxford University Press, 2020), 566.

31 Ashley Walsh, "'A great heathen fist from the North': Vikings, Norse Mythology, and Medievalism in Nordic Extreme Metal Music," (M.A. thesis, University of Oslo, 2013), 8.

32 Andy Bennett, "Paganism and the Counter Culture," in *Pop Pagans: Paganism and Popular Music*, eds. Donna Weston and Andy Bennett (New York: Routledge, 2014), 18.

33 David Perry, "White supremacists love Vikings. But they've got history all wrong," *Washington Post*, May 31, 2017, www.washingtonpost.com/posteverything/wp/ 2017/05/31/white-supremacists-love-vikings-but-theyve-got-history-all-wrong/

34 Dorothy Kim, "White Supremacists Have Weaponized an Imaginary Viking Past. It's Time to Reclaim the Real History," *Time*, April 15, 2019, https://time.com/5569399/viking-history-white-nationalists/

35 Kevin Moberly and Brent Moberly, "Reincorporating the Medieval: Morality, Chivalry, and Honor in Post-Financial-Meltdown Corporate Revisionism," *Studies in Medievalism XXI: Corporate Medievalism*, ed. Karl Fugelso (Cambridge: D.S. Brewer, 2012), 11–25.

36 Trent Reznor, "[Interview] Trent Reznor Discusses 'The Girl with the Dragon Tattoo,'" interview by Jack Giroux, The Film Stage, December 12, 2011, https://thefilmstage.com/interview-trent-reznor-discusses-the-girl-with-the-dragon-tattoo/

37 Jason Guerrasio, "It took the entire making of 'Thor: Ragnarok' for Marvel to finally nab the rights to a Led Zeppelin song," *Business Insider*, November 6, 2017, www.businessinsider.com/led-zeppelin-immigrant-song-in-thor-ragnarok-2017-11

38 Dina AlAwadhi and Jason Dittmer, "'We come from the land of the ice and snow': De-Colonising Superhero Cinema through Music," *Politik* 23, no. 1 (2020): 88–93.

39 Ibid., 91.

References

Akkerman, Gregg. *Experiencing Led Zeppelin: A Listener's Companion*. Lanham, MD: Rowman and Littlefield, 2014.

AlAwadhi, Dina and Jason Dittmer. "'We come from the land of the ice and snow': De-Colonising Superhero Cinema through Music." *Politik* 23, no. 1 (2020): 88–93.

Barnes, Geraldine. "Nostalgia, Medievalism and the Vinland Voyages." *Postmedieval: A journal of medieval cultural studies* 2 (2011): 141–54.

Bennett, Andy. "Paganism and the Counter Culture." In *Pop Pagans: Paganism and Popular Music*, edited by Donna Weston and Andy Bennett, 13–23. New York: Routledge, 2014.

Bergmann, Eirikur. *Iceland and the International Financial Crisis: Boom, Bust and Recovery*. London: Palgrave Macmillan, 2014.

Carlos, Caitlin Vaughn. "'Ramble On': Medievalism as Nostalgic Practice in Led Zeppelin's Use of J.R.R. Tolkien." In *The Oxford Handbook of Music and Medievalism*, edited by Stephen C. Meyer and Kirsten Yri, 530–43. Oxford: Oxford University Press, 2020.

Cederlund, Carl Olof. "The Modern Myth of the Viking." *Journal of Maritime Archaeology* 6, no. 1 (2011): 5–35.

Charlesworth, Chris. "Led Zeppelin at the Bath Festival, June 28, 1970." *Just Backdated: A Blog by Chris Charlesworth*, June 27, 2018. http://justbackdated.blogspot.com/2018/06/led-zeppelin-at-bath-festival-june-28.html

Child, Francis James and George Lyman Kittredge, eds. *The English and Scottish Popular Ballads*, vol. 2, part 2. New York: Houghton, Mifflin, 1886.

Fast, Susan. "Rethinking Issues of Gender and Sexuality in Led Zeppelin: A Woman's View of Pleasure and Power in Hard Rock." *American Music* 17, no. 3 (1999): 245–299.

Fast, Susan. *In the Houses of the Holy: Led Zeppelin and the Power of Rock Music*. Oxford: Oxford University Press, 2001.

Frith, Simon and Angela McRobbie. "Rock and Sexuality." In *On Record: Rock, Pop and the Written Word*, edited by Simon Frith and Andrew Goodwin, 317–32. New York: Routledge, 1990.

Guerrasio, Jason. "It took the entire making of 'Thor: Ragnarok' for Marvel to finally nab the rights to a Led Zeppelin song." *Business* Insider, November 6, 2017. www.businessinsider.com/led-zeppelin-immigrant-song-in-thor-ragnarok-2017-11

Halsall, Paul. "Medieval Sourcebook: Abbo of Fleury: The Martyrdom of St. Edmund, King of East Anglia, 870." Internet History Sourcebooks Project, 1998. https://sourcebooks.fordham.edu/source/870abbo-edmund.asp?fbclid=IwAR0 kF4rIo_cwgvywuU-C_Bmjbb6Lwti2qHD5nLTqeJpes5bL7cofJCt-JoQ

Karlsson, Gunnar. "Iceland: Finance." *Encyclopedia Britannica*, last updated Sept. 14, 2020. www.britannica.com/place/Iceland/Finance#ref752815

Keynes, Simon and Michael Lapidge, eds. *Asser's Life of King Alfred the Great.* New York: Penguin Books, 1983.

Kim, Dorothy. "White Supremacists Have Weaponized an Imaginary Viking Past. It's Time to Reclaim the Real History." *Time*, April 15, 2019. https://time.com/5569 399/viking-history-white-nationalists/

Led Zeppelin. "June 22, 1970 - Laugardalsholl Hall." *Led Zeppelin.* www.ledzeppelin.com/show/june-22-1970

Lewis, Dave. *Led Zeppelin: The Complete Guide to Their Music.* London: Omnibus Press, 2010.

Marlow, Lee. "Getting the inside story behind Led Zeppelin's 'lost' film." *Louder*, July 19, 2017. www.loudersound.com/features/getting-the-inside-story-behind-led-zeppelins-lost-film

McLaughlin, Mark, dir. *The Led Zeppelin Story.* DVD. Port Washington, NY: Koch Vision, 2004.

Moberly, Kevin and Brent Moberly. "Reincorporating the Medieval: Morality, Chivalry, and Honor in Post- Financial-Meltdown Corporate Revisionism." *Studies in Medievalism XXI: Corporate Medievalism*, edited by Karl Fugelso, 11–25. Cambridge: D. S. Brewer, 2012.

Perry, David. "White supremacists love Vikings. But they've got history all wrong." *Washington Post*, May 31, 2017. www.washingtonpost.com/posteverything/wp/2017/05/31/white-supremacists-love-vikings-but-theyve-got-history-all-wrong/

Plant, Robert. "Led Zeppelin - Robert Plant Interview (Iceland 1970)." YouTube video. Uploaded by Led Zeppelin, April 16, 2008. www.youtube.com/watch?v=Qpij-eSKIBk

Reykjavik Arts Festival. "Led Zeppelin at the Reykjavik Arts Festival 1970." Vimeo video posted April 24, 2014. https://vimeo.com/92853792

Reznor, Trent. "[Interview] Trent Reznor Discusses 'The Girl with the Dragon Tattoo.'" interview conducted by Jack Giroux. *The Film Stage*, December 12, 2011. https://thefilmstage.com/interview-trent-reznor-discusses-the-girl-with-the-dragon-tattoo/

Smith, Erin Sweeney. "Post-Imperialism, Imaginary Geography and the Women of Led Zeppelin's IV." *Popular Music* 36, no. 3 (2017): 410–26.

Snyder, Christopher A. "'To be or not to be'—King: Clive Donner's *Alfred the Great* (1969)." In *The Vikings on Film: Essays on Depictions of the Nordic Middle Ages*, edited by Kevin J. Harty, 39–45. Jefferson: McFarland, 2011.

Spanos, Brittany. "The Tao of Kurt Cobain: 12 Great Quotes from the Nirvana Frontman." *Rolling Stone*, February 20, 2017. www.rollingstone.com/music/music-news/the-tao-of-kurt-cobain-12-great-quotes-from-the-nirvana-frontman-112939/

Spraklen, Karl. "Leisure, Popular Culture and Memory: The Invention of Dark Age Britain, Wales, England, and Middle-Earth in the Songs of Led Zeppelin." *International Journal of the Sociology of Leisure* 1 (2018): 139–52.

Swanton, Michael J., ed. *The Anglo-Saxon Chronicle*. New York: Routledge, 1998.

Trafford, Simon. "Viking Metal." In *The Oxford Handbook of Music and Medievalism*, edited by Stephen C. Meyer and Kirsten Yri, 564–85. Oxford: Oxford University Press, 2020.

Wall, Mick. "Collapsing stages, Hell's Angels, and a band called Led Zeppelin." *Louder*, September 2, 2019. www.loudersound.com/features/collapsing-stages-hells-angels-and-a-band-called-led-zeppelin

Walsh, Ashley. "'A great heathen fist from the North': Vikings, Norse Mythology, and Medievalism in Nordic Extreme Metal Music." M.A. thesis, University of Oslo, 2013.

5   David Bowie—"Rebel Rebel" (1974)

Glenn Hendler

The version of David Bowie's "Rebel Rebel" familiar to most listeners is propelled for four and a half minutes by a driving, melodic rock guitar riff. If the title doesn't trigger the riff in your memory, just hearing the distinctively large interval between its first two notes, from a D up to a high E, may do the trick. The opening couplet ("You've got your mother in a whirl / She's not sure if you're a boy or a girl") of the (repeated) verse is memorable, too, both for its simple melody and for its celebration of gender ambiguity. So is the chorus, which accentuates the doubling of the word "rebel" in the title, as is the shout: "Hot Tramp! I love you so." "Rebel Rebel" is built almost entirely on such memorable instrumental, vocal, and lyrical hooks.[1]

This essay's starting point is that more familiar "Rebel Rebel,"[2] which closes side one of Bowie's 1974 album *Diamond Dogs*, and which in a slightly different mix reached #5 in the UK singles charts before the album was released. But this essay's destination is an analysis of the less widely known US single release.[3] That track is recognizably the same song, but it constructs a different soundscape. To start with, it cuts the first iteration of the verse, refrain, and chorus, making the song 90 seconds shorter. The guitar riff is processed through a phase shifter, which smooths some of its rock 'n' roll edges. There are vocal additions: an additional set of backing vocals singing the same ten-note series of "lie-lie-lie" in melodic interplay with the guitar riff; backmasking effects; some ululations toward the end. Crowding the riff and making it slightly less prominent are several added percussion instruments, all played by Bowie's friend Geoff MacCormack. It is a busier, noisier, livelier, and more concise version of "Rebel Rebel."

Why did Bowie, his collaborators, and his management create this very different single for his US audience?[4] Why did they release it as a single in the US in late May 1974, three months after the release of the UK single, and after that track had faded from the UK charts?[5] Why did this version not become the breakthrough hit that was hoped for? It peaked at #64, dropped off the charts, and was then withdrawn, to be replaced by the UK mix.[6] Did Bowie and his management simply misread the American public in 1974? This misstep occurred after two years of Bowie's dominating the UK singles charts like no one since the Beatles, and just a year before he would reach #1 on the

DOI: 10.4324/9781003093206-6

US *Billboard* charts for the first time with "Fame." Why, in between these two career milestones, was Bowie's aim less than true?

As these questions indicate, this essay tells a story about the production, release, and marketing of different versions of one particular song. However, like other contributors to *One-Track Mind*, I believe that a single track can open up broader issues. By paying close attention to the US single release of "Rebel Rebel," we will learn more about Bowie's emerging engagement with US soul music, R&B, and what was then called "Latin soul." "Rebel Rebel" can also teach us something about the rapidly shifting and racialized distinctions between AM and FM radio audiences and their formats, as well as the equally racialized divergence between rock and other genres of popular music. Bowie's efforts to negotiate the changing meanings of race, genre, and musical style in 1974 thus took place on shifting terrain that this essay aims to map.

By the time Bowie composed "Rebel Rebel," his recently "retired" Ziggy Stardust persona had made him the biggest rock celebrity in the UK for nearly two years, Ziggy, though, had been a largely national phenomenon, dominating the UK singles and albums charts. Bowie had long understood that the path to global success led through the United States; he had toured there twice, only sometimes filling the arenas that had been booked for him, and receiving more media attention than sales. He had even made America the subject matter of his 1973 *Aladdin Sane* album, which he sometimes called "Ziggy Goes to Washington."[7] But none of his string of UK top-ten hits from 1972–73—"Starman," "The Jean Genie," "Drive-In Saturday," and "Sorrow," as well as re-releases of 1971's "Life on Mars?" and even his very silly early song "The Laughing Gnome"—had cracked the US singles charts. And while his US album sales were respectable, they did not approach the heights he had reached in the UK. Bowie was thus in early 1974 a long way from the transatlantic stardom he would attain over the following two years when the hits "Fame" and "Golden Years" topped the US charts, and even further from the global superstardom he would reach in 1983 with the *Let's Dance* album, its string of hit singles, and the worldwide Serious Moonlight Tour.

This was not for lack of trying. In 1970 Bowie had dumped his longtime manager Ken Pitt in favor of an American lawyer named Tony Defries, who made Bowie the central cog in a complex financial apparatus called the MainMan Group of Companies. MainMan had helped create Bowie's stardom in the UK as well as what inroads he had made into the US, starting with the 1970 tour of radio stations Bowie did in support of *The Man Who Sold the World*. Indeed, within the company Bowie was seen as Defries's creation. According to MainMan's president, Tony Zanetta (Defries had no official title), "All the members of 'the MainMan family' considered Tony Defries—not David Bowie—to be the real star. He had *manufactured* David Bowie, who existed to generate the funds necessary to enable the MainMan machine to thrive."[8]

MainMan became a transatlantic entity before Bowie became a major transatlantic star. The singer's record and concert sales enabled Defries to set up offices on both sides of the Atlantic and to establish, for instance, a film division that never made any films. And in late 1973 and early 1974, when Bowie was writing and recording "Rebel Rebel" and the rest of the *Diamond Dogs* album, MainMan was gearing up to promote Bowie for the US mass audience once again.

The earliest move in this campaign was perhaps the oddest. In October 1973 Defries persuaded a US television crew to fly to London to film three days of Bowie at the Marquee Club playing alongside an eclectic assortment of other performers. The result was a 90-minute extravaganza called *The 1980 Floor Show*, which has still never aired in the UK. In the US this episode of *Midnight Special* aired twice on NBC: in fall 1973, and then again in fall 1974. Though a viewing of that rebroadcast cemented my own Bowie fandom,[9] there is little evidence that this apparent parody of a variety show did much to build Bowie's mass audience in the US.

The 1980 Floor Show was only the first salvo in a larger transatlantic media blitz Defries orchestrated in 1974, now in support of the *Diamond Dogs* album. MainMan put up giant billboards for the album in New York City and Los Angeles; Defries also placed national television ads. In all media and on the album cover, Bowie was referred to without his first name, in an effort to make him a one-word brand like Cher or Liberace. Later in 1974, Bowie launched the most expensive and elaborate tour ever mounted up to this point; the Year of the Diamond Dogs Tour, too, was only ever seen in North America. Nearly all MainMan's energy in 1974—like Bowie's—was aimed at expanding his US audience.

"Rebel Rebel" was not at first part of these efforts. Every theory about Bowie's original intention for the song underscores that it was aimed squarely at a UK audience. For instance, he announced more than once that he was working on a musical theatre version of the *Ziggy Stardust* story.[10] But the post-Ziggy project Bowie pursued most seriously was the least likely to have had a place for "Rebel Rebel": a musical version of George Orwell's *1984*. In the October 1973 issue of *Disc* magazine, Bowie's erstwhile co-author, playwright Tony Ingrassia, noted that they had not yet acquired the rights to *1984*, and that "it is still possible that we may [have] to call it 1983 or something like that." Bowie himself, *Disc* said, would play the role of Winston, and the cast would likely include "drag rock star" Jayne County and "Geoffrey MacCormack, who plays congas in Bowie's current band."[11] Performer and publicist Cherry Vanilla is named as another potential member of the cast, and is quoted as saying that Bowie's version was likely to be "unrecognizable from the original."

Though—with the exception of Bowie and MacCormack—those mentioned in the *Disc* story were Americans (and veterans of Andy Warhol's Factory), the *1984* musical was planned for the West End in the UK and not for Broadway in the US. Then, in December 1973, Sonia Orwell denied Bowie and MainMan the rights to *1984*. From then on, Bowie stopped writing songs that, from their titles, must have been originally intended for that musical ("We Are the Dead," "1984," and "Big Brother"), blended their lyrics and imagery with elements drawn from Bowie's reading of American writer William Burroughs's work as well as his own creative worldmaking, and came up with the more hybrid and original concept that became *Diamond Dogs*—a framework in which "Rebel Rebel" still seems anomalous.[12]

The production process of "Rebel Rebel" is at least as fuzzy as the song's conceptual and lyrical origins. The track may have been laid down at any or all of four London studios: Trident, Olympic, Island, or Morgan. Bowie worked at all of them while making *Diamond Dogs*, partly because MainMan was not paying its bills on time, and thus there were stretches when Olympic was threatening to ban Bowie.[13] Ava Cherry—who was involved with Bowie at the time—told me that he came up with the song's chord sequence and opening couplet at a quiet moment when the two were sitting in the studio. In her memory the band Bad Company was working across the hall, suggesting that they were likely at Island.[14] Despite the song's apparently spontaneous sound, it was, like the rest of *Diamond Dogs*, a studio concoction, with its different parts recorded at different times. The guitar riff was partly composed by Bowie, but with several notes and a bend added by session guitarist Alan Parker. Parker has said he not only composed about "25 percent" of the riff but also played it, producing the guitar sound we are familiar with. Though the album credits Bowie with all guitars other than Parker's on "1984," and many commenters have attributed the riff to him, in fact Bowie has largely confirmed Parker's claim.[15]

While most of *Diamond Dogs* mixed at Brooklyn-born producer Tony Visconti's home studio in London, Keith Harwood is credited with mixing "Rebel Rebel" at Olympic Studios. Visconti may have done some final work on the song at a studio in Hilversum, Netherlands, where Bowie traveled on February 12, 1974.[16] While there, Bowie debuted "Rebel Rebel" on the Dutch television show *TopPop*, lip-synching the lyrics with gusto in front of a green screen (see Figure 5.1). While he occasionally strummed his bright-red electric guitar, more often he treated the obviously unplugged instrument as a prop—leaning on it, lifting it over his head, tucking it under his arm, and extending it directly in front of him like a weapon. Dressed in high-heeled boots, bright-red overalls, a complexly patterned top, and a polka-dotted scarf, he still sported his red Ziggy-style mullet. The black patch Bowie wore over his eye produced a piratical look that has become iconic, but in fact its presence was a matter of medical necessity as he had conjunctivitis. That evening Bowie received an award, displayed the one word of Dutch he knew (*jazeker*, an enthusiastic affirmative), and sampled a shot of a spiced regional liqueur called Schelvispekel.[17]

"Rebel Rebel" was released in the UK two days later. The single debuted at #6, and remained on the charts for the next seven weeks, peaking at #5. During that time Bowie completed work on *Diamond Dogs*, its Guy Peellaert outside cover, and the Leee Black Childers photo collage on the inside. He

Figure 5.1 David Bowie performs "Rebel Rebel" on Dutch TV, February 12, 1974. Credit: Gijsbert Hanekroot/Alamy Stock Photo.

also worked on plans for the upcoming Year of the Diamond Dogs Tour with Fisher, Ravitz, and Basil.

In the meantime, a few copies of the UK single made it to the US. Bowie had inspired a Los Angeles DJ named Rodney Bingenheimer to start a club called Rodney's English Disco, and sent along an acetate of the UK mix of the single.[18] "Rebel Rebel" was for a time played at the club every half hour, regularly drawing patrons to the dance floor. But there was not yet a domestic US single or album available for sale or AM radio airplay before the end of May.

Back in London, Bowie was ready to follow his song to the United States. The simple version of the story is this: Because in these years Bowie refused to fly, he and companion Geoff MacCormack left from Cannes on the *SS France* to New York City on April 3. The boat trip gave the two friends more time to talk about music—and to decide to create a new version of "Rebel Rebel" for the American market. On landing in New York City on April 11,

1974, they greeted fans at the dock, checked into their hotel, and from there, MacCormack told me, they went "straight to the studio to add vocals and percussion" to "Rebel Rebel."

But the story really starts before they left the UK, when Bowie was developing several plans for what might come next. Most of these plans involved collaborations with one of his oldest friends, MacCormack, and a newer friend, Ava Cherry.[19] The US single of "Rebel Rebel" has to be contextualized in relation to those plans, and with reference to both MacCormack, Bowie's childhood friend, and Cherry, who was involved with Bowie both romantically and artistically. Cherry and MacCormack encouraged Bowie in both a revival of his long-standing interest in various forms of Black music and his burgeoning interest in soul music in particular. And, I'll argue, the US single bears a complex relation to those cultural forms and, through them, to a project that involved both of his friends, the soul band called the Astronettes. "Soul" is a kind of keyword that can help us understand many of Bowie's activities and ideas in 1974, including his engagement with the Latin soul music of his youth and of the early 1970s.[20] The UK releases of "Rebel Rebel" seem untouched by soul in any of its meanings, but the concept may help us understand the changes Bowie and MacCormack made to the US single.

Bowie and MacCormack had been friends since their childhood, but their musical collaboration began in earnest during the recording of *Aladdin Sane* in 1973. That collaboration is most audible on the track "Panic in Detroit." Bowie had asked the drummer of his *Ziggy*-era band Spiders from Mars, Mick "Woody" Woodmansey, to play a Bo Diddley beat. Woodmansey at first demurred, calling the beat "too simple." Ultimately, the drumming on "Panic in Detroit" sounds as if Woodmansey settled somewhere between his original rock intention and what Bowie wanted,[21] but it is MacCormack's modulated but frenetic congas that propel the song, giving it a lively, urgent, distinctive feel.

This is one of several times when MacCormack supported Bowie's desire to play something other than straightforward rock 'n' roll, to produce music that sounded—especially to white English ears—more "soulful" and thus perhaps more appealing to Americans. In January 1974, at around the same time Bowie was recording the original "Rebel Rebel," he also recorded "Rock 'n' Roll with Me," co-written with MacCormack (credited under his pseudonym, Warren Peace). Soul influences were audible in the song from the start; its opening chord progression, contributed by MacCormack, evoked Bill Withers's "Lean on Me." In live performances on the Diamond Dogs Tour, the backing vocals by Ava Cherry, Luther Vandross, Robin Clark, Diane Sumler, and—always— MacCormack himself would increasingly accentuate the song's soulful, even gospel-tinged aspect.[22]

Ava Cherry had met Bowie in New York at a party following a Stevie Wonder concert, attracting the attention of the pale red-haired singer by being the only Black women he'd ever seen with her hair dyed blonde. She reconnected with him later in France, and then joined him in London, first moving into the Bowie household with his wife Angie, their son, and a few others, and then relocating to her own apartment nearby.[23]

Cherry told me that in London, Bowie asked her advice on how to form "a soul band." Her reply was that they would have to go to New York City and visit the Apollo Theater. Before they did so, though, they formed the vocal group called the Astronettes. The trio—Cherry, MacCormack, and Jason Guess—first appeared under that name as backing vocalists on the *1980 Floor Show*. Then Bowie got MainMan to sign them as a band, touting Cherry as "the next Josephine Baker." The instrumentation for the band was provided by some of Bowie's best musicians—Aynsley Dunbar, Herbie Flowers, Mike Garson, and Marc Pritchard, and the Puerto Rican arranger Luis Ramirez was engaged to do brass and string arrangements.[24] However, the album remained unfinished—Bowie seems to have abandoned the idea—and went unreleased until Tony Defries put it out in 1995, to the surprise of everyone involved (including Cherry, who was on the cover).

The timing and location of the Astronettes' recording sessions are as hard to pin down as those of the recording of the original "Rebel Rebel." Some sources claim there were studio sessions with the band in late 1973, others that they only recorded in the first few days of January 1974, and still others that there were sessions later in January—all in London. If these sources are correct, then the Astronettes provide an interesting pre-history for the US single version of "Rebel Rebel."

Contradicting these sources, however, Ava Cherry tells me that while there may have been some preliminary sessions in early January, she has vivid memories of extensive Astronettes sessions at RCA studios in New York. These would have to have taken place after Bowie and MacCormack's arrival, and thus after the additions to "Rebel Rebel" were made—reversing the relation of pre-history and history. If Cherry is correct—and I think she is—then the Astronettes recordings would represent developments in Bowie's relation to soul beyond what he and MacCormack added to "Rebel Rebel" on April 11, 1974. It is also possible, Garson told me, that the instrumental tracks were recorded in London and the vocals added later. No one's memory of these events is entirely clear.

Whatever the chronology, the Astronettes represented Bowie's first effort to produce a soul album. The Bowie-penned tunes evince influences from Marvin Gaye and others. "I Am Divine" is probably Bowie's earliest effort to produce the "Philly soul" sound that he would approach more closely later in 1974 when recording songs for the *Young Americans* album with Philadelphia and New York musicians at Sigma Sound Studios in Philadelphia, where he would incorporate elements of "I am Divine" into "Somebody Up There Likes Me."

The selection of artists covered by the Astronettes—Annette Peacock, the Beach Boys, Frank Zappa, and Bruce Springsteen, among others—hardly read as the track list for a soul record. Cherry describes trying many songs to see what would work with her voice, and says that Bowie himself selected this quite eclectic list. But despite the Whiteness of this list of covers, it was in fact not uncommon for soul artists to do what scholar Emily Lordi calls "soul covers," often of "white songs," such as Aretha Franklin's version of Simon and Garfunkel's "Bridge over Troubled Water" and similar covers by Nina Simone, Donny Hathaway, and Minnie Riperton's band Rotary Connection.[25] Even the least likely of the Astronette's covers, then, could have been part of the project of a "soul band."

"Soul" was not only a name for the kind of music Bowie and Cherry would eventually go hear at the Apollo Theater in Harlem. Bowie and MacCormack also had a long-standing shared interest in Latin soul. I asked MacCormack if their shared interests had included Latin music and soul music. The reply was emphatic. MacCormack told me that he and Bowie had shared "an early appreciation and knowledge of American 'Black' music from when they were eight years of age onwards." He also noted that he bought his "first Latin track in 1964," and presumably shared it with his friend. That single was Ray Barretto's "El Watusi."

Barretto was a crucial figure in the rise of the various forms of music that eventually coalesced under the name "salsa." The megahit "El Watusi" came out before that coalescence, though, during a stylistic transition in the New York scene between the *pachangas*, exemplified by Johnny Pacheco, and the *boogaloo* style. The difference between these two styles, according to scholar Juan Flores, is that while Pacheco's pachangas "evidenced little African American influence," boogaloo was a full-fledged "vernacular Latin African American fusion." Flores names Barretto's "El Watusi"—along with Willie Torres's ballad "To Be with You" and "Mongo Santamaría's "Latinized" version of Herbie Hancock's 'Watermelon Man'"—as prefiguring the boogaloo movement, which he describes more broadly as "Latin soul."[26] Indeed, "El Watusi" appeared on Barretto's album *Latin Soul Man*.

The Astronettes' recordings make audible for the first time Bowie's interest in Latin soul. Up to that point, little if any of that sound had affected his own music. Indeed, during the 1973 recording sessions for *Aladdin Sane*, Mike Garson had offered to play a "Latin-style" piano solo at the center of the track, but Bowie had rejected that idea, pushing Garson toward the avant-garde solo that takes up the middle section of the song. Perhaps the closest Bowie had come to integrating "Latin" sounds into his own music was Mick Ronson's Spanish-style guitar stylings on "Lady Grinning Soul" (also on *Aladdin Sane*). He had also featured the flamenco-rock band Carmen on *The 1980 Floor Show*.

Probably the most "Latin"-sounding song Bowie ever wrote was the Astronettes' track "Things to Do." Mike Garson's piano on that track, he told me, was influenced by Latin music pianists who had been at their peak in the 1960s—Eddie and Charlie Palmieri, Larry Harlow—and writer Chris O'Leary has aptly described the song's rhythm as drawing on the boogaloo style, which Bowie and MacCormack had been familiar with since hearing "El Watusi." Indeed, there is some rhythmic and sonic resemblance to that tune, though the Astronettes' vocals—while quite rough and preliminary—are far more melodic than the half-sung Spanish spoken word of the Ray Barretto hit.

"Soul," in all these senses, was thus on David Bowie's mind before, during, and after the transatlantic boat voyage. On an earlier boat trip to Japan, Bowie had brought along his collection of Latin records; he may have done the same on the *SS France* in April 1974, for MacCormack has reported that "David and I got very heavily into Latin music" on that trip. While on the boat, he continued, Bowie decided "we should put down a new backing vocal and have some congas all the way through 'Rebel Rebel.'" With that in mind, they headed straight to the studio to set about "remodeling" the existing track by adding additional vocals, instrumentation, and effects. In addition to the congas that MacCormack had also added to "Panic in Detroit," the other instruments they overdubbed were a güiro, tambourine, and castanets, each of which MacCormack seems to have played himself. The other changes include the phase shifter added to the lead guitar, an additional backing vocal line, and the backmasking added to some vocals. Also added, toward the end, were a set of high-pitched vocal trills.

MacCormack says their goal was to "liven up" the song with percussion and these other elements, not to "import any 'Latin vibe.'" Whether or not such a vibe was intended, the US single of "Rebel Rebel" has since been described as "Latinized," "Latin dub," "funky," and even "flamenco." Just phase-shifting the guitar subdued its rock 'n' roll edge, making it sound less like something that could have appeared in a Rolling Stones song. Though some of the percussion instruments added, such as castanets, were associated with Latin music, they were common enough in pop music that they were unlikely to have produced such impressions on their own. The one possible exception is the güiro—a hollow object, often a gourd, with grooves that are scraped rhythmically by a stick or metal tines.[27] Though it has long been part of folk music from Spain (including flamenco), and though it has occasionally appeared in popular tunes such as the Drifters' "Under the Boardwalk," by the 1970s the güiro was closely associated with Puerto Rican and Cuban musical traditions. These two styles were converging as boogaloo in New York City when MacCormack and (presumably) Bowie were listening to "El Watusi"—a song that prominently features a guiro—in Bromley in the early 1960s, and by the time the two arrived in New York City had recombined in new ways to produce a lively salsa scene.[28]

Working on another project with Bowie and the Scottish singer Lulu at those same sessions was the Puerto Rican guitarist Carlos Alomar. Alomar had toured with James Brown, played with Chuck Berry and the O'Jays, and opened for Sly and the Family Stone before becoming part of the band the Main Ingredient. He met Bowie for the first time at the Lulu sessions, and the two hit it off despite, or more likely because of, their contrasts. "He had orange hair and he was white," Alomar wrote later; "I had an Afro and I was black." Soon after, Alomar invited Bowie to his mother's home in Queens for a home-cooked meal, and also invited Bowie and Ava Cherry to shows at the Apollo Theatre, including one featuring Richard Pryor, the Temptations, and the Spinners.

Alomar also accompanied Bowie to Latin clubs such as the Hunts Point Palace, a Latin club in the Bronx that had been crucial in the development of several musical trends.[29] As MacCormack told me, and Ava Cherry confirmed, they "visited the Latin dance club Corso in NYC a few times" in this period. The Corso was on the second floor of a building on East 86th Street between Second and Third Avenues. At both venues, the English friends could in 1974 have seen performers such Ray Barretto, of "El Watusi" fame, but also Johnny Pacheco, Hector LaVoe, Tito Puente, Larry Harlow, Pete "El Conde" Rodriguez, Luis "Perico" Ortiz, and others.[30] They were thus exposed to the stars of their own youth as well as to the burgeoning salsa movement.

They went to these concerts and clubs *after* the recording of the US single of "Rebel Rebel," so these performers cannot have influenced that track. However, in thinking back to 1974, Bowie drew a distinction that can make these experiences relevant, noting that his exposure to Black and Latin music started with knowledge of the music but ignorance of its cultural context. As he put it, "I was like most English who come over to America for the first time, totally blown away by the fact that the blacks in America had their own culture, and it was positive and they were proud of it."[31] Bowie underscored the importance of this encounter with "their own culture" when he said later:

> With people like Carlos Alomar and a few of my girlfriends at the time, I was really seeing a lot of American nightlife, including the Latin clubs, and it was terribly exciting to me. It rekindled the affection for soul and R&B which I had in the '60s. In fact the reason I left my very first band, The Kon-rads, was that they wouldn't do Marvin Gaye's "Can I Get A Witness?" It had been a major thing for me in my youthful days. And it all came back with a vengeance, seeing it for real in the States. It was unlike anything I'd seen or witnessed before.[32]

In short, the US single of "Rebel Rebel" was produced just as Bowie and MacCormack were "rekindling" their engagement with soul and related cultural formations. That they were very early in that transition when they recorded the track—that they were just starting that more vivid experience of "seeing it for real in the States"—is audible in its soundscape. Assuming Ava Cherry's chronology is accurate, the Astronettes sessions took place a bit later in that process of rekindling, thus informing Bowie's more sophisticated engagement with boogaloo sounds and rhythms on "Things to Do." But my guess is that that encounter was audible to the single's listeners.

While the US single of "Rebel Rebel" was produced by Bowie and MacCormack during a transition in the artists' relation to soul, R&B, and Latin music, it was released into a US market that was in the midst of other racialized transitions. In 1974, top-40 music was still played almost exclusively on AM radio. FM stations that played rock and related genres could be categorized as "progressive" or "freeform"; they were starting to shift to a format that came to be known as AOR, or "album-oriented rock." AOR defined itself in direct opposition to top 40 in highly racialized ways. Top-40 radio was extraordinarily diverse racially, ethnically, and in the genres of music it played, which could include funk, soft rock, R&B, and early disco. The AOR format characterized the genre it was aligned with as "rock," which was often defined in opposition to soul, R&B, and Latin music. Put bluntly, AOR was increasingly white. Even when a performer like Santana would "cross over" into AOR air play, the fact that there was a gap to cross underscored the supposed distinctiveness of rock.[33]

This context can help explain why the US single of "Rebel Rebel" only barely charted in the US. Again, in the UK, David Bowie had had several top-ten singles by 1974, while in the US only a 1973 reissue of his 1969 song "Space Oddity" had appeared in the top 20. Bowie was by no means an obscure figure in the United States, but only his albums had charted, never his singles. *Diamond Dogs* was the first Bowie album to break into the US top ten. It went to #5, despite the relative unpopularity of the US single release from that album: "Rebel Rebel."[34] Put simply: an album that charted higher than its associated single most likely owed its success to FM radio. And a single that aimed for top-40 status but missed it did not get AM airplay.

The marketing of "Rebel Rebel" in the US shows that Bowie—or, more likely, MainMan and RCA—misjudged this transitioning music market in 1974. To promote the "Rebel Rebel" single, on May 4 they placed a full-page ad in *Billboard*.[35] Following Tony Defries's script, it referred to the singer as "Bowie," without a first name. The ad also asserted in its headline that the song was "soon to be released, because it's already a hit," presumably referring to imported discs like the one Rodney Bingenheimer was playing at his English Disco. It tried to produce still more vicarious desire by claiming that a big magazine and "six of this country's most powerful rockers" had paid "out of their pockets to have [the single] shipped all the way from Europe."

MainMan and RCA told their readers that they expected this song to be Bowie's US breakthrough, calling "Rebel Rebel" "the first Bowie single since 'Space Oddity' with mass appeal." That breakthrough would take the form of growing Bowie's audience share from niche appeal to mass popularity: the ad quotes a writer from *Creem* as saying that the song "will amaze and delight even the people who were never in the Bowie camp in the past."

Bowie's existing audience, implied the ad, was locatable both geographically and on the radio dial. Enthusiastic testimonials came from programmers and music directors at radio stations in places such as Cleveland, Detroit, and Philadelphia—each a place where Bowie had an early and passionate fan base. It is thus plausible, for instance, that "Rebel Rebel" was already "the most requested song on WMMS" in Cleveland. Crucially, all the radio stations referenced were on the "progressive" end of the FM programming spectrum: along with WMMS, there was WABX in Detroit, WMMR in Philadelphia, and similar stations in San Francisco, Baltimore, and Los Angeles.

Most importantly, MainMan's marketing hopes were expressed in a quotation from Ben Edmonds of *Creem*: "It would be a joy to hear this single on AM radio." This is the first in the list of quotations; the last one tells us what they thought they were going to be marketing and hearing. "Good ole' rock & roll, that's what it's about." That is perhaps what "Rebel Rebel," in all its versions, is "about"—after all, "You love bands when they're playing hard." And what these music programmers had heard on the import single, on the album, and on FM radio—what those WMMS listeners were requesting— sounded like "good ole' rock & roll."

When the advertised US single arrived in stores and at radio stations, programmers, DJs, and listeners got something else. It was still a rock song, but it was overlaid with several signifiers of Latin music: castanets, a güiro, those vocal trills at the end. The marketing did not match the product, at least not in a context in which rock was being starkly differentiated from soul music, R&B, dance music, and Latin music. It is not that the song had been thoroughly Latinized; but listeners would have heard sounds that signified something other than "good ole' rock & roll."

Ultimately, not even enthusiastic endorsements from progressive and AOR programmers could produce the "joy" of hearing "Rebel Rebel" on AM radio, at least not very often. The US single version of the song had revised its soundscape to fit Bowie's just-emerging understanding of the multi-racial, multi-cultural American audience, but it was marketed to an audience that was being trained by AOR—perhaps even by some of the very programmers quoted in the ad—to appreciate a narrower sound defined as rock. The album version of "Rebel Rebel" was created to fit into that Whiter soundscape, while the US single was produced by an artist who arrived in the US with a knowledge of some of the forms of Black and Latin music that would make up that merging, less "rockist" AM radio landscape, but who was only days from beginning the fuller immersion into these cultural contexts that would lead him toward the chart success, months later, of "Fame" and the *Young Americans* album.

Thus, the single debuted at #85 in June 1974, took three weeks to reach its peak of #64, and then dropped off the top 100. In the meantime, the division between AOR and top-40 AM radio was widening. I was 12 years old in 1974, and in my hometown of New Haven, Connecticut, I listened both to WAVZ-AM and to the emerging progressive/AOR powerhouse WPLR-FM. On the AM station, I don't recall hearing any David Bowie at all—except perhaps that 1973 reissue of "Space Oddity"—until 1975, when "Fame" topped the charts. On FM, I heard the album version of "Rebel Rebel," but never the US single version. The FM station also increasingly played earlier Bowie songs that became AOR standards: "Suffragette City," "The Jean Genie," and "Changes." They very occasionally played "Fame," even though it was an AM hit with a groove so funky that James Brown cribbed it for one of his own songs soon thereafter.[36] But the US single of "Rebel Rebel" largely fell between the cracks of race, culture, format, and genre. The shape of those cracks would define the US music market for years to come.

Notes

1 Several of the astonishingly various definitions of a "hook" are ably summarized in Gary Burns, "A Typology of 'Hooks' in Popular Records." *Popular Music* 6, no. 1 (January 1987): 1–20. See also Tom Cole, 'You Ask, We Answer: What's a Hook?" *NPR*, October 15, 2010; and Karen Tongson, "Earworms, Touchstones, Inversions." In *Confessions of an ACA Fan*, edited by Henry Jenkins. 2011. http://henryjenkins.org/blog/2011/08/aca-fandom_and_beyond_karen_to_1.html

2 For analysis of the album version see Glenn Hendler, *Diamond Dogs*. New York: Bloomsbury, 2020. 87–93.

3 There are later versions as well. On the next several concert tours Bowie often performed shortened versions of "Rebel Rebel" that most closely resemble the US single, giving that mix and edit a kind of afterlife. However, what appeared on greatest-hits collections was, until the 2000s, usually the album mix or perhaps the very similar UK single mix. Then, in 2003, Bowie recorded a much different version of "Rebel Rebel" for the soundtrack of the movie *Charlie's Angels: Full Throttle*. Finally, the 2015 mashup titled "Rebel Never Gets Old" blends "Rebel Rebel" with Bowie's 2003 song "Never Get Old." For most of this track, the guitar riff signals the presence of the older tune. The original vocals come in only toward the end; they are kept relatively low in the mix.

4 For an overview of singles that have been released with different mixes and edits, see Walter Everett, "'If You're Gonna Have a Hit': Intratextual Mixes and Edits of Pop Recordings." *Popular Music* 29, no. 2 (2010): 229–50.

5 The timeline throughout this article relies heavily on Roger Griffin, *David Bowie: The Golden Years* (London: Omnibus Press, 2016).

6 The contemporaneous audience for the US single mix and edit thus consisted of a limited number of US fans who either purchased it during the short period it was available or heard it on the radio as infrequently as a #64 single would have gotten airplay. However, it has since then resurfaced on later compilations—starting with 1989's *Sound + Vision* box set—and as a bonus track on twenty-first-century remixes of the *Diamond Dogs* album.

7 Rob Sheffield, "How America Inspired David Bowie to Kill Ziggy Stardust With 'Aladdin Sane.'" *Rolling Stone*, April 13, 2016.

8 Henry Edwards and Tony Zanetta, *Stardust: The David Bowie Story* (New York: McGraw Hill, 1986), 217.

9 My own viewing of the 1974 rebroadcast was the first time I ever saw Bowie perform. I discuss that experience at some length in Hendler, *Diamond Dogs* 1–4.

10 Nicholas Pegg, *The Complete David Bowie* (London: Titan Books, 2011), 330.

11 "Bowie 1984 AD," *Disc*, October 27, 1973. Cited at www.bowiegoldenyears.com/press/73-10-27-disc.html

12 For more on the complex ways Bowie integrated Orwell and Burroughs and made something different from both of them, not merely song-by-song but even within the songs with titles drawn explicitly from *1984*, see Hendler, *Diamond Dogs* .

13 Kevin Cann, *Any Day Now: David Bowie, The London Years: 1947–1974* (Croyden, Surrey, UK: Adelita, 2010), 318.

14 Ava Cherry, *All that Glitters: The Ava Cherry Story*. Detroit: Aquarius Books, 2022.
15 Parker has detailed memories of the precise equipment he played on. See David Buckley's liner notes for the 30th-anniversary release of *Diamond Dogs*, as well as Chris O'Leary, *Rebel Rebel: All the Songs of David Bowie from '64 to '76* (Winchester, UK: Zero Books, 2015); and David Cantello, "The Year of the Diamond Dogs." *The Year of the Diamond Dogs*, 2017 (https://theyearofthediamonddog.webs.com/diamonddogssessions.htm). They—and I—thus believe the album credits are wrong, and attribute the lead guitar on "Rebel Rebel" to Parker, not Bowie.
16 The album credits say *Diamond Dogs* was "recorded at Olympic and Island Studios, London"—with no mention of Trident or Morgan—"and Studio L Ludolf" in Hilversum, Netherlands.
17 The video and awards ceremony are on YouTube: www.youtube.com/watch?v=9MAez6oC5F4
18 One consequence of the energy crisis of the early 1970s was that even the UK single of "Rebel Rebel" was pressed in the United States, and thus had "Made in the USA" on the label. It is not clear whether Bingenheimer's copy of the single had traveled to the UK and then back to the US, or if he got it more directly.
19 MacCormack kindly agreed to answer some questions via email, Cherry generously agreed to a phone interview, and pianist Mike Garson responded to email queries as well. Thanks are due to all three of them, to Jo MacCormack for mediating one email exchange, to Mark Bakalor for helping with another, and to Raquel Cion for facilitating the phone call. Otherwise unsourced quotations from Cherry, MacCormack, and Garson are drawn from those conversations.
20 My usage of the word "soul" in this article is heavily informed by Emily J. Lordi, *The Meaning of Soul: Black Music and Resilience Since the 1960s* (Durham: Duke University Press, 2020); on "keywords," see Bruce Burgett and Glenn Hendler, eds. *Keywords for American Cultural Studies*. Third Edition. (New York: New York University Press, 2020).
21 Woody Woodmansey, *Spider from Mars: My Life with Bowie* (New York: St. Martin's, 2016), 1978.
22 Chris O'Leary writes about some marvelous recordings of Bowie rehearsing an early version of this on his *Pushing Ahead of the Dame* blog, and also provides a link: https://bowiesongs.wordpress.com/2020/04/06/24359/
23 These biographical details come from various sources. Cherry recounts most of them in this interview: www.youtube.com/watch?v=_ppyUA828po
24 Miles Charlesworth and Chris Charleworth, *David Bowie Black Book*, (London: Omnibus Press, 2013), 71.
25 Lordi, *The Meaning of Soul*, 46–73.
26 Juan Flores, *Salsa Rising: New York Latin Music of the Sixties Generation* (New York: Oxford University Press, 2016), 130.
27 The güiro is a New World instrument, probably developed by the Taino, the indigenous Arawak who dominated Cuba, Hispaniola, Jamaica, Puerto Rico, and other islands of the Caribbean before the European invasion.
28 In addition to Flores, *Salsa Rising*, 3026, see Benjamin Lapidus, *New York and the International Sound of Latin Music, 1940–1990* (Jackson: University Press of Mississippi, 2021).
29 Carlos Alomar, "A Transitional, Generational Artist." *Billboard*, May 4, 1974: 9.
30 Pete Bonet, *The Corso: The Real Nuyorican Salsa Story* (Conneaut Lake, PA: Page Publishing, 2020).

31 David Bowie, "Interview with Bowie," conducted by Paul Du Noyer. *Q*, April 1990.
32 David Bowie, "Interview with David Bowie," conducted by Paul Du Noyer. *Mojo*, July 2002.
33 See in particular Eric Weisbard, *Top 40 Democracy: The Rival Mainstreams of American Music* (Chicago: University of Chicago Press, 2014), from which I am drawing the distinction (and connection) between "format" and "genre."
34 On the strength of the top-ten singles "Fame" and "Golden Years" from the *Young Americans* and *Station to Station* albums respectively, in 1976 RCA released a retrospective collection called *ChangesOneBowie*. Its popularity—it reached #10 on the album charts—is probably responsible for many US listeners' familiarity with earlier UK Bowie hits such as "Changes" and "The Jean Genie." *ChangesOneBowie* was less a greatest-hits collection than it was a tool for educating new Bowie fans on his past, since it contained several songs that had not even been A sides of singles, such as "Ziggy Stardust" and "Suffragette City," as well as songs that were relative flops as singles, such as "Diamond Dogs." The album also included the album version of "Rebel Rebel."
35 Alomar, "A Transitional, Generational Artist."
36 I'd speculate that John Lennon's presence on that song helped justify categorizing it as within the bounds of rock.

References

Alomar, Carlos. "A Transitional, Generational Artist." *Billboard*, May 4, 1974: 9.
Bonet, Pete. *The Corso: The Real Nuyorican Salsa Story*. Conneaut Lake, PA: Page Publishing, 2020.
Bowie, David. "Interview with Bowie," conducted by Paul Du Noyer. *Q*, April 1990. www.pauldunoyer.com/david-bowie-interview-1990/
Bowie, David. "Interview with David Bowie," conducted by Paul Du Noyer. *Mojo*, July 2002. www.pauldunoyer.com/david-bowie-interview-2002/
Burgett, Bruce, and Glenn Hendler, eds. *Keywords for American Cultural Studies*. Third Edition. New York: New York University Press, 2020.
Burns, Gary. "A Typology of 'Hooks' in Popular Records." *Popular Music* 6, no. 1 (January 1987): 1–20.
Cann, Kevin. *Any Day Now: David Bowie, The London Years: 1947–1974.* Croyden, Surrey, UK: Adelita, 2010.
Cantello, David. "The Year of the Diamond Dogs." *The Year of the Diamond Dogs*, 2017. https://theyearofthediamonddog.webs.com/diamonddogssessions.htm
Charlesworth, Miles, and Chris Charleworth. *David Bowie Black Book*. London: Omnibus Press, 2013.
Cherry, Ava. All that Glitters: The Ava Cherry Story. Detroit: Aquarius Books, 2022.
Cole, Tom. 'You Ask, We Answer: What's a Hook?" *NPR*, October 15, 2010. www.npr.org/sections/therecord/2010/10/15/130588663/you-ask-we-answer-what-s-a-hook
Disc, "Bowie 1984 AD," Disc, October 27, 1973.
Edwards. Henry, and Tony Zanetta, *Stardust: The David Bowie Story*. New York: McGraw Hill, 1986.
Everett, Walter. "'If You're Gonna Have a Hit': Intratextual Mixes and Edits of Pop Recordings." *Popular Music* 29, no. 2 (2010): 229–50.

Flores, Juan. *Salsa Rising: New York Latin Music of the Sixties Generation.* New York: Oxford University Press, 2016: 130.

Griffin, Roger. *David Bowie: The Golden Years.* London: Omnibus Press, 2016.

Hendler, Glenn. *Diamond Dogs.* New York: Bloomsbury, 2020.

Lapidus, Benjamin. *New York and the International Sound of Latin Music, 1940-1990.* Jackson: University Press of Mississippi, 2021.

Lordi, Emily J. *The Meaning of Soul: Black Music and Resilience Since the 1960s.* Durham: Duke University Press, 2020.

O' Leary, Chris. "Pushing Ahead of the Dame: David Bowie, Song by Song." *BowieSongs.* https://bowiesongs.wordpress.com

O'Leary, Chris. *Rebel Rebel: All the Songs of David Bowie from '64 to '76.* Winchester, UK: Zero Books, 2015.

Pegg, Nicholas. *The Complete David Bowie.* London: Titan Books, 2011.

Pek, Norbert. "Aardapels Voor David Bowie." *Perfects*, 3 October 2013. www.perfects.nl/weblog/aardappels-david-bowie/

Sharp, Ken. "Travels With Bowie" (interview with Geoff MacCormack). *Record Collector*, October 2008. https://recordcollectormag.com/articles/travels-with-bowie

Sheffield, Rob. "How America Inspired David Bowie to Kill Ziggy Stardust With 'Aladdin Sane.'" *Rolling Stone*, April 13, 2016. www.rollingstone.com/music/music-news/how-america-inspired-david-bowie-to-kill-ziggy-stardust-with-aladdin-sane-230827/

Thompson, Dave. *Your Pretty Face is Going to Hell: The Dangerous Glitter of David Bowie, Iggy Pop, and Lou Reed.* New York: Backbeat Books, 2009.

Tongson, Karen. "Earworms, Touchstones, Inversions." In *Confessions of an ACA Fan*, edited by Henry Jenkins. 2011. http://henryjenkins.org/blog/2011/08/aca-fandom_and_beyond_karen_to_1.html

Weisbard, Eric. *Top 40 Democracy: The Rival Mainstreams of American Music.* Chicago: University of Chicago Press, 2014.

Woodmansey, Woody. *Spider from Mars: My Life with Bowie.* New York: St. Martin's, 2016

6 Donna Summer—"I Feel Love" (1977)

Simon Reynolds

There are songs that divide pop history into before and after. Some are incontestable: "She Loves You," "Anarchy in the UK," "Rapper's Delight." Sometimes a song splits pop time in half without that many people noticing its revolutionary implications, the impact emerging fully only later (think Phuture's 1987 single "Acid Trax." which pioneered the Chicago acid house genre that in turn ignited the British rave scene into existence). Other times, the rupture in business-as-usual happens in plain view, at the peak of the pop charts, and the effect is immediate.

One single whose status as a world-historical pop event is incontestable—and that was felt as a real-time future-shock—is "I Feel Love." Released in early July 1977, the song was a global smash, reaching #1 in several countries (including the UK, where its reign at the top lasted a full month) and rising to #6 in *Billboard*. Its impact reached far beyond the disco scene in which singer Donna Summer and her producers Giorgio Moroder and Pete Bellotte were already well established. Postpunk and new wave groups admired and appropriated its innovative sound, the maniacal precision of its grid-like groove of sequenced synth pulses.

Even now, long after discophobia has been disgraced and rockism defeated, there's still a mischievous frisson to staking the claim that "I Feel Love" was far more important than other epochal singles of '77 such as "God Save the Queen," "Sheena Is a Punk Rocker," or "White Riot." But really there should be nothing provocatively heretical or historically revisionist about that opinion. It's a simple statement of fact. For if any one song can be pinpointed as where the '80s began, it's "I Feel Love."

Within club culture, "I Feel Love" pointed the way forward and blazed the path for genres of the '80s and '90s such as Hi-NRG, Italo, house, techno, and trance. All the residual elements in disco—the aspects that connected it to pop tradition, show tunes, orchestrated soul, funk—were purged in favor of brutal futurism: mechanistic repetition, icy electronics, a blank-eyed, fixated feel of posthuman propulsion.

"'I Feel Love' stripped out the flowery, pretty aspects of disco and really gave it a streamlined drive," says Vince Aletti, probably the very first music critic to take disco seriously. In the club column he wrote for *Record World* at

DOI: 10.4324/9781003093206-7

the time, Aletti compared "I Feel Love" to "Trans-Europe Express/Metal on Metal" by Kraftwerk, another prophetic piece of electronic trance-dance that convulsed crowds in the more adventurous clubs, if not conquering the pop charts like Summer's song did.[1]

The reverberations of "I Feel Love" reached far beyond the disco floor, though. Then unknown but destined to be synth-pop stars in the 1980s, the nascent Human League completely switched their direction after hearing the song. Blondie, equally enamored, became one of the first punk-associated groups to embrace disco. Brian Eno famously rushed into the Berlin recording studio where he and Bowie were working on creating new futures for music, waving a copy of "I Feel Love." "This is it, look no further," Eno declared breathlessly. "This single is going to change the sound of club music for the next fifteen years."[2]

In the wake of "I Feel Love," Giorgio Moroder became a name producer, the disco equivalent of Phil Spector. He even appeared on the cover of Britain's leading rock magazine, *New Musical Express*.[3] The Moroder hit factory was widely considered the Motown of the late '70s, with Donna Summer as its Diana Ross.

Summer and Moroder, with his iconic black mustache, were the public face of the operation. But inside his Munich-based Musicland studio, Moroder led a team of brilliant musicians and technicians. Most significant of these was Pete Bellotte, Moroder's silent partner—silent in the sense that he never did interviews and shied from the limelight. But Bellotte played a crucial role as catalyst of song concepts as well as musical and production ideas: it was he who had originally spotted Summer's vocal gifts. The crack squad also included man-machine super-drummer Keith Forsey, a series of keyboard players including Þórir Baldursson, Sylvester Levay, and Harold Faltermeyer, the brilliant engineer Juergen Koppers, and a slightly mysterious figure known as Robbie Wedel, whose occult command of the inner workings of the Moog made a crucial contribution to the construction of "I Feel Love."

In a business fueled by ego, Moroder has always been unusually gracious and generous when it comes to acknowledging the collective nature of the magic that typically still gets attributed to him alone. Former colleague Keith Forsey recalls Moroder as being "good at delegating, at finding talents that were compatible." But he also stresses that Moroder called the shots. Moroder "was the leader, and you had to follow. Giorgio was boss."

Step into Moroder's apartment in Los Angeles's upscale Westwood neighborhood and the scene screams "Mr. Music." There's a white grand piano, a special shelf for his Grammys and Oscars, and a wall laden with gold discs. Profuse with glass ornaments, the living room's predominantly white décor floats somewhere between *Scarface* (a movie for which Moroder made the soundtrack, as it happens) and the sleek interiors of *10*, that '70s period piece in which Dudley Moore plays an LA-based songwriter undergoing a midlife crisis. In a corner there's a bronze Buddha draped in chiffon scarves, while an entire wall is mostly taken up with a gigantic and slightly garish painting of Elizabeth Taylor.

Twinkly and avuncular, Moroder still has his famous mustache, although it's now Santa Claus white rather than coal black. Aged 77 when the meeting took place in May 2017, his memory is not what it used to be: some patches of his history he recalls crystal clear, but others—like the 1978 album *Once Upon A Time*, the apex of the Summer-Moroder-Bellotte symbiosis, in my opinion—are totally blank.

Moroder grew up in the Alpine valleys of South Tyrol, a region of northern-most Italy that for five centuries was part of Austria until it passed into Italian control after the First World War. His native tongue is the regional Ladin language, although he is fluent in German and Italian. "In my hometown Urtijëi, we would speak three languages during any day, depending on whoever you're talking with. But with my brothers, I would still speak Ladino."

In his youth Moroder performed live in clubs, then started releasing and producing records from the mid-60s onwards, scoring hits in a few European countries with bubblegum singles like "Moody Trudy" (1969) and "Looky Looky" (1969). In the early '70s he partnered with Pete Bellotte, a British expat who'd spent much of the '60s clawing unsuccessfully for a commercial breakthrough as guitarist in the band Linda Laine and the Sinners while earning a solid living playing rough nightclubs in Germany. Although Moroder and Bellotte's bouncy, synth-laced ditty "Son of My Father" (1972) became a smash when covered by Chicory Tip, there was little to indicate that the pair would become the presiding pop geniuses of the late '70s.

Along the way, Bellotte stumbled on the extraordinary voice of a Black American singer who'd also moved to central Europe and stayed for the work opportunities. Boston-born Donna Gaines had graduated from fronting the rock group Crow in her hometown to musical theater work in Europe as part of the cast of *Hair*, gigs at the Vienna Folk Opera in productions of *Porgy and Bess* and *Showboat*, and studio work as a session singer. After marrying an Austrian actor, she took his name: Sommer. When her vocal on a Bellotte song demo unexpectedly led to record industry interest, she anglicized her married name to Summer and formed a three-way musical partnership with Moroder and Bellotte.

The team achieved modest success in Europe with singles and a debut Summer album, but the real breakthrough came with the disco-erotica epic "Love to Love You Baby," which reached #2 in *Billboard*, #4 in the UK, and went top-20 in 13 other nations in 1976. Summer's gasps and groans had journalists nicknaming her the Black Panter and "the Linda Lovelace of pop."[4] Crowning Summer the queen of "Sex Rock," *Time* magazine counted no less than 22 simulated orgasms across the record's almost 17-minutes-long span.[5] Neil Bogart, boss of the legendary disco label Casablanca, had asked Moroder to extend the song to a full album side because—the story goes—he wished to soundtrack an orgy. Bogart enthused about the first side of the album *Love To Love You Baby* as "a beautiful, great balling record," telling people to "take Donna home and make love to her—the album, that is" and encouraging radio stations to play the track at midnight as a catalyst for home-listener romance.[6] The sultry schlock of Summer's live performances of this era played up the softcore erotica sound of "Love to Love You Baby." The singer would often be carried onstage by two men clad in loincloths, while backing-dancer couples simulated copulation in ever-changing positions

Huge as it was, "Love to Love You Baby" initially seemed like a risqué novelty hit rather than the start of a long-term career for any of the participants. Nor did the production and arrangement on Summer's first three disco albums (lush, luxuriant, deftly executed but quite conventional in sound) presage any kind of giant musical leap forward from Moroder and Bellotte.

There was a clue to a secret experimental streak, though: a Moroder solo album quietly released in 1975 to almost zero attention. *Einzelgänger* (the title is roughly equivalent to "lone wolf") teems with pitter-pattering drum machine beats and unsettling processed vocal stutters that recall the ethereal whimsy of Cluster's mid-70s albums like *Zuckerzeit* or the three records Kraftwerk made before their pop move *Autobahn*.

But it's possible that Moroder's latent interest in electronic music might never have blossomed so spectacularly with "I Feel Love" if not for the conceptual spark that came from Bellotte. The Englishman was in charge of lyrics, and his passion for literature drove him to organize Summer's early records around big themes. One of those concepts was an album in which each song stylistically corresponded to a different decade of the twentieth century. Almost as an afterthought, Bellotte and Moroder decided to end the album, titled *I Remember Yesterday*, with a song that represented the future: "I Feel Love." (See Figure 6.1)

Gaunt and sunburned, with long swept-back gray hair and light stubble, Pete Bellotte exudes a wry, semi-detached air sitting in the café of a London bookstore in May 2017, as if faintly bemused by the abiding interest in the Moroder Summer era. At the same time the 73-year-old self-described recluse is clearly proud of the achievements in which he played an indispensable role. This interview is a vanishingly rare occurrence: back in the day, Bellotte did no press at all, and there appear to be only a few photographs of him from that era, in which he sports an almost identical mustache to Moroder's.

Bellotte's love affair with the written word started aged nine when his uncle gave him a copy of Charles Dickens's *A Christmas Carol*. "By eleven, I'd read everything Dickens had written." Unlikely as it seems, Bellotte's bookworm tendency fed directly into Donna Summer's discography. *A Love Trilogy*, the 1976 follow-up to *Love To Love You Baby*, got its structure because he'd just read British fantasy writer Mervyn Peake's *Gormenghast* trilogy. "I thought, we could have three songs, and they'd go into a fourth song combining all three." *Four Seasons of Love*, the next album, was similarly shaped by Bellotte's reading of novelist Lawrence Durrell's *Alexandria Quartet*.

Figure 6.1 The cover of Donna Summer's album *I Remember Yesterday*. Credit: Vinyls/
Alamy Stock Photo.

Then, in 1977, came *I Remember Yesterday*. "Originally it was going to be called *A Dance to the Music of Time*, because I'd just read Anthony Powell's twelve-volume cycle of the same name. Those novels go through a whole period of British history, and from that I got the concept of the album: each song would relate to a different decade." So the title track and opening number featured the swinging horns of a 1940s dance band. "Love's Unkind" jumped to the early '60s girl-group era. Motown pastiche "Back in Love Again" was a lovely lost cousin to the Supremes' "Baby Love." The '70s were represented by the Labelle-like funk of "Black Lady" and the bang-up-to-date disco of "Take Me," featuring unfeminist lyrics but gorgeous singing from Summer, a macho-man backing vocal that fills the mind's eye with chest hair and gold chains, and a deliciously nubile groove of bouncy bass and chattering clavinets.

The Anthony Powell–inspired concept for *I Remember Yesterday* tapped into disco's retro leanings as manifested by groups like Dr. Buzzard's Original Savannah Band and the Pointer Sisters whose early image and sound were steeped in 1940s nostalgia. But in a beautiful irony, the most famous track on this concept album proved to be "I Feel Love": the reverse of retro.

For Moroder and Bellotte, the idea of a song and a sound from tomorrow meant synthesizers and machine rhythm. So they called on a fellow whose services they'd used sporadically before: Robbie Wedel, an electronics wizard who assisted the Munich-based composer Eberhard Schoener with the operation of the Moog that the latter had bought. Wedel turned up, recalls Bellotte, with

> three big units, roughly two and half feet by two feet, full of oscillators and voltage controls, the wires hanging out like one of the old telephone exchanges. And he brought a fourth box too, which was the arpeggiator and trigger for the machine.

The three men set to building the rhythm track. "It was done in reverse," says Moroder, referring to how he broke with his usual approach of writing a song first on a keyboard, then arranging in the studio. "Donna came in later and we composed the melody that would fit in. And 'I Feel Love' is a difficult song to sing."

While Moroder and Bellotte concentrated on building the tune's classic locomotive bass line, they didn't notice that Wedel had asked engineer Jurgen Kuppers to lay down a signal on track 16 of the tape, "a reference pulse," or as Moroder now calls it, the Click. "We've laid the first track down and Robbie says, 'Would you like to synch the next track to this?' And we don't know what he means," recalls Bellotte.

> So Robbie explained that because of the signal on the tape, each part of the tune created on the Moog will link up to exactly the same tempo. And the timing was exactly spot on. Robbie had worked out this methodology himself—it wasn't something the machine's inventor Bob Moog knew about. It was through Robbie that we managed to get the track—he's the reason why, when you hear "I Feel Love" today, those sounds in there are so solid and fantastic.

Another reason why "I Feel Love" pummels along so propulsively is the bright idea that emerged somewhere in the process, probably from Wedel or Kuppers, of putting a delay on the bassline: this created a strobing flicker effect, intensified by the equally clever trick of putting the original bass-signal through the left speaker channel and the minutely delayed pulse through the right speaker. The whole track seems to shimmer convulsively, like controlled and channeled epilepsy. Moroder recalls that the effect created problems in big clubs where the stereo separation was wide, because "if you were dancing next to the left speaker, the groove emphasis was on the 'up' and the feel was off." But that glitch doesn't appear to have diminished the track's absolute dominion over disco dance floors then and to this day.

Wedel also showed Moroder and Bellotte how to turn Moog noise into percussion by clipping it. "You take white noise," says Moroder, imitating the hissing sound, "and you put it into an envelope, so it sounds like a hi-hat, or a snare. And then you say this sound should be just one eighth of a bar long. So from white noise you can create most of the drum sounds."

The only problem was that despite its famously "fat" and full sound, the Moog couldn't deliver the right punch for the kick drum, and so, compromising their all-electronic conception for "I Feel Love," Moroder and Bellotte were forced to call on the human, hands-on services of Keith Forsey. A veteran drummer who'd played with the chaotic acid-rock collective Amon Duul II before drifting into session work (and who would later achieve fame and fortune producing Billy Idol's '80s MTV smashes and writing Simple Minds only US #1, "Don't You Forget About Me"), Forsey was renowned for his incredibly precise timekeeping. "I was never one of those 'chops' players," Forsey says, meaning that he didn't go in for drum solos or flashy fills but concentrated on ultra-tight groove maintenance.

Forsey recalls "I Feel Love" as the start of a period in which Moroder recorded each drum in the kit individually for complete separation of sound: this "totally clean sound, no bleed through, no overheads, no room sound" had more impact on the dance floor. For Forsey, it was rather an unnatural, counter-intuitive procedure, frustrating the natural way of playing, where every limb in the body is engaged. "Your body has to dance if you want the people to dance," he says. Forsey would find himself playing the kick or the snare "for fifteen to eighteen minutes solid—the other guys would leave the studio booth and go off to make a cup of tea, leaving me to it." Sometimes he'd put a phone book on the hi-hat so he could it tap silently, to preserve some element of groove and feel in his otherwise disembodied and deconstructed performance.

The rhythmic chassis of "I Feel Love" now complete, it was time for the rider of the runaway train to play her part. Moroder and Bellotte both pay tribute to Summer's intuitive feeling for what a song required. A typical session, Bellotte recalls, involved the vivacious singer coming in and talking for several hours—she loved to gossip, joke, talk about what was going on in her life—before realizing that time had flown and she had to dash off. She would then lay down her vocal in just one or two takes. Her variegated work experience—rock, gospel, musical theater, light opera—gave her a wide range of modes to draw on, and "she loved doing funny voices," recalls Bellotte. "I've sung gospel and Broadway all my life and you have to have a belting voice for that," Summer told *Rolling Stone* in 1978. "They categorize me as a black act, which is not the truth. I'm not even a soul singer. I'm more a pop singer."[7]

For "I Feel Love," Summer pushed beyond the softcore of "Love to Love You Baby" with a vocal that sounds more cosmic than carnal. She uses what's known as a "head voice," breathy and angelic, rather than the kind of husky "chest voice" you associate with grainy, groin-y R&B. That explains why the song's vibe is unearthly rather than earthy: this is love as out-of-body experience and rapt mystic levitation rather than hot between-the-sheets action. As Vince Aletti puts it, "It's like she's coming from some other place."

The song's feeling of suspension from time, of being lost in a loop of ecstasy or reverie, comes also from the incredibly simple and short lyric, in which phrases like "heaven knows" or "fallin' free" are each repeated five times. The melodic plateau of the verse shifts to a gently ascending chorus of the title phrase: itself an odd utterance, since "I feel love" is not really something you'd find yourself saying in any real-world amorous situation. Intransitive and open-ended, it's suggestive of a rhapsodic state of being "in love with love."

Which is pretty much where Summer's head and heart were when the words were written. As Bellotte recalls it, "I Feel Love" was

> the first time Donna wanted to be involved in a lyric. She was in LA, so I'd gone round to her house one evening and she answered the doorbell with a phone in her hand. She told me she was on the phone to New York and I should come in, help myself to coffee, she'd be down in a second. I sat there with my notebook ready to write the lyric, and half an hour later, she came downstairs and said, "Won't be long!" So I waited and waited, and it went on for about an hour and half, during which she came down and said, "Make a start, make a start."

Finally, around 10.30 or 11:00 PM, Bellotte recalls, Summer finished her phone call, which had been to her astrologer. Summer was a firm believer in the oracular power of horoscopes and had once canceled a private jet chartered by her manager because of a last-minute warning from her astrologer that she shouldn't fly. Forsey remembers sessions where he would be informed that "Donna isn't coming to the studio today, her astrologer told her not too." The reason for that night's intensive phone consultation was that she had just met Bruce Sudano, the guitarist and singer in Brooklyn Dreams, an R&B outfit who would later work as her backing group.

"Donna had fallen for Bruce, deeply," recalls Bellotte. Summer and her astrologer had been examining her and Sudano's star signs, and comparing those alignments with the sign of her current (and as it turned out, literally ill-starred) Austrian boyfriend Peter.

> When she came downstairs, Donna announced that her astrologer had told her, "This is the man." That was the night "I Feel Love" was written: when she'd changed her whole life. And it was the best thing that ever happened to her, she and Bruce were together for the rest of her life. So when Donna flew back to Munich to record the vocal, that was the feeling she gave the song.

That real-life, slightly kooky, and very '70s story brings a human dimension to the genesis of this technologically turbo-charged monster track. But in other respects Summer's performance has a woman-machine quality that looks ahead to the looped diva samples of house and rave music (tracks like Orbital's "Halcyon + On + On," for instance, with its blissed spirals of trilling upper-octave feminine vocals) while also prophesying twenty-first century fembots like Kylie Minogue and Britney Spears. Summer's live performances of "I Feel Love" sometimes played up this android aspect: *Rolling Stone*'s Mikal Gilmore described her dancing "in angular, jerky motions," her face "a dazed, mechanical mask."[8]

Many rock fans and critics seemed to believe that the electronic Eurodisco pioneered by Moroder and his team was actually robot music that literally played itself. Interviewed by *NME* in 1978, Moroder mocked the notion that the machines were in charge. "Even if you use synthesizers and sequencers and drum machines, you have to set them up, to choose exactly what you are going to make them do. It is nonsense to say that we make all our music automatically." Sometimes it was easier to get the sound you were looking for with the new technology, he added, "but as often as not it is at least ten times more difficult to get a good synthesiser sound than on an acoustic instrument."[9] On the cover of his 1979 solo album *E=mc²*, Moroder appears with his white, rolled-up-sleeves jacket open to reveal a computer circuit board, as if having a little fun with the idea of electro-disco as machine-made, while also reinforcing the album's boast to be the first fully digital recording.

Still, there's no denying that it was precisely the *precision* of "I Feel Love" that made it so stark and startling to listeners in 1977. Moroder and his team had assimilated the logic immanent within Black dance music (think James Brown's "Sex Machine") and German motorik rock (think Neu! and Kraftwerk), then taken it the next level of clockwork exactitude. Human ingenuity and creativity drove the decisions at every step, but to listeners it sounded like the machines had taken over: a thrilling breakthrough for some, a disturbing development for others.[10]

Revolutionary tracks like "I Feel Love" carry a retrospective aura of inevitability, like they were ordained to be. And certainly the way technology was going, a track along the lines of "I Feel Love" would have been made by somebody around that time. But as we've seen, the precise shape the song took has an element of circumstance and accident: the convergence of Moroder's interest in synths with Bellotte's literary obsessions and Summer's heightened emotional state. The stars aligned and history happened.

Ironies abound in this tale. The first is that none of its creators thought much of "I Feel Love." Intended as an ordinary album track, the primary recording process for the song took just three hours (the mixing took much longer). "Once we'd finished the song, and the whole album, it didn't mean anything to us, in terms of us thinking we'd done anything special," recalls Bellotte. Indeed, initially "I Feel Love" was consigned to the lowly status of B side to the single release in early May 1977 of "Can't We Just Sit Down (And Talk It Over)," another track off *I Remember Yesterday*.

It was Casablanca boss Neil Bogart—an archetypal music-biz "record man" insofar as he wasn't a musician but had a matchless instinct for which songs had commercial potential—who insisted that "I Feel Love" should become a single in its own right. In an echo of his intervention with "Love to

Love You Baby," Bogart pinpointed three crucial edits that would extend the song's length and expand its trippy, out-of-time feeling.

The other great irony of "I Feel Love" is that its makers not only failed to see the import of what they'd created, they didn't really see its impact either. Moroder and Bellotte hardly ever went to discotheques, so they didn't witness the frenzy it incited on dance floors across the world, the feeling of a sudden leap into tomorrow. "Neither Giorgio nor I can dance," laughs Bellotte. When asked how he had such a feel for dance music if he never danced, Moroder says, "I would just tap my feet in the studio."

According to Bellotte, the pair were just too busy for clubbing. In their heyday as hitmakers, they lived extremely regular lives: starting work in the studio at around 10:00 a.m., they finished promptly at six, and repaired to one or other of the finest restaurants in Los Angeles (by mid-1978, the operation had moved from Munich to the entertainment capital of the world). Fine dining was their solitary vice: although photos exist of Moroder wearing a gold razor-blade necklace of the "chopping out lines"-type nestling amid his chest hair, neither partner participated in the disco era's rampant hedonism. Bellotte says they didn't smoke, drink, or take drugs. Moroder says he was in bed by the time fans of the music were dervish-whirling to the sounds they'd made.

The impact of "I Feel Love" on the sound of disco was immediate and immense. A spate of electronic dance hits followed swiftly: Space's "Magic Fly," Dee D. Jackson's "Automatic Lover," Cerrone's "Supernature." The song, says Moroder, received a particularly strong response from the gay community. "Even now, millions of gay people love Donna and some say, 'I was liberated by that song.' It is a hymn."

The song's gay anthem status was enshrined in 1985 when Bronski Beat covered "I Feel Love" in a medley with "Love To Love You Baby" and '60s melodrama pop hit "Johnny Remember Me." Frontman Jimmy Somerville's stratosphere-shattering falsetto entwined with the high camp of guest vocalist Marc Almond from Soft Cell, and the video was impishly homoerotic. "Jimmy told me he became a singer *because* of 'I Feel Love,'" says Moroder. "He heard that 'oooh'"—he imitates Summer's helium-high soprano—"and he said, 'That's my career!'"

Another gay musician propelled on his journey by "I Feel Love" was the producer Patrick Cowley. Described as the "American Giorgio Moroder"—a tag that certainly fits his sound if not his mainstream impact—Cowley's work has in recent years been rediscovered by the hipster archival industry, with reissues of his Moog-rippling porno soundtracks. But his larger impact at the time was as a pioneer of Hi-NRG, the gay club sound that would dominate the '80s and reach the mainstream with hits like Dead or Alive's "You Spin Me Round" (1984). Based out of San Francisco, Cowley produced hits like "You Make Me Feel (Mighty Real)" (1978) for trans diva Sylvester, co-founded the "masculine music" label Megatone, and scored solo on the dance floor with anthems like "Menergy" (1981). But his disco career actually started with an unsanctioned 15-minute long remix of "I Feel Love" that circulated furtively on acetate among select favored DJs on the gay scene. An inspired expansion, punctuated by hallucinatory breakdowns of swaggeringly inventive Moog-play and percussive delirium, Cowley's "I Feel Love Megamix" almost eclipses the original. Finally released officially in 1982, it made the UK top 30.

By that point Moroder & Co.'s innovations underpinned large swathes of contemporary pop music in the UK and Europe. For some, hearing "I Feel Love" was a life changer. Phil Oakey told me that when Martyn Ware came round to his Sheffield apartment in 1977 to recruit him into the Future—the group that became the Human League—Ware brandished copies of "I Feel Love" and "Trans-Europe Express" and announced, "We can do this."[11] The group instantly shifted from its early Tangerine Dream–like abstraction towards poppy and boppy accessibility, as heard on the manifesto-like song "Dance like a Star" (original 1977, released in 2002), which bears more than a passing resemblance to "I Feel Love." Eight years later, and now a pop star, Oakey would honor the debt by teaming up with Moroder for the hit single "Together in Electric Dreams" (1984).

Another outfit who had a Damascene conversion to electronic disco was glam-era oddballs Sparks, who hooked up with Moroder for 1979's brilliant *No. 1 in Heaven* album and its UK hit singles "No. 1 Song in Heaven" and "Beat the Clock." Originally from Los Angeles, the anglophile brothers Ron and Russell Mael had become pop sensations in the UK in 1974, but by the time punk kicked off they'd lost their way. Looking for an aesthetic reboot, Sparks were the first established rock band to embrace disco at album length, as opposed to the one-off disco-influenced hits made by rockers like the Rolling Stones and Rod Stewart. In interviews, Ron and Russell invented anti-rockism, loudly dismissing guitars as passé and deriding the very concept of "the band" as exhausted. They burbled about the thrillingly modern impersonality of the Moroder-Summer sound, in particular "I Feel Love" and its "combination of the human voice and this really *cold* thing behind it."[12] Electronic disco, Sparks proclaimed, was the true new wave, whereas most actual skinny-tie new wavers were merely retreading the '60s.

Probably the Maels had the likes of Blondie in mind when they made that swipe. But Blondie themselves were converts to the new sound. Talking to *NME* in early 1978, Debbie Harry praised Moroder's sound as "the kind of stuff I want to do,"[13] and the group covered "I Feel Love" at a benefit concert later that spring. "Heart of Glass" (1979) was their slinky first stab at disco, followed by tracks like "Atomic" (1980) and "Rapture" (1981), with its Summer-like swirl of a chorus. But "Call Me" (1980), the Blondie track that Moroder actually produced, was brashly rocking in the Pat Benatar style.

Alongside obviously indebted postpunk and synthpop groups like New Order, Visage, and Eurhythmics, the aftershocks of "I Feel Love" reached into all kinds of odd corners. Progressive jazz-rock veterans Soft Machine, of all people, released the Moroder-style single "Soft Space" in 1978. Apocalyptic Goth doom-mongers Killing Joke underpinned several of their singles with clinical Eurodisco pulse-work. And while they were later synonymous with stadium-scale bluster, early on Simple Minds fused cinematic post-Bowie art rock with hypnotic sequenced synth patterns on "I Travel" (1980) and their Euro-infatuated lost masterpiece *Empires and Dance* (1980).

Moroder took the "I Feel Love" template further with Sparks and with his Academy Award–winning score *Midnight Express* (1978, which produced the club hit "The Chase"). But surprisingly, with Donna Summer he cut barely half a dozen tracks in the fully electronic vein. 1978's *Once Upon A Time*—another themed album, with a narrative updating the Cinderella story to the modern metropolis—dedicated the second of its four sides to synths. "Now I Need You" and "Working the Midnight Shift," the first two panels in a seamless side-long triptych, ripple with a serenely celestial beauty rivaled only by Kraftwerk's "Neon Lights." Also a double album, 1979's *Bad Girls* shunted the synth-tunes to side four, frontloading the album with ballsy raunch and balladsy romance. But "Our Love," "Lucky," and the fabulous "Sunset People" (an inexplicable failure as a single) made for a fine swan-song finale for the electronic style that made Summer famous and turned Moroder into an in-demand soundtrack composer.

Summer was eager to transcend the disco category, though, and *Bad Girls'* rock moves shrewdly repositioned her as a "credible" artist in America. For the first time she received critical plaudits from rock journalists who'd previously belittled Eurodisco with descriptions like "sanitized, simplified, mechanized R&B."[14] Now they were placated by Donna taking a more active role in the song-writing and by crossover ploys like the screeching solo from LA axeman-about-town Jeff Baxter that punctuated "Hot Stuff" (four years before Michael Jackson tried the same maneuver with "Beat It"). "Hot Stuff" reached #1 and remains Summer's biggest hit by far in the USA.

"Donna Summer Has Begun to Win Respect" announced a *New York Times* headline.[15] Respect ain't much use, though, when the magic vanishes. Breaking with the disco-tarnished Casablanca and signing to Geffen, Summer strove to become a radio-format crossing all-rounder, resulting in a series of increasingly barren albums: the confused *The Wanderer* (1980); one last Moroder/Bellotte produced album, *I'm A Rainbow* (1981) that Geffen suppressed and which finally saw release in 1996; and the dried-up gulch that was 1982's *Donna Summer*, a fraught and largely fruitless collaboration with Quincy Jones. In Britain, where popular taste preferred her clad in glistening synthetics, that album produced an unlikely hit with her last great single, a cover of "State of Independence" written by Yes-man Jon Anderson and Vangelis. With *Chariots of Fire* and *Blade Runner*, Vangelis was starting to eclipse Moroder in the Hollywood electronic score soundtrack stakes.

Moroder spent three years on his pet project: restoring Fritz Lang's 1927 futuristic dystopia *Metropolis* and finding lost footage, only to spoil the silent classic with colorization and a score that could have worked if it had picked up where "Now I Need You/Working the Midnight Shift" and "Beat the Clock" left off, instead recruiting the unsuitable talents of Bonnie

Tyler, Pat Benatar, Freddie Mercury, and Loverboy. After the movie's hostile reception in 1984, he drifted away from music for many years, putting his energy and resources into quixotic ventures like the Moroder-Cizeta luxury sports car and a scheme to build a pyramid in Dubai. Meanwhile Bellotte had moved back to England, where he set up his own recording studio, but devoted most of his energy to parenting and to his literary interests: an unfinished biography of Mervyn Peake, a book of his own stories titled *The Unround Circle*, and a CD of prose-poem "rhythm rhymes," *The Noisy Voice of the Waterfall.*

But then—just like a classic-era disco album—came the reprise.

Moroder got a call from Daft Punk, then working on the album that would be released in 2013 as *Random Access Memories*—their perverse vision-quest attempt to time travel back to the '70s, the lost golden age when dance music involved super-slick musicianship and heroic struggles to get results out of electronic technology that is crude and cumbersome by the standards of digital equipment today. Rather than collaborate with Moroder musically, though, Thomas Bangalter and Guy-Manuel de Homem-Christo had something more unusual in mind. They interviewed Moroder for a couple of hours, discussing the length and breadth of his career, and then isolated two short extracts: a vignette from his very early days as a struggling performer, and a potted history of the making of "I Feel Love." Sandwiching these soundbites between wedges of synth-burble modeled on the classic Munich sound, the result was "Giorgio by Moroder": a poignant paean to the lost future that inevitably couldn't be sonically futuristic itself (indeed, the Eurodisco pastiche fashioned by Daft Punk is distinctly weak sauce). Instead the song is conceptually innovative, inventing a new genre: memoir-dance.

"One day I'll type out the whole interview and that'll be my biography," Moroder told me at the time, joking but half-serious.[16] But rather than commemorate his past glories, what the collaboration with Daft Punk really did was restart his life as a producer. Since *Random Access Memories* came out he's released his first solo album in 23 years, 2015's *Déjà vu*, teeming with collaborations with contemporary pop stars like Sia and Charlie XCX. The critical response was mixed, the commercial performance lackluster compared to his heyday (although the Britney-fronted cover of "Tom's Diner" hit the top 20 in Argentina and Lebanon). But Moroder is now an in-demand DJ: when we speak at his Westwood apartment, he's just about to head off to play a string of dates.

"They pay for your flights and the money is *great*," Moroder enthuses. In his set, he always plays "I Feel Love"—a tweaked version in which he's finally fixed the left-right speaker fluctuation in the bass pulse that always bothered him. DJ-ing is something that he never did at the time, and as a result—in a final irony—this means that nowadays he spends far more time in the clubs, up way past his customary bedtime, than he ever did back in the day. For the first time really, Moroder also gets to feel the love of his audience—three generations of them now—in the flesh.

Notes

1   Vince Aletti, *Record World*, May 28, 1977. Republished in Vince Aletti, *The Disco Files 1973–78* (U.K.: DJhistory.com, 1998), 294.
2   Brian Eno, quoted by David Bowie, in the Kurt Loder, "Liner notes," *Sound + Vision* box set (Rykodisc, 1989).
3   Angus MacKinnon, "Giorgio Moroder cover story interview." *New Musical Express*, December 9, 1978.
4   Richard Cromelin, "Donna Summer: Love on the Road," *Rolling Stone*, March 25, 1976.
5   Uncredited, "Sex Rock," *Time*, December 29, 1975, 39.
6   Mikal Gilmore, "Donna Summer: Is There Life After Disco?" *Rolling Stone*, March 23, 1978, 16.
7   Gilmore, "Donna Summer: Is There Life After Disco?" 18.
8   Gilmore, "Donna Summer: Is There Life After Disco?" 19.
9   MacKinnon, "Giorgio Moroder cover story interview."
10   A typical negative opinion expressed by rock fans and rock critics would be this verdict from Bill Holdship: "The music totally lacks emotion. It's a mechanical, machine-like music for a generation of mechanical, machine-like robots…": Uncredited, "Disco: If This Is Culture, Then I Want Out," *Michigan State News*, September 26, 1978.
11   Phil Oakley, "Interview with Phil Oakey of The Human League," conducted by Simon Reynolds, July 2002, Sheffield, UK. *Totally Wired: Postpunk Interviews and Overviews*, 281. New York: Soft Skull Press, 2010.
12   Harry Doherty, "Sparks interview." *Melody Maker*, April 7, 1979.
13   Harry, Debbie. "Debbie Harry and Blondie interview," conducted by Tony Parsons. *New Musical Express*, February 4, 1978.
14   Dennis Hunt, "Article on Eurodisco," *Los Angeles Times*, March 26, 1978.
15   John Rockwell, "Donna Summer Has Begun to Win Respect," *The New York Times*, July 26, 1979.
16   Simon Reynolds, "Daft Punk Gets Human With a New Album," *The New York Times*, May 15, 2013, www.nytimes.com/2013/05/19/arts/music/daft-punk-gets-human-with-a-new-album.html

References

Aletti, Vince. "Column in *Record World*, May 28, 1977." Republished in Aletti, Vince, *The Disco Files 1973–78*, 294. U.K.: DJhistory.com, 1998.
Aletti, Vince. Interview with the author. May 12, 2017. New York (by telephone).
Bellote, Pete. Interview with the author. May 25, 2017, Piccadilly, London, UK.
Cromelin, Richard. "Donna Summer: Love on the Road." *Rolling Stone*, March 25, 1976.
Doherty, Harry. "Sparks interview." *Melody Maker*, April 7, 1979.
Esposito, Jim, "Donna Summer and Sex Rock." *Oui*, September, 1976.
Forsey, Keith. Interview with the author. May 14, 2017. Los Angeles (by telephone).
Gilmore, Mikal. "Donna Summer: Is There Life After Disco?" *Rolling Stone*, March 23,1978.
Harry, Debbie. "Debbie Harry and Blondie interview," conducted by Tony Parsons. *New Musical Express*, February 4, 1978.

Hunt, Dennis. "Article on Eurodisco." *Los Angeles Times*, March 26, 1978.

Loder, Kurt. "Liner notes." Sound + Vision box set. Rykodisc, 1989.

MacKinnon, Angus. "Giorgio Moroder cover story interview." *New Musical Express*, December 9, 1978.

Moroder, Giorgio. Interview with the author. May 10, 2017. Westwood, Los Angeles, CA.

Oakley, Phil. "Interview with Phil Oakey of The Human League," conducted by Simon Reynolds, July 2002, Sheffield, UK. *Totally Wired: Postpunk Interviews and Overviews*, 281. New York: Soft Skull Press, 2010.

Reynolds, Simon. "Daft Punk Gets Human With a New Album." *The New York Times*, May 15, 2013. www.nytimes.com/2013/05/19/arts/music/daft-punk-gets-human-with-a-new-album.html

Rockwell, John. "Donna Summer Has Begun to Win Respect." *The New York Times*, July 26, 1979.

Uncredited. "Sex Rock." *Time*, December 29, 1975.

Uncredited. "Disco: If This Is Culture, Then I Want Out." Michigan State News, September 26, 1978.

7 X-Ray Spex—"Oh Bondage! Up Yours!" (1977)

Helen Reddington

Beginning with a distinctive truncated laugh, then the baby-voiced "Some people think little girls should be seen and not heard, but I think…[yelling] OH BONDAGE, UP YOURS!" this track by X-Ray Spex redefined British punk as humorous and not exclusively male and white: it is sung by a young, Black female Londoner. From the very start the song parodies "girliness," morphing from a confidential-sounding, childlike beginning into a satisfying full-throated bellow hollered over a chaotic and energetic punk track featuring, unusually, a saxophone. In this chapter I will examine the background of the song, the lyrics, its reception by the press at the time, Poly Styrene's persona, and the song's legacy (see Figure 7.1). Released as a single in September 1977, the song was embedded in the British punk moment as a symbol of the times, yet it has become an anthem of female punk empowerment for successive generations of young women. For female listeners in particular, it has embodied punk as a subculture that was inclusive of *us*, in all our glory of different body shapes and different heritages.

It was first recorded earlier that year at London's Roxy club, one of the city's most iconic punk venues, and released as a live recording on a compilation album, *The Roxy London WC2*, before the stand-alone release of a new version later in the year. Although a subsequent single, "The Day the World Turned Dayglo," was the first chart hit for the band in 1978, it is "Oh Bondage! Up Yours!" that has endured: within its defiance is the definition of the original punk music of 1977. The song uses irony to skewer the role of the British newspapers in their attempt to turn punk's impact into a parody of itself; its lyrics reflect straight back at the tabloids their own attempts to ridicule and disempower punk and hold up only its sexual fetishes to the public. The relationship between punk and the press will be explored in greater detail later in the chapter, using "Oh Bondage!" as an illustration of the different ways that journalists (some of them music journalists) and local press reporters tried to define and control the music that sprang from the punk community in Britain.

Context

Poly was born Marion (later changed by deed poll to Marianne) Elliott to a British mother and a Somali father. She was raised mainly in Brixton, which,

DOI: 10.4324/9781003093206-8

although it was a multicultural area at the time, had enough of a disgruntled white working-class element to make life difficult for her as a biracial child. In an interview with Lucy Toothpaste, she described the difficulties of interracial prejudice and the strategies she tried in order to fit in.[1] For young British women raised in the 1960s and 1970s, Poly's speaking and singing voice struck a chord. We too had spent our childhoods in chilly asphalt school playgrounds, bonding with each other through skipping, chanting, and communicating in our piping voices, in competition with the more assertive noise of the boys. In our co-educational setting, unlike in previous educational eras when we really would have been seen but not heard, girl children were now both seen *and* heard, to the apparent disgruntlement of more conservative sectors of society.

Subversive playground songs have long been part of the vocabulary of little girls.[2] As a child, Poly adapted this playground behavior, trying to attract the attention of TV producers at Granada TV by singing and dancing as she walked past their premises after school. Even at primary school, she challenged the hierarchy through the vehicle of songwriting. The school authorities insisted on the children eating meat at lunchtime, and Poly, a vegetarian from an early age, taught her classmates a subversive song she had written, "Old Mother Johnson, coming this way, who do you think you are?" and wrapped the meat that was served for school dinner in her handkerchief to throw away later.[3] She had already been singled out for praise back then: "I performed in my school assembly and I was told by my headmaster I had a great future."[4] The effective simplicity of her playground chant was a precursor to the melodies that she created as a songwriter in X-Ray Spex: singable tunes that delivered simple and powerful slogan-like messages through melodies that did not require extensive vocal skills or experience to replicate. Poly's compositional technique with the band was simple: "I just work out what I want to say then sing the tune to the others. It's up to us all to take it from there."[5]

Poly's subversive nature is apparent right from the start of the track. She sends up girly niceness with impressive passive aggression, choosing a cloying platitude that many young girls of her generation would have been silenced by, underpinned by a faux-gentle delivery. The sarcastic usage of speech repertoire is identified by musicologist Philip Tagg:

> The sudden application of sing-song motherese intonation, featuring a descending third delivered in a highish register, on to a particular disabyllic in utterances like: "Baby go *bye-byes*!," "Oh-*oh*!," "That's *naughty*!," "You'll be *sor-ry*," "[I] *love you*!," "*Bo-ring*!," (sing-song disyllabics in italics). This use of over-intoned "kiddie-speak" can have effects ranging from humorous and childish to rude and patronising.[6]

Paradoxically, the beginning of the song echoes, both in timbre and delivery, a speech made by Margaret Thatcher to the Conservative Party

Conference in 1975 in which she delineated her scorn for those whose political perspective she disagreed with.[7] Thatcher's sometimes patronizing, sometimes forceful speaking voice was a familiar feature of news and current affairs TV programmes throughout her term in the British Conservative Party, even before she became its leader.[8] It is not unreasonable to think that Poly appropriated the timbre of her spoken introduction to the song from a powerful woman in another field of activity.[9]

Once the song has taken off from its misleadingly "calm" launch pad, the force of the track is continuous. The main melody itself is just as close to the cadences of everyday speech as the intro, but in an entirely different way. It can be muttered, snarled, chanted, yelled, or sung by practically anyone regardless of gender, age, or experience. Its range of pitches is very narrow, and word-rhythms are prioritized over the melody and marked by plenty of repetition. The singing style is declamatory and employs the energy and volume that previous generations of young women might well have used for screaming at bands like the Beatles.[10]

Poly had an altogether different kind of agency: she hollered in order to express and articulate feelings from *within herself* as a response to her position in society, unlike the herd emotions of screaming fans responding to a concert by young male performers, or the male equivalent, a football crowd chanting at a match. In "Oh Bondage! Up Yours!" Poly demonstrates anger as play,[11] thereby gaining agency from the situation where not only her gender but also her race set her aside from her peers. Anger allowed Poly to foreground her inner self as opposed to the preconception people might have of her. "Anger might be thought of as the act of recognizing ethical claims to selfhood, rather than as the demand that that moral code fulfill its promise, a promise never made to racialized women."[12] For many young women, punk enabled them to make considerable progress from the "bedroom lives" of teenage girls described by Simon Frith and Angela McRobbie.[13]

Poly's open-throated, declamatory singing defies previous definitions of Western singing styles offered by cultural commentators such as Roland Barthes[14] and John Shepherd.[15] It is closest in timbre to early hillbilly artists such as Rose Maddox, who had to shout to be heard above the combined din of her large band and the urban noise pollution of dive bars where her band performed in the 1940s. Lyrically, as Laing observes, "Oh Bondage! Up Yours!" is a song where there is a "mismatch" between the subject[s] of the énonciation and the énoncé. The way this happens is that the subject of the énoncé "is presented as contradictory, with verse one presenting as 'masochistic' followed by a 'rebellious' chorus…the lyric worked rather like a classic narrative, with the first sections posing a major enigma—how can these two utterances be reconciled?"[16]

The second verse resolves the song by clarifying that the bondage referred to in the chorus is that of slavish adherence to capitalism; in other words, it actually appears to be *voluntary*. Laing concludes that the lyrics of the song act as a drama between two speakers, and indeed the relationship between the message, its delivery, and Poly herself exemplifies Simon Frith's analysis of the usage of song lyrics: "Songs are more like plays than poems; song words work as speech and speech acts, bearing meaning not just semantically, but also as structures of sound that are direct signs of emotion and marks of character."[17] Poly also references the simplicity and memorability of the advertising jingles that were daily fodder for 1970s children, parodying the industry that wanted to enslave us, to control us with their own seductive messages delivered in musical bites. The use of the vulgar slang term "up yours" made perfect sense to a generation raised on *Carry On* films;[18] there was a certain Sid James–ness to the statement that also underlined the very cockney referencing in its lyrics.

"Oh Bondage!" had actually been written before punk, in 1974 or 1975, according to Poly in an interview with John Robb, and was originally recorded with the rock guitarist Gary Moore; its reworking as a punk song was serendipitous and timely. She felt that the original recording was too sophisticated, virtuoso, and progressive, and wanted a different approach:

> I was into the three-minute instant amphetamine thing: I wanted it quick and fast and short because we were getting quite bored at all the progressive rock things, with the endless guitar solos. I used to go and see that and used to think wouldn't it be better just short and snappy and fast and you don't talk too much to the audience. I'd been around and I'd done my homework before I put X-Ray Spex together.[19]

The X-Ray Spex version, which featured guitarist Jack Stafford, bass player Paul Dean, and drummer Paul Hurding, also showcased the 15-year-old Lora Logic on sax. Using similar harsh timbral techniques to Poly's vocals, the majority of Lora Logic's sax lines counterpoint the simplicity of the sung melody, repeating bluesy motifs and supporting Poly's voice by playing throughout the song, satisfyingly out of tune. After its release, the BBC, having listened only to *their idea* of the song and not the lyrics themselves, banned it from airplay.[20]

The Press Reception

The press response to the song was crucial, because it set the scene for what appeared to be the later ritual sacrifice of Poly, the girl who had spoken out of turn, wanting to be *heard* as well as *seen*. The Svengali-figure Falcon Stuart was an expert at music PR, using the strategy of soliciting reviews in many local papers around the UK as well as in music and trade papers. Yet, one has the sense of Poly being thrown to the wolves, with her youth, beliefs, and a certain naivety about what life should deliver simultaneously protecting her and leaving her open to attack. In this respect, Poly's relationship with Stuart echoed Johnny Rotten's relationship with Malcolm McLaren, a similarly manipulative manager figure.

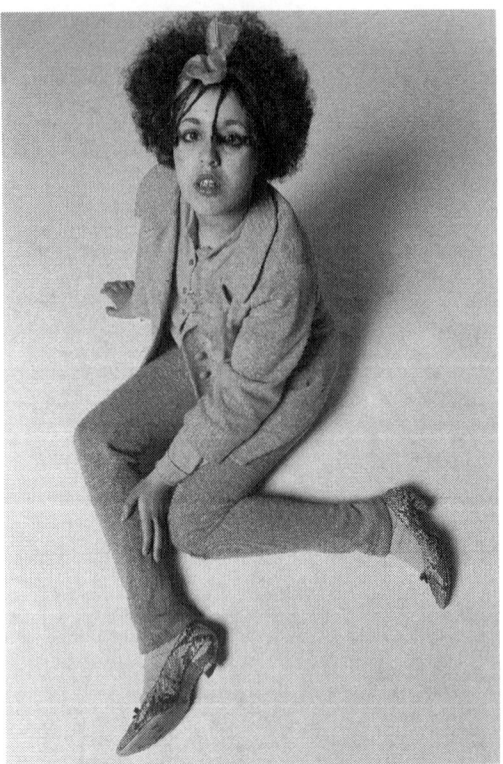

Figure 7.1 Poly Styrene, lead singer with the punk group X-Ray Spex, December 18, 1977. Credit: Trinity Mirror/Mirrorpix/Alamy Stock Photo.

Looking through Stuart's archive at John Moores University, Liverpool, I was appalled at the license taken by reporters and journalists at the time as they tried to fight back against the aggression of punk with aggression of their own. Journalists and reporters insulted the band, the music, and most importantly, Poly; the sheer nastiness and misogyny are deeply saddening. Even positive articles could include a snide sting in their tail. Nonetheless, the descriptions of the record are accurate and illuminating, regardless of the negative opinions of the critics. From the outset, Poly's presence both as a person and as the creative force behind X-Ray Spex was analyzed forensically by the media, who often portrayed her as an upstart in an upstart genre of music. Inevitably, remarks about her persona were interlinked with reviewers' comments about the record itself. En masse, they give a strong indication of the ways in which she was defined in, and defined herself against, a hostile and alien culture. In chronological order, a selection of articles illustrates the rise and fall of the band.

Poly had first used faux naivety as a vehicle for subversive lyrical subject matter in 1976, when she released the song "Silly Billy" on the label GTO. Steve Barrow of the monthly *Black Echoes* was unimpressed, writing disparagingly:

> This is one for all fans of "little girl" reggae. Tuneless vocals, novelty story line, dated rhythm and mariachi type horns don't add up to much.
>
> [On the] Flip [side] is an early 60's type song, faintly reminiscent of groups such as the Crystals etc., but without the power. This side features a nice flute solo that is the most memorable thing about the record.
> Miss.[21]

In contrast, to the female journalist Caroline Coon writing in *Melody Maker*, the message in the lyrics and the way in which the message was delivered were much more important factors. Coon commented that the single had a "ja-rootsy" feel about the fictitious Billy impregnating a girl and denying it, and that it was "one of the most outstanding little reggae quips for months. Keep an eye out for this new, talented singer."

The idea of Poly's lyrics as being purely "novelty" or comedy was used as a defensive listening strategy by other male reviewers later when "Oh Bondage! Up Yours!" was released. The sarcasm in her lyrics and the way in which they were delivered completely bypassed many of these reviewers, who appeared to consider themselves a cut above the "silly girl" they were listening to. Some journalists hedged their bets, not sure whether to support or criticize the single, exemplified by this review of the track in *Sounds*, a representative of the "inky" music press, in October 1977:

> The saxophone is a dead giveaway on this, of course. Who else can it be but X-Ray Spex with a classic little toon [sic] that brought tears of nostalgia for the early days of the Roxy Club to my eyes. Delivered with the subtlety and tact of a lawnmower at a flower arranging exhibition, this plea for freedom from male domination, I think, is remarkable more for its musical immediacy than its lyrical content. But I don't care, I love it. "Some people say little girls should be seen but not heard" says Poly Styrene in a baby-doll voice at the start of the record. X-Ray Spex should be seen and heard.[22]

The remark about the lawnmower is notable; Poly often talked about using the sounds of everyday commodities on future recordings. Asked in a radio interview on a visit to EMI how she saw her music developing, she remarked, "maybe to the sound of a hoover,"[23] and in an interview with *Trick* magazine in 1977 she said, "If I wanted to put a washing machine on it I would."[24]

The sheer gutsiness of including a saxophone in a punk lineup was extraordinary in itself: Lora was exceptionally brave to apply to play in the first lineup of the band, and Poly was brave to take her. As an instrument it referenced much more mainstream styles of pop music, and indeed this led to retro-spective comparisons to the glam rock band Roxy Music.[25] Poly valued the sax as part of the sonic signature of the band, highlighting its importance as a lead instrument in an interview with *Melody Maker*'s Ian Birch: "The sax makes all the difference. Also, it's good to use it as a lead instrument. The lead guitar is a bit less interesting."[26] This was appreciated by at least one reviewer:

> Never thought a sax would work with a punk group—remember those dreary combos with intellectual jazz pretensions? In this group its use is sheer genius and matches Poly Styrene's high, but strong voice perfectly. A very competent and individual group amongst the new wave.[27]

and hated by Bob Edmands from *New Musical Express*:

> Just the sort of person suburban studs would like to invite to their wife-swapping parties. As for her vocals, they're strident without getting hys-terical, and as a bizarre counter-point, a truly weird woodwind player hams along beside her.[28]

Other journalists resorted to sting-in-the-tail reviewing, thereby hedging their bets on the future of the single and the band, as exemplified here by Philip Hall in the *Record Mirror* "Singles of the Week" section:

> Yet another new wave classic. This time fun is the essential factor coupled with incredible originality. Poly Styrene's high-pitched "scream" has been captured effectively by the "live" production which makes it sound as though she's sitting in your speaker. The screeching sax adds the final touch of weirdness to what is destined to be the anthem of sad-masochists [sic] everywhere.[29]

Some of the later reviews were much savvier, such as this one from local paper *The Redditch Indicator*:

> Now this is new wave proper. Poly Styrene rants against male dominance in her charming cockney slur, above a backing that keeps threatening to dissolve into total psychotic disorder and featuring an utterly crazy saxo-phone sound. Bizarre but wonderful.[30]

Lora Logic's early breakaway from the band was triggered by a media report that focused on Lora rather than Poly.[31] This alone illustrates the potentially destructive power of the pop music press, who as we have seen, tore at the band and its first release. Logic's replacement, Glyn John fared a little better:

> This band is likely to be grouped under the collective heading of "new wave" but its sound is in fact totally unique, with effervescent vocalist

Poly Styrene's piercing wails contracting [sic] sharply with the mellow sax work of Glyn John. Unusual and captivating music.[32]

The unpleasantly patronizing Bob Hart in the *Sun* thought it amusing to allude to Poly's braces in an article entitled "Poly is Bracing Herself for Hits":

Poly Styrene is a sturdy little 19-year-old who has become a Punk rock cult figure for the bitter little songs she sings through the rather cumbersome braces on her teeth.
    She is the lead singer and songwriter with X-Ray Specs [sic], and one of the most distinctive figures on the British Punk scene.
    She is fascinated with the thoroughly Punk topics of bondage and boredom. They crop up in her songs.[33]

Certain journalists appeared to be cheerleading for her before resorting to the aforementioned sting in the tail, as illustrated by the journalist Thompson Prentice of the *Daily Mail*:

There is little in punk music that is to my liking, but Poly Styrene's message—warning, if you like—sums up the real malaise among today's teenagers—confusion... .
    She admits that she is still confused herself, but what may lead to her salvation, she feels, is that she *recognizes* it... .
    Her lyrics are blunt, harsh and astonishingly urgent. For people like Poly Styrene, those are the preferable qualities today... .
    Poly is reluctant to reveal her real name. "It would spoil the fun if I did," she says. "besides, my real name is a bit silly anyway."
    Her real name is Marion.[34]

He continues to predict that just like teddy-boys and flower children, Poly will grow up to be "normal," and concludes: "Poor, unpretty Poly. How many of us want to be like her? The point we're left to ponder is that she doesn't want to be like us, either." Perhaps the clumsiest attempt to meet Poly halfway was this interview, published in *New York Rocker*, in which Michael Porteus tries to transcribe her Cockney accent verbatim, thus destroying the message of the interview, possibly deliberately:

I wrote "Oh Bondage Up Yours" afta a Pistols gig last year. There were these girls that useta chain 'emselves together wif 'andcuffs and things, about ten of 'em. But I dinnit write it bout them. I just used that kinda bondage theme to express repression. When people, see these people wearing bondage they think they're for bondage- but they're not. 'Cos by wearin' it or singin' about it, ya against it. Ya don't pretend that ya not chained up and everythink. Ya admit ya repressed.[35]

The journalist later observes nastily, reiterating the obsession with Poly's braces: "Even her teeth are in bondage."[36]

Despite the apparent attempts by some reviewers to influence the band's fortunes, the track had a tremendous resonance in parts of the US, where the poppy sounds of X-Ray Spex introduced American audiences to punk music that was more appealing than the darker, thrashy, male-fronted singles that emerged from the subculture. The journalist Alan Rubenfeld observed that the band (whose single was played repeatedly at a 24-hour "New Wave" marathon in Michigan)

> helped [to] demonstrate to the uninitiated that the New Wave is a lot more than ugly, screaming people wearing safety pins in their cheeks.
>
> In fact the Spec's [sic] single "Oh Bondage, Up Yours," was undoubtedly the most requested song of the marathon. Listener response was so overwhelming that several DJ's had to disconnect their request lines in order to program their shows.[37]

The death knell of the band was forecast, if not created, by the press. Tim Lott at *Record Mirror*, who seemed to be pursuing a personal vendetta against the band,[38] led the backlash:

> Propped by Laura's divine sax squeal, loveable image and in-a-dream eyelids, it was incredibly peculiar and so exciting.
>
> Now Laura's in front of a blackboard and X-Ray Spex got their backs to the wall. Glyn John is a bad sax player. Sure, Laura was probably technically not that hot but she made the right noises. John is orthodox, old, and hits a lot of very, very bum notes. He ruined "O Bondage Up Yours" and it takes a lot to ruin that "song".... Poly's mind might still be like a plastic bag and the world might still have turned dayglow. But Laura's missing and half the magic with her.
>
> X-ams have subtracted the X-factor, So who's gonna argue now about the evils of academia?

Punk music itself challenged traditional rock criticism and demanded a new approach to listening, as Holly Kruse notes (2002: 134–55). The ferocious engagement of critics with this track attests to the strength of feeling engendered by a simple song on a simple record. Poly, as a female punk artist, disrupted what Kembrew MacLeod describes as "1960s authenticist ideology" (2002: 107), which male rock writers used to approve or critique the music they listened to.

Poly in Person

Much has been written about the relationship with Jamaican music and the appropriation of reggae styles by white male punk bands such as the Clash,[39] but little about the Black women who were pioneering presences within punk rock itself.[40] Poly Styrene, Rhoda Dakar, and Pauline Black were all living out and living through social and political changes that made life deeply uncomfortable for young Black people in Britain. Musically they were all very different, but they were all significant figures in the original London punk subculture. Like Rhoda and Pauline, Poly Styrene defied the white male aura of punk. Rather than being White, wan, spiky haired, aggressive, and slender, she was of dual heritage, with curly hair, normal proportions for a woman of her age, and a communicative personality both on- and offstage. She was defined by what she did as much as by the way she looked. As Lucy O'Brien noted, in terms of body size and clothing, for most women in the subculture, "Punk was a place where women felt free to express difference."[41] Poly situated herself in a no-man's-land midway between art and punk, acknowledging the lack of barriers between cultural activities in the marginal world of young people in the 1970s: "We were like art punks. If it hadn't been for Beaufort Market, and me being there doing all the fashion stuff, I wouldn't have started playing live half as fast."[42] Through her active example of transcending the white male aura of punk, Poly gave other girls permission to participate in the punk subculture.[43]

Other pop bands in the British charts at the time featured women who demonstrated much more traditional performances of womanhood: the manufactured pop group Brotherhood of Man's twee song "Save All Your Kisses for Me," which won the 1976 Eurovision Song Contest in the Netherlands;[44] Julie Covington's "Don't Cry for Me Argentina" in 1977; and in 1978, Kate Bush's "Wuthering Heights." Bush was a rare British example of a woman rock *songwriter*, but her record label used her youth to exploit her gamine sexuality relentlessly at this time when many women performers were actively resisting the focus on the way they looked rather than the way they sounded.[45] Poly's feisty pop persona had much in common with the spirited bass-playing chart artist Suzi Quatro, who was also a hollerer; however, Suzi was a mouthpiece for the songs of the male songwriting team of Nicky Chinn and Mike Chapman (and was also an ardent capitalist).

In common with fellow punk front woman Siouxsie, Poly had a powerful drive, but unlike Siouxsie her visual image was not designed to intimidate. She possessed a similar girly charm to that of the American girl groups (cited as an influence), but her identity was strongly British and her songs weren't romance-focused. To the forefront of Poly's songwriting was her message: This is what it feels like to be a young *person* at this time in history. This is what people of my culture see, this is what we hear, and this is what we feel. She simultaneously voiced the idealism and disillusionment of a generation who had been brought up with the nostalgic post-WWII "Englishness" idealized by Enoch Powell, Eric Clapton, and David Bowie (who eventually became the catalysts for the Rock Against Racism movement) and the contrasting narrative of pop groups like Blue Mink, whose 1969 single "Melting Pot" envisaged a future where different races blended to such an extent that racism was obsolete, despite some rather clunky lyrics written by the white male writing team, with the world populated by "coffee-colored people by the score."[46]

Our generation wanted to be liberated from the weighty postwar expectations of our parents. Consumerism had become a new religion, and the future appeared to be bleak: ours was a world of detergent swans and artificial mashed potato. Poly's statement that she "chose the name Poly Styrene because it's a lightweight disposable product" made perfect sense.[47] She appeared to have a direct link to the energy of childhood, the defiance, strong will, and challenging behavior that must have made her a great companion in the playground. It was this kind of lived authenticity that survived Falcon Stuart's reported attempts to control and isolate her. An article in 1978 in *Cosmopolitan* magazine by Yvonne Roberts documented Poly's sources of inspiration, followed by the conundrum faced by a dual-heritage artist creating pop music at the time:

> Poly is no safety-pin addict. She founded the group, acquired a backer, orchestrates rehearsals in an empty room above a furniture store—and writes the words and music too.
>
> "A lot of punk lyrics have a single phrase or a good line but the rest isn't worked out," she says. "I start with an idea—it might come from a word on a tin of Savlon—and build on it. It may take a few hours, it may take a couple of months but I think the words are important. I couldn't sing someone else's words, just like a musician couldn't play someone else's instrument…. Everyone does something for money nowadays. No-one does anything for *interest*."
>
> At school, Poly says, she did try being black, then white, then she realised that, as she was a nobody, she might as well be herself. "You see what I mean?"[48]

The Legacy of the Song

Punk is sometimes defined as white man's music,[49] and although some of it was recuperated in the early 1980s by skinheads, Poly was a pioneer of the strong "anyone can do it" impetus behind the social movement. As a symbol of positive, articulate, and powerful girlhood/womanhood she was extraordinary. Where the tabloid newspapers in the UK focused on the sexualized side of female punks' appearance, Poly reflected punk's arty side, the DIY, home-made, and hence *empowered* side. While Vivienne Westwood was making well-crafted clothing that parodied furtive British sex fetishes and that had excited moral panic in the media, Poly approached punk from an entirely different direction, resisting the Westwood and McLaren machine as much as the contemporary mainstream.

Poly's authenticity as an artist incorporated the irony of early punk, creating music under the umbrella of punk fulfilling a folk definition of authenticity that "came about not only because of a musical experience, but also because of a cultural need."[50] Writing on Woody Guthrie, Willhardt continues: "It is personal history and personal affect which combine to authenticate music."[51] Allan Moore, inspired by Gilbert and Pearson's definition of authentic rock whereby the singer's "fundamental role is to *represent* the culture from which he [sic] comes,"[52] defines authenticity as the way that artists speak the truth of their own situation, that they speak the truth of the situation of (absent) others; and that they speak the truth of their own culture, thereby representing (present) others.[53]

Perhaps Moore's later comment encapsulates the impossibility of divorcing individual emotional reactions to music from its manipulative effects: "A seemingly artificial text may also be an authentic expression of true life experiences in an artificial society."[54] The early activity of punk intersected neatly with the Situationist philosophy of Guy Debord, and was articulated by its ethos. Nils Stevenson, the manager of Siouxsie and the Banshees, perfectly summarizes their core beliefs:

> They felt that in what they dubbed the Society of the Spectacle people had turned into consumers of mediated events, mediated ideas and mediated actions, and that their role was to challenge that enforced passivity by breaking down the barriers between direct and mediated experience. The artist depicting situations and feelings was merely colluding with the forces that created the Society of the Spectacle. The role of the artist, as they saw it, was to create challenging situations.[55]

Poly's role as a mediator and challenger of contemporary consumer culture was exhausting for her, and exhaustive. In the film *She's a Punk Rocker* (2010), she underlines the role of the press in promoting spitting at concerts, shrugging it off with a remark about her plastic clothes being practical (the spit is easy to clean off), and in the 2021 film *I'm a Cliché* we see just how damaging her life in the music industry was for her in her life after punk. Yet young women saw themselves reflected in the mirror she held up to them; she was the personification of the future they wanted, the embodiment of their social, political, and cultural desires. As Lauraine Leblanc observes, by "depicting herself as both an agent of and resister to her submission, she created a parody of both positions, juxtaposing them powerfully against each other."[56]

"Oh Bondage! Up Yours!" was our battle hymn, an articulation of punk that spoke to us and included us; the band performed the song as part of their set at the 1978 Rock Against Racism concert at Victoria Park in Hackney, London, to more than 80,000 people, with Poly as a significant female presence on the stage. She was a universal defiant schoolkid, grown up and out there battling against the machinations of not just the music industry but also the entrenched capitalism within it that assumes that fame and money will always win over principle and moral authority. And as she herself noted: "Journalists make you what *they* want you to be. They never really write about you, they write about *themselves*, just using you."[57] It is difficult to read the vitriolic reviews of the single and Poly herself, and all the more remarkable that she managed to achieve any sort of life. In conversation with the writer Lucy O'Brien at the launch of her and Zoë Howe's book *Dayglo* at Rough Trade East in 2019, Poly's daughter Celeste Bell said that Poly's love of bright colors was a personal antidote to the darkness that she perceived around her.

X-Ray Spex broke up in 1979 after Poly joined the Hare Krishna movement. She continued to make art and music, and her final album, *Generation Indigo*, was made with the producer Youth (formerly of Killing Joke) in 2011. She exhibited her artwork alongside fellow punk Gaye Black from the Adverts, also now an artist, and died of cancer in 2011. Her funeral was attended by members of punk bands, London friends, her family, members of the Hare Krishna religion, and a small dog, and was conducted by a Catholic priest. It was a very Poly occasion.

The legacy of the song continues to this day. The punk label Damaged Goods released the Shadracks homage to the original single (complete with the original B side, "I Am a Cliché") in 2018,[58] and Gina Birch (of the Raincoats) and I, co-directors of the 2018 documentary *Stories from the She-Punks: music with a different agenda*, use the song to introduce and close the film. The song was covered spontaneously at a screening of a work in progress at the British Library to mark the 40th anniversary of punk.[59] It has also been covered by the bands Armitage Shanks,[60] Free Kitten,[61] the Ukulele Orchestra of Great Britain,[62] and also by musician and cultural commentator John Robb's band Goldblade on the day Poly died.[63] To use the words of Kathleen Hanna, lead singer of the American feminist punk band Bikini Kill:

> Poly lit the way for me as a female singer who wanted to sing about ideas. She taught me, by example, that fame was less the goal than something to back away from when it started to invade your core. Her lyrics influenced EVERYONE I KNOW WHO MAKES MUSIC.[64]

Writing this chapter has triggered the inevitable irony of being duped by Marx's "commodity fetishism"[65] and simultaneously being won over by the power and charm of a manufactured artifact, regardless of the political and cultural power ascribed to it. In a moment of sublime irony, the 1979 Arena documentary *Who Is Poly Styrene?* features a voiceover during Poly's visit to the EMI factory where the single was being mass-produced: "Plastics play an essential role in reproducing sound and vision, and in recording it too."

Notes

1 C. Bell and Z. Howe, *Dayglo: the Poly Styrene Story* (London and New York: Omnibus, 2019), 26.
2 See for instance, Opie, I., and Opie, P. *The Lore and Language of Schoolchildren*, (New York: NYRB Classics, 2001); and V. Thorpe, "Subversive Rhymes are Child's Play," *The Observer*, December 12, 2007.

3 Poly, Styrene, "Interview with author." 2010.

4 John Robb, "Episode 7." *The John Robb Tapes*, podcast. July 12, 2019.

5 Unattributed, "'It's Great Fun Being In A Band', A Jackie Pop Special On X-Ray Spex." *Jackie* 761 (August 5, 1978): 13.

6 P. Tagg, *Music's Meanings: A modern musicology for non-musos* (Larchmont and Huddersfield: The Mass Media Music Scholar's Press, 2013), 368.

7 www.youtube.com/watch?v=cVje4C1nTt0

8 Thatcher later had elocution lessons to pull her voice into a more gentle and persuasive timbre, not wishing to sound like a "strident female." Wendy Webster, *Not a Man to Match Her: The marketing of a Prime Minister* (London: The Women's Press, 1990).

9 Later, Poly voted for the Labor Party, but she was originally impressed by Thatcher's achievements as a specifically *female* MP, because Poly was a natural entrepreneur whose ambitions were echoed to an extent by Thatcher's enterprise culture; Poly had been a fashion designer and a market trader alongside her musical career. Thatcher had visited Poly's school when she was minister for education, and Poly was photographed sitting in the chair she'd just vacated. This had a strong impact on Poly, who appreciated Thatcher's later work with Gorbachev that led to the ending of the Cold War era. Poly Styrene, "Conversation with author," interview conducted by Helen Reddington, August 27, 2000.

10 Dave Laing, *One Chord Wonders: Power and meaning in punk rock* (Oakland: PM Press, 2015), 73–4

11 Jayna Brown, "'Brown Girl in the Ring': Poly Styrene, Annabella Lwin, and the Politics of Anger," *Journal of Popular Music Studies* 23, no. 4 (2011): 459.

12 Ibid., 458.

13 Simon Frith, and Angela McRobbie, "Rock and Sexuality," *Screen Education* 29 (1978).

14 Roland Barthes, *Image, Music, Text* (London: Fontana, 1977).

15 John Shepherd, *Music As Social Text* (London: Polity, 1991).

16 D. Laing, *One Chord Wonders: Power and meaning in punk rock* (Oakland: PM Press, 2015), 86.

17 Simon Frith, *Why Do Songs Have Words?* In *Lost in Music*, ed. A. Levine White. (London: Routledge, 1987), 97.

18 The *Carry On* films are a British institution of (mainly) the 1960s. They are smutty, boisterous, set in familiar British settings (campsites, hospitals), and have a cast of stereotypes often played by the same actors. Each one was prefixed by "Carry On...," for instance, *Carry On Cabbie, Carry On Doctor*, and so on.

19 John Robb, "Episode 7." *The John Robb Tapes*, podcast. July 12, 2019.

20 It was not unusual for the BBC to censor pop records, sometimes claiming political reasons (as they had with Paul McCartney's "Give Ireland Back to the Irish" in 1972), but more often for "moral" reasons (for example, Donna Summer's "Love to Love You, Baby" in 1975 and Jane Birkin's "Je t'Aime" in 1976). Martin Cloonan notes that the lack of sexual content in punk lyrics meant that there was little *overt* censorship of the genre itself, but in the case of the Stranglers' "Peaches," Buzzcocks' "Orgasm Addict," and Ivor Biggun's "Winker's Song," "the main censorship that punk suffered was being marginalized and played only on the 'specialist' weekend and evening programmes." M. Cloonan *Banned! Censorship of Popular Music in Britain: 1967–92* (Aldershot: Arena/Ashgate, 1996), 113).

21 Steve Barrow, "Mari Elliott: Silly Billy," *Black Echoes*.

22 Unattributed, "NOT VERY FAR BEHIND SINGLES OF THE WEEK," *Sounds*, October 14, 1977.

23 Alan Yentob, dir. *Who is Poly Styrene?* (London: BBC, 1979.)

24 Unattributed, *Trick*, December 1977.

25 NME, *NME Book of Modern Music* (London: NME, 1978), 62. Musically, the rich cacophony of X-Ray Spex was redolent of a garageland Roxy Music, though their series of singles was produced by Falcon Stuart with a somewhat unsavoury heavy metal frame of reference.

26 Ian Birch, "On Spex." *Melody Maker*, August 20, 1977, 32.

27 Unattributed. *Sennet*, November 23, 1977.

28 Bob Edmands, "Singles Raises a Cheer for BEARDS AND BONDAGE!" *New Musical Express*, October 22 1977, 27.

29 Tim Lott, "Tell Laura I Love Her X Ray Spex." *Record Mirror*, October 1, 1977.

30 Unattributed, *The Redditch Indicator*, November 4, 1977.

31 Helen Reddington, *The Lost Women of Rock Music: Female musicians of the punk era* (Sheffield: Equinox, 2012), 55.

32 Unattributed, *Worksop Guardian*, November 25, 1977.

33 Bob Hart, "Pop Shop," *The Sun*, November 25, 1977, 23.

34 Thompson Prentice, "The Most Unlikely Face of a Budding superstar," *Daily Mail*, October 29, 1977, 7.

35 Michael Porteus, "Looking Through X-Ray Spex," *New York Rocker*.

36 The obsession with Poly's braces was extraordinary. In the Arena documentary Poly visits the EMI records factory, where she is asked by a woman packing LPs: "Are your teeth real? Only on telly you look as though you've got steel teeth. Nice." The fact that the metal-toothed James Bond villain Jaws first appears in 1977 in the film *The Spy Who Loved Me* may have something to do with the focus on Poly's dental braces by so many interviewers and reviewers.

37 Alan Rubenfeld, "WCBN Catches New Wave," *Michigan Daily*, February 3, 1978.

38 See Unattributed, "NOT VERY FAR BEHIND SINGLES OF THE WEEK," 40 for a scathing live review, for instance.

39 D. Hebdige, *Subculture: the meaning of style* (London and New York: Routledge, 1979).

40 Paul Gilroy, *There Ain't No Black in the Union* Jack (London and New York: Routledge, 1992).

41 L. O'Brien, "The Woman Punk Made Me," in. *Punk Rock: So What?* ed. R. Sabin (London and New York: Routledge, 1999), 191

42 Poly Styrene, "Poly Styrene Interview," interview conducted by A. Ogg. *Punk and Post-Punk* 2, no.2 (2013): 200.

43 Annabella Lwin of the band Bow Wow Wow was one of the earliest artists to be directly influenced by Poly. See Brown, "Brown Girl in the Ring."

44 The contrast between the lyrical naivety of this and other Eurovision songs and what was happening politically at the time in the region is noted somewhat lightheartedly in Chris West's book: Chris West, *Eurovision: A history of modern Europe through the world's greatest song contest* (London: Melville House, 2017).

45 Mavis Bayton's book *Frock Rock* examines this in greater detail than the author has space for here: Mavis Bayton, *Frock Rock: Women Performing Popular Music* (Oxford and New York: Oxford University Press, 1998).

46 See www.discogs.com/Blue-Mink-Melting-Pot/master/237588. Ironically this song was written by Roger Cook and Roger Greenaway, two white men whose lyrical vocabulary reflects the casual racism of the time.

47 Yentob, dir. *Who is Poly Styrene?*
48 Yvonne Roberts, "Can We Dispose of Poly Styrene? Or is the High priestess of 'punk built to last?" *Cosmopolitan*, February 1978.
49 R. Sabin, *Punk Rock: So What?* (London and New York: Routledge, 1999).
50 M. Willhardt, "Available rebels and folk authenticities: Michelle Shocked and Billy Bragg," in *The Resisting Muse: Popular Music and Social Protest*, ed. L. Peddie (London and New York: Routledge, 2006), 31.
51 Ibid., 32.
52 J. Gilbert. and E. Pearson, *Discographies: dance music, culture and the politics of Sound* (-London and New York: Routledge, 1999), 164–5.
53 Allan Moore, *Authenticity as Authentication* Popular Music Volume 21/2 (Cambridge: Cambridge University Press, 2002), 209.
54 J. Fornas, *Cultural Theory and Late Modernity* (London: Sage, 1995); paraphrased in Moore, *Authenticity as Authentication*, 220.
55 N. Stevenson, *Vacant: A diary of the punk years 1976–79* (London: Thames and Hudson, 1999), 8.
56 L. Leblanc, *Pretty in Punk: Girls' Gender Resistance in a Boy's Subculture* (New Jersey: Rutgers University Press, 1999), 45–6.
57 Unattributed article, Falcon Stuart's archive, University of Liverpool
58 https://damagedgoods.co.uk/discography/oh-bondage-up-yours/
59 www.youtube.com/watch?v=5NrFckg-WAA, also accompanied by Tessa Politt of the Slits and Jane Woodgate of the Modettes on vocals, Zoe Howe drumming on a cardboard box, Kat Five from Feral Five on bass guitar, and Karina Townsend of Mike Flowers Pop on tenor sax.
60 Armitage Shanks Sing And Play Twenty Punk Hits Of The Seventies - 1995 - Vinyl Japan - Cat No ASKLP-51.
61 Free Kitten 1992 Sympathy of the Record Industry –SFTRI 256
62 www.youtube.com/watch?v=SKvNiOnswZ0&t=3s
63 www.youtube.com/watch?v=7U01IK6Envo
64 KathleenHanna.Com, "Poly Styrene." *KathleenHanna*, April 26, 2011.
65 T. Bloomfield, "*Resisting Songs: Negative Dialectics in Pop,*" *Popular Music* 12, no. 1 (1993): 13–31.

References

Barthes, R. *Image, Music, Text*. London: Fontana, 1977.
Bayton, Mavis. *Frock Rock: Women Performing Popular Music*. Oxford and New York: Oxford University Press, 1998.
Bell, C. and Howe, Z. *Dayglo: the Poly Styrene Story*. London and New York: Omnibus, 2019.
Bloomfield, T. "*Resisting Songs: Negative Dialectics in Pop.*" *Popular Music* 12, no. 1 (1993): 13–31.
Brown, Jayna. "'Brown Girl in the Ring': Poly Styrene, Annabella Lwin, and the Politics of Anger." *Journal of Popular Music Studies* 23, no. 4 (2011): 455–78.
Cloonan, M. *Banned! Censorship of Popular Music in Britain: 1967–92*. Aldershot: Arena/Ashgate, 1996.
Fornas, J. *Cultural Theory and Late Modernity*. London: Sage, 1995.
Frith, Simon. *Why Do Songs Have Words?* In *Lost in Music*, edited by A. Levine White. London: Routledge, 1987.

Frith, Simon and Angela McRobbie. "Rock and Sexuality" *Screen Education* 29 (1978): 3–19.

Gilroy, Paul. *There Ain't No Black in the Union* Jack. London and New York: Routledge, 1992.

Gilbert, J. and E. Pearson. *Discographies: dance music, culture and the politics of Sound.* London and New York: Routledge, 1999.

Harris, Kenneth. *Thatcher.* London: Wiedenfeld and Nicholson, 1998.

Hebdige, D. *Subculture: the meaning of style.* London and New York: Routledge, 1979.

Kruse, Holly. "Abandoning the absolute: transcendence and gender in popular music discourse" in Steve Jones, *Pop Music and the Press.* Philadelphia: Temple Music Press, 2002.

Laing, Dave. *One Chord Wonders: Power and meaning in punk rock.* Oakland: PM Press, 2015.

Leblanc, L. *Pretty in Punk: Girls' Gender Resistance in a Boy's Subculture.* New Jersey: Rutgers University Press, 1999.

Levine White, A. ed. *Lost in Music.* London: Routledge, 1987.

Moore, Allan. *Authenticity as Authentication* Popular Music Volume 21/2. Cambridge: Cambridge University Press, 2002.

NME. *NME Book of Modern Music.* London: NME, 1978, 62.

O'Brien, L. "The Woman Punk Made Me." In. *Punk Rock: So What?* edited by R. Sabin, 186–98. London and New York: Routledge, 1999.

Opie, I. and Opie, P. *The Lore and Language of Schoolchildren.* New York: NYRB Classics, 2001.

Peddie, I., ed. *The Resisting Muse: Popular Music and Social Protest.* London and New York: Routledge, 2006.

Reddington, Helen. *The Lost Women of Rock Music: Female musicians of the punk era.* Sheffield: Equinox, 2012.

Sabin, R. *Punk Rock: So What?* London and New York: Routledge, 1999.

Shepherd, John. *Music As Social Text.* London: Polity, 1991.

Stevenson, N. *Vacant: A diary of the punk years 1976–79.* London: Thames and Hudson, 1999.

Styrene, Poly. "Conversation with author," interview conducted by Helen Reddington. August, 27, 2000.

Styrene, Poly. "Interview with author," interview conducted by Helen Reddington. 2010

Styrene, Poly. "Poly Styrene Interview," interview conducted by A. Ogg *Punk and Post-Punk* 2, no. 2 (2013): 197–204.

Tagg, P. *Music's Meanings: A modern musicology for non-musos.* Larchmont and Huddersfield: The Mass Media Music Scholar's Press, 2013.

Webster, Wendy. *Not a Man to Match Her: The marketing of a Prime Minister.* London: The Women's Press, 1990.

West, Chris. *Eurovision: A history of modern Europe through the world's greatest song contest.* London: Melville House, 2017.

Willhardt, M. "Available rebels and folk authenticities: Michelle Shocked and Billy Bragg." In *The Resisting Muse: Popular Music and Social Protest*, edited by L. Peddie. London and New York: Routledge, 2006.

Web

KathleenHanna.Com. "Poly Styrene." *KathleenHanna*, April 26, 2011. www.kathleenhanna.com/poly-styrene/

Robb, John. "Episode 7." *The John Robb Tapes*, podcast. July 12, 2019. https://thejo hnrobbtapes.podbean.com/e/episode-seven-poly-styrene/

Video and Film

Ahsworth, Zillah, dir. *She's a Punk Rocker*. London: She Rocks Punk, 2020. www.yout ube.com/watch?v=LHoJHMV0ybA
Sng, Paul and Celeste Bell, dirs. *I'm a Cliché*. London: Modern Films, 2021. www.modernfilms.com/polystyrene
Thatcher, Margaret. "Free Society," speech to the 1975 Conservative Conference, London, October 10, 1975. www.youtube.com/watch?v=cVje4C1nTt0
Yentob, Alan, dir. *Who is Poly Styrene?* London: BBC, 1979.

Articles

These articles form part of Falcon Stuart's archive at The University of Liverpool; some details are missing because many of them are simple press clippings.
Barrow, Steve. "Mari Elliott: Silly Billy." *Black Echoes*.
Birch, Ian. "On Spex." *Melody Maker*, August 20, 1977, 32.
Coon, Caroline. *Melody Maker*, April 24, 1976, 3.
Edmands, Bob. "Singles Raises a Cheer for BEARDS AND BONDAGE!" *New Musical Express*, October 22, 1977, 27.
Hall, Philip. "Poly Fills Your Life With Fun." *Record Mirror*, October 22, 1977
Hart, Bob. "Pop Shop." *The Sun*, November 25, 1977, 23.
Lott, Tim. "Tell Laura I Love Her X Ray Spex." *Record Mirror*, October 1, 1977.
Prentice, Thompson. "The Most Unlikely Face of a Budding superstar." *Daily Mail*, October 29, 1977, 7.
Porteus, Michael. "Looking Through X-Ray Spex." *New York Rocker*.
Roberts, Yvonne. "Can We Dispose of Poly Styrene? Or is the High priestess of `punk built to last?" *Cosmopolitan*, February 1978.
Rubenfeld, Alan. "WCBN Catches New Wave." *Michigan Daily*, February 3, 1978.
Thorpe, V. "Subversive Rhymes are Child's Play," *The Observer*, December 12, 2007.
Unattributed. "Review of Roxy Live album." *Kentish Times*, July 28, 1977.
Unattributed. *Radio and Record News*, October 14, 1977.
Unattributed. "NOT VERY FAR BEHIND SINGLES OF THE WEEK." *Sounds*, October 14, 1977.
Unattributed. *The Redditch Indicator*, November 4, 1977.
Unattributed. *Sennet*, November 23, 1977.
Unattributed. *Worksop Guardian*, November 25, 1977.
Unattributed. *Trick*, December 1977.
Unattributed. "'It's Great Fun Being In A Band', A Jackie Pop Special On X-Ray Spex." *Jackie* 761 (August 5, 1978): 13.

8 Prince—"When You Were Mine" (1980)

Scott Poulson-Bryant

I

When I was a college freshman, I spent two semesters as a DJ, spinning records in a hot, cramped, and tiny booth at WBRU's small AM station. The first record I played in the debut show of my very short career as a DJ was Prince's "When You Were Mine," the second track on his third album, 1980's *Dirty Mind* (see Figure 8.1). This was in 1985, a few months after the release of *Purple Rain*—the film and its hit soundtrack—launched Prince from respected, hitmaking artist to globally chart-topping, crossover superstar, a few months after I'd experienced the singularly teenage sensation of loss that happens when, by some trick of marketing, production, or songwriting, "your" favorite artist becomes the world's favorite artist. This is, often, an experience specific to a particular kind of teenager: the kind of too-cool-for-school teen who eschews the mainstream and wields their taste in underground hipness as a badge of pride, or on the flip side, the kind of not-so-cool teenager who shields himself from scrutiny with music—mainstream or otherwise—that he believes speaks to him, echoing his deepest thoughts, while also speaking for him.

I was the latter kind of teen, in high school at least. And even as college meant a new terrain upon which to stride more confidently, music remained one of the main ways I articulated myself in the world. So, even as Prince was no longer just the falsetto-singing oddball who'd managed to court audiences as the post-disco R&B seducer of "I Wanna Be Your Lover" before he mutated into an ethereal, Edwardian-frocked, post-new wave one-man funk band, it was important for me to endorse the Prince who'd most deeply spoken to me and echoed my deepest inchoate thoughts: the rebel, the mysterious, sexually suspect Prince of *Dirty Mind* (1980) and *Controversy* (1981). Even though *Purple Rain* had just ended its run at number one on the *Billboard* chart (and would stay on the chart for another 80 weeks or so), "When You Were Mine"—my favorite Prince song, back in 1985 and today—introduced my radio show. This was my rebellious act. It was a message of sorts, an 18-year-old's declaration of musical independence: I meant to express to the world—or, at least, the handful of listeners the small AM station attracted—that Prince had, indeed, at one point, alone in the suburbs, been mine.

DOI: 10.4324/9781003093206-9

When I interviewed Prince in 1991, I told him that story, sitting in a small candlelit studio in his Paisley Park recording complex after listening to his upcoming *Diamonds and Pearls* album.[1] He gave me a coy smile and nodded. At the time I believed that nod was less about approval and more about a shared understanding of what music did for teenagers, cool ones and not-so-cool ones.

I open here with this personal anecdote about my own relationship to Prince because thinking about the history of a pop song is also an act, I believe, of thinking about the history of the pop song's critics and listeners, the ones who may not (in the strictest sense) give the song life, but do, nonetheless, participate in its living. Thinking about (and writing about) the history of a pop song also means, in many cases, that there isn't a deep and formal body of literature to access in order to bolster claims or structure argument. Though there is a body of literature about Prince, which has grown rapidly in the wake of his unexpected death in 2016, the song "When You Were Mine"—described as "a cult favorite among knowledgeable Prince fans" in the original liner notes of his 1993 greatest hits package *The Hits/The B-Sides*[2]—has not maintained much of a presence within it. Perusing several reviews of the *Dirty Mind* album from the year of its release, "When You Were Mine" is often not even discussed as part of the critical analysis. More often than not, attention at the time was paid to the album's more salacious offerings, including "Sister" (the song in which Prince insists, "Incest is everything it's said to be"), only considered as just another example of the album's suggestively rendered content. One critic, in Prince's hometown of Minneapolis, called the album and its songs "seedy and vulgar," a "jungle of teen-age lust and heavy breathing."[3] Despite this early critical erasure, however, the song has grown in stature over the years, particularly through Prince's concert performances of it, various cover recordings, and extensive reviews, recollections, and retrospectives in the growing body of Prince blogs and fan sites. In 2018, Will Harris at Diffuser. com resisted the dated liner-notes description of the song: "You can probably forget the cult at this point," he wrote. "It's just a straight-up classic."[4] The year before that, Dance/Music/Sex/Romance (D/M/S/R), a website devoted to "the Prince oeuvre, song by song, in chronological order," wrote that the song "wasn't Prince's first classic song...but it was his first standard: timeless, durable..."[5] D/M/S/R also did something quite different than some of the other blogs: it directly engaged with the one aspect of the record I found, and still find, to be the most fascinating thing about it—how bravely, defiantly queer it is. "Prince may not have been a gay artist," the critic wrote, "but he was undeniably a queer one; and 'When You Were Mine' is one of the great queer pop songs, by Prince or anyone else."[6]

Rather than paying sustained attention to the queerness that adheres to and in the song, much of the literature I found about "When You Were Mine" grapples with just how "different" the song and its album were from the R&B-inflected albums of Prince's earlier recorded output, thinking through Prince's slippery way with musical genres and—putting Prince in conversation with

Figure 8.1 Cover of Prince's 1980 album *Dirty Mind*. Credit: Vinyls/Alamy
Stock Photo.

artists like Elvis Costello, Joe Jackson, and Blondie—reading the song and
its combination of edgy, sardonic lyrics and surf-rock, Farfisa organ-inspired
rhythms as a defining critical moment in Prince's sonic and aesthetic progression from R&B wunderkind to new wave artist. The song, according to D/M/
S/R, was "his first real foray into crossover territory: a masterful capital-'P'
pop song with all the literary value of contemporary New Wave troubadours
Elvis Costello and Joe Jackson."[7] "If ever there was a point where Prince
can be said to have gone new wave," Diffuser.com's Will Harris wrote, "then
'When You Were Mine' is probably it."[8] Intellectually I understand the insistence on defining Prince through such genre-specific lenses as attempts to make
him legible within the popular music canon, yet I also know that the historical
and cultural imprecisions of genre—and Prince's seeming investment in these
imprecisions—are what attracted me to Prince (and "When You Were Mine")
in the first place. "When You Were Mine" is, indeed, "one of the great queer
pop songs," but not just because of its lyrics.

II

According to stories told by members of his band, Prince wrote "When You
Were Mine" in Orlando, Florida, while they were on tour opening for Rick

James. Keyboardist Matt Fink told a BBC documentary team that after Prince decided not to join the rest of the band on a day trip to Walt Disney World, they headed off, leaving Prince hanging out on the balcony of the hotel room with his guitar. "By the time we came back," Fink recounted, "he'd written [it]."[9] Reportedly, Prince did not enjoy the two months opening 42 dates for Rick James on James's "Fire it Up Tour" in early 1980.[10] Apparently he and James did not get along, and though he and the band were received well, he felt constricted by the set list, made up of approximately seven songs from his first two albums—records that had garnered him some popularity in the R&B market, including the hit "I Wanna Be Your Lover" (1979) from his second album. He also felt constricted by what he regarded as the industry expectations of him and his work, not just as a Black artist but as a more musically expansive artist than his work up until that moment had expressed.

Upon returning home to Minnesota after the tour, Prince—the rising star who'd not only signed, just before turning 18, a six-figure deal with Warner Brothers but had negotiated a contract that specified that he could produce himself and that he would not be relegated to just the "Black music" arm of the label[11]—holed up in his home studio and finished writing and recording the songs that would become *Dirty Mind*. According to journalist Carol Cooper, Prince was eager to move out of the "cozy ghetto exclusivity of the black teen [market]."[12] As Michaelangelo Matos describes the time, it was "the dark ages of r&b crossover" in the early '80s, before Michael Jackson and MTV (and Prince) opened the record sales floodgates.[13]

Asked about the lyrical content of the album in an interview with *New York Rocker* in 1981, Prince described the raw, sexually-charged collection of songs he'd recorded as "just what I was feeling at the time," attributing the itchy, propulsive sound of it to having written most of the songs on a "raggedy guitar" that just sounded "real cool" to him.[14] But when he brought *Dirty Mind* to Warner Brothers, expecting the label to react negatively to the rough edges of the production's DIY sound, he got a different response: "The sound of it is fine," Prince recalled the record execs telling him. "The songs we ain't so sure about. We can't get this on the radio. It's not like your last album at all." Prince's response to them was, "But it's more like me."[15] He told *Melody Maker* in 1981 that while working on *Dirty Mind* he experienced a "revelation," a realization that he "could write just what was on [his] mind…that [he] didn't have to hide anything." The lyrics on the album were "straight from the heart."[16]

"More like me." "Didn't have to hide." In many of the analyses of Prince as a new wave artist, there are questions regarding his motivation for the very clear and obvious sonic shift away from the radio-friendly, danceable, rock-inflected R&B he'd produced on his first two albums. These analyses ask whether Prince's artistic shift was purely creative or more ruthless in origin, a way to re-establish himself in the public eye as a provocative artist and to market himself anew, draw eyes to himself beyond the R&B cage his race has placed him in. Cooper suggests there *was* some sense of strategy to Prince's new style. "Storming the rock press with the renegade allure of incest, oral sex, and soul-rock fusion, *Dirty Mind* did indeed cultivate the critical attention to the Nuevo wavo crowd."[17] Zachary Hoskins locates a new wave, post-punk ethic in the sartorial shifts that mapped along the terrain of the sonic shifts in Prince's sound, pointing out Andy Schwartz's reading of Prince's album cover choice to don bikini briefs as an Iggy Pop influence. He also close-reads Prince's deployment of a "Rude Boy" button as a "reappropriation of the phrase's appropriation by the post-punk '2-tone' ska revival, which turned a term for stylish Jamaican street toughs into one for a predominantly white English subculture." Removing it from its "postcolonial subculture," Prince "Americanizes" the symbol, "turning it into a synonym for a hypersexual hedonist, the subject in possession of a 'dirty mind'…reclaiming 'Rude Boy' as a specifically Black brand of outlaw."[18] Hoskins' astute analysis rescues Prince from the canonizing frame of the new wave label, recognizing Prince as a participant in a much larger, global landscape of influences, able to revise, in the most Hebdigean of ways, the subcultural impulses of popular culture to mark himself as "different" in an industry deeply invested in commercial "sameness."[19] Being a music fan of the precise age to appreciate Prince's "Rude Boy" reference—recalling it not just as a musically and culturally generic marker of Gen-X Americanized fandom but also as the title of a 1980 rockumentary film about the Clash—and perhaps as the kind of "wandering spirit" who needed music like Prince's to develop myself, there is probably something of the "rude boy" in my critical and historical rehearsal here, a desire to think about Prince outside of music critic rubrics of genre and style.[20] Perhaps there is also something of the queer, Black "rude boy" in my thinking, a desire to consider Prince through the intimate parameters of my own Black, queer ear, a desire to imagine him outside of the confines of critical taste and gatekeeping. By which I mean: whether or not Prince merely observed the sonic and sartorial (and popular) nuances of new wave and (as Michaelangelo Matos cogently described him[21]) exploited its "openness as a beacon of the future" to achieve the next level of success, I flash back on teen me, the lost kid who found himself in Prince, and I understand that revision of whatever post-punk or new wave impulses were there in his work as one of the quintessentially queer aspects of Prince and "When You Were Mine."

III

What if we did not (as the D/M/S/R website smartly considers it) think through Prince's new wave moment as an alignment with Elvis Costello or Joe Jackson but as a queering of Stevie Wonder or Smokey Robinson? What if—after hearing that Prince told an AOL Live group in 1997 that he wrote "When You Were Mine" "after listening to John Lennon"—we didn't consider the "sing-song backing vocals" of "When You Were Mine" through the frame of the Beatles but instead considered the influence of girl groups like the Supremes who pre-dated and influenced the Fab Four?[22] What if we did not, as Matos does, think of "When You Were Mine" as "*pure* new wave" (italics mine)?[23]

Purity—of sound, of form, of content—is not something I associate with "When You Were Mine." It is introduced with a two-kick drumbeat, immediately synched with a subtle but propulsive bass, a tinny keyboard, and a skittishly itchy guitar strum. Prince sings the first verse, which manages to be both sweet and raunchy, recounting the story of a breakup. With an added "Oh girl" to kick it off, the second verse starts on the same lyrical note, repeating the song's title, but introduces Prince's multi-tracked vocals. He isn't just the one-man band of instrumentalists, he is his own set of backup singers. As the verses progress, we learn about the girl who's walked away from our narrator: we know—despite his describing the relationship as being "like a dream"—that he gave her all his money even though he says she'd "done [him] wrong." But that "dream"? Does he mean "dream" in the fantasy sense of dream, as in a dream-state of perfection? It is hard to tell, as the "dream" line is the first line of the third couplet, connected to "You let all my friends come over and meet"—is that what made this girl "dreamy"? Her openness to his friends hanging out at the crib? But is "hanging out" all that happens? We wonder because the first line of the *next* couplet describes this girl as "strange." And why is she strange? "Because [she] didn't have the decency to change the sheets." Is she merely non-hygienic? Or are those sheets in need of changing because "all of [his] friends" have been there, so to speak, to "meet"? It is unclear. It is confusing. But it is also, oddly, expertly sketched and sung, compelling in the way that a story should be, inviting you in and holding you, even as you're dubious about where the story will lead.

By the second chorus, the one in which multi-tracked Prince is now singing, in places, as part of a group in the call-and-response nature of classic girl-group camaraderie and support, we find out that the narrator's girl is "fine." But we also find out that he let her wear all his clothes. Is her level of attraction connected to this cross-dressing?

In the chorus, we learn that not only is she gone but she's found another guy. But our narrator doesn't care, because he is still in love with this potentially un-hygienic, cross-dressing girl. He is, in fact, *more* in love with her than when they were together.

It is later in the song, in the third verse and the first bridge, that the song performs what a screenwriter might call a plot twist. Our narrator allowed his ex-girl—who was, he tells us, "kinda sorta [his] best friend"—to fool around… when he was there in bed as well. But he wasn't picky: he "never was the kind to make a fuss / when he was there sleeping in between the two of us." It's the positioning here that matters. The other man, as it were, isn't just sleeping in the bed, he's sleeping between the two lovers, which compels one to ask: Has he been the sexual object of them both? We do not find out. Instead what we find out is this: he still loves his girl, this sexually free vixen, he even loves her more now than he did when she was his, but now he spends his time following the new guy—was he the one who'd shared their bed?—whenever he's out with our narrator's former girl. She's liberated him.

It's a loaded moment, that plot twist. It's ripe with mystery. It begs, after hearing it for the first time, multiple listens. Partly because the song is a sonic pop marvel, a feat of songwriting in the way that it manages to be both louche and spirited, jaunty but decadent, bopping along on its throwback beat. Had there been a song since, perhaps, the Kinks' "Lola" that was so brazen and plain spoken in its embrace of queer sexuality? Or perhaps since Bowie's "John, I'm Only Dancing"? The kind of freewheeling, sexually liberated (and liberating) themes at play in the song had indeed been located in "Black music"—from the Moroder-moderated moans of Donna Summer, to the Caribbean-influenced rhythms of Grace Jones, to the brilliantly bold and outright gayness of Sylvester. But those records mined the cultural and sonic spaces of disco, which produced and provided a soundtrack of sexual desire and expression, giving space beyond the parameters allowed to women and LGBTQ performers before (and during) the 1970s. There most definitely hadn't been a song like "When You Were Mine" written and performed in the defiantly cross-genre, crossover lane in which Prince trafficked by a Black cisgender male artist, had there? Might we have to reach back to the blues? To Little Richard?

Yet what made the song such a sonically queer experience for me, as a teen, hearing the song for the first time on a mix tape given to me by an old friend from sleepaway camp on whom I'd crushed since I was 13 years old, who I thought had a crush on me, though he would never say it? Not with *his* voice at least. But possibly with music: he was the one, in fact, who'd prepped me for the queer masculinities of Prince by introducing me to the eccentricities of Bowie, who'd told me, "I think you'll like how he looks and what he sings about." But there was another queering at play, which perhaps I only hear through that Black queer ear I referenced earlier. Perhaps, growing up in a Black household, inundated with the pop brilliance of Smokey Robinson and Holland-Dozier-Holland, I could only hear Prince's buoyant pop melody overlaid with sad lyrics of loss through the calliope-laced harmonic frame of "Tears of a Clown"? Had my Black queer ear taken to Prince because I thought I could hear in it the sturdy elegance of Motown songwriting (and a cultural imperative to sometimes think of music as representative of identity, as indicative of racial progress even)? Despite the tendency of critical analysis of Prince to regard him—the formal and genre aspects of his work—as in-between Blackness and Whiteness, as performing crossover as a racialized artistic achievement, it is impossible for me to think about Prince and his music outside of a Black context, outside of a legacy of Black excellence that did not transcend race—as it was so often asked to do or implied to be doing—simply because of those formal and generic elements of his work. My pathway to doing that, to understanding his songwriting gift and its way of seeming so necessary to my own development, was to hear it as my invitation to engage the sturdy elegance of Smokey and H-D-H, yet remixed: an almost relentless attention to the craft of melodic and harmonic detail suffused with a reach for a modern performance (and critique) of Black masculinity. Smokey wrote a kind of urban poetry of heterosexual love and romance, and sang it with a falsetto. "When You Were Mind" is Prince's new wave remix of that broken-hearted balladry, punked up and rude, queer as fuck, inviting the rest of us into the groove.

I think here now of the time I read John Rockwell's review of *Parade*, Prince's 1986 album. In a fairly positive review thematically built around an argument about Prince's maturation as both a man and a musical artist in the context of some "luridly reported incidents" that had occurred in the wake of *Purple Rain*'s success, Rockwell's analysis of Prince devolves into a psychological close-reading of the man, critiquing what he understands as a sexual solipsism coursing throughout his work, part publicity ploy, part adolescent fantasy generator. Referring to him as a "mere facile pop trickster with a dirty mind" (playing on the 1980 album's title and calling it one of Prince's best), Rockwell nonetheless believes that Prince's musical mingling of sexuality with themes such as "God, apocalypse, and political injustice" made his work seem "hollow," commenting on the "prosaic and naïve" quality of Prince's "less-than-sure gift for lyric writing." Yet, according to Rockwell, none of this managed to subsume or preclude Prince's ability to break racial barriers through his sonically stylistic experiments, his "brilliant attempts to blend black and white musical influences and every manner of rock, soul, and disco."[24] There is, however, something fascinating in Rockwell's ability to read Prince as a hero in breaking the chains of the "de facto" segregation of "early 80s radio," to locate a kind of renewed hope for the miscegenated future of popular music in Prince's "experimentation," while also considering, later in the review, the way in which—on "tougher" songs like "Kiss" and "New Position"—Prince "chooses to play up the black side of his multi-faceted music sensibility."[25]

The combination of "tougher"/"black side" perked up my Black queer ear. By 1986, Prince had been regarded as biracial—thanks partly to the narrative of *Purple Rain*, which depicted Prince's character, the Kid, as the son of a Black father and a white mother, and partly to a 1981 *Rolling Stone* profile which described him as "the son of a half-black father and an Italian mother."[26] This myth of his supposed mixed heritage became part of the myth of his musical mastery; his vaunted ability to cross genres and styles, dabbling in the Whitenesses of guitar rock and the Blacknesses of funk with equal ease, became a controlling narrative, a way to explain not just his abilities but him as well. But as Stereo Williams wrote in a *Daily Beast* tribute shortly after Prince's passing, "Prince was a black artist."[27] "He was," Williams wrote, "the musical heir to legends like Little Richard, James Brown, and Sly Stone—and also a student of the Staple Singers, Thom Bell and Linda Creed, the Meters, and Rufus. He deconstructed black music and reshaped it."[28] In the process, he deconstructed Black masculinity and the myriad, iterative ways in which it has been both celebrated and erased in the hothouse of popular culture. As

Williams quotes singer Alexander O'Neal, "Like Prince says, 'It's all about being free.'" I do not, ultimately, disagree with the critical desire to insert Prince's sonic ambitions into racial rubrics of genre, to locate the new wave nuances of his early '80s transitions. I just find it difficult to disentangle the insistence on it from his "black side."

There may be no better way to conclude a history of "When You Were Mine," and the history, as I wrote earlier, of the fans and critics who gave it life, than by taking a moment to think about the ways in which the song transcends its erasure from early critiques of Prince by living on as a much-covered song, confirming its sturdiness and the way it speaks, as Prince did, across genre, gender, race, and audience. Reportedly, English singer-songwriter Iain Matthews, who'd been an original member of Fairport Convention, was the first artist to record a cover of "When You Were Mine," in 1981. Bette Bright recorded a single the same year, deeply mining the throwback groove, turning the song into a boppy '50s-style rocker not dissimilar from her band's cover of the Angel's girl-group classic "My Boyfriend's Back." Matthews left the gender play in the lyrics intact; Bright made the lyrics more hetero-gender clear. Detroit rocker Mitch Ryder reached *Billboard's* Top 100 with a version in 1983 (produced by John Mellencamp, a notorious Prince fan, who, according to rumor, loved Prince's "Little Red Corvette" so much that he once played it over a boom box for his audience during a concert). Though the video starred Ryder and a series of leggy female strippers, he left the lyrics intact, probably scrambling many adolescent sexuality signals when the video ran on MTV. Later that same year, Cyndi Lauper released a version of the song on *She's So Unusual*, the album that catapulted her to pop fame. More mid-tempo than Prince's version (and the prior covers), Lauper's recording has a dark, churning synth feel similar to her hit "She Bop," yet becomes a keening ballad of teen love—singing the original lyrics as written, Lauper seems to sings of losing and loving her queer boyfriend, who wore *her* clothes, who had another guy sleeping in between them.

There's something in the variety of geographic, gendered, and sonic landscapes at play in the many versions of the covers. The song's ability to travel these circuitous routes, across various fan bases and generic representations, speaks not just to Prince's power as a songwriter but to his ability to provide globalness out of the localness of a song, written and produced in the cross-racial, multi-gender musical mélange of "Uptown"— as the liner notes of *Dirty Mind* tell us—which can be read as Prince's affectionate description of an area of Minneapolis but also the many terrains of his imagination.

My Black queer ear hears, in the reach of those covers, more analysis of Prince in those cover recordings than we find in all the writing about the man, this essay included. The queerness I've emphasized might only be my reading, the post-adolescent musings of a middle-aged man who's lived with a song for over 40 years. But maybe not: I'd heard this queerness before, this reach away from normative masculinity in the lyrics and vocal chords of Prince himself.

Indeed, the narrator of "I Wanna Be Your Lover" had intoned that he didn't merely want to make his lover come…running; he wanted to be her brother, her mother, and her sister, too. And I'd hear it again: his vocal-matching with Sheila E. on "The Glamorous Life"; his vocalizing as "Camille" on *Sign O' the Times*; the queer questions that line the lyrics of "Anna Stesia" and "Controversy." Was he Black or white? Was he straight? Or gay? He was not ashamed of articulating his pop-savvy R&B notes and rhythms in this genderqueer way that pushed against the expectations of Black male bravado expected to be performed in popular music, from the church-trained vocal star to the lover-man balladeer.

That is just what Prince did. He queered not just the performance of Black masculinity on the pop landscape; he queered the sonic contours, by chafing against the corporate, label-driven expectations of R&B and by Blacking up the rebel yell of post-punk and the sleek, barbed mannerisms of new wave.

He made pop history by not allowing pop history to define him. Or his listeners, before the parade of post-*Purple Rain* accolades and after. Especially the queer ones who thought of him as theirs.

Notes

1 Spin, "Fresh Prince: Spin's 1991 Cover Story." *SPIN*, September 1991.
2 Prince. *Prince - The Hits / The B-Sides*, CD box set. Los Angeles: Warner Bros, 1993.
3 Michael Anthony, "Seedy, Vulgar sex songs don't make Prince charming," *The Minneapolis Star Tribune*, November 7, 1980, 17.
4 Will Harris, "'When You Were Mine' Was a Hit - For Other People," *Diffuser*.
5 Zach Hoskins, "When You Were Mine," *Dance / Music / Sex / Romance* (blog), June 16, 2017.
6 Ibid.
7 Ibid.
8 Harris, "'When You Were Mine' Was a Hit."
9 Michaelangelo Matos, "Do It All Night: The Story of Prince's Dirty Mind," *Pitchfork*, October 6, 2015; Hoskins, "When You Were Mine"; Harris, "'When You Were Mine' Was a Hit."
10 Matos, "Do It All Night."
11 Bob Protzman, "From the Archives: 18-Year-Old Prince Signs First Record Deal," *Twin Cities* (blog), April 21, 2016.
12 Carol Cooper, "Someday Your Prince Will Come (1983)," *The Beat Patrol* (blog), May 6, 2009.
13 Matos, "Do It All Night."
14 Andy Schwartz, "A Dirty Mind Comes Clean: Interview with Andy Schwartz," in *Prince: The Last Interview*, ed. Hanif Abdurraqib (Brooklyn: Melville House, 2019), 24
15 Schwartz, "A Dirty Mind Comes Clean," 25.
16 Zachary Hoskins, "Rude Boy: Prince as Black New Waver," *Spectrum: A Journal on Black Men* 7, no. 2 (2020), 92.
17 Cooper, "Someday Your Prince Will Come."
18 Hoskins, "Rude Boy."

19 Dick Hebdige, *Subculture: The Meaning of Style* (London; New York: Routledge, 1991).
20 For more on Prince as operating in a global context of style and citation, please see Adrian A. Bautista's essay "A Flâneur in the Erotic City," in which Bautista used Prince's mid-80s filmic and musical work to theorize Prince as a "postmodern flâneur" using "signifiers that convey gender ambiguity/bending…and transformative creativity." Adrian A. Bautista, "A Flâneur in the Erotic City: Prince and the Urban Imaginary," *Journal of African American Studies* 21, 3 (2017), 353–372.
21 Matos, "Do It All Night."
22 Hoskins, "When You Were Mine."
23 Matos, "Do It All Night."
24 John Rockwell, "Prince's 'Parade' stakes a claim to popularity," *The New York Times*, March 30, 1986.
25 Rockwell, "Prince's 'Parade' stakes a claim to popularity."
26 Bill Adler, "Rolling Stone (#337)," *Prince Interview Archive*, February 19, 1981.
27 Stereo Williams, "Prince Was Not 'Biracial.' He Loved His Blackness—and Yours," *The Daily Beast*, April 24, 2016.
28 Williams, "Prince Was Not 'Biracial.'"

References

Adler, Bill. "Rolling Stone (#337)." *Prince Interview Archive*, February 19, 1981. https://sites.google.com/site/prninterviews/home/rolling-stone-337-19-february-1981

Anthony, Michael. "Seedy, Vulgar sex songs don't make Prince charming." *The Minneapolis Star Tribune*, Nov 7, 1980, 17. www.newspapers.com/image/187647470/?terms=Prince%20%22When%20You%20Were%20Mine%22&match=1

Bautista, Adrian A. "A Flâneur in the Erotic City: Prince and the Urban Imaginary." *Journal of African American Studies* 21, no. 3 (2017).

Cooper, Carol. 'Someday Your Prince Will Come' (1983)." *The Beat Patrol* (blog), May 6, 2009. https://beatpatrol.wordpress.com/2009/05/06/carol-cooper-someday-your-prince-will-come-1983/

Harris, Will. "'When You Were Mine' Was a Hit - For Other People." *Diffuser*, February 1, 2018. https://diffuser.fm/prince-when-you-were-mind-cyndi-lauper/

Hebdige, Dick. *Subculture: The Meaning of Style.* London: Routledge, 1991.

Hoskins, Zach. "When You Were Mine." *Dance / Music / Sex / Romance* (blog), June 16, 2017. https://princesongs.org/2017/06/16/when-you-were-mine/

Hoskins, Zach. "Rude Boy: Prince as Black New Waver." *Spectrum: A Journal on Black Men* 7, no. 2 (2020): 83–109.

Matos, Michaelangelo. "Do It All Night: The Story of Prince's Dirty Mind." *Pitchfork*, October 6, 2015. https://pitchfork.com/features/from-the-pitchfork-review/9731-do-it-all-night-the-story-of-princes-dirty-mind/

Prince. *Prince - The Hits / The B-Sides*, CD box set. Los Angeles: Warner Bros, 1993.

Protzman, Bob. "From the Archives: 18-Year-Old Prince Signs First Record Deal." *Twin Cities* (blog), April 21, 2016. www.twincities.com/2016/04/21/prince-signs-first-record-deal/

Rockwell, John. "Prince's 'Parade' stakes a claim to popularity." *The New York Times*, March 30, 1986. www.nytimes.com/1986/03/30/arts/prince-s-parade-stakes-a-claim-to-popularity.html

Schwartz, Andy. "A Dirty Mind Comes Clean: Interview with Andy Schwartz." In *Prince: The Last Interview*, edited by Hanif Abdurraqib. Brooklyn: Melville House, 2019.

Spin. "Fresh Prince: Spin's 1991 Cover Story." *SPIN*, September 1991. www.spin.com/2016/04/prince-cover-story-1991-diamonds-and-pearls/

Williams, Stereo. "Prince Was Not 'Biracial.' He Loved His Blackness—and Yours." *The Daily Beast*, April 24, 2016. www.thedailybeast.com/prince-was-not-biracial-he-loved-his-blacknessand-yours?ref=scroll

9 Neil Young—"Transformer Man" (1982)

George Plasketes

"The computers and the heartbeat all have to come together—where chemistry and electronics meet."[1]

(Neil Young)

In the wane of 1982, on December 29, Neil Young released a technotronic album, *Trans*. His resourceful rationale was systematic and straightforward. There were few favorable first impressions of the record itself, and the "acquired taste" assurances were limited. The album's cover design is intriguing and foretelling, as it invites interpretation as an illustrated indicator of the music content inside—its setting, strange sound, and story that surround the set of tracks (see Figure 9.1). The clean-edged composition is reminiscent of science fiction graphic design, whether movie poster or pulp, from the 1950s or 1960s. It portrays two distinct realms or spheres, separated by a freeway's broken center line—the digital divide—with the suggestion of crossing over from one world or space to another. A hippie and a hologram robo-figure are hitchhiking on opposite sides of the two-lane blacktop; each headed in different directions, perhaps destined for their respective utopias. The image contrast is sharp, the interface plain: Nature and science. Past and future. Traditionalist and technophile. A forest with tall trees and a tail-finned vintage sedan on the human highway, juxtaposed with the information superhighway, occupied by a timely DeLorean-design auto, angular, futuristic Metropolis architecture, and a sonic jet droning in the sky above.

The visual on *Trans*'s back sleeve provides further foreshadowing, the artwork expressing the computer and cardiovascular in colorful convergence, a heart and its aortic valves, vessels and chambers with circuitry, a rendering of Young's vision of "where chemistry and electronics meet."

Completing the cover's composition, the record's title, *Trans*, banners a fitting computer-age caption and also postures as a pertinent prefix for relevant variants: *Trans*form, *Trans*ition, *Trans*parent, *Trans*fer, *Trans*figure, *Trans*port, *Trans*lation, *Trans*mit, *Trans*mission, *Trans*action, *Trans*gression, *Trans*cend, among other usages. The most overarching consonance may be,

DOI: 10.4324/9781003093206-10

Transcribe/Transcript, as the album is Young's computerized chronicle of the period.

Young's improbable album inaugurated a curious and conflicting creative course for the prolific singer-songwriter that persisted through much of the new decade. *Trans* was clearly conspicuous, countering the comforts of Young classics such as *Harvest* or *Comes a Time*. The aberrant album's divergence from Young's common career progression was striking. Dating back to Buffalo Springfield in the 1960s, Young had established a fairly consistent acoustic-electric pattern with his recordings, with album releases alternating between folk-rock and country-tinged strumming, piano, and harmonica, and rock powerchording, jamming, and thrashing noisily with Crazy Horse. The duality perhaps peaked with *Rust Never Sleeps* (1979), an exemplar integrating Young's two distinct stylistic sides. Young's peculiar post-*Rust* path initially proceeded on cue from the 1970s into *Hawks and Doves* (1980) and *Re-ac-tor* (1981), before he abandoned that blueprint for a mystifying zigzag through multiple and varied genres. On his sequence of subsequent 1980s albums, Young assumed different personas and bands for each record—the vocoder and "Neil 2" on *Trans* (1982), the Shocking Pinks on *Everybody's Rockin'* (1983), International Harvesters on *Old Ways* (1985), and Blue Notes on *This Note's for You* (1988)—before circling back to his steadfast sidekicks Crazy Horse.

Figure 9.1 Cover of Neil Young's *Trans* album. Credit: Alamy Stock Photo.

Beginning with *Trans*, Young's genre-careening series of albums released on Geffen Records routinely bewildered Young's most devoted fans, critics, and even some of his band members along the way. In the revealing Young biography *Shakey* (2003), author Jimmy McDonough astutely observed that "it was starting to feel like Neil Young was on a kamikaze mission."[2] Other resigned reviewers shrugged, "Well Mr. Weird is at it again," while wondering, "What's next?"[3] The few who were willing to attribute any value to the records rationalized the albums as products of Young's singular vision and exploration as an auteur. The run of recording randomness was so erratic that it eventually provoked a lawsuit filed by Young's longtime canyon-turned-corporate colleague David Geffen on behalf of his new record label, which improbably sued the rock legend on the unusual grounds that the enigmatic artist was being "uncharacteristic Neil Young."[4]

Across *Trans*'s 40-minute span, Young employs electronica prominently steered by two tech toys—a Sennheiser vocoder and Synclavier sythensizer—in computerized collaboration as the central sound sources and vocal devices that distort and digitize two thirds of the album's nine tracks. Even Young's Buffalo Springfield standard "Mr. Soul" receives a mechanized makeover.

The experimentation on *Trans* was instigated in part by Young's technological inquisitiveness. The method in the mechanized madness was also profoundly personal, particularly the track "Transformer Man," a reflective response by Young based on his and his wife Pegi's parental quest for communication channels with their incapacitated son Ben. Born in 1978, Ben is Young's second child to be diagnosed with cerebral palsy. His son Zeke, born in 1972 during Young's previous lengthy live-in relationship with late actress Carrie Snodgress, was also afflicted with the same disability. However, Ben's condition was rare and more severe than his older brother Zeke's. Ben diagnosis was spastic paraplegia, rendering him non-oral/verbal. Ben's disability and the quest for connectivity became foundational for *Trans*. "*Trans* is about communication, about not getting through. And that's what my son is," Young explicitly explained. "You can't understand the words on *Trans* and I can't understand my son's words."[5]

"Transformer Man" is Young's unassuming yet resounding thesis statement on *Trans*. The track is the basis, the essence, of the album, which Young considered "the beginning of my search for communication with a severely handicapped non-oral person."[6] The track is summary and signpost. Ode and odyssey and "Once upon a time." Science fiction and fairy tale. Ben and Neil. The hippie and the hologram, hitchhiking across the digital divide. Singular as a distorted and doting disability ditty. A son song and unsung song—figuratively and literally—that stands out on multiple levels and is highly emblematic of the post-disco era and the emergence of electronica, dance strands, and new wave within the MTVortex. Sequenced serenely as *Trans*'s side one's fourth track, "Transformer Man" is the album's heartbeat and soul, its spirit and circuitry, core and emotional centerpiece. Its totality surreptitiously embodies Young's personal struggles and professional conflicts during the period, particularly parenting with Ben's disability and the accompanying quest for communication and connectivity through intense pattern programs. The track's rich contextualization encompasses technological, musical, artistic, organizational, and legal dimensions, more broadly situated within the shifting economic, cultural, and creative currents of the early 1980s. Music's corporate climate of the times was characterized by *New York Times* critic Jon Pareles as "Rock Reaganomics," part of the industry's response to the arrival of MTV and the accompanying emergent music-video aesthetic in August 1981, with the emphasis on branding artists, genres, and record labels alike.[7]

Transition and *Transformation*: Rust, *Re-ac-tor*, Reprise

Neil Young entered the 1980s carrying considerable cachet and creative capital. The previous decade had been an extraordinarily prolific period for Young, highlighted by some of his most critically acclaimed and commercially successful solo records, released at an astounding album-a-year pace. Young led off the 1970s with cohorts Crosby, Stills, and Nash (CSN) on *Déjà Vu* in March, and six months later solo with *After the Gold Rush* (1970). The hallmark *Harvest* (1972) ensued, along with the Kent State shooting anthem "Ohio" released as a stand-alone single with the CSN trio in between, and a double-LP soundtrack to his film *Journey Through the Past*. Live new material on *Time Fades Away* (1973) was followed by *On the Beach* (1974), mid-decade darkness and brooding with *Tonight's the Night* and *Zuma* (both in 1975), and a collaboration with Stills on *Long May You Run* (1976). Then came *American Stars 'n' Bars* (1977) and back-to-back top-ten albums with *Comes a Time* (1978) and *Rust Never Sleeps* (1979), as well as its same-year concert companion, *Live Rust*, to punctuate Young's abundant era. Young's impressive body of work during the span earned him and his music widespread recognition among critics and fans in a range of categories on year-end and decade lists, from artist and album to songwriter and vocalist, in publications from the *Village Voice* to *Rolling Stone*.

Young's productivity sustained itself into the new decade before swerving sharply with *Trans*, two albums and two years in. His initial 1980s recordings, *Hawks & Doves* (1980) and *Re-ac-tor* (1981), followed form, remaining relatively consistent with Young's career-long acoustic/electric rotation. The ideological *Hawks & Doves* tracks included the modest lead "Little Wing," which was retrieved from a batch of songs intended to be among the sequence on *Homegrown*, a set recorded mid-1974 into early 1975 between Young's albums *On the Beach* and *Zuma*. The *Homegrown* project and its plentiful playlist mysteriously vanished into the void of Young's vast vault, where it remained for decades, exiled in limbo as one of Young's legendary long-lost recordings in absentia archive. While a sampling of songs such as "Little Wing" along with "Love is a Rose," "Star of Bethlehem," and "Homegrown" were scattered across Young albums (*Hawks & Doves*, *Decade*, *American Stars 'n Bars*), the

Homegrown recordings from the mid-1970s sessions did not resurface collectively until 45 years later in 2020.

Though *Trans* was an undeniably sharp stylistic swerve for Young, there were some audible hints of a sound shift from Young that started to surface with its predecessor, *Re-ac-tor*. More precursor than pure musical prelude to *Trans*, *Re-ac-tor*'s effects and noises were in part attributed to Young's initiation with one of the music machines he had become intrigued with—the Synclavier—an early-model digital synthesizer and polyphonic sampling system. Young was among the early adopters of the costly and cutting-edge component. The initial design and development of the digital device originated at Dartmouth College's School of Engineering before its distribution in the consumer market in the late 1970s. The pioneering prototype was a collaboration between professors Jon Appleton and Frederick Hooven and hardware/software programmers Sydney A. Alonso and Cameron Jones. The versatile sampling, recording, and sequencing system was the ultimate one-person band, with sound-coloring capacities and a giant memory capable of storing an abundance of sounds and instruments.

Re-ac-tor is 39 minutes long (or short), with its two sides in four-song symmetry, each encumbered with two excessive tracks—"T-Bone," in relentless repeat for 9 minutes of side one, and an intense electric reworking of the previously acoustic ballad "Shots" occupying the album's closing 7:42. The record's machine-gun overdubs provided an aural glimpse of production possibilities and sound pursuits that Young would expand upon in *Trans*, continuing to a lesser degree on his other projects through the decade, among them *Landing on Water* (1986).

Re-ac-tor's songwriting and recording, which took place on Young's fabled Broken Arrow Ranch in Half Moon Bay, California, and the album's subsequent release, coincided with an intensely stressful period personally for Young. Less than two years after Ben's birth and the heartbreaking repeat disability diagnosis, his wife Pegi underwent successful surgery for a life-threatening brain abnormality. In October 1980, following Pegi's recovery, the Youngs enlisted in a special-needs program on Ben's behalf. Recommended to them by a friend, the patterning system, sponsored by the Philadelphia-based Institute for Achievement for Human Potential, specialized in assisting parents to engage in developmental tasks with disabled children. Following considerable deliberation, the Youngs signed on, and for the next 18 months they were passionate participants in the program.[8]

The patterning program, which Young called "the most difficult thing I've ever done," was rigorous, with a 12-hours-a-day, seven-days-a-week schedule of seclusion, preparation, and active supervision.[9] The prodigious level of immersion took a cumulative toll on Young physically, mentally, emotionally, and creatively. The *Re-ac-tor* sessions began a downward spiral as Young detached from his constants, Crazy Horse. "Neil didn't encourage Crazy Horse during those years," said his longtime producer David Briggs. "He lost control of his personal life, and everything went along with it."[10] The program's restrictive parameters and protocols inevitably impacted his music pursuits and finances, totally supplanting touring and only allowing for a limited block of time during the afternoons for arranging studio recording time. Throughout his career, Young preferred, if not insisted on, synchronizing his studio sessions with the lunar cycles, routinely recording his albums at night, if possible under a full moon.

Interestingly, with his minimal allotment of spare time from Ben's program, Young chose to devote much of that free time to film projects. Young scored the film, *Where the Buffalo Roam* (1980), based on the life of Dr. Hunter S. Thompson, with Bill Murray cast as the Gonzo journalist. Young's soundtrack contributions included an a capella rendition of the standard "Home on the Range," a series of four "Ode to Wild Bill" interludes, and a "Buffalo Stomp" and its refrain accompanied by the Wild Bill Band of Strings.

Young was also finalizing *Human Highway*, another in his series of "art films." Produced under his cinematic pseudonym, "Bernard Shakey," the project was preceded by the concert fantasy *Journey through the Past*, his directorial debut in 1973 (released in theatres in 1974), shot on 16mm, which was followed by *Rust Never Sleeps* in 1979, featuring oversized stage props, amplifiers, and Devo-inspired costuming. At its 1950s B-movie best (or worst), the wry, improvisational *Human Highway* was perhaps Young's *Renaldo & Clara* matinee moment. Set in a small town situated near a nuclear power plant, Shakey cast alter ego Young as Lionel (a model-train-line-inspired name), a mechanic who drifts into a rock-star delusion after being struck in the head. The film premiered in limited distribution to predominant thumbs-down reviews on August 16, 1982, the fifth anniversary of Elvis's death.

Film was a diversion for Young, a parallel pursuit that he hoped would help keep his music fresh. His rock-star mythology and music-making had become subservient to survival mode, with his primary focus as a father and husband being taking care of his sons and wife. Years later, when looking back with some clarity on the calamity of the period, Young stated: "I closed down so much that my soul was completely encased. I didn't even consider that I needed a soul to make my music. I shut the door on my music."[11]

Lyrics on *Hawks & Doves*, in songs such as "Lost in Space," with its ramblings about "the unknown dangers of the ocean floor," invited interpretations suggesting indications of a person in pain, with detectable traces of despair and disillusion. The implications persisted. *Re-ac-tor*'s stark, angular black-and-red back-cover design included the serenity prayer printed in Latin, presumably a cryptic inner glimpse of Young's emotional state, managing and coping with the overwhelming conditions surrounding him. As Young told *Rockline*, "It was too much of a personal trip to lay on everyone in English."[12] Throughout the process and stressful sequence of circumstances, Young protected his family's privacy. The Young sons' cerebral palsy was no secret. Zeke's and Ben's conditions were common knowledge that was occasionally referenced, though seldom emphasized or made the focal point of Young's interviews or coverage in the rock press.

Re-ac-tor's intense, guitar-heavy, punk-blues sound was largely received with indifference in the rock critical sphere, with consensus characterizations such as "shaggy," "disheveled" "rackety." and "thrown together."[13] Beyond its overall critical inconsequence and marginal-to-poor sales, *Re-ac-tor* became noteworthy as the album that marked the end of Young's affiliation with Reprise Records, a lengthy residence which resulted in a rich run of Young solo recordings following Buffalo Springfield's breakup in 1968. During that span, Young released 13 albums in 17 years on the legendary label, which was founded in 1960 by "the Chairman of the Board," Frank Sinatra. The major downside of the split from the Warner Group was that it meant Young was parting with renowned producer Mo Ostin. Young, promptly signed with another iconic music industry figure, David Geffen, who was forming Geffen Records following his founding and fostering of the prominent Asylum Records, a haven for Southern California's 1970s Laurel-and-Topanga-scene singer-songwriters. Young was among a troupe of high-profile Geffen roster recruits that included his canyon cohort Joni Mitchell, Elton John, and disco diva Donna Summer. The four were projected as star cornerstones of the nascent label and signed deals to receive one million dollars per album with Geffen Records.

*Trans*formation and *Trans*lation: Vocoder as Voice and Veil

"I've been Neil Young for years."[14]

(Neil Young)

Neil Young admittedly "needed the change." And not simply that of signing with a new record label, but musical as well as individual change also. One of the most significant shifts for Young personally occurred in early 1982, when the Youngs decided to leave the Philadelphia Institute Program. Despite 18 months of total absorption and "being programmed" along with Ben, the Youngs were simply worn out, physically, mentally, emotionally, and spiritually. They remained tangled in doubt, fear, and glimmers of hope while attempting to balance Ben's needs with their own. Ben's lack of progress on certain levels stirred skepticism from Neil and Pegi regarding the program's effectiveness. After attending a seminar sponsored by the National Academy of Child Development (NACD) in February, the Youngs found the organization's approach to be much more suitable. Though similar in some ways, the NACD's program, at four hours a day, was notably less rigorous. In addition, the Youngs believed the organization's emphasis on mental processes and communication skills would better benefit Ben and his specific needs.[15]

Amid the engulfing personal chaos and its accompanying challenges, Young had grown wary of his perceived public persona, as intimated in his late 1970s declaration, "Better to burn out than to rust." Interviews in the rock press during 1981, and his subsequent emergence from the virtual seclusion of Ben's consuming pattern program, revealed an undercurrent of an inner yearning for reinvention. Young contemplated "being Neil Young" and the nuances of legacy and longevity. He was resolved to avoid rock-dinosaur syndrome and settling "where Crosby, Stills, and Nash are": stuck in the past and "the same old," playing it safe and unable to adapt, without experimenting or offering something different musically.[16]

Young was ready and willing to take some chances and explore some new directions. He incongruously bought into the brave new world, embracing computer technology. This peculiar path of sound pursuit was at once pleasantly perverse, precise, and packed with possibility. There was an undeniable sheer contrariness to Young—the rustic, ragged rocker in foot-stomping flannel with presumed neo-Luddite leanings—being exposed as a curious accomplice with shiny machines and tech wizardry. However, the experimentation with *Trans* may not have been as extreme a departure for Young as it appeared to be on the stereotypical surface to fans, friends, and fellow musicians. Young may have been open minded and receptive rather than indifferent to technology's siren song, a posture perhaps partially rooted in his twin transport fixations—vintage cars and toy trains. The latter hobby evolved into such an obsession that Young had to construct a separate barn on his Broken Arrow Ranch to accommodate his elaborate model-train track designs, layouts, and installations. Beyond the playful toward the professional, Young was keenly aware of computer technology, its possibilities, developments, applications, and influence on sounds, trends, and developments, and its place and presence in music and the recording industry. Among his musical peers who came of stage during the 1960s, Young was the loner keenly tuned into the times, listening forward and actively extolling the virtues and value of exposure to new music. In 1981, he was particularly captivated by Kraftwerk's innovative *Computer World*, taking courage and conceptual cues from the German electronica group's breakthrough into the American music marketplace. The album appeared to prod and reaffirm Young's musical wanderlust, planting a sense of permission and the possibility of traveling the technological terrain.

Young was attracted to, if not strangely fascinated with, the unearthly precision, timing, and emotion of computer-generated music. His tone in interviews during the period was more contemplative than whimsical, as if delivering a new music manifesto. Among his ponderings, Young found the mechanized manipulation of music to be soulful rather than soulless, and a viable, evocative channel of expression that heightened rather than hindered the human spirit.

> Now people are living on digital time, they need to hear something perfect all the time or they don't feel reassured everything's okay ... Electronic music is lot like folk music to me ... it's a new kind of rock and roll—it's so synthetic and anti-feeling that it has a lot of feeling.... So I think this new music is emotional—it's very emotional—because it's so cold. I have my synthesizers and my computers and I'm not lonely.[17]

That summer, Young, restless and not completely satisfied with some of the vocals he had recorded for *Re-ac-tor*, acquired another pricey piece of technology to complement the Synclavier—a Sennheiser vocoder. The small audio machine analyzed and synthesized human voice signals, compressing, encrypting, multi-layering, and transforming, allowing any vocalist to play with octaves and to hit virtually any note, any tone or timbre. Invented in the late 1930s at Bell Labs, the device signaled a technological turning point for the country-folk rocker Young. "I feel that with all the new digital and computerized equipment I can get my hands on now, I can do things I could never do before," he said. "I know this is just the beginning for me."[18]

The vocoder was a revelation, and promptly became Young's "weird and unmusical" partner processing his frail wail, enabling him to sing with somebody else's voice or make it his own. "It's still my melodies, my enunciation, my feeling," he insisted. "It just lifts a restriction—why should I have to sing with my own voice in 1982, when I can stretch out in different directions?"[19] Young, enamored with techno tinkering between the two components, instantly began composing computer-world-themed songs for vocoded vocals. Young's positivity and the pragmatism of his technological turn were undoubtedly framed and inspired by his parental experience with his son Ben.

As a variant voice, the vocoder was a veil for Young. Biographical and autobiographical accounts suggest that Young's mental and emotional states at the time of *Trans* may not have been conducive to his producing a worthy and relatable album that was based on his firsthand experience with a child with a disability. While Young assuredly wanted to express his thoughts musically, he was circumspect and ardently aware, and tuned into his own and his family's feelings. Young was suspended in an emotional and artistic limbo of parallel purposes. He simultaneously wanted to express his deeper feelings and to suppress them, the latter impulse reinforcing his pre-existing inclination to hide himself in roles and styles, to "stop being Neil Young." He did not want the message of these songs to be clear or direct. The vocoder proved to be a compatible, if not ideal, creative accomplice, enabling Young to conceal his true voice in computerized distortion when channeled through the Synclavier and into music, "Just putting little clues in there as to what was really on my mind."[20]

Young's distorted vocal approach throughout the record was intended to replicate, or at the most minimal to echo, his son Ben's communication. Routing Young's voice through a machine such as the vocoder made it difficult to decipher what he was singing/saying. "I felt like it was art, an expression of something deeply personal," explained Young. "It was a very deep and inaccessible concept."[21]

*Trans*mission: Music from Another World

Trans was Young's Geffen-label debut. In its formative stages, the album evolved alongside, and with tracks extracted from, another Young work in progress, the provisionally titled *Island in the Sun*. Young concisely characterized the *Sun* set as being about the planet Earth, accented with some mellow, acoustic, swaying South Pacific lap-steel love songs. Geffen was underwhelmed during a first listen to the demos that came out of the Hawaii sessions, and he suggested that Young do something else. Young's compromise was to seek a middle ground that allowed him to salvage some of the *Island in the Sun* songs by incorporating them within another record that he "was already hearing in (his) head to follow up."[22] The material in mind translated into *Trans*.

The *Trans* album was completed in the summer of 1982, though it was not released until late December. Six of the albums nine tracks feature Young's vocoded vocals, with the remaining three being standard, non-programmed songs from the *Island in the Sun* session in Hawaii. Another song, "If You Got Love," was suddenly withdrawn from the album, though it remained printed in the track listing and on the lyric sheet. The last-minute reshuffling of the tracks in the running order was symptomatic of *Trans*'s unsettling under-current. In addition to the discordancy of the tracks delivered in distinctly different styles, the album was rushed to completion, leaving co-producer dis-satisfied with the mixes.

True to Young's well-documented passionate-artist posture and tempera-ment, he "went overboard" with his new techno devices. According to *Trans* co-producer Briggs, the album started out with the usual two guitars, bass, and drum. "Next thing we knew, Neil stripped all our music off, overdubbed all this stuff—the vocoder, weird sequencing, and put this synth shit on it," said Briggs. Young's stalwart Crazy Horse bandmates Frank "Poncho" Sampedro, Billy Talbot, and Ralph Molina were indifferent loyalists. "They played on the stuff, but they didn't think it was music," added Briggs.[23]

The song sequencing on *Trans* is sporadic, with the predominant set of computer tracks providing the album's most coherent portion. Both sides of *Trans* (mis)lead with "normal voice" tracks, with the remaining non-computer compositions placed as punctuation to conclude the record. The opening tracks to each side—the convincingly catchy "Little Thing Called Love" and the synth swirls of "Hold On to Your Love"—do not prepare the listener for the subsequent song sequences that complete each side. The lead tracks create a false impression or suspicion that Young may have been concealing the com-puter content for at least the album's initial three minutes. The remainder of side one consists of four techno tracks—"Computer Age," which incorporates a stray Rolling Stones riff, "We R in Control," "Transformer Man," and "Computer Cowboy (AKA Skycrusher)," a cyber-crime foretelling of a twenty-first-century outlaw lifting data from memory systems.[24] Similarly, side two's four tracks are centered by two more computer songs: "Sample and Hold," a wry new-mate design scenario,[25] and a reimagined version of the Buffalo Springfield classic "Mr. Soul," with a backward guitar and Young duet with his computer collaborator. *Trans*'s nine-song cycle closes with affection for allegory and the ancients in "Like an Inca." The sprawling syn-thesis of the apocalyptic jungle journey evokes Young's "Like a Hurricane" and "Cortez the Killer," with an echo of Dylan-via-Hendrix's "All Along the Watchtower." The brisk Latin rhythms, in a narrative that runs slightly longer than eight minutes, summon a suitable time-warp soundtrack for a Bill Moyers–produced myth-and-civilization documentary, while featuring a Dylan homage with the lyric "Like a skipping rolling stone."

Young biographers David Downing (*A Dreamer of Pictures* (1994), and Jimmy McDonough (*Shakey* (2002)) aptly title their *Trans* chapters "Music from Another World" and "A Voice No One Could Recognize" respectively. *Trans*'s six computer tracks collectively possess a futuristic tenor and sci-fi sensibility as they explore settings and themes central to the relationship between humans and technology. The prevailing point of view is impartial, a neutral shade of technological spectatorship that straddles slender suspicion and positivity. The medium is mostly the message, with minimalist lyrics contorted and coded in the mechanized modes, intentionally difficult to decipher without following the vocoded verses printed in the liner notes. The filtered, beeping textures throughout complement the technological terminology ("signal, "unity," "data banks") that thread the *Trans* tracks and frequently exude a ghostly ambience, simultaneously sad and strange, lost and lonely, swimming and suspended, floating in an ether, as if trapped between dimensions.

*Trans*cript

"Transformer Man" is the proverbial buried lead, a transcript inconspicuously situated as *Trans*'s fourth track. The placement was purposeful, part of Young's preference and plan to mask the message. The most concise of the completely computer compositions at 3:22 (the tech-straddling "Mr. Soul" is six seconds shorter; "We R in Control" is six seconds longer), "Transformer Man" is overtly biographical of Ben. And of Neil as well. Ben may be operating the transformer, but Neil is transformed. The track is a caring love letter from father to son, a poetic and poignant parental portrait, a gentle hymn of hope amid a caring quest to find common convergence, interface, even if in code. Young is explicit about "Transformer Man" being a "song for my kid." "If you read the words and look at my child in his wheelchair," he told McDonough, "with his little button and switch on his head, his train set and his transformer, the whole thing is for him."[26]

A pulsing heartbeat and intermittent modulation—"Transformer Man, Transformer Man, doo-ta-doot-doot-doot-doot-doot"—provide a chorus-like chant and cadence. Young's vocoded delivery, though distant and desolate, is intimate. There is a Frankensteinian subtext that conjures the pattern-program channeling of devoted parental presence. In addition to a toy-train association, the "Transformer Man" designation possesses a kid-nickname quality, a substitute for "Sonny Boy" standards such as "Junior," "Buddy," "Little Man," or "Big Guy." Neil's fatherly gaze at "Transformer Ben" reveals his son "run[ning] the show, [by] remote control, direct[ing] the action with the push of a button ... power in your hand." Neil offers his son a "sooner or later" lesson, that "you'll have to see the cause and effect." The line echoes a familiar phrase, though in a less constrained context, from Young's "Walk On" from *On the Beach* (1974): "Sooner or later it all gets real / Walk on."

The affection in the connection is discernable, the tone strikingly tender: "Every morning when I look in your eyes / I feel electrified by you." Naturally, hopes and dreams pervade—"So many things still left to do"— coupled with affirmations of support—"But we haven't made it yet." In its closing stanza, the song's circuitry enters David Bowie's "Space Oddity" orbit, floating with otherworldly wistfulness and resolve—"Still in command, your eyes are shining on a beam through the galaxy of love / Unlock the secrets / Let us throw off the chains that hold you down."

"Transformer Man's" concealment clearly contains a cathartic context as well. Young stated that, with everything he had been keeping inside, he "dumped the load on *Trans* and told the whole fucking story."[27] More precisely, the essence of that story resides and reverberates in "Transformer Man" as transcript.

The sweet sorrow and heart-wrenching nature of "Transformer Man" was largely concealed, if not long lost in translation, due in large part to Dad's determination to disguise his discerning nature and use of discretion discussing Ben's disability. Young maintained that he did not want the message of "Transformer Man," or any of the computer songs, to be clear and direct. Yet, amid the unfathomable mystery of *Trans*'s method and its puzzle pieces personified throughout the tracks, Young appeared situated in a self-inflicted quandary, perhaps more so with "Transformer Man," the album's most personal track. Though its vocoding was calculated and intentionally camouflaged, Young, fairly or unfairly, seemed to halfway hope or fully expect that the listening audience would grasp the meaning. And when they didn't "get it," and the record flopped, he took it personally. Young was incongruously and passionately aware that he purposely presented something as intimate as Ben's condition in an obscure way, admitting that "they [the audience] didn't have a fuckin' chance in the world. It was so well disguied, you could never fuckin' recognize it ... only I really knew what it was."[28]

Though not entirely suppressed or secretive, the Ben backstory was not widely circulated at the time of *Trans*'s release, and remained in the background for many years. Once the listener becomes familiar with Ben's biography and his challenging condition, the track becomes profoundly poignant and powerful, and potentially a genuinely transformational experience.

*Trans*action and *Trans*gression: The Geffen-Young Courtship

"There was a new Neil every year. Not only did you not know which Neil you were going to get, you didn't even know if you were gonna get Neil."

(Elliot Roberts, Neil Young's long-time manager)[29]

While Young may have been a self-saboteur despite his gallant artistic intentions with *Trans*, there was also a somewhat unanticipated undercurrent of corporate conflict early on with his new record label. David Geffen had a well-earned reputation for being an artist-friendly executive, with Asylum Records founded on the principle of creative freedom. However, already in the formative stages of his fledgling label, the emphasis had shifted somewhat to a more corporate stance.

With Young's Geffen Records' debut, Geffen chose not to support production and distribution of a music video to promote *Trans*, despite the form's ascendance as the visual version of the 45-RPM single. Music video had become a primary music marketing method in the burgeoning MTV era that launched on cable television in 1981. Young was disappointed by the lack of support, and perhaps felt creatively betrayed considering his and Geffen's history, not to mention Geffen's artist-advocacy posture in the Southern California music ecology. Young insisted that a music video would have provided essential conceptual context for *Trans*'s complex computer-centric content, its subtleties, its themes, and its digital delivery. In Young's view, any promotion for the album done by his new record label was incomplete, if not ineffectual, without accompaniment by videos, which would have provided a manual with context for the high-concept tracks. Young had conceptualized a visionary video with a simultaneously strange, humorous, and sad shade. His science-fiction narrative's surreal state featured a hospital setting with a cast of robotic half-humans, scientists, and doctors whose primary goal was to teach a baby named Tabulon to touch a button.[30] Lyric-specific to "Transformer Man," and based on Ben, the baby figure has a keypad face that he keeps striking in frustration, trying to unlock the secret of a little being who has so much to say but is incapable of communicating. That quest for interface, of course, is at the core of *Trans*.

Young acknowledged that, with or without his big-concept music video, the *Trans* album was "definitely out there" and "went way over everybody's head."[31] Though frustrated by the perplexing and poor reception to the album, he expressed few regrets and no apologies for his technological explorations. Young did, however, recognize his miscalculation with the *Trans* tracks, conceding that the song selection sabotaged the album's intent. Combining the songs from the *Island in the Sun* sessions with the computer-based tracks diluted and distracted, inevitably interrupting *Tran*'s track continuity and undermining its tech-communication concept. Young's second-guessing arrived at the obvious conclusion, that releasing *Trans* as a separate EP consisting solely of the computer set of songs "would have been a cooler thing," not to mention smarter and smoother, but he conceded that he "wasn't really thinking that clearly" at the time.[32]

> So the lesson from that is I should not have caved to Geffen in the first place. I should have put out *Island in the Sun* in its original form and then should have done *Trans*, with more room for *Trans* songs to establish

themselves as a complete atmosphere. I had betrayed myself by not staying true to my art and following the muse.[33]

Young's bandmates and longtime music associates may have been just as bewildered, though less dismissive, as critics and fans were at Young's electronic, experimental eccentricities and the strangeness emanating from *Trans*. Some of Young's cohorts appreciated his artistic instincts and creative courage. Stated co-produced David Briggs:

> You tell me any established artist that did something new and different in the eighties. Nobody was doin' that vocoder stuff, and that's what artists do—they go out there and plow new ground, and in rock and roll it's hard to find new ground … *Trans* was a success in the fact that a major established artist took music to a place that was as abrasive and grating to listeners as *Tonight's the Night*. When a major established artist puts his whole career on the line to go to new ground, the critics should at least applaud the guy—as opposed to dismissin' it.[34]

David Geffen's executive response to Young's "plowing new ground" resonated above, below, and beyond the indifferent critical reviews and the compassionate creative community. In November 1983, the *Trans* script became a legal document. Less than one year after *Trans*'s release and reception, Geffen filed a $3.3 million lawsuit against Young, claiming that his first two records for Geffen Records—*Trans* and the retro-rockabilly *Everybody's Rockin'* in 1983—were "non commercial." Geffen alleged that the erratic endeavors were "musically uncharacteristic of Young's previous recordings." The company was expecting "Neil Young records." Presumably, by Geffen's standards, "characteristic Neil Young records" were tantamount to Young's most commercially successful, accessible, and/or critically acclaimed 1970s works such as *Harvest, Comes a Time*, and *Rust Never Sleeps*.[35]

Geffen was a captivating character who brought an intriguing personal and professional context to the odd lawsuit. Geffen was one of the most prominent non-artist figures of the fabled 1960–70s Southern California music scene, swiftly ascending from a William Morris agent to establish himself as one of the leading record-industry entrepreneurs and eventual multimedia moguls, forming the DreamWorks Entertainment empire with Steven Spielberg and Jeffrey Katzenberg in 1994. In 1970, Geffen created Asylum Records, which merged with Elektra in 1972 and became the touchstone label of the thriving Los Angeles–vicinity singer-songwriter circle, particularly the folk/rock/country symbiosis.

During that time period, Geffen connected with Young's manager, Elliot Roberts of Lookout Management. That agency morphed into the Geffen-Roberts Company, a partnership which sought to redirect the music business to become more artist friendly in its dealings both creatively and financially. Geffen and Roberts refused to repeat the fleecing of rock's first generation by agents, managers, and record labels. The duo was committed to providing a nurturing, protective, indulgent environment for emerging artists. The agency became the core of the LA-neighborhood music scene, selling millions of records and extracting richer royalty rates and prerequisites from record labels for artists. In his 2006 music-canyon chronicle, Michael Walker writes of the Geffen-Roberts presence: "Everywhere you looked, it seemed there was evidence that Los Angeles, thanks in no small part to the Laurel Canyon/ Geffen Roberts stable [of artists], had eclipsed San Francisco as the music capital of America."[36]

The Geffen-Roberts relationship was a swaying factor in Young's decision to sign with Geffen's new label in the early 1980s. Geffen offered Young the same financial deal that he had with Warner-Reprise. Though the amount was a far less lucrative offer than what RCA was proposing, Young's familiarity with Geffen and the promise of total creative control were among the deciding factors for his signing with Geffen's label. In a 1982 interview with the fanzine *Broken Arrow*, Roberts' positive projection of the partnership is revealing, if not prophetic:

> David had worked with Neil for a very long time. He totally relates to Neil as an artist and has no preconceived notions. He knows that he's capable of doing anything at any point in time … Neil's not concerned with selling large numbers of his records; he's concerned with making records he's pleased with. Unfortunately, they are not always commercial from the record company's point of view. David Geffen relates to that.[37]

Young's case and creative course did not benefit from the unexpected underperformance of the debut albums of his fellow high-profile Geffen roster recruits, whose record releases preceded Young's. Sales fell flat on Donna Summer's *The Wanderer* (1980), Elton John's *The Fox* (1981), and Joni Mitchell's *Wild Things Run Fast* (1982). As the most striking of the four major debuts, Young's *Trans* did not alter the label's launch trajectory. Geffen took the collective inauspicious inauguration as a reflection on him. He was predictably distressed, feeling financial and peer pressure, aware that Mo Ostin had produced successful records with the key artists that Geffen had recruited to his label.

One record in with Geffen and Young was already expressing Reprise regrets, saying that he was wrong and stupid for leaving the legendary label. His proclamations that Reprise was the "greatest record company" and that it would have supported any of his projects "whether it was commercial or not" amplified the widening Geffen-Young divide. The tension carried over from the production of *Trans* into Young's next record, the sparse, early-era *Everybody's Rockin'*, which Young "almost vindictively gave Geffen" after he denied Young studio time and rejected his plans to record a country album, which would survive to become Young's next Geffen record, *Old Ways* (1985).[38]

The entangled triangulation involving Geffen, Young, and intermediary Roberts promptly collapsed under mounting pressures. Trust and communication disintegrated, with all sides feeling betrayed. Young obviously had been in a difficult place personally, dealing with Ben's condition and financial issues. Geffen was not only working to establish a new company within a highly competitive music industry, he also had empire aims that dramatically altered his company brand from the trademark Asylum artist sanctuary of the 1970s. Geffen signed Young (among others) to be a megastar, not an unpredictable artist who expected total support from the record company for the kind of music he wanted to produce, no matter the commercial outcome. Business as *un*usual. Young received $1 million each from Geffen for two atypical albums (computer, rockabilly) which alienated his audience and systematically fragmented his record-sales base.

Considering the long-standing personal and professional dynamic between Geffen, Young, and Roberts, a lawsuit seemed as excessive as Young's genre meandering. By most accounts, both Geffen and Young took the failure personally. Roberts, hopelessly caught between his strong-willed friends, said they all overreacted, while steering the situation with stubbornness and irrationality. Geffen, partly paranoid and in poor-sale panic mode, was convinced Young was taunting him and deliberately producing esoteric albums (such as *Trans*) with substandard material while hiding a *Harvest Two* in his pocket. Upon realizing that no one, including Roberts, could ever approach the resolute Young about the kind of material he should write and record, Geffen decided he had no other option but to pursue legal action over Young's *trans*actions, a last-resort means of making a point to the obstinate artist.

Young responded to the record-label litigation with sarcasm and a countersuit. In an interview with long-time music critic Bill Flanagan published in *Musician* magazine in November 1985, Young commented:

> That was confusing to me because I always thought that I was Neil Young. But it turns out that when I do certain things, I'm not Neil Young. Well, to get sued for being noncommercial after 20 years of making records I thought was better than getting a Grammy.[39]

The Geffen-Young conflict lingered, its contemptuous undercurrent simmering since Geffen's non-support for Young's music video for *Trans*, which became a resentful (micro-) chip that Young carried on his shoulder through the decade. While the Geffen-Young legal case may not have dominated music headlines, it did provide the rock press with an engaging short-term narrative with long-lasting implications. Geffen was cast as the corporate villain, with Young the iconoclast artist-victim, and commerce versus creative control at the conflicting core. Perhaps due to the unfavorable attention brought on by the ongoing discord, Geffen eventually backed off the lawsuit pursuit. Both sides softened and reached a compromise. An apologetic Geffen expressed regret for his mishandling of the episode and his awkward attempt to bring Young "back to track." Young agreed to complete his country album (*Old Ways*) and to make a "real" record that was more "characteristic Neil Young" at some point. The Geffen and Young lawsuits and countersuits were dropped, with dismissals filed in Los Angeles Superior Court fittingly on April Fools' Day, 1985.[40]

Perhaps the most unusual part of the settlement was Young's instructing his manager, Roberts, to change his million-dollar deal with Geffen to $500,000 per album for his three remaining records with the label. The self-imposed half-million reduction was unprecedented, and was essentially an idiosyncratic attempt by Young to buy creative control. "Neil was on such a trip about the money and about the pressure it brought with it," said Roberts, whose longtime friendship with Geffen was severely strained during the dissension. "Neil felt that for a million bucks, maybe they're right, but for five-hundred thousand, I should be able to do what I want to."[41]

In the aftermath, Young released three more records on Geffen's label—the country *Old Ways* (1985), guitar-rock *Landing on Water* (1986), and an uneven reunion with Crazy Horse on *Life* (1987), which featured a "record company man" tirade, "Prisoners of Rock and Roll"—before returning home to Reprise Records. There, Young's prolific album-per-year pace persisted, though with an initial Geffen hangover, as the flagrant genre-sampling continued. *This Note's for You* (1988) was anchored by a ten-piece, horn-based rhythm-and-blues band. It was not until the end of the decade with *Freedom* (1989) that Young returned to a recognizable, original brand, one that more closely resembled "Neil Young."

*Trans*cendence

> "Whatever one thinks of the *Trans* material, this
> ['Transformer Man'] was surely one of Young's gentlest,
> most beautiful love songs."
>
> (Neil Young biographer Jimmy McDonough)

In the nearly 40-year aftermath since their arrival in 1982, "Transformer Man" and its aberrant transporter *Trans* have progressively aged gracefully, gradually attaining various levels of awareness and acceptance and contributing an incongruous and indelible mark upon the vast and varied Neil Young Recording Archive. There have been an intriguing number of routine, random, and recent revisitations of *Trans*, richly (re)contextualized in writings across an array of musical, cultural, critical, and technological spheres. Among the columns and essays, the writings range from a spirited defense of aesthetic choices at *We Are the Mutants*,[42] to explorations of the record's commercial afterlife in the online *Vinyl Me Please Magazine*,[43] to prophecy at UDiscoverMusic.com[44] and philosophy in Bruce Umbaugh's chapter, "Extended Mind and the Music of *Trans*," in the volume, *Neil Young and Philosophy*, edited by Douglas L. Berger [45] The recent accumulation of critical views generally arrives at a more affirmative stance than previously, with terms such as "overlooked" prevalent. The themes of transcending boundaries and prescience are common reflections, offset by an occasional and unfortunate "robo-rock" reference.

Despite the notable strands of enriched appreciation and reconsideration, "Transformer Man" still upholds its unsung status, occasionally overshadowed by other *Trans* tracks. In a 2014 *Rolling Stone* Special Collector's Edition devoted to Neil Young, "Transformer Man" did not place among "Neil Young's 100 Greatest Songs," while a pair of its companion computer tracks from *Trans* were ranked on the list—"Sample and Hold" (at number 49) and "Computer Age" (number 93). Predictably, *Trans* crowned the category of Young's "Weirdest Albums."

"Transformer Man" is a gentle gem worthy of a special place in Young's extensive catalog of love songs. On a broader scale, Young's doting, distorted ode is a distinctive entry in the father-son song sampler, a catalog that includes, among other son songs, Cat Stevens' (Yusuf Islam) conversational classic "Father and Son" (1970), Jackson Browne's "The Only Child" (1977) from *The Pretender*, John Lennon's "Beautiful Boy (Darling Boy)" (1981), Eric Clapton's "Tears in Heaven," (1991)—a Grammy-winning, heartbreaking hit, written with Will Jennings in the aftermath of the death of Clapton's four-year-old-son Conor—and Bruce Springsteen's "Pony Boy," (1991), a deep-track adaptation on his *Human Touch* album.

Another meaningful aspect of "Transformer Man's" legacy resides in its symbolic presence as an ideal soundtrack/anthem/theme song for the Bridge School Benefit, a weekend charity concert initiated by Neil and Pegi Young four years post-*Trans* in 1986. For the next thirty years, through 2016, the all-acoustic music event, which featured a high-profile lineup, was held every October at the Shoreline Amphitheater in Mountain View, California. Proceeds from the annual Bay Area benefit consistently reached the million-dollar range, and were the primary means of funding for the non-profit organization the Bridge School, also co-founded by the Youngs in 1987 in their continual commitment to Ben's special needs and development. Located in Hillsborough, the innovative school specializes in assisting children with severe speech and physical impairments, utilizing advanced augmentative and alternative communication and assistive technology.

Technology was not a passing fancy, impulse, or one-off with Young. The inner technophile has remained an active part of Young's music makeup, outlook, and agenda. In 2012, three decades after *Trans*, Young, discontent with digital sound quality, particularly Apple's iTunes and the compressed audio inferiority of MP3s, founded Pono (Hawaiian for "righteousness" and "proper"), a portable high-resolution download technology and service. Pono Music's 24-bit musical mission was to present songs in their purest state, "as they first sound during studio recording sessions." In an interview in *Wired* magazine, Young said he considered his entrepreneurial effort at developing the sound-source ecosystem a gallant preservationist "attempt to rescue the art form that I've been practicing for the past 50 years."[46] Young was committed to the cause, and always ready, willing, and informed to make the case, whether on late-night cable talk shows, during interviews, or in passages and chapters in his memoirs. In *Waging Heavy Peace: A Hippie Dream* (2012), Young, adhering to the myth that "technology is supposed to make life better for everyone. That's its aim," promoted his PureTone sound and its user-interface feature called the Revealer.[47] Pono Music's run was brief. Production of PonoPlayers began in 2014, with distribution of the digital device to the general public the following year. Young pulled the plug on Pono in 2017, a fate he mainly attributed to record companies' inflated charges for high-resolution formats.

*Trans*figures: Computer Coda

In mid-1993, just over ten years after *Trans*, Young selected "Transformer Man" to be part of his *MTV Unplugged* set. Young recontexualized the *Trans* computer track into a strumming, vocoderless version, with sweetly swaying backing vocals harmonized between Young's half-sister Astrid and Nicolette Larson, well-known for her hit cover of Young's "Lotta Love" in 1978. The recircuited song settles seamlessly into a typical Young soft-and-steady, romantic rhythm and moonlit mode. The acoustic adaptation is arresting and lovely. And decipherable. Being sung and heard in a new place, nothing is lost in translation. Something is maybe gained. The heartbeat is a steady backbeat brush. There is a lightness in the lyrics. The chemistry and electronics meet, even if unplugged. Perhaps the clarity is simply another concealed Youngian code referencing son Ben's seeing the "sooner or later," the cause and effect; his progress as a teenage "Transformer Man". And for Neil Young, his own deliverance on display from what he called "the invisible shield" of the 1980s, his most difficult decade: "That whole era there's always something between me and what I was trying to say."[48] Neil and Ben Young, father and son, Transformer Men transfigured.

Notes

1 Jimmy McDonough. *Shakey: Neil Young's Biography* (New York: Anchor Books 2003), 556.
2 Ibid., 93.
3 Ibid., 617.
4 See George Plasketes, "Geffen Records v Neil Young: The Battle of the Brands," in *B-sides, Undercurrents and Overtones: Peripheries to Popular in Music* (Burlington, VT: Ashgate 2009), 51–67.
5 David Downing, *Neil Young: The Man and His Music* (New York: De Capo Press), 161.
6 Ibid., 162.
7 Jon Pareles, "Work Hard, Play Hard," *Rolling Stone*, January 4, 1985: 137.
8 Downing, *Neil Young: The Man and His Music*, 155.

9 Ibid.

10 McDonough, *Shakey: Neil Young's Biography*, 550.

11 Downing, *Neil Young: The Man and His Music*, 152.

12 McDonough, *Shakey: Neil Young's Biography*, 550.

13 See William Ruhlman, "*Re-ac-tor*: Neil Young and Crazy Horse." All Music Guide; and Greg Kot, "Greendale's a Trip Through Neil Young's Career," *Chicago Tribune*, August 24, 2003.

14 Downing, *Neil Young: The Man and His Music*, 160.

15 See Downing, *Neil Young: The Man and His Music*, 159 and McDonough, *Shakey: Neil Young's Biography*, 550–1.

16 Downing, *Neil Young: The Man and His Music*, 160.

17 McDonough, *Shakey: Neil Young's Biography*, 553.

18 Downing, *Neil Young: The Man and His Music*, 161.

19 Ibid.

20 Ibid., 162.

21 Neil Young, *Waging Heavy Peace: A Hippie Dream* (New York: Blue Rider Press), 284.

22 Ibid.

23 McDonough, *Shakey: Neil Young's Biography*, 551.

24 "Skycrusher" adapts conventions of the traditional western and a nod to Michael Crichton's 1973 film *Westworld* featuring Yul Brynner as an amusement park android cowboy wearing black. Young amusingly punctuates the song with, "Come a ky ky yipiie yi ay ye."

25 The phrase "sample and hold" is drawn from a phrase rooted in Young's toy train passion, specifically work on a digital system for controlling speed of the trains and for increasing accessibility for the disabled.

26 McDonough, *Shakey: Neil Young's Biography*, 558.

27 Ibid.

28 Ibid.

29 Ibid., 587.

30 Downing, *Neil Young: The Man and His Music*, 161.

31 McDonough, *Shakey: Neil Young's Biography*, 556.

32 Ibid.

33 Downing, *Neil Young: The Man and His Music*, 285.

34 McDonough, *Shakey: Neil Young's Biography*, 557.

35 George Plasketes, "Geffen Records v. Neil Young: The Battle of the Brands." In *B-Sides, Undercurrents and Overtones: Peripheries to Popular in Music, 1960 to the Present* (Burlington, VT: Asghate: 2009), 58.

36 Michael Walker, *Laurel Canyon: The Insider Story of Rock and Roll's Legendary Neighborhood* (New York: Fraser & Fraser, 2006), 114.

37 McDonough, *Shakey: Neil Young's Biography*, 554.

38 Ibid., 557.

39 Bill Flanagan, "The Real Neil Young Stands Up," *Musician*, November 1984: 34.

40 McDonough, *Shakey: Neil Young's Biography*, 592

41 Ibid., 593.

42 Richard McKenna, "More than Just a Number: Defending Neil Young's *Trans*," *WeAreTheMutants*, January 16, 2017.

43 Gary Suarez, "*Trans* An Album So Controversial, the Label Sued Neil Young Over It." *VPM (Vinyl Me Please Magazine)*, February 6, 2018.

44 Brett Milano, "*Trans*: The Overlooked Prescience of Neil Young's Electro Album," *UDiscoverMusic*, December 29, 2020.
45 Douglas Berger, Neil Young and Philosophy (Lanham: Rowman and Littlefield, 2019).
46 Michael Calore, "Why Neil Young hates MP3s -- and what you can do about it," Wired, 2012.
47 Young, *Waging Heavy Peace*, 94–5.
48 McDonough, *Shakey: Neil Young's Biography*, 543.

References

Berger, Douglas. Neil Young and Philosophy. Lanham: Rowman and Littlefield, 2019.
Calore, Michael. "Why Neil Young hates MP3s -- and what you can do about it." *Wired*, 2012.
Downing, David. *A Dreamer of Pictures: Neil Young: The Man and His Music.* New York: Hachette, 1994.
Flanagan, Bill. "The Real Neil Young Stands Up." *Musician*, November 1984.
Kot, Greg. "Greendale's a Trip Through Neil Young's Career." *Chicago Tribune*, August 24, 2003.
McDonough, Jimmy. *Shakey: Neil Young's Biography*. New York: Anchor/Random House, 2002.
McKenna, Richard. "More than Just a Number: Defending Neil Young's *Trans*." *WeAreTheMutants*, January 16, 2017. https://wearethemutants.com/2017/01/16/more-than-just-a-number-defending-neil-youngs-trans/
Milano, Brett. "*Trans*: The Overlooked Prescience of Neil Young's Electro Album." *UDiscoverMusic*, December 29, 2020. www.udiscovermusic.com/stories/trans-the-overlooked-prescience-of-neil-youngs-electro-album/
Pareles, Jon. "Work Hard, Play Hard." *Rolling Stone*, January 4, 1985.
Plasketes, George. "Geffen Records v. Neil Young: The Battle of the Brands." In *B-Sides, Undercurrents and Overtones: Peripheries to Popular in Music, 1960 to the Present*, 51–67. Burlington, VT: Asghate: 2009.
Ruhlman, William. "*Re-ac-tor*: Neil Young and Crazy Horse," review. *All Music Guide*. www.allmusic.com/album/re-ac-tor-mw0000717742
Suarez, Gary. "*Trans* An Album So Controversial, the Label Sued Neil Young Over It." *VPM (Vinyl Me Please Magazine)*, February 6, 2018. https://magazine.vinylmeplease.com/magazine/trans-album-so-controversial-label-sued-neil-young-over-it/
Umbaugh, Bruce. "Neil Young and *Trans*." In *Neil Young and Philosophy*, edited by Douglas L. Berger. Washington D.C.: Lexington Books, 2019.
Walker, Michael. *Laurel Canyon: The Insider Story of Rock and Roll's Legendary Neighborhood.* New York: Fraser & Fraser, 2006.
Young, Neil. *Waging Heavy Peace: A Hippie Dream.* New York: Blue Rider Press, 2012.

10 The Replacements—"Unsatisfied" (1984)

Gina Arnold

These days it's hard to remember how much we hated Ronald Reagan and everything he stood for. In retrospect, he seems like a kindly old duffer—wrongheaded, for sure, politically insufferable, but not full-on evil like others we could mention. But make no mistake: Ronald Reagan was an abomination of a president, and we were well aware of it at the time. Tax cuts, deregulation, re-militarization, "Star Wars" (the Strategic Defense Initiative), trickle-down economics … it was all a cover for making rich people richer, and the fact that people could look at his frozen, dyed-black hair and see into his stone-cold heart and still think otherwise was appalling. This is the man, remember, who ordered troops to fire on peaceful protesters at UC Berkeley in 1969, killing one person; who, in 1981, fired 11,345 striking air traffic controllers rather than negotiate with their union; and who once claimed that voting for the Civil Rights Act—and later, the Voting Rights Act (that is, dismantling Jim Crow)—would cause the US to become "an antheap of totalitarianism."[1] In 1985, Reagan went to Europe to commemorate the end of World War II by visiting the gravesite of Waffen-SS Officers—that is, Nazi war criminals—who'd been buried there.[2] The Ramones even had a song, "Bonzo Goes to Bitburg" (1985), about it, and hell, if the *Ramones* were bothered by the sight of a president's foreign diplomacy, then it must have been pretty bad.

Ronald Reagan was the winner of the first presidential election I ever voted in, and the eight years of his reign coincided with the exact period of my coming of age—that era when you form all your most important political opinions and aesthetic tastes, and of course discover the music you love the most. It's also the age when you're at your most judgy, which is probably why everything I associate with that time now—preppie chic, presidential anti-AIDS statements, pro-South African apartheid remarks, date rape—is still utterly abhorrent to me. I hated people who were into him (and by proxy, those things) as much as I hate them now, but on the flip side, I still love what I loved back then with a passionate intensity, because that time also encompasses when I was in college, when I worked on a college radio station, and when I first found out about the independent underground music scene. In 1984 I volunteered to be a DJ at a college radio station, and the experience turned the decade which Bill Clinton (of all people) later called "a gilded age

DOI: 10.4324/9781003093206-11

of greed, selfishness, irresponsibility, and neglect" into one that, for me personally, was one of glorious, memorable, abandon.[3]

It was the year that Michael Jackson toured off *Thriller* (1982), and the two biggest singles were "Born in the USA" and "Like a Virgin." But for me, the Replacements' song "Unsatisfied" is the real anthem of the Reagan era. "Family values." "It's morning in America." "Let's make America great again." Those were the catchphrases of the time, and everything about them felt smarmy and disingenuous, like the opening sequence to the Netflix biopic *The Dirt* (2019), which begins with a montage meant to evoke how conservative the Reagan years were—shoulder pads, the moral majority, and fluffy haircuts—and then falsely credits the truly abysmal band Motley Crüe with being some kind of a liberating antidote to it all. Ugh. The Replacements song "Unsatisfied," recorded and released in 1984, stands in direct opposition to that time. It crashed right into that era's massive self-confidence and twisted it into the meaningless shards of puffed-up rhetoric that it was all along.

In an article in the *Journal of Popular Music Studies* on subcultural identity formation in alternative music, Holly Kruse explains how, in the 1980s, a loose network of college radio stations in cities across America created

> the possibility that a band could break through to at least cult popularity without the aid of a major record label (and now can achieve mainstream success by graduating from the ranks of independent labels to the majors: witness REM and Nirvana).[4]

This tight-knit network of musicians, listeners, labels, and fans (myself included) would at the time have described itself as being radically in opposition to the mainstream. As Kruse reminds us, Laclau and Mouffe state that "all values are values of opposition and are defined only by their difference"; similarly, Simon Reynolds has explained how, thanks to the college radio network, "[a] noise band in Manchester can have more in common with a peer group in Austin, Texas, than with one of its 'neighbours' two blocks away."[5] So it was that while the mainstream world was listening to music by Madonna and Bruce Springsteen, my friends and I were digging deep into a post-punk treasure trove of independent music, most of it made by bands of American white boys with four instruments and a shitty amplifier.

If you put it that way, it sounds boring and awful, but the times were different then. Today, artists can potentially use new technologies and forms of dissemination to overcome barriers like gender and genre, but back then everything was pretty white and bland, which may be why the Replacements' playful take on songs by the Bay City Rollers, Kiss, and the Monkees seemed so funny: live, they mocked that bland whiteness with dry acumen, while simultaneously contributing songs like "Androgynous" and "Sixteen Blue" that elevated the form to something far deeper and more true. When the Replacements arrived in my town to play live, they blew up all my notions about what "good" music was and where "good" bands could come from.

Before I heard the Replacements, whose hometown of Minneapolis barely registered in my consciousness, I thought only English people wearing tons of black eyeliner and New Yorkers were hip and cool, and that every band should cover the Velvet Underground. After, I wasn't so sure. The Replacements were Midwestern goofs. But in the course of 18 months between 1983 and 1985, I had heard at least 12 original songs by them that would have gone—I mean, that *go*—on my top-twenty songs of all time ever. After a lifetime of thinking musical excellence was the province of the Beatles and the Stones, it was so revelatory to see it appear in my own peer group. It was like hearing profundity pop out of the mouth of the class clown.

The Replacements' oeuvre—or perhaps I should say, the mood that their oeuvre incited—was a revelation to me, but at the time I came to hear of them, the Replacements were already going on five years old (see Figure 10.1). They had come together in Minneapolis in 1979 and had recorded one EP (*Stink*) and two other long-play albums for the local label Twin/Tone, which also put out music by local favorites the Suburbs and the Suicide Commandos, among others. The Replacements had a vexed reputation in Minneapolis due to their habitual drunken snarkiness and unreliably antic live shows, but there was no doubt they were wildly popular with locals, in part just because one never knew what they would do next. Appear naked? Wear a tutu? Cover a song by Jethro Tull? Break your heart? They were anarchic and bipolar, but few would dispute that they were also geniuses (genii?). Lead guitarist Bob Stinson, speaking to *Goldmine* magazine a little before his death in 1995, described their shows as "like watching Alfred Hitchcock with the cartoons on."[6]

During those years, the band played a lot in the Midwest, but they didn't come to California until 1984, when the Replacements released *Let It Be*, their third full-length album, and began a tour of America that went around it twice. I saw them at least seven times between October 1984 and late 1985—in cities that included Palo Alto, San Francisco, San Jose, Fresno, and Davis— and in 1986, when I was in Europe, I saw them play in both London and Paris. At the latter show, I was one of only a handful of people, all American, and I didn't have enough francs to pay for a beer.

By that year, the band had signed to Warner Brothers Records, made a truly disastrous appearance on *Saturday Night Live*, and pretty much shot themselves in the foot on many a stage across America. This was a trend that would continue until their acrimonious breakup in 1991, and which was probably most apparent in their infamous opening slots for Tom Petty in 1989.[7] But the shows I remember best came before that, and I remember their atmosphere as irreverent, defiant, explosive, and just plain *fun*. More accurately, as one writer once memorably put it, the overwhelming effect of the Replacements is homesickness. "Everybody in the band has cried in the van on the way to the show," Westerberg has said.[8] Exactly. I too have cried, both on the way to the show and on the way home, and for a wide variety of reasons. Very often when I saw them, the Replacements played like shit. Indeed, over the years I saw way more bad shows than good ones, and yet, there was something about the

Figure 10.1 From left to right: Bob Stinson, Tommy Stinson, Chris Mars, and Paul Westerberg of the Replacements, in 1984. Credit: Corbis Premium Historical/Getty Images.

experience of seeing them live that captured what it was like to be alive and human, something about them that was just so poignant and true. And for me, "Unsatisfied," the lead-off song on side two of *Let it Be*, is the song that exemplifies that feeling. Mixing perfect '80s jangle pop with the kind of vocal angst that would later populate the jukebox of grunge, it is, simply put, the sonic apex of that era. And possibly of any era.

This might sound like surprisingly high praise since, although the '80s had its fair share of rock stars, the Replacements could not conceivably be counted among them. Despite being legends among college radio aficionados, their music got very little airplay, and no wonder: while with Warner Brothers, during the height of MTV's reign of terror, rather than create a pretty-boy cliché of themselves standing in the desert with their hair waiving back or whatever, they stubbornly released a video for the song "Bastards of Young" which was essentially a still shot of a speaker emitting the music. This was because, as singer Paul Westerberg told David Fricke of *Rolling Stone*, if they had to do a video, it would only be one that "nobody would want to watch all the way through, much less twice," and it is difficult to overstate just how perverse that gesture was.[9] It is probably one of the main reasons the Replacements aren't more widely known today, but it is that attitude—that is to say, their adamant belief, in the face of every possible sign otherwise, that rock was sonic, not visual, and that MTV was stupid—that is captured so poignantly on "Unsatisfied." If you think about it, it is also the emotional, political, and ideological opposite of the Rolling Stones' far better known "(I Can't Get No) Satisfaction" (1965). The latter is a tricksy, nasty piece of work, a whiny lament by an ultra-privileged douchebag who is sick of hearing advertisements and is flabbergasted to note that he has been turned down by a girl. The double negative in its chorus gives it away: "I can't get no ..." meaning you *can*, right, Mick? *You can* get satisfaction, but you want to complain about it anyway.

As Derrida says, we don't speak language, it speaks us. Linguistically speaking, a song titled "Unsatisfied" ought to mean the same thing as one that proclaims "(I Can't Get No) Satisfaction," but there's no question that the Replacements' version of that phrase is an entirely different proposition. Just for starters, can you even imagine Mick Jagger asking anyone else if *they* were satisfied? I could leave the whole thing right there and have delineated the difference between the two songs for good and all. But "Unsatisfied" is a bigger and better song than "Satisfaction" for more reasons than that. It's better because rather than refer solely to the singer's life and feelings, it refers explicitly to *yours*. This singer isn't just frustrated by advertisements or disappointed in his current romantic circumstances. He's disillusioned with the world itself. And why shouldn't he have been, given that era? There is a story that the Replacements' manager, Peter Jesperson, called the Replacements— back in the days before cell phones—to find out the final lyric to "Unsatisfied" for publishing rights' purposes, and that Paul Westerberg took the call at a payphone on the highway. Reception being bad, as it usually was in those days, he was forced to scream his answer into the phone.

When I think about the Replacements, I like to think of that apocryphal moment: the barren highway, the empty gas station, the grubby young man yelling the truth into the cold Midwestern night. "What is the last line you sing, the one after when you say, 'I'm so dissatisfied?'" asks Peter. "It's 'Liberty is a lie!'" Paul yells into the telephone. "No, I said, "*Liberty is a lie!*'"[10]

And liberty *is* a lie. We know that now, to our cost, and if I were a better historian, or perhaps a professor of political science, I would now use this space to explain to you exactly how the election of Ronald Reagan presaged the situation we find ourselves in now. But I am only a professor of critical race studies. I can argue that the civil rights movement and the counterculture caused a turn to the radical right. I can see the moments when liberty slipped away. But I can't do more than suggest to you the recognition—or *pre*cognition—that the whole post-World War II era that my cohort and I came of age in (when there were lots of jobs and pensions, no wars for the boys fight in, and you could go to a state college practically for free) was in fact not a permanent condition but a very brief lull that would be irrevocably changed by specific Reagan policies like deregulation, union busting, and (especially) the bogus war on drugs.

According to Genius.com, the heavily frequented site for explaining lyrics, Westerberg wrote that song about how unsatisfied he felt with music, not with democracy: "It was just the feeling that we're never going anywhere and the music we're playing is not the music I feel and I don't know what to do and I don't know how to express myself."[11] Doubtless, that *is* what he felt, but what I felt then, and still feel now, whenever I hear it, is as if someone is clutching my heart. The song told me that I was not alone in feeling that there was no point in playing along with the rich kids and the status quo, that it was a loser's game to do so, and therefore I, a bona fide loser, was fully justified in quitting it.

"Unsatisfied" also typifies the Reagan era because of the way the song was positioned against larger cultural movements. A band on an independent record label cast adrift in a major-label world is a great allegory for many of the Reagan era's signature changes. Reagan's great mission was to deregulate all kinds of industries, including the media and the airwaves. Theoretically, that wasn't a bad thing for independent record labels, as a plethora of new stations and media formats would allow for new niche markets and audiences. In actuality, it did nothing of the sort. Rather, the majority of those stations and formats peddled the same stuff to the same people. Besides, one of the things we always forget about the '80s is that they weren't just pre-internet, pre-peer-to-peer, pre-streaming, they were even pre-CD.

Think about that for a minute, and all that it implies. Just for starters, in order to purchase music to play at home, people still had to drag their asses to dedicated record stores and interact with the clerks there (which often wasn't the most pleasant experience). Then they had to take their purchases home and stack them somewhere safe where they wouldn't warp. And remember the trouble we had to take in order to transport our collections between our dorms and apartments? For years, my record collection accounted for the majority of my belongings. It weighed the most and used up the most space, and yet living without it was unthinkable.

No wonder so many people were just not up for the commodity-fetishistic practices a record collection required, instead just listening to the radio and whatever it decided to play for them. And the radio was tyrannical. If you weren't into top forty, you could curate your listening in one of three or four ways: talk radio, country, hair metal, or its British opposite, new wave. It goes without saying that it was all super White. All of hip-hop, then at its best, was unavailable to be heard on commercial radio. Prince was practically censored for referring to actual sex acts, and the rest was impersonal dross, full of squeals and angles, like the Missing Persons song "Walking In LA" (1982), which is about impersonality itself and sounds like it was sung by a fembot. Whether it was the Thompson Twins, Human League, and Soft Cell, or Def Leppard, Quiet Riot, and Motley Crüe, it all sounded as clean as a whistle— and, incidentally, as White as wherever it was that the colonial rulers lived in the midst of the Indian city of Lucknow … in 1885.

Looking back, the idea that commercial radio would be entirely responsible for a person's listening fare seems crazy and depressing, but back then, we didn't know any better. On the fell day in one's teen years that you realized you were in thrall to some corrupt corporation's choice of artists, the shock was visceral. The minute you realized, you went left of the dial, to where the college radio stations resided, to engage with music that sounded like it was made somewhere—anywhere—not in a studio vacuum. This is what people forget. At that time, the jangle of a Rickenbacker being strummed by an actual hand was just totally antithetical to the smooth, synthetic sounds of '80s pop of any kind.

"Unsatisfied" opens with an especially good example of that raw, human sound. In contrast to radio fare of the '80s, the recording is so intimate that your fist almost cramps from the feeling of fingers clenching the fretboard to form the chords. About 30 seconds in, there's an electric chord that keens over the top of that jangle, and it sounds like it was made by a violin bow on top of electrified honey. One upward swoop, and then—faintly, in the background, as if by accident—a voice kind of upchucks into the music: "*Ny'..uh?*"

And in come the drums. "Look me in the eye and tell me that I'm satisfied," growls the singer, and his voice sounds exactly as if it came straight out of that boy you saw out of the corner of your eye when you were looking out the window of the bus. It's as if he looked straight back at you and asked you, personally, "*Are you satisfied?*" It's the rhetorical question to end all rhetorical questions. In Latin, it would start with the particle "num." Even today, I'd stake that first 45 seconds of music against anything ever recorded, and the next three minutes aren't bad either. Every time I play it, the song catches at my heart. It's everything I ever dreamed of, right in front me, and, well, you probably know the punch line.

One way you know that "Unsatisfied" is more than a song, and more than a feeling, is that despite its brilliance, it's all but uncoverable. The trans artist Laura Jane Grace once sang "Androgynous," a song from the same album, and I've heard Freedy Johnston do a good cover of "I Will Dare" on a ukulele, but covers of "Unsatisfied" (by, for example, the bands Hole and Calexico) merely underline the truth that it's uncoverable. Sure, a person can play the chords and sing its lyrics, but it's impossible to recover, reinsert, or change its import to listeners, because its emotional weight was sunk largely in the way that it contrasted with other songs of the era. It was a time when inhumanity in music was considered cool, and this was the actual opposite: authentic. This singer, this song, this sentiment are so utterly honest it's almost shocking to hear them, like seeing someone in kindergarten wet their pants in front of the whole class, or a guy get turned down in public after proposing to his girlfriend on the big screen at a ballpark. At first you have to look away, rather than suffer that secondhand embarrassment. But if you have the guts to look back, you'll be a changed person.

The Replacements' history bookends the 1980s nicely. Although they'd gigged around Minneapolis earlier, they handed their first cassette to Peter Jesperson, the manager of the record store Oarfolkjokeopus, in May of 1980; their last show was in 1991, but the writing was on the wall well before that.

In the course of the decade, they released a bunch of records and played thousands of gigs, but despite receiving ecstatic press, the records were only moderately successful, even by the standards of the day—according to the *New York Times* archive, *Let It Be* only sold a total of 120,000 copies in six years—and the bulk of the gigs were in nightclubs rather than arenas (though in 1989 they did a tour as the opening act for Tom Petty).[12] The sum total of people who saw them in those years was probably diminished even more by the fact that many of them, like me, simply went to see them over and over again. The Replacements were an addiction, an obsession, almost a way of life for their fans, but they were never a household name, and their music wasn't played much (if at all) on commercial radio. Disappointed, the band broke up under a cloud of bad fortune at the Taste of Chicago Festival in Grant Park in Chicago on July 4, 1991, in a legendary gig which ended with their roadies finishing the set. Four years later, one of their founding members, guitarist Bob Stinson, died of a drug overdose.

The band had long since vowed they'd never play again, but in 2013, two of its members, Paul Westerberg and Tommy Stinson, reunited under the name, just for a few gigs to benefit their ailing guitarist, Slim Dunlop, who'd suffered a debilitating stroke. Later, they took the show on the road as the Back by Unpopular Demand Tour, and in 2015, on April 13th, the tour came to my town, San Francisco.

At first I thought I did not want to go. I thought their history—my history with them—was over, and I didn't want to sully it. But at the last minute I changed my mind, purchasing a ticket on Stubhub and sneaking there without a companion. If there was one thing I knew, it was that I wished to be alone in their presence—that is, alone in the midst of 3,300 people who loved them as much as I do. In the old days, I wouldn't have believed there were that many people in the *country* who did so, much less that those people regarded them with the same Yeats-ian passionate intensity as I. I wouldn't have believed it, because there weren't.

But now there are, and this set of fans is better than the last set. The last set made a huge fuss when there were horns on "Can't Hardly Wait;" talked about the Replacements being sellouts for signing to Warner Brothers, dissed *Tim* and *All Shook Down*, records that have proved their worth over and over again. This set of fans didn't judge the Replacements on anything but their music. And this set of fans was earned fairly and squarely, through the beauty of technological change—MP3s and YouTube and blogs and Pitchfork and social networking and that one last unquantifiable ingredient of music that sometimes, but only sometimes, allows listeners entry into the most romantic and remote little portals of the past. Remember that when you're cursing Apple Music or selling a CD collection or wishing that some record store was still open or just generally maligning this generation: the internet has allowed the Replacements to survive when their contemporaries all either died or over-toured or simply faded away into obscurity. And that is so precious and lucky, like everything to do with the Replacements—it's just so goddamned right.

As for the show ... how did I ever think I could talk sentiently, or write sentiently, about a *show*? How does one talk sentiently about true love? It reminded me of the time I had a crush on a guy and I said to my friend, "I like him so much that what I can't understand is why *you* don't have a crush on him too!" And she pointed out that if she and I, and everyone else, had crushes on the same person, the world would literally stop turning: "We'd be like bees or ants or something ... not even human."

But at the Replacements' last show, we *were* like bees or ants or something. There were times during that show when the air was like one big love balloon wafting up around the stage, when the ecstasy of the crowd was peaking. You know the break in "Can't Hardly Wait"? The silent part? The balloon actually popped at that moment, and the love went spilling out all over, enveloping the whole place, causing tears to start out of people's eyes. "Bastards of Young?"? "Alex Chilton"? "Left of the Dial"? Forget about it. Puddles, *actual* pools, of live, goopy, human sentiment were visibly forming below me on the floor. During "Skyway," the guy next to me literally burst into tears, and he was very much not alone. The band didn't play "Unsatisfied," and I for one am glad. I don't think anyone—they or I—could have handled it. The next day, a friend wrote on Facebook, "They did it in Minneapolis and I died." Yup. That is what I was afraid would happen. We would all have died. True, it would have been a Romeo and Juliet–like death; that is, death by love. But still. We'd be dead.

F. Scott Fitzgerald (who grew up in St. Paul) once said that American lives have no second acts, but he was wrong as hell about this one. What we always loved about the Replacements was their down-home-ness; the way they tied country music to punk, saw the beauty in cheesy top-forty tunes, and took minute pleasure in the most manufactured and daunting aspects of life in these United States at a time in the country when to do so was an act of daring. I went into the show thinking, "What on earth made me ever think indie rock was important?" and I came away thinking, "Oh now I remember!"

I think that in the modern world it takes an incredible amount of courage, and is almost unbelievably honorable, to actually suck a little bit. To take a chance. *To not care.* That's what the Replacements did; that singular thing that we all envied so much. They really didn't care. Paul Westerberg just burns talent. He drips it off him in great globs and squanders it in front of your face. But that is all he does with it. Then he lets it go. At the time, and even now, it seems like a positively noble gesture, a grandiose "Fuck you" to a world of expectations and aspirations and responsibilities and tension: a giant sigh of relief. Loving the Replacements during the Reagan '80s was like that too: it was a way to just let go of desire and doubt, an antidote to phoniness and bullying and bluster. We loved and we love them, and our love is always unrequited, but that's the best kind of love: the secret loves, the sacred loves, the things you'd love anyway, with no possible reward except the fact that you're allowed to do it.

That's what rock 'n' roll music is for, in my opinion. It allows us to experience that absolutely selfless feeling of love which could honestly pass us by if we didn't have a place to experience it. That's what I get from hearing "Unsatisfied," both then and now … in that seemingly endless era before the invention of CDs and then Napster and iTunes … when what you chose to listen to was a way to define who you were. To choose the Replacements was to declare yourself somehow outcast from the mainstream, against the massive conventionality that characterized the era, against Reagan's consolidation of the media, against being against drugs, against everything that would soon coalesce into the institutionalized forces that are holding our society in check.

The Replacements weren't very popular in their time, but they ushered in grunge. With Nirvana, that sound and the scene that spawned it became large enough—and profitable enough—to be co-opted by the mainstream, and so the sincerity, the authenticity, the very values that sound originally enunciated got lost. Maybe listening to "Unsatisfied" now doesn't quite signal the call to arms that it once did, but it's the song that made the '80s less unbearable for me. Is there a band that's doing that for the young people of this era?

Notes

1 Douglas C. Rossinow, *The Reagan Era: A History of the 1980s* (New York: Columbia University Press, 2017).
2 Ronald Reagan, *Reagan: A Life in Letters* (New York: Free Press, 2004).
3 Bill Clinton, *The New Covenant: Responsibility and Rebuilding the Community*. The New Covenant Speeches.
4 Holly Kruse, "Subcultural Identity in Alternative Music Culture." *Popular Music* 12, no. 1 (January 1993): 33–41.
5 Kruse, "Subcultural Identity in Alternative Music Culture."
6 Ralph Heibutzki, "Brats in Babylon: The Replacements, 1980–1991." *Goldmine*, October 29, 1993.
7 Bob Mehr's meticulously reported biography *Trouble Boys* does a deep dive into the darkness that underpins the band's career, exploring among other things the suburban family dysfunction that most likely underpins so many bands of that era.
8 Stephen Metcalf, "Revisiting the Replacements' Let It Be on the Album's 25th Anniversary." *Slate Magazine*, December 17, 2009.
9 David Fricke, "The Gospel according to Paul Westerberg." *Rolling Stone*, May 22, 1986.
10 This story was told to me by the Replacements manager, Peter Jesperson. It appears in my book *Route 666: On the Road to Nirvana*.
11 The Replacements. "Unsatisfied." *Genius*. genius.com/The-replacements-unsatisfied-lyrics
12 David Browne, "POP MUSIC; the Independents See Vultures Circling Overhead." *The New York Times*, October 27, 1991.

References

Arnold, Gina. *Route 666: On the Road to Nirvana*. New York: St. Martin's Press, 1993.
Browne, David. "POP MUSIC; the Independents See Vultures Circling Overhead." *The New York Times*, October 27, 1991. www.nytimes.com/1991/10/27/arts/pop-music-the-independents-see-vultures-circling-overhead.html

Clinton, Bill. *The New Covenant: Responsibility and Rebuilding the Community*. The New Covenant Speeches.

Fricke, David. "The Gospel according to Paul Westerberg." *Rolling Stone*, May 22, 1986. www.rollingstone.com/music/music-news/the-gospel-according-to-paul-westerberg-108802/

Hale, Grace Elizabeth. *COOL TOWN: How Athens, Georgia, Launched Alternative Music and Changed American Culture*. North Carolina: University Of North Carolina Press, 2020.

Heibutzki, Ralph. "Brats in Babylon: The Replacements, 1980–1991." *Goldmine*, October 29, 1993.

Kruse, Holly. "Subcultural Identity in Alternative Music Culture." *Popular Music* 12, no. 1 (January 1993): 33–41.

Mehr, Bob. *Trouble Boys - the True Story of the Replacements*. New York: The Perseus Books Group, 2017.

Metcalf, Stephen. "Revisiting the Replacements' Let It Be on the Album's 25th Anniversary." *Slate Magazine*, December 17, 2009. slate.com/culture/2009/12/revisiting-the-replacements-let-it-be-on-the-album-s-25th-anniversary.html

Reagan, Ronald. *Reagan: A Life in Letters*. New York: Free Press, 2004.

Rossinow, Douglas C. *The Reagan Era: A History of the 1980s*. New York: Columbia University Press, 2017.

Smith, R. J. "Going down with the Replacements." *The Village Voice*, November 12, 2020. www.villagevoice.com/2020/11/12/going-down-with-the-replacements/

The Replacements. *Unsatisfied*. Twin/Tone Records, 1984.

The Replacements. "Unsatisfied." *Genius*. genius.com/The-replacements-unsatisfied-lyrics

11 NWA—"F- tha Police" (1988)

Austin McCoy

As Ice Cube, MC Ren, Eazy-E, Dr. Dre, and DJ Yella, members of Niggaz Wit' Attitudes (NWA) (see Figure 11.1) performed at Detroit's Joe Louis Arena, people in the crowd egged on the group to perform its controversial anti-police-brutality track. "Fuck the Police! Fuck the police! Fuck the police!" the crowd screamed.

O'Shea "Ice Cube" Jackson had just finished performing "I Ain't tha 1" and was looking to Dr. Dre, who served as one of the DJs, for the cue to start the group's final song of their set. However, Ice Cube noticed MC Ren and Dr. Dre discussing the closer. Then MC Ren began to instruct the 20,000 in attendance: "Everybody say fuck the police!"

The crowd chanted back, "Fuck the police!"

Dre instructed Cube, "Come in on two." Dre threw on the beat to "F- the police" and Ice Cube started to perform his legendary verse.

Meanwhile, nearly two hundred officers from the department's gang unit positioned themselves throughout the venue because, as retired sergeant Larry Courts told attendees at a Black Lives Do Matter forum in Ypsilanti, MI, in 2015, the police were there to "keep the peace." Yet, while Courts admitted that the gang squad always worked rap concerts at large venues, the DPD's gang squad was there to police NWA as well. According to Courts, "We were strategically placed...we didn't think there was going to be a riot. But we had our marching orders. We were told that under no circumstance that they were to perform the song."[1] Less than a minute into their performance, plainclothes officers started to rush the stage. Then everyone heard "pop, pop, pop." Believing someone fired a gun, thousands of concertgoers as well as the members of the group fled. Eazy-E, Ice Cube, Dr. Dre, MC Ren, and DJ Yella ran in different directions as Detroit police officers ventured backstage looking for them, confronting members of LL Cool J's entourage. Eventually the group's security spirited them back to the hotel, where DPD officers eventually caught up with them. The DPD detained them for 15 minutes, when one officer allegedly told the group, "We just wanted to show the kids that you can't say 'Fuck the Police' in Detroit."[2]

This episode in August 1989 underscores how NWA's pathbreaking anti-police-brutality song "F- tha Police" became a tool of defiance and resistance

DOI: 10.4324/9781003093206-12

for the group and its listeners. Law enforcement's reaction to "F- tha Police" also illustrates how the police saw the song as a piece of propaganda that threatened their authority. Initially NWA refrained from performing the song during their tour because law enforcement launched a national fax campaign encouraging other police forces to boycott working the group's tour.

Historian Felicia Angeja Viator writes in her book on the rise of West Coast rap that "'Fuck tha Police' was, of course, grounded in local grievances. But it also spoke directly to a problem plaguing all of Black America."[3] Members of NWA understood this. The recording of "F- tha Police" emerged out of the group's experiences, especially Dr. Dre's and Eazy-E's encounters with Los Angeles law enforcement. Yet the group also recognized that the song would appeal to other African Americans living in South Central Los Angeles and throughout the country due to the persistence of police brutality and state violence inflicted on them.

"F- tha Police" especially resonated with Detroiters at that concert, since police brutality cast a long shadow in the city's history. Black Detroiters endured a long history of police abuse, especially during the 1960s, when they erupted in open rebellion, and during the 1970s, when a single police unit killed 19 residents in two years of operation.[4] While it is possible Black concertgoers were not thinking of this history as they pled for NWA to perform their hit song, they would not miss an opportunity in the concert to give the Detroit police a metaphorical, or even literal, middle finger. Like Ice Cube said, "'Fuck tha police' was something everyone wanted to say, but felt they couldn't."[5]

As NWA produced one of the most incendiary pieces of rap music and popular culture ever released, the group did not view itself as a political outfit like Boogie Down Productions (BDP) and Public Enemy (PE). NWA was not shy about their desire to use music to attain wealth. They saw the controversy as providing a boost to their popularity and stature within popular culture, as well as to record sales. And unlike BDP, PE, and other groups like Eric B and Rakim, NWA were not afraid to produce retrograde songs steeped in misogyny, homophobia, and nihilism. However, in a blistering five-minute-and-forty-five-second song, Ice Cube, MC Ren, Dr. Dre, Eazy-E, and DJ Yella popularized a rallying cry that captured years, if not decades, of frustration with an institution often seen as a racist "occupying force" in Black communities. Thus, like the Black Panther Party for Self-Defense, the group sought to delegitimize law enforcement and question their presumed monopoly over violent force.[6]

In political culture, the FBI and other local police departments saw "F- tha Police" as a threat, and thus they sought to utilize organized labor actions and threats to censor NWA. Particular law enforcement agencies like the Los Angeles Police Department (LAPD) spent decades developing and articulating the "thin blue line" ideology justifying its need to professionalize, expand, and militarize its force. LAPD chiefs like William Parker, who led the police force from 1950 until his death in 1966, believed that law enforcement did not just "serve and protect" people and enforce laws but that they

Figure 11.1 From left to right: Eazy-E, DJ Yella, MC Ren, and Dr. Dre of NWA at the Eighth Annual MTV Video Music Awards at Universal City, California, on September 5, 1991.

also functioned as the "thin blue line" between order and anarchy, whether that anarchy represented political radicals or criminalized Black and Brown people. For law enforcement who saw themselves as guardians of the US republic, "F- tha police" gave Black and Brown people license to not just question their authority but to actually attack them, as did groups such as the Black Panthers.

Historical Context of "F- tha Police"

As with the creation of hip-hop culture in South Bronx during the early 1970s, economic restructuring, political repression, the emergence of street gangs, and transformations in policing laid the groundwork for the emergence of West Coast rap, NWA, and the recording of "F- tha Police." A wave of plant closings decimated the South Central Los Angeles area. Between 1978 and 1982, factory closings cost the city close to seventy thousand jobs. The jobless rate rose to 11 percent during the 1983 recession, while youth unemployment in South Central reached 50 percent.[7] Street gangs like the Crips and Bloods and the drug trade emerged to fill the vacuum left by the industrial sector and the suppression and decline of Black radical political organizations such as the Black Panthers.

The LAPD pioneered the professionalizing, politicizing, and militarizing of policing during the twentieth century. Chief William Parker built the LAPD into a political organization with his ability to propagandize the function of law enforcement in the city and in the US. Chief Parker formalized the political function of the police and its role in defending the nation from domestic threats in his articulations of the "thin blue line" ideology. Grounded in Manichean, Cold War thinking, Parker claimed the LAPD represented the thin blue line between order and disorder. With this, the police established themselves as a vital arm of governance in a liberal capitalist society built upon histories of racial exclusion and the exploitation of workers. This, along with material support from the federal government, would have larger ramifications as police across the country developed into a political-interest group.[8]

The federal government played a key role in the transformation of policing. President Lyndon Johnson declared a war on crime in March 1965, and Congress passed the Safe Streets Act of 1968, which established the Law Enforcement Assistance Administration, which distributed resources to states in an effort to support police forces. Subsequently, Richard Nixon declared a war on drugs in 1971, in which Los Angeles emerged as a flashpoint.[9] This war further drove the militarization of police departments, and the passage of anti-drug legislation allowing the state to incarcerate more people for longer periods of time devastated Black and Brown communities.

The bipartisan Anti-Drug Abuse Act of 1986 doubled the level of funding for crime and drug-control programs from Ronald Reagan's first term. The law, which was supported by many Democrats such as progressive congressman Ronald Dellums and Charles Rangel from New York, established mandatory minimum sentences for heroin, cocaine, and crack cocaine possession. Much of the funds to fight the drug war, or to persuade youngsters to "Just Say No," contributed to the militarization of police forces as they went to the purchase of helicopters, airplanes, and intelligence-gathering systems. Reagan's drug and crime policy led to a considerable increase in arrests and incarceration.[10]

Conflating the war on drugs with a war on gangs, the LAPD sought to fight this conflict with a police force that outfitted itself with military weaponry. The police department established the nation's first SWAT team in 1967, which deployed a tank borrowed from the California National Guard. Supported by the federal government, the police department then created Community Resources Against Street Hoodlums (CRASH) in 1972, joining other special crime units such as Detroit's Stop the Robberies, Enjoy Safe Streets (STRESS). CRASH spearheaded the LAPD's battle against gangs during the 1970s.[11]

Chief Daryl Gates oversaw the department's war on gangs as the LAPD came to symbolize racist policing in the midst of this escalation. The police killing of Eula Mae Love in January 1979, involving a dispute over a $22 gas bill, stirred discontent among African Americans and accelerated organizing and calls for the LAPD to revisit their use of deadly force policies. In the midst of debates around police tactics and racialized violence, Gates remarked infamously that Hispanics and Latino/a officers were "lazy" and said African Americans were more susceptible to death by chokehold, which elicited outrage from Black and Brown residents.[12]

NWA was not the first rap act to diss the LAPD. Police militarization inspired local rapper Todd "Toddy Tee" Howard to record an anti-LAPD track called "Batterram" in 1984. "Batterram" was a local hit, named after the military-style vehicles Gates and the LAPD acquired from the federal government as the city prepared for the 1984 Olympics.[13] The LAPD's Operation Hammer represented Chief Gates and the police's principal initiative to stop gangs. Gates remarked, "This is war ... We want to get the message out to the cowards out there ... that we're going to get them."[14] The LAPD's offensive would come to be seen as an assault on whole Black communities. This was the case on August 1, 1988, as NWA prepared to release *Straight Outta Compton*, when the police raided several apartments on Dalton Avenue, ransacking homes and brutalizing some of the tenants. The LAPD's gang sweeps inspired the group's "Straight Outta Compton" music video.[15]

NWA emerged out of the war on gangs and from various sources in the local music scene during the mid-1980s.[16] Seeking an exit from hustling and drug dealing, Eric "Eazy-E" Wright spearheaded the formation of the group in 1986. He recruited Andre "Dr. Dre" Young and Antoine "DJ Yella" Carraby from another local electronic R&B group, the World Class Wreckin' Cru, and O'Shea "Ice Cube" Jackson and Lorenzo "MC Ren" Patterson, two local rap upstarts, to the group. Kim "Arabian Prince" Nazel, who eventually left the group before their release of *Straight Outta Compton*, and Dallas, Texas, rapper Tracy "The DOC" Curry rounded out the group—although he served as a writer for the group, Curry would not appear on the album.

Wright stumbled into his rap career by recording "Boyz-n-the Hood" after members of the NYC-based rap group Home Boys Only (HBO) refused to recite Ice Cube's narrative of street life in South Central Los Angeles.[17] After releasing the record in 1987, Wright linked with independent label Macola for distribution, then eventually connected with rock manager Jerry Heller to form Ruthless Records in the same year. The following year, Eazy-E and Heller struck a deal with Priority Records to distribute Ruthless's music. Up until that point, Priority had little experience with rap music, as their claim to fame was producing California Raisins albums.[18]

While the business acumen of Bryan Turner, Mark Cerami, and Steve Drath impressed Eazy-E and Heller, the three Priority founders eagerly encouraged their Ruthless signees to continue to "present their versions of LA's 'ghetto truths' to +provoke audiences."[19] This drive to articulate what they saw as their "ghetto truths" eventually earned NWA the "most dangerous group" moniker. They sought to push boundaries around acceptable discourse and imagery in popular music. The group recorded songs degrading women and threatening their enemies with violence in an explicit manner unheard of in rap music before. But the group's challenge to police is what caught law enforcement's and the nation's attention.

"F- tha Police"

According to Soren Baker, the song, "F- tha Police" almost did not happen. Ice Cube wrote a verse for it but threw away the lyrics because of Dr. Dre's skepticism. "He [Dr. Dre] didn't want no songs talking about the police," Ice Cube said. Dr. Dre told Ice Cube, "Nobody gave a fuck about that, about hearing about the police."[20] Despite Ice Cube's desire to create the song, he admitted that Dre expressed hesitation because of his time in county jail. However, Dr. Dre's resistance did not stop Ice Cube from raising the idea with the rest of the group, and the other members agreed that the song would appeal to Black hip-hop fans especially. DJ Yella later recalled how he thought the song reflected many Black Americans' authentic experiences: "The song was true to the ghetto. Everybody hated the police."[21]

Eazy-E's antics actually led to an encounter with law enforcement that inspired "F- tha Police." Police officers caught him and Dr. Dre performing drive-by paintball-gun shootings at pedestrians. Dr. Dre later told the *Irish Examiner* that the police catching them and forcing them to lay face down in the streets with guns drawn motivated the group to record the song. "We thought it was bullshit. So we went to the studio and recorded the song," Dr. Dre said.[22]

In "F- tha Police," the group turns the tables and places law enforcement on trial in "NWA court." With an instrumental sampling Public Enemy's "Bring the Noise" (1987), Dr. Dre introduces the "case of the NWA vs. the police department" and identifies MC Ren, Ice Cube, and "Eazy motherfuckin' E" as the "prosecuting attorneys[23] who would testify against the police. Then Ice Cube launches into the group's revenge fantasy after record scratches and the beat drop.

Cube's first line, "Fuck the police comin' straight from the underground," and the other elements of his revenge fantasy wherein he taunts and threatens police with violent retaliation most likely raised listeners' hairs, especially those who could not fathom publicly addressing law enforcement in such a violent fashion. Cube fantasized about fighting an officer in a jail cell and beating "a police out of shape" until, eventually, they would have to "bring the yellow tape."[24]

Ice Cube's famous verse castigating and threatening police addressed a myriad of issues related to race and policing—profiling, stop-and-frisk, and violence. Even though Cube's reference to stop-and-frisk policies is laced with homophobia, he honed in on how police might use particular tactics to humiliate Black Americans. Black Americans and advocacy groups have reported officers groping those they frisked on numerous occasions. Some officers even taunt detainees. Legal scholar Bernard Harcourt described an encounter in an appendix of a police study written by Jon Gould and Stephen Mastrofski: "The cop then said to the black man: 'I bet you are hiding [drugs] under your balls. If you have drugs under your balls, I am going to fuck your balls up'."[25] These incidents recall another horrific police-brutality incident that took place in New York City less than ten years later. In 1997, NYPD officers forcibly sodomized Haitian immigrant Abner Louima with a broken broomstick in a bathroom.[26]

Starting his verse with the same refrain as Cube, "Fuck the police," MC Ren reverses Ice Cube's contention about law enforcement exercising their "authority to kill a minority." "Fuck the police and Ren said it with authority," Ren raps, "because the niggas on the street is a majority."[27] Ren not only states the obvious—that Black residents often outnumber the police, especially white law enforcement—his lyric underscores an older, anti-racist, anti-colonial, and anti-imperial argument: that Black and Brown people are the majority and that police serve as mere occupiers in their areas of jurisdiction. MC Ren could be saying, "Fuck the police" with authority, or force, or he could be uttering the statement with the authority derived from his experience with police and as a "street reporter," as the group often claimed.[28]

The idea of MC Ren, Ice Cube, and Eazy-E recording a song as "underground street reporters" underscores the notion that they were not just speaking about their experiences, or for themselves, but expressing a view about law enforcement that other Black Americans shared but were afraid to say publicly. And, obviously, the song's popularity, and listeners' desire for NWA to perform the track at their concerts, highlight how fans invested NWA with the authority to voice their collective grievances about police harassment and violence. NWA, positioning themselves as journalists, underscored Public Enemy frontman Chuck D's 1989 claim that rap was "the Black CNN." For Chuck D, NWA, and others engaged in "reality rap," they did not see established media outlets as concerned with providing a panoramic view of Black America, only the aspects that emphasized criminal behavior.[29]

Out of all of the in-song skits and verses, Eazy-E's highlighted the city's war on gangs. The skit dramatizes the police executing a warrant for Eazy-E's arrest. While Eazy-E answers the door, the police use a ram to barge into the place and then pin the lyricist on the floor. "Sweatin' my gang, while I'm chillin' in the shack, and shinin' the light in my face, and for what?" Eazy-E asked.[30] While Eazy-E boasted of his criminal credentials, he showed how the police and law criminalized Black people. "They put out my picture with silence / 'Cause my identity by itself causes violence."[31] Again, the group locate racism and violence at the heart of policing in the US.

"F- Tha Police" is a sonic attack on law enforcement as well. Dr. Dre and DJ Yella captured the group's sense of urgency from the onset with the Public Enemy sample from "Bring the Noise." However, it's Roy Ayers Ubiquity's "The Boogie Back" wailing over the beat that resembles sirens, giving the track its menacing mood. There's little chance a familiar listener would fail to recognize the group's signature song. Historian Robin D. G. Kelley articulates the importance of rappers utilizing sound to assert their presence in public space and to challenge power, especially in the case of "F- tha Police":

> Their music and expressive styles have literally become weapons in a battle over the right to occupy public space. Frequently employing high-decibel car stereos and boom boxes, black youth not only "pump up the volume" for their own listening pleasure, but also as part of an indirect, ad hoc war of position. The "noise" constitutes a form of cultural resistance that should not be ignored, especially when we add those resistive lyrics about destroying the state or retaliating against the police ... We cannot easily dismiss Ice Cube when he declares, "I'm the one with a trunk of funk / and 'Fuck the Police' in the tape deck."[32]

Even while sampling Public Enemy's production collective, the "Bomb Squad," NWA distinguish themselves from their sonic counterparts from Long Island. "F- tha Police" was less chaotic than the Bomb Squad's compositions on *It Takes a Nation of Millions to Hold Us Back* (1988), but it was no less sample-heavy and funky. Yet it still had more in common with New York than the West Coast productions that followed. Dr. Dre and DJ Yella also relied on James Brown samples, one of which, "Funky Drummer" (1970), was an East Coast (and eventually rap-wide) staple.

By questioning police power, NWA unknowingly tapped into a tradition of peoples' justice—whereby oppressed and marginalized people dramatize the criminality of the state by either appealing to international authorities or organizing peoples' tribunals. In 1951, the Civil Rights Congress took their petition, *We Charge Genocide: The Historic Petition to the United Nations for Relief From a Crime of The United States Government Against the Negro People*, to the United Nations in an effort to hold the US government accountable for the systemic oppression and killing of Black people due to various forms of racial discrimination.[33] After Detroit police officers were acquitted for torturing and killing three Black Detroiters and tormenting two white women in a room at the Algiers Motel in the midst of the 1967 uprising, local activists held a peoples' tribunal where they tried the officers themselves.[34] NWA followed by holding their own tribunal, on record, where everyone who listened participated as spectators, or even as members of the jury.

While NWA's "F- tha Police" might have featured vulgar lyrics, their desire to put the police on trial highlighted the criminal legal system's inability to hold police accountable for brutalizing Black Americans. It also suggested that true justice in the event of state-sanctioned violence could only arise from the grassroots, where citizens are able to judge those who police them. The most accountable criminal legal system is one that is inherently democratic. And the democratic form of justice just happened to meet one of the most democratic and transgressive forms of art, next to punk rock, that arose during the late twentieth century. Black Panthers Huey Newton and Bobby Seal believed the "brothers on the block," as the Panthers referred to Black urbanites, or the lumpenproletariat, as Karl Marx called them, actually represented the most authentic agents for meting out justice against the state.[35]

With "F- tha Police," NWA discarded the order/anarchy dichotomy upon which the "thin blue line" ideology rests. MC Ren, Ice Cube, and Eazy-E argued that it was the police who acted in an anarchistic manner when they failed to follow the law. Thus, for them, retaliatory violence and peoples' justice was a legitimate response to police lawlessness. The indiscriminate violence at the center of the LAPD's Operation Hammer in its war on gangs underscored the haphazard and anarchic aspects of law enforcement. The LAPD sought to wrap the thin blue line around the neck of the Black population until it submitted to its will in its fight to take down street gangs. Yet, for NWA, the people, in the context of the song, should defend themselves and wield power to hold police accountable.

If the US political, economic, and legal systems rely on the consent of the governed, MC Ren, Ice Cube, and Eazy-E all stated for the court that they refuse to recognize the legitimacy of law enforcement. They would not allow police to brutalize them, nor would they respect the symbolism of law enforcement like the officers' badges. For them, these symbols are meaningless as long as the police continue to commit crimes, something that many Black critics of law enforcement, such as James Baldwin, the Black Panthers, and Angela Davis, have pointed out. In fact, "F- tha Police" is a descendant of the Panthers' "Off the Pigs" slogan and the group's use of art to illustrate the police's role as oppressors in American society.

What is ironic is that law enforcement was right; NWA's lyricism is violent. And the group sought to question and undermine law enforcement's authority to exercise violence over them, other Black Americans, and all Americans, generally. Ice Cube retorts, "A young nigga got it bad 'cause I'm brown. And not the other color so police think they have the authority to kill a minority." MC Ren threatens to go for his weapon "for the so-called law."[36] Ren also refers to Miranda rights as "all junk" and the officer's "fake-ass badge."[37]. And Eazy-E asks, "Without a gun and a badge, what do ya got? A sucker in a uniform waitin' to get shot."[38] However, NWA suggests that the only language the police understand is violence. It is no accident that songs like "F- tha Police," "Batterram," and Ice-T's "Cop Killer" (1992) appeared as the war on drugs continued to ramp up in response to the drug epidemic during the 1980s and early 1990s. America's response to the emergence of the crack cocaine trade in inner cities was violence, and no civil rights movement existed on the scale of the 1960s to stop police violence and job loss. A Black-led culture helped fill a leadership and political void, and it did so in the most direct, if not militant, way possible, even if these artists were imperfect.

NWA's violent lyrics and attempts to undermine law enforcement highlight a more important reality—police violence was, and continues to represent, an existential threat for Black Americans due to legal protections law enforcement officers enjoy, their position in everyday governing, and their political and cultural power. Ultimately, Ice Cube, MC Ren, and Eazy-E, raised the same questions about policing in the United States as the Black Panthers and other like-minded groups—do Black Americans not have the right to defend themselves when law enforcement harass and brutalize them, especially when police are rarely held accountable? Can society hold police accountable? Should Black and Brown people continue to recognize and respect police authority and power in the United States? The title of the song, like the Black Panthers calling the police "pigs," suggests otherwise.

The Afterlives of "F- tha Police"

In his last book, *Blood in My Eye*, prison activist George Jackson wrote:

> Power responds to all threats. The response is repression. If the threat is a small one, the fascist tactic is to laugh it off, ignore it, isolated with its defense mechanism—media. The greater the threat, the greater the corresponding violence from power.[39]

NWA may not have positioned themselves as the heir apparent to the Black Panther Party, but the FBI's assistant director at the time, Milt Ahlerich, and the nation's law enforcement saw the song as an attack. In August 1989, Ahlerich sent Priority Records a letter expressing concern that music "advocating violence and assault" against police officers was "wrong ... and such recordings such as the one from NWA are both discouraging and degrading to these brave, dedicated officers." Ahlerich punctuated the letter by admitting that "music plays a significant role in society" and that his remarks "reflect the opinion of the entire law enforcement community." While Ahlerich did not name the song specifically, Priority Records president Brian Turner, Eazy-E, Ice Cube, the rest of the group, as well as music journalists, all knew what song the assistant director referenced.[40]

The backlash to "F- tha Police" coalesced quickly as police departments launched a campaign by fax to encourage departments and security workers to boycott working the group's shows. Law enforcement's attempt to silence and isolate NWA reignited a debate about artists' first amendment rights. Yet NWA essentially won the fight with the backing of their record label, music writers, and the ACLU.[41] The FBI's letter censuring the song effectively boosted the group's popularity.[42]

The controversy inspired NWA to capitalize on their outlaw image on the group's follow up EP, *100 Miles and Runnin* (1990). By the time of the release of this project, Ice Cube had left the group due to a dispute over his pay. Yet, Eazy-E, Dr. Dre, MC Ren, and DJ Yella proved more than capable of taking on law enforcement with "100 Miles and Runnin'" and a proper "F- tha Police" sequel, "Sa Prize (Part 2)." Structured similarly as "F- tha Police" as a song and skit, the song "100 Miles and Runnin'" depicts NWA trying to evade authorities after the "F- tha Police" controversy. Yet in "Sa Prize," Eazy-E, MC Ren, and Dr. Dre perform a revenge fantasy skit wherein they collaborate with another person from the streets to ambush two police officers, one of them named, "Sgt. Kickass." And while Dr. Dre, Eazy-E, and MC Ren recite verses speaking out against racist harassment and laced with threats against the police, they incorporate short vignettes from other Black and Brown people who discuss their contempt for the police. With this addition, NWA's protest against police brutality is more inclusive, as they not only include people who are presumed to be African American but also Latina/o people, and they also highlight the problem of police committing sexual assault against Black women.[43]

"F- tha Police" took on a different valence after the 1992 uprising following the beating of Black motorist Rodney King by LAPD officers Laurence Powell, Timothy Wind, Theodore Briseno, and Stacey Koon. After the videotape of the beating aired, it became apparent that police brutality was an indisputable fact of life for Black Americans, and NWA and Ice Cube appeared more as prophets than as provocateurs who questioned the LAPD's authority. After a jury acquitted Powell, Wind, Briseno, and Koon, LA erupted in violence and property destruction. In the midst of the uprising, the song emerged as a slogan and tool of mass resistance against the state. Rioters scrawled it on walls in the riot zone.[44] NWA member MC Ren reacted to the rebellion positively, stating, "Everybody looks at black people different now."[45]

Even though Eazy-E and Dr. Dre poked fun at Rodney King for the beating in an interview with *Spin Magazine*, the members contended that the incident validated the group's anti-police music. However, they also expressed skepticism as to whether or not the beating and the videotape would elicit changes in policing.[46] The Rodney King incident also fueled Ice Cube's continued focus on police conduct as well as racial tensions in South Central Los Angeles. Ice Cube seemed to predict that tensions would boil over on his second album, *Death Certificate*, released in December 1991. The xenophobic "Black Korea" represented Ice Cube's clearest warning that Black people in South Central Los Angeles might rebel against structural racism and economic exploitation—addressing the killing of Latasha Harlins by Soon Ja Du, a Korean store owner, three days after the Rodney King beating.[47]

In the years following the King beating and 1992 uprising, gangsta rap, in all of its forms, engulfed the rap music market. Gangsta rap's takeover during the early 1990s and the backlash against anti-law-enforcement lyrics marginalized overt political rap acts and performances. Law enforcement, with the help of actor Charlton Heston, forced Ice-T to remove "Cop Killer" from his rock group Bodycount's album, and Tommy Boy Records dropped Paris after the Bay Area rapper sought to release songs critical of law enforcement and President George H. W. Bush ("Bush Killa") on his album *Sleeping With the Enemy* (1992).[48] Dr. Dre and Ice Cube still included songs with social commentary on their subsequent releases. However, they and their record labels pushed more commercial-friendly songs focusing on partying, misogyny and sexual conquests, and inner city violence. Tracks like "It Was a Good Day"

(1993) and "Nuthin' but a 'G' Thang" (1992) became smash hits, opening the door for more artists to strike gold with sample-heavy and melodic radio hits.

As hip-hop culture has accumulated more generations of fans, aging artists have embraced becoming nostalgia acts—booking tours based upon their hit albums and songs and rereleasing expanded versions of their most acclaimed work. NWA has not done this, but they reintroduced themselves to younger generations of music fans with the release of their critically acclaimed biopic *Straight Outta Compton* in 2015. The making of "F- tha Police" and the dramatization of their Detroit performance represented one of the high points of the film. The trailer also recalls how the song and NWA responded to the Rodney King rebellion, playing on the notion that the song remained a significant tool of resistance and solidarity after law enforcement and the right sought to censor it.

"F- tha Police" in the Age of Black Lives Matter

Political context distinguishes the difference between hearing and saying "fuck tha police" in 1989 and 2020. While one should not minimize opposition to police brutality during the 1980s and '90s, whether through protest or art, NWA, as well as Public Enemy and Boogie Down Productions, filled a vacuum left by the repression of Black radical politics and the war on drugs. The solidarity campaigns led by African Americans to push corporations and universities to divest from apartheid-era South Africa and call for Nelson Mandela's release from imprisonment represented the only social movement grounded in mass protest politics. Unfortunately, no national social movement arose to take on police brutality, and African Americans were left relying on art and episodic campaigns.[49]

However, "F- tha Police" stretches into the present moment with the emergence of Black Lives Matter as a slogan and a banner for a movement against anti-Black state violence in the aftermath of the deaths of Trayvon Martin, Eric Garner, Michael Brown, Aura Rosser, and Sandra Bland between 2013 and 2015, cresting again in 2020 as hundreds of thousands took to the streets throughout the US and worldwide in response to the murders of George Floyd and Breonna Taylor.

Criticism of the roles the police play in US politics and culture persists into the present, whether through vulgar slogans such as "Fuck 12" and anti-police-brutality songs such as Compton-based rapper YG's "FTP," or through more academic and activist critiques of "copaganda" and the political and cultural messages upholding "thin blue line" understandings of policing.[50] The list of television shows presenting police as the only legitimate guardians of society is endless.[51] The recent emergence of "Blue Lives Matter" symbolism has taken the political and cultural conflict to a new level. It is important to note that the "Blue Lives Matter" slogan is a reactionary response to the Black-led movement against racist state violence. The slogan is grounded in an erroneous conflation of occupation and identity that mocks Blackness and sees racial identity and racism as inconsequential in lived experiences with policing, surveillance, and incarceration while trying to elevate the occupation of law enforcement to a legally protected category like race, gender, sex, and ability. The attempts of law enforcement and their political allies to elevate occupation to the level of a legally protected identity has the potential to produce some dangerous legislative consequences for marginalized peoples and dissidents.[52]

The re-emergence of "F- tha Police" in the era of Black Lives Matter converged with changes in technology and distribution over the last two years. "F- tha Police" went from a song that law enforcement and politicians wanted to ban to a song that listeners have streamed hundreds of millions of times. Now, with streaming platforms such as Spotify, Apple Music, and Tidal, anyone, anywhere in the world, can include NWA's anthem in their curated soundtracks to their marches and demonstrations against state violence. Utilizing this technology, however, means that these movements do not escape the profit motives of record companies, streaming services, and hardware producers like Apple, since they all have to receive a cut.

Yet these technologies intersect with histories of resistance to illustrate how art, in this instance through the menacing sounds of "F- tha Police," reverberates in protest culture. The resurgence of "F- tha Police" also highlights how protest culture is not only cumulative but anticipatory.[53] George Lipsitz quotes Frantz Fanon to underscore this point about hip-hop's politics of sound.

> Speaking about times when desires for radical change permeate popular culture even though no political movement has yet arrived to challenge the established order, Fanon argues: "Well before the political fighting phase of the national movement, an attentive spectator can thus feel and see the manifestation of a new vigor and feel the approaching conflict, He [sic] will note unusual forms of expression and themes which are fresh and imbued with a power which is no longer that of an invocation but rather of the assembling of the people, a summoning together for a precise purpose. Everything works together to awaken the native's sensibility and to make unreal and unacceptable the contemplative attitude of the acceptance of defeat."[54]

"F- tha Police" is a song that found a movement. One is likely to hear the song in a soundtrack while chanting "Say Her Name" and "Black Lives Matter." However, one is also likely to hear the song while marching in the streets, probably among others recorded by artists inspired by NWA, such as Paris, KRS-One, Bone Thugs-n-Harmony, Scarface, and newer artists like Rapsody, Run the Jewels, and Kendrick Lamar.[55] "F- tha Police" captured the anger of generations of Black youth forsaken by civil rights gains, economic restructuring and job loss, cuts to social services, and the growth of police forces and prisons. The most recent three-word demand to emerge at protests, "Defund the Police," builds on the anger but also provides an action step in seeking to address all of the conditions that inspired NWA to record their iconic song.

Notes

1 John Counts, "Retired Detroit sergeant recalls telling N.W.A. they couldn't play 'F*** tha Police' at 1989 concert," *MLive.com*, April 3, 2019; Gerick D. Kennedy, *Parental Discretion Iz Advised: The Rise of N.W.A. and the Dawn of Gangsta Rap* (New York: Atria Books, 2017).

2 Counts, "Retired Detroit sergeant recalls telling N.W.A. they couldn't play 'F*** tha Police' at 1989 concert"; Kennedy, *Parental Discretion Iz Advised*; Rich Goldstein, "A Brief History of the Phrase 'F*ck the Police,'" *The Daily Beast*, April 14), 2017; Steve Knopper, "The True Story of N.W.A. Playing 'Fuck Tha Police' Live in Detroit," *GQ.com*, July 21, 2020.

3 Felicia Angeja Viator, *To Live and Defy in LA: How Gangsta Rap Changed America* (Cambridge: Harvard University Press, 2020), 218.

4 Dan Georgakas and Murvin Surkin, *Detroit, I Do Mind Dying: A Study in Urban Revolution* (New York: Haymarket Books, 2012); Joe T. Darden and Richard W. Thomas, *Detroit: Race Riots, Racial Conflicts, and Efforts to Bridge the Racial Divide* (Michigan: Michigan State University Press, 2013).

5 Soren Baker, *The History of Gangster Rap: From Schoolly D to Kendrick Lamar* (New York: Abrams Image, 2018).

6 James Baldwin, "A Report from Occupied Territory," *The Nation*, July 11, 1966; Joshua Bloom and Waldo E. Martin Jr, *Black Against Empire: The History and Politics of the Black Panther Party* (Los Angeles: University of California Press, 2013).

7 Jeff Chang, *Can't Stop, Won't Stop: A History of the Hip Hop Nation* (New York: Picador, 2006); Max Felker-Kantor, *Policing Los Angeles: Race, Resistance, and the Rise of the LAPD* (North Carolina: University of North Carolina Press, 2018).

8 Heather Thompson, "Why Mass Incarceration Matters: Rethinking Crisis, Decline, and Transformation in Postwar American History," *The Journal of American History* 97 no. 3 (2010): 703–34; Elizabeth Hinton. *From the War on Poverty to the War on Crime* (Cambridge: Harvard University Press, 2017).

9 Hinton. *From the War on Poverty to the War on Crime*.

10 Donna Murch, "Crack in Los Angeles: Crisis, Militarization, and Black Response to the Late Twentieth Century War on Drugs," *The Journal of American History* 102, no. 1 (2015): 163–72.

11 Georgakas and Surkin, *Detroit, I Do Mind Dying*; Murch, "Crack in Los Angeles," 165; Felker-Kantor, *Policing Los Angeles*.

12 William Raspberry, "The Chief and the Choke Hold," *The Washington Post*, May 17, 1982; Felker-Kantor, *Policing Los Angeles*.

13 Viator, *To Live and Defy in LA*.

14 Murch, "Crack in Los Angeles," 168.

15 NWA, "F tha Police." *Straight Outta Compton* (Los Angeles: Ruthless Records, 1989); Murch, "Crack in Los Angeles"; Felker-Kantor, *Policing Los Angeles*.

16 Loren Kajikawa, *Sounding Race in Rap Songs* (Los Angeles: University of California Press, 2015).

17 Kennedy, *Parental Discretion Iz Advised.*
18 Viator, *To Live and Defy in LA.*
19 Ibid.
20 Baker, *The History of Gangster Rap.*
21 Ibid.
22 Korey Grow, "N.W.A's 'Straight Outta Compton': 12 Things You Didn't Know," *Rolling Stone*, August 8, 2018.
23 Viator, *To Live and Defy in LA.*
24 NWA, "F tha Police."
25 Bernard E. Harcourt, "Unconstitutional Police Searches and Collective Responsibility," *Criminology and Public Policy* 3, no. 3 (2004): 366.
26 Beth Fertig and Jim O'Grady, "Twenty Years Later: The Police Assault on Abner Louima and What it Means," *WNYC News*, August 9, 2017.
27 NWA, "F tha Police."
28 NWA, "F tha Police"; Viator, *To Live and Defy in LA.*
29 Rohan B. Preston, "Chuck D Says Rap Tells About Black Sensibilities," *Chicago Tribune*, September 16, 1993.
30 NWA, "F tha Police."
31 Ibid.
32 Robin D.G. Kelley, *Race Rebels: Culture, Politics, and the Black Working Class* (New York: The Free Press, 1994).
33 For a discussion of the We Charge Genocide petition, see Carol Anderson, *Eyes Off the Prize: African Americans, the United Nations, and the Struggle for Human Rights, 1944–1955* (New York: Cambridge University Press, 2003).
34 Danielle McGuire, "Murder at Algiers Motel." In *Detroit 1967: Origins, Impacts, Legacies*, edited by Joel Stone, 173–83 (Detroit: Wayne State University Press, 2017).
35 Judson Jeffries, *Huey P. Newton: The Radical Theorist* (Jackson: University Press of Mississippi, 2006); Bloom and Martin Jr, *Black Against Empire.*
36 NWA, "F tha Police."
37 Ibid.
38 Ibid.
39 George Jackson, *Blood in My Eye* (New York: Bantam Books, 1972).
40 Dave Marsh and Phyllis Pollack "Wanted for Attitude: The FBI Hates This Band," *The Village Voice*, September 2, 2020.
41 Law enforcement's and the right's attempts to censor rap acts for anti-police and lewd lyrics is well documented. For more see Viator, Chang, and Dan Charnas, *The Big Payback: The History of the Business of Hip-Hop* (New York: New American Library, 2010)
42 Kennedy, *Parental Discretion Iz Advised.*
43 NWA, "Sa Prize (Part 2)." *100 Miles and Runnin,'* (Los Angeles: Ruthless Records, 1990).
44 Viator, *To Live and Defy in LA.*
45 Ibid.
46 Ibid.
47 Ice Cube continued his critique of urban affairs and US politics on the critically acclaimed album. His targets included George H. W. Bush, Jesse Jackson, McDonald's, and the US Military. He also advocated for Black gun ownership and gang unity. He then released *The Predator* in November 1992, which was his

most successful album to date. Ice Cube also addressed the Rodney King beating and the uprisings. The album featured another revenge fantasy, "Say Hi to the Bad Guy," but *The Predator* represented Ice Cube's confirmation that his warnings of a racial conflagration were warranted.

48 Dan Charnas, *The Big Payback: The History of the Business of Hip-Hop* (New York: New American Library, 2010), 385–7, 394. Paris's early label woes encouraged him to embark on a successful career as an independent rap artist who calls himself the "Black Panther of Rap."

49 Robin D.G. Kelley, "'Slangin' Rocks...Palestinian Style': Dispatches from the Occupied Zones of North America," in *Police Brutality: An Anthology*, ed. Jill Nelson, 21–59 (New York: W.W. Norton & Company, 2000).

50 The "12" in the slogan, "Fuck 12" is a slang reference for law enforcement. See, "Fuck 12," *Rap Dictionary*, https://rapdictionary.com/meaning/fuck-12/. Several rap artists have released songs titled, "Fuck 12," including Gucci Mane, Migos, and Young Thug.

51 Micha Frazer-Carroll, "Copaganda: Why film and TV portrayals of the police are under fire," *The Independent*, July 9, 2020.

52 Elahe Izadi, "Louisiana is the first state to offer hate crime protections to police officers," *The Washington Post*, May 26, 2016.

53 See Mary Frances Berry, *History Teaches Us to Resist: How Progressive Movements Have Succeeded in Challenging Times* (Boston: Beacon Press, 2018) for her analysis of how political outlooks, organizing and protest tactics, and progressive politics reverberate through protest culture over long periods of time. For a discussion of the cumulative nature of movements, see Nathan Robinson, "Keeanga-Yamahtta Taylor on Why Racism Has Been Profitable," *Current Affairs*, July 25, 2020.

54 George Lipsitz, *Dangerous Crossroads: Popular Music, Postmodernism and the Poetics of Place* (New York: Verso, 1994).

55 See songs such as KRS-One's "Sound of Da Police," Bone Thugs-n-Harmony's "Fuck Tha Police," Scarface's, "Look Me In My Eyes," Kendrick Lamar's, "Alright," Run The Jewels', "Early," and Rapsody's "12 Problems."

References

Anderson, Carol. *Eyes Off the Prize: African Americans, the United Nations, and the Struggle for Human Rights, 1944–1955*. New York: Cambridge University Press, 2003.

Baker, Soren. *The History of Gangster Rap: From Schoolly D to Kendrick Lamar*. New York: Abrams Image, 2018.

Baldwin, James. "A Report from Occupied Territory." *The Nation*, July 11, 1966. www.thenation.com/article/archive/report-occupied-territory/

Berry, Mary Frances. *History Teaches Us to Resist: How Progressive Movements Have Succeeded in Challenging Times*. Boston: Beacon Press, 2018.

Bloom, Joshua and Waldo E. Martin Jr. *Black Against Empire: The History and Politics of the Black Panther Party*. Los Angeles: University of California Press, 2013.

Chang, Jeff. *Can't Stop, Won't Stop: A History of the Hip Hop Nation*. New York: Picador, 2006.

Charnas, Dan. *The Big Payback: The History of the Business of Hip-Hop*. New York: New American Library, 2010.

Counts, John. "Retired Detroit sergeant recalls telling N.W.A. they couldn't play 'F*** tha Police' at 1989 concert." *MLive.com*, April 3, 2019. www.mlive.com/news/ann-arbor/2015/08/former_detroit_sergeant_recall.html

Darden, Joe T. and Richard W. Thomas. *Detroit: Race Riots, Racial Conflicts, and Efforts to Bridge the Racial Divide.* Michigan: Michigan State University Press, 2013.

Felker-Kantor, Max. *Policing Los Angeles: Race, Resistance, and the Rise of the LAPD.* North Carolina: University of North Carolina Press, 2018.

Fertig, Beth and Jim O'Grady. "Twenty Years Later: The Police Assault on Abner Louima and What it Means." *WNYC News*, August 9, 2017. www.wnyc.org/story/twenty-years-later-look-back-nypd-assault-abner-louima-and-what-it-means-today/

Frazer-Carroll, Micha. "Copaganda: Why film and TV portrayals of the police are under fire." *The Independent*, July 9, 2020. www.independent.co.uk/arts-entertainment/tv/features/police-brutality-tv-copaganda-brooklyn-nine-nine-paw-patrol-cops-george-floyd-a9610956.html

Georgakas, Dan and Murvin Surkin. *Detroit, I Do Mind Dying: A Study in Urban Revolution.* New York: Haymarket Books, 2012.

Goldstein, Rich. "A Brief History of the Phrase 'F*ck the Police.'" *The Daily Beast*, April 14), 2017. www.thedailybeast.com/a-brief-history-of-the-phrase-fck-the-police

Grow, Korey. "N.W.A's 'Straight Outta Compton': 12 Things You Didn't Know." *Rolling Stone*, August 8, 2018. www.rollingstone.com/feature/n-w-as-straight-outta-compton-12-things-you-didnt-know-707207/

Harcourt, Bernard E. "Unconstitutional Police Searches and Collective Responsibility." *Criminology and Public Policy* 3, no. 3 (2004): 363–78.

Hinton, Elizabeth. *From the War on Poverty to the War on Crime.* Cambridge: Harvard University Press, 2017.

Izadi, Elahe. "Louisiana is the first state to offer hate crime protections to police officers." *The Washington Post*, May 26, 2016. www.washingtonpost.com/news/post-nation/wp/2016/05/26/louisianas-blue-lives-matter-bill-just-became-law/

Jackson, George. *Blood in My Eye.* New York: Bantam Books, 1972.

Jeffries, Judson. *Huey P. Newton: The Radical Theorist.* Jackson: University Press of Mississippi, 2006.

Kajikawa, Loren. *Sounding Race in Rap Songs.* Los Angeles: University of California Press, 2015.

Kelley, Robin D.G. *Race Rebels: Culture, Politics, and the Black Working Class.* New York: The Free Press, 1994.

Kelley, Robin D.G. "'Slangin' Rocks...Palestinian Style': Dispatches from the Occupied Zones of North America." In *Police Brutality: An Anthology*, edited by Jill Nelson, 21–59. New York: W.W. Norton & Company, 2000.

Kennedy, Gerrick D. *Parental Discretion Iz Advised: The Rise of N.W.A. and the Dawn of Gangsta Rap.* New York: Atria Books, 2017.

Knopper, Steve. "The True Story of N.W.A. Playing 'Fuck Tha Police' Live in Detroit." *GQ.com*, July 21, 2020. www.gq.com/story/nwa-fuck-the-police-live-detroit

Lipsitz, George. *Dangerous Crossroads: Popular Music, Postmodernism and the Poetics of Place.* New York: Verso, 1994.

Marsh, Dave and Phyllis Pollack. "Wanted for Attitude: The FBI Hates This Band." *The Village Voice*, September 2, 2020. www.villagevoice.com/2020/09/02/crackdown-on-culture-the-fbi-hates-this-band/

McGuire, Danielle. "Murder at Algiers Motel." In *Detroit 1967: Origins, Impacts, Legacies*, edited by Joel Stone, 173–83. Detroit: Wayne State University Press, 2017.

Murch, Donna. "Crack in Los Angeles: Crisis, Militarization, and Black Response to the Late Twentieth Century War on Drugs." *The Journal of American History* 102, no. 1 (2015): 163–72.

NWA. "F tha Police." *Straight Outta Compton*. Los Angeles: Ruthless Records, 1989.

NWA. "Sa Prize (Part 2)." *100 Miles and Runnin*,' Los Angeles: Ruthless Records, 1990.

NWA. *Straight Outta Compton (Official Music Video)*. YouTube, 2009 [1989]. www.youtube.com/watch?v=TMZi25Pq3T8

Preston, Rohan B. "Chuck D Says Rap Tells About Black Sensibilities." *Chicago Tribune*, September 16, 1993.

Rap Dictionary. "Fuck 12," *Rap Dictionary*. https://rapdictionary.com/meaning/fuck-12/

Raspberry, William. "The Chief and the Choke Hold." *The Washington Post*, May 17, 1982. www.washingtonpost.com/archive/politics/1982/05/17/the-chief-and-the-choke-hold/e17fa90f-c692-43c2-935f-463da9cab500/

Robinson, Nathan. "Keeanga-Yamahtta Taylor on Why Racism Has Been Profitable." *Current Affairs*, July 25, 2020. www.currentaffairs.org/2020/07/interview-keeanga-yamahtta-taylor-on-why-racism-is-profitable

Thompson, Heather. "Why Mass Incarceration Matters: Rethinking Crisis, Decline, and Transformation in Postwar American History." *The Journal of American History* 97 no. 3 (2010): 703–34.

Viator, Felicia Angeja. *To Live and Defy in LA: How Gangsta Rap Changed America*. Cambridge: Harvard University Press, 2020.

Viator, Chang, and Dan Charnas. *The Big Payback: The History of the Business of Hip-Hop*. New York: New American Library, 2010.

12 Salt-N-Pepa—"Shoop" (1993)

Amy Coddington

"Hey yeah, I want to shoop, baby."

So begins Salt-N-Pepa's 1993 song "Shoop," the first single from their fourth album, *Very Necessary*. Written and performed by the group, made up of rappers Salt and Pepa and DJ Spinderella, the song features the two MCs slinging metaphor after metaphor about good-looking men and what they would like to do with them. All this talk about men was noteworthy—following its release, the song garnered widespread attention in relation to a national debate regarding female sexuality. As critic Leonard Pitts Jr. wrote, "Publications as frothy as *Entertainment Weekly* and as serious as *Newsweek*" used "Shoop" as provocation for conversations about women openly expressing sexual desire, what they inflamingly called "reverse sexism."[1] Did the group's declaration of sexual agency make them feminists? Or did their tight clothing and seductive dancing in the song's music video—their "gyrating shamelessly in scanty clothes," as one critic worded it—negate the power of their bold lyrics?[2]

This debate did nothing to slow the success of this song; all publicity is good publicity, after all. The song was a veritable smash, climbing the charts throughout the fall of 1993 and eventually reaching number four on the *Billboard* "Hot 100" in early December, a higher chart position than any of the group's previous releases. After steady airplay on music video channels and radio stations across the United States, the single went gold, setting up their October 1993 album *Very Necessary* to be the most successful of the group's career.

All of this popularity and controversy might seem like a lot for a song that, judging by the nonsensical title alone, has very little meaning. What about "Shoop" made it so good at drawing listeners in and provoking conversation? And what does it mean to shoop? In this essay, I use these questions to interrogate the context and substance of the song, arguing that Salt-N-Pepa's song takes a seemingly nonsense word and gives it meaning: shoop comes to mean desire, power, and success. In the following sections, I'll explore each of these definitions in turn, using them as a framework through which to interpret this song, to listen carefully to its artistry, and to think through its impact more broadly.

DOI: 10.4324/9781003093206-13

To Shoop Is to Articulate Desire, and to Act on That Desire

The most obvious lyrical precedent for the song is from nearly 30 years prior, a number-six *Billboard* "Hot 100" hit called "The Shoop Shoop Song (It's in His Kiss)." Initially offered to the Shirelles and originally recorded by Merry Clayton, the song was made famous by Betty Everett in 1964. Engaging in call and response with her backup singers, the Opals, Everett acts as a wiser female friend and confidante, explaining to the Opals that the telltale sign of whether a man loves you is not how he looks or how he acts but is instead how he reacts to physical affection: kissing, holding, and squeezing. The evidence, she sings, will be "there in his kiss." As she sings these words, the Opals, in multipart harmony, loudly sing the word "shoop" over and over, a moment of lyrical nonsense that inspired the song's name. Jacqueline Warwick writes that vocables in songs by groups of female artists like "The Shoop Shoop Song" draw from similar nonsense word usage in the mostly male genre of doo-wop as well as girls' musical games like skipping rope and handclapping—influences that these songs share with hip-hop.[3] Indeed, Kyra Gaunt notes that understanding these lineages reasserts the participation of women within hip-hop culture, highlighting a version of hip-hop history wherein female rap groups such as Salt-N-Pepa are not side notes but rather an integral part of the culture's fabric.[4]

Nonsense words, Warwick argues, allow female singers to talk about sexuality without naming it as such; they can be understood as articulating sexual desire while "'passing' as charming and childish gibberish."[5] In "The Shoop Shoop Song," she writes, shoop has a physical meaning rather than a literal one, as singing this word required the Opals to pucker their lips in the circular closed-lip shape frequently used when kissing.[6] Two 1960s cover versions of this song by male musicians perhaps corroborate the feminine coding of this nonsense syllable; the background vocalists in both of the gender-swapped versions of the song by the Beatles-esque groups the Searchers and the Hollies, retitled as "It's In Her Kiss," replace all instances of "shoop" with the lead singers' lyrics. But by the 1990s, as Warwick notes, using a vocable like "shoop" had a substantially different meaning thanks to the loosening of societal norms that restricted conversations about female sexuality. Rather, in Salt-N-Pepa's song, the word "should not be understood as a sly allusion to what 'nice' girls can't say directly, but rather as a reference to girl talk about sexuality, an acknowledgement of an earlier generation's strategic language."[7]

Indeed, the rhetorical possibilities of musical girl talk had recently resurfaced in popular culture with the release of Cher's cover of "The Shoop Shoop Song" for the end credits of the 1991 movie *Mermaids*. A comedy featuring Cher as a single mother raising two girls, the film, like the song, narrates a story about the unspoken complexity of female sexuality. Featuring footage from the movie, the music video for the song highlights the power of female friendship and shows a parallel between the girl talk of the 1960s and the 1990s. The video begins in black and white, with Cher and her daughters imitating Black girl groups of the 1960s; by the end, it transitions into color, showing them laughing while graffitiing an urban landscape. Using Black culture as a vehicle for multigenerational bonding, the white female characters in the video continue the long history of white appropriation of Black musical traditions throughout the nineteenth and twentieth centuries, and in particular, underscore how appropriating Black culture has been used to unite non-Black populations with competing interests. The song reached #33 on the *Billboard* "Hot 100" in January 1991, seven months before "Let's Talk about Sex," Salt-N-Pepa's highest-charting single prior to releasing "Shoop," first appeared on the charts.

"Shoop" does just that: talk about sex. A "sexy little tribute to the male bodies that drive these rappers crazy," the song recasts the word "shoop" as something far more innuendo-laced; the title of the song, according to the press, was "a new hip hop term for sex."[8] As these quotations indicate, and as Warwick notes, this song is more explicit than the girl-group songs of the 1960s. Rather than revolving around "first base," about a kiss revealing a man's love, Salt-N-Pepa's song moves below the belt, discussing how well-endowed men might wield their precise weaponry to delight the rappers. Over a sample from "I'm Blue" by the girl group Sweet Inspirations, the rappers talk about sex without ever mentioning the word: in the second verse they obliquely reference penises, discussing Uzis and then asking, "What's up with that thang? / I wanna know, how does it hang?"; elsewhere they insinuate wanting to have sex, saying that they want to "slip slide to it swiftly" and have a man give them "some of that yum yum chocolate chip, honey dip."[9] A unique account of flirtation, pursuit, and sex, the song makes clear that when a woman asks a man "what you wanna do," as Salt does at the end of the song, the only acceptable response is to turn the question around, to center female desire and female choice.

Importantly, this song talks about sex on a Black woman's terms. Prior to the release of "Shoop," the group regularly garnered positive attention for their bold reclamation of the too often male-dominated genre. Tricia Rose noted in 1990 that female rappers such as Salt-N-Pepa "effectively changed the interpretative framework" of hip-hop and that the "distinctly Black, physical and sexual pride" the group exhibited upended white beauty ideals.[10] By 1993, when "Shoop" was released, mainstream hip-hop was dominated by the male-centered perspectives of gangsta rappers. In "Shoop," however, the two women take center stage, only briefly sharing the spotlight with an uncredited male rapper, Big Twan. The song centers the experiences of Black women, highlighting and celebrating Black female agency and pleasure: in the first verse Pepa takes the lead, asking a man for "his digits"; in the second verse Salt initiates an encounter, inverting the typical direction of catcalling by inviting a man into her car; later Pepa insinuates that being with her requires effort, as she will "make you get hot, make you work up a sweat"; and when Big Twan comes in with his guest verse, he notes that he never rushes past foreplay, a sex act commonly understood as distinctly pleasurable for women, claiming that he "hit skins but never quickly."

The conceit of "Shoop," wherein women look freely at the men around them, make their own decisions about who to talk to, and call the shots once they have made contact, contributed to a national conversation about changing gender roles. If women were the ones looking, wrote critic Tom Maurstad, were the tables turning?[11] Salt-N-Pepa certainly made it seem that way: during their 1994 tour, they brought male audience members up on stage and pretended to whip them for "leaving the toilet seat up," a skit that did not go unnoticed by some male reviewers of their shows.[12]

Some critics noted that the group uniquely balanced what they considered to be the opposing poles of power and sexuality. In the rather sexist words of one male critic, the group was "sexy, not sex objects; bold, not raunchy; strong, not brittle or witchy."[13] The song's video displayed this nuance clearly. Taking place in the city, on the beach, and in the club, the video shows off the women in the group's gorgeous bodies, dressed in form-fitting, stylish outfits including swimsuits, short jean shorts, and tight shirts. In the club, they dance in front of a neon sign proclaiming the main act: girls. But these girls aren't just awaiting male attention; they also assertively approach men that they find interesting—they are powerfully "sexy" while at the same time "not sex objects." But other critics found this distinction hard to reconcile, and noted that the group embodied a long-standing tension regarding the political power of female sexuality. As *Newsweek* put it in a headline about girl groups including Salt-N-Pepa, could a woman "grind in [her] videos and still be a feminist?"[14]

This question misses the point, for the group was well on their way toward articulating a new type of feminism, one that Joan Morgan in 1999 termed hip-hop feminism.[15] The apparent tension embedded in the question of whether a feminist could be openly sexual fails to account for the history of Black female sexuality in the United States. Informed by the legacy of centuries of chattel slavery, white supremacy dictates Black female sexuality as either non-sexual or hypersexual; Black women, as Hortense J. Spillers notes, have rarely been afforded space to define their sexuality—she writes that "black women are the beached whales of the sexual universe, unvoiced, misseen, not doing, awaiting *their* verb."[16] Continuing, she notes that one of the few times that a Black woman's "sexual experiences are depicted ... by the subject herself [is] often in the guise of vocal music." And indeed, as Hazel V. Carby, Angela Davis, Susan Douglas, and Tricia Rose have noted, music has offered Black women a space to honestly discuss sexuality: from the blues, through Betty Everett and other girl-group music of the 1960s, and into the innuendo-laden rhymes of Salt-N-Pepa, Black female musicians have carved out spaces to articulate their sexual desires, perhaps less rigidly bound by the stereotypes created and replicated by centuries of systemic racism in the United States.[17]

In songs like "Shoop," Salt-N-Pepa articulated a fiercely independent Black sexuality. As the executive editor of *Rap Pages* Sheena Lester stated, the group "personif[ied] the empowerment of young Black women."[18] Key to this empowerment was their articulation of what Cheryl Keyes terms a "fly girl" identity, whereby sexuality was foregrounded and a woman could be "an erotic subject rather than an objectified one."[19] Sitting on the beach in perfectly fitted swimsuits, thirstily looking at men around them, Salt-N-Pepa were no longer "awaiting their verb," they were, well, shooping: they were articulating and acting on their sexual desires.

The hip-hop feminism that Salt-N-Pepa articulated was one that, in Morgan's words, was "brave enough to fuck with the grays," one that didn't require women to stick to previously defined notions of sexuality.[20] Salt-N-Pepa were feminists without minimizing their sexiness; Salt claimed that the group stood for "being a woman and not being weak. Not being so strong that you act like a man, because I feel there's nothing wrong with being sexy and being feminine. But being strong."[21] Perhaps it was precisely this feminist perspective that gave the group the tools to articulate what critics misunderstood as unreconcilable ways of being: Aisha Durham, Brittany C. Cooper, and Susana M. Morris write that hip-hop feminism provides Black women with a framework to engage with the contradictions of the social categories that they encounter, helping them make sense of their lived realities.[22] Charting the developing terrain of hip-hop feminism, "Shoop" spoke directly about sex without being explicit, floating above the boundaries of white feminism and respectability politics to declare that grinding in the video was exactly what a feminist looked like.

To Shoop Is to Take Charge, to Take Control

Despite all of this female-centered rhetoric, the song actually starts with what sounds, at least to my ears, like *male* desire: "Hey yeah, I want to shoop, baby," is sung by an overdubbed, deep-pitched voice. This vocal line might set the listener up for a male-centered perspective, standard in early 1990s hip-hop. But when Pepa starts talking, saying that she's not interested in "you" but instead "the bow-legged one," she instantly clarifies who has control. And from there, both female rappers pull the spotlight away from the low-pitched hook, reducing the male voice to a mere supporting role while claiming their rightful place at center stage.

The gender roles in the song differ from those in many mainstream hip-hop songs from this era, in which often-uncredited women sang hooks for male rappers. For example, a few years before "Shoop" was released, singer Martha Wash sued multiple male producers after they refused to credit her vocal hooks in various hip-house songs, including C+C Music Factory's number-one hit "Gonna Make You Sweat (Everybody Dance Now)" and Black Box's "Strike It Up."[23] The song that replaced "Shoop" at the top of *Billboard*'s "Hot Rap Songs" chart in late 1993, Snoop Doggy Dogg's "Who Am I (What's My Name)?," also failed to credit the female vocalists who sang the song's melodic hook. While the identities of the female singers still remain unverified, Nanci Fletcher, the backing vocalist on many of the other songs on *Doggystyle*, claims that pioneering female rappers J. J. Fad sang the hook.[24] If this is the case, it's a telling reversal of the unique gender dynamics in "Shoop." In Salt-N-Pepa's song, a male singer supports the female rappers by vocalizing his desire in the melodic hook; Snoop Doggy Dogg's raps, on the other hand, are accompanied by a hook sung by women who quite possibly had been famous female rappers just a half-decade earlier. What's more, Snoop's song ends with a strong articulation of the stereotypical gender roles in mainstream hip-hop, as a deliriously enraptured woman sings about Snoop and his male Dogg Pound. By inverting these gender dynamics, "Shoop" underscores the group's agency, making it clear that women are in control of the song.

It wasn't just *this* song that the women took charge of; rather, "Shoop" appears on the first album that the women in the group had full artistic control over. Cheryl James (Salt) and Sandra Denton (Pepa) (see Figure 12.1) became friends over lunch at their local community college, and met Hurby "Luv Bug" Azor while working at a Sears department store in College Point, Queens, selling service contracts to appliance customers. This Sears was a veritable

Figure 12.1 From left, Sandra Denton and Cheryl James at the Sixth Annual Soul Train Music Awards on March 10, 1992, at the Shrine Auditorium in Los Angeles, California. Credit: Barry King/Alamy Stock Photo.

talent hot spot: working alongside Salt, Pepa, and Azor were Chris Martin and Chris Reid of Kid 'n Play and actor and comedian Martin Lawrence. Azor and Salt began dating soon after they met, and after Azor taught Salt how to rap, the two of them enlisted Pepa to help them record a response track to Doug E. Fresh & the Get Fresh Crew's "The Show" in 1985.[25] A couple of months later, after their song "The Show Stoppa (Is Stupid Fresh)" proved moderately successful thanks to initial airplay on the New York radio show *Mr. Magic's Rap Attack*, and after the song was released on a small label, the group (including producer Azor and a DJ dubbed Spinderella) signed a deal with Next Plateau Records. Their first major hit, the B side "Push It," was recorded in a friend's bathroom and eventually made its way to the top 20 on the *Billboard* "Hot 100" in early 1988, a feat achieved by only a handful of rap songs at that point, and surpassed by only one song featuring a woman rapping, Blondie's "Rapture."[26] Over the next half-decade, the group put out a number of successful singles, including "Expression," "Do You Want Me," and "Let's Talk about Sex," which all peaked in the top 30 of the "Hot 100."

But it took a change of personnel and vision to achieve the chart success of "Shoop." Despite the group's accomplishments, the women were not adequately compensated. Prior to releasing *Very Necessary*, the women in the group—contrary to the female-empowerment rhetoric on their records—had very little artistic control and received a smaller share of the profits than Azor. Early on in their career, Azor started his own production and management company and negotiated the group's contracts to his benefit. As their manager, producer, songwriter, and in Salt's case lover, Azor exerted almost Motown levels of control over his artists, telling them what to wear, what songs to release, and who to hang out with.[27] "In the beginning," he recalled, "there was no compromise. I wrote, they rapped. Nobody asked anything."[28] This meant that the group released songs that they weren't entirely comfortable with, such as a partially sung cover of "Twist and Shout."[29] Deidra Roper, who joined the group as Spinderella in 1987 when the original Spinderella left, claimed that in the early years "we were like his babies, his creations."[30] Azor was well compensated for "his creations." It was reported that over the five years the group was signed to Next Plateau Records, the label paid Azor's company around five million dollars; Azor took half, and divided the other half among the three women in the group, an unfair arrangement that underscored his role as visionary and devalued theirs as performers and laborers.[31]

As the group became successful and made friends in the music industry, things changed. "Everybody got wiser," Azor claimed.[32] According to Salt, the women "just woke up … [and] made a big ruckus," reacting to their feeling that the label "saw us as ditsy little girls that should be lucky they could get a car."[33] The group renegotiated their contract with Azor, and when it came time to work on *Very Necessary*, the group split artistic control with him, writing half of the tracks. One of these songs was "Shoop," which Salt has said Azor didn't think would do well.[34] But he was wrong, meaning that either the group had internalized his hit-making methods or the musical landscape had shifted to the point that his artistic impulses weren't always correct. Perhaps it was both: while the sound of popular music had indeed changed since the group's last album, the group shows tremendous talent in creating such a catchy song.

To Shoop Is to Succeed on Your Own Terms

One of hip-hop's central concerns in the early 1990s had to do with crossing over into the mainstream. As hip-hop became more and more popular with white audiences throughout the late 1980s, and as record companies began encouraging rappers to create songs for these same audiences, the relationship between hip-hop artists and their core Black fans became increasingly complicated. Artists and fans worried about—to paraphrase A Tribe Called Quest—rap turning into pop—or in the words of 3rd Bass—hit pop getting turned into hit pop. Salt-N-Pepa were very much a part of this process; songs like "Push It" ushered in the era of hip-hop becoming hit pop, and Azor intentionally courted pop audiences by having the group release rapped covers of oldies classics such as the Turtles' "You Showed Me." As the hip-hop community distanced itself from the most overt crossover rappers like MC Hammer, who critic Bill Stephney claimed was not a rapper but instead a "major entertainer," Salt-N-Pepa worried about their reputation, as they easily could have been lumped in with Hammer and other crossover rappers due to their catchy singles and dance-laden music videos.[35] In a 1994 *Rolling Stone* feature, Salt articulated concern about the group's audience in the years leading up to the release of *Very Necessary*, saying that the group "got to the point where [they] were only being played on pop radio." She continued, noting that at a concert "there was nothing but white people in our audience. And that hurt me because I'm black, and I want my people there, too."[36] On the new album, given their new roles as writers and producers, the group didn't have to go along with Azor's pop vision. According to Azor, they were free to make "Shoop" and the rest of their half of *Very Necessary* " 'street'; they wanted it to sound 'black'."[37]

Even though the group crafted "Shoop" in opposition to Azor's pop-adjacent sound, the song had all of the right components to become a pop hit, with easy-to-understand, innuendo-laced lyrics atop a melodic hook and a mid-tempo shuffling beat. Released as the up-tempo styles of hip-house and new jack swing were fading from popularity after dominating radio airwaves for the previous half-decade, the song's slow yet danceable groove fit well on pop radio stations trying to find songs that matched the slowing tempos of G-Funk, R&B ballads, and grunge-adjacent pop and rock music.[38] Including melodic sung hooks such as the one in "Shoop" helped rappers get played on pop radio, as radio programmers were hesitant to program songs that lacked the melodic nature of the pop and R&B songs that the stations usually played. Programmers liked clean, easy-to-understand rhymes: the laid-back lilt of the lyrics in "Shoop" allowed casual listeners to catch what the rappers were saying, with the swung rhythm of the rhymes mimicking the natural lilt of spoken English by lending additional time to stressed syllables.[39] In addition, programmers often liked songs that were titillating but not too provocative. Despite the sexual subject matter, the lyrics of "Shoop" are blatantly clean, as evinced by Salt cleverly playing as though she catches herself about to swear, avoiding filling in the rest of the line "You're a sexy mutha ..." by halting a bit before changing the subject.[40] Salt's catch is a signal, letting the listener know that that she is cool, that she is fly: provocative, not profane.

A half-decade earlier, getting played on the radio as a rapper meant having to, in Ice-T's words, "bend to the format" to fit in on pop radio playlists.[41] But by 1993 the sound of pop had changed, in large part thanks to those very rappers who did "bend to the format."[42] By creating radio-friendly rap in the late 1980s, artists like Salt-N-Pepa participated in a monumental shift in the sonic landscape of pop, bringing the Black sounds of hip-hop into the White-coded mainstream of pop. By 1993, rappers didn't have to bend to the sound of the White mainstream to fit on pop radio stations, because the sounds of rap—the beats as well as the rhymes—were all over pop radio. This meant that Salt-N-Pepa could nuance their pop appeal; rather than dumbing down their flow, making their rhyme schemes and phrasing more regular, the rappers' expert delivery guides listeners through a rather complex battery of distinct flow patterns, pointing listeners to important moments.

Switching flows and alternating between a swung and straight feel, stepping in and out of more metrically aligned moments with ease, Salt-N-Pepa deliver their bars with creative acumen and versatile agility. The lyrics are simul-taneously assertive and hilarious, walking an odd line between potentially serious—the song is off an album called, after all, *Very Necessary*—and deli-ciously absurd, the type of one-liners that you wish your best friend was witty enough to spout. The song is full of their trademark snarl, with the rappers pouncing on initial consonants and dynamically changing pitches to lend a sassy delivery to lines like "You're a shotgun, bang / What's up with that thang/I want to know, how does it hang?" The rappers' immaculate timing helps highlight their sass, lending the lyrics a striking candidness and showing their sense of humor. In the aforementioned lyrics, for example, Salt waits a moment before articulating the final parts of the last two lines, coyly making the listener wait for the innuendo-laced rhyme. This small, repeated displace-ment not only gives the line personality but also catches listeners' attention, pulling them in and encouraging them to remember the line.

Creating a hit involves more than skill; the song must be accessible and memorable to novice listeners. "Shoop" is exemplary in this regard, as both rappers effortlessly land catchy lyrics by switching up their flow to point casual listeners towards memorable phrases. For example, in the first verse, Pepa sets up a regular pattern of single-syllable swung rhymes prior to the line "Don't know, how you do, the voodoo that you do so well." When she begins this line (interpolated from a Cole Porter song), she switches to two-syllable straight quick-fire rhymes.[43] This change in flow directs listeners to the lines in question, guiding them to an important part and then ushering them into the return of the hook and the titular line of "Makes me wanna shoop." Similarly, in the second verse, Salt sets up the line comparing a man to eating ice cream by creating an uneven rhyme pattern prior to it. Once she asks the man to "come and give me some of that yum yum chocolate chip, honey dip," the rhyme scheme evens out, drawing listeners' attention to the extended metaphor. By changing their flow to point listeners to these and many other catchy lines, both rappers ensure that their intricate flow is easy to follow.

Conclusion

In "Shoop," the group created a hit on their own terms by rapping how they wanted, about what they wanted, atop the style of beat they wanted. And listeners wanted in; "Whatever 'Shoop' meant," Clover Hope writes, "everyone wanted to do it."[44] The success of this song and their two following singles, a collaboration with En Vogue entitled "Whatta Man" and the Grammy-winning pro-sex anthem "None of Your Business," catapulted the group to new heights of stardom: *Very Necessary* went platinum in the United States five times over the next two years.[45] While their next album failed to achieve the same success, thanks to lacking promotion by their bankrupt record label, the group has remained within the public eye thanks to appearances in a reality TV show, movies and advertisements, and multiple throwback hip-hop concert tours; most recently the group executive produced a biopic about their career, and received the Lifetime Achievement Award at the 2021 Grammys. And the word "shoop" has had an afterlife, as it once again gave voice to the inexpressible complexity of female experience in Whitney Houston's "Exhale (Shoop Shoop)," which debuted atop the *Billboard* "Hot 100" in late 1995.

Salt and Pepa began their careers a decade earlier by offering a response to Slick Rick's verse on the "The Show," which documents Slick Rick talking to a pretty woman on the train. "The Show Stoppa," their answer record, talked back, telling the story from the woman's point of view and turning Slick Rick's advances into a laughable tale of unwanted attention from, as the lyrics go, a dupe. But the irony of this record was that the women didn't write their rhymes, they didn't pick the subject matter, and they didn't choose their beat; despite its female-driven narrative, the song's aesthetics were bound by men. Nearly a decade later, however, everything had changed. "Shoop" demonstrated that female rappers could and would demand desire, control, and success: they would shoop. And given all this, who wouldn't want to shoop?

Notes

1 Leonard Pitts, Jr., "Don't Ask Salt-N-Pepa to Act Like Sugar 'n' Spice," *Greensboro News Record*. June 3, 1994, W11.
2 Leonard Greene, "Weld Could Find Betta Role Models," *Boston Herald*. December 8, 1995, 1.

3 Jacqueline Warwick, *Girl Groups, Girl Culture* (New York: Routledge, 2007).

4 Kyra D. Gaunt, "Translating Double-Dutch to Hip-Hop: The Musical Vernacular of Black Girls' Play," in *That's the Joint!: The Hip-Hop Studies Reader*, eds. Murray Forman and Mark Anthony Neal (New York: Routledge, 2004), 261.

5 Warwick, *Girl Groups, Girl Culture*, 36.

6 Ibid., 37.

7 Ibid.

8 Touré, "The Hips vs. the Head," *The New York Times*. January 16,1994, H28; Siegmund, "Parental Distraction Advised," *Los Angeles Times*. January 23, 1994, F68.

9 This song, released in 1967, is itself a cover of Ike Turner's "I'm Blue (The Gong-Gong Song)," first recorded in 1961 by The Ikettes.

10 Tricia Rose, "Never Trust a Big Butt and a Smile," *Camera Obscura* 8, no. 23 (May 1, 1990), 128.

11 Tom Maurstad, "Role Reversal," *San Antonio Express-News*, March 30, 1994, 6D.

12 Bill Eichenberger, "Salt-N-Pepa Deliver Sound Messages With Spunk," *Columbus Dispatch*, August 6, 1994, 3H.

13 Michael Saunders, "Salt-N-Pepa Is Now Seasoned and Slick," *The Province*, June 10, 1994, B30.

14 John Leland and Marc Peyser, "Our Bodies, Our Sales," *Newsweek* 123, no. 5 (January 31, 1994), 56.

15 Joan Morgan, *When Chickenheads Come Home to Roost: A Hip-Hop Feminist Breaks It Down* (New York: Simon & Schuster, 1999).

16 Hortense J. Spillers, *Black, White, and in Color: Essays on American Literature and Culture* (Chicago: University of Chicago Press, 2003), 153.

17 See Hazel Carby, "It Jus Be's Dat Way Sometime," in *The Jazz Cadence of American Culture*, ed. Robert G. O'Meally (New York: Columbia University Press, 1998); Angela Y. Davis, *Blues Legacies and Black Feminism: Gertrude "Ma" Rainey, Bessie Smith, and Billie Holiday* (New York: Pantheon Books, 1998); Douglas, "Why the Shirelles Mattered," in *Where the Girls Are: Growing Up Female with the Mass Media* (New York: Three Rivers Press, 1995); and Rose, "Never Trust a Big Butt and a Smile."

18 Lester is quoted in Jeanine Amber, "Salt 'n' Pepa," *YSB*, March 31, 1994, 34.

19 Cheryl L. Keyes, "Empowering Self, Making Choices, Creating Spaces," in *That's the Joint!: The Hip-Hop Studies Reader*, ed. Murray Forman and Mark Anthony Neal (New York: Routledge, 2004), 269.

20 Morgan, *When Chickenheads Come Home to Roost*, 59.

21 Quoted in Pitts, Jr., "Don't Ask Salt-N-Pepa to Act Like Sugar 'n' Spice," W11.

22 Aisha Durham, Brittney C. Cooper, and Susana M. Morris, "The Stage Hip-Hop Feminism Built: A New Directions Essay," *Signs* 38, no. 3 (2013), 721. Angela Davis writes, similarly, about the blues, that "what gives the blues such fascinating possibilities of sustaining emergent feminist consciousness is the way they often construct seemingly antagonistic relationships as noncontradictory oppositions." See Davis, *Blues Legacies and Black Feminism*, xv.

23 Jason Newman, "Martha Wash: The Most Famous Unknown Singer of the '90s Speaks Out," *Rolling Stone*, September 2, 2014.

24 Quoted in 2Pac Forum Channel, "Nanci Fletcher Interview Part 1: About Deathrow, Snoop Dogg, Nate Dogg, Dr. Dre, 2Pac & More," YouTube, June 16, 2013, https://youtu.be/VvXFzt4KrTU, 9:39–9:44.

25 Dinitia Smith, "Straight Outta Queens: How Salt-N-Pepa Turned Rap on Its Head," *New York Magazine*, January 17, 1994, 36.

26 Ibid., 37.

27 Joy Duckett Cain, "The Growing Pains of Salt 'N' Pepa," *Essence*, October 1994, 130.

28 Quoted in Jancee Dunn, "The Spice of Life," *Rolling Stone*, June 30, 1994, 21.

29 Christopher R. Weingarten, "Salt-N-Pepa: Our Life in 15 Songs." *Rolling Stone*, September 5, 2017.

30 Quoted in Tony Green, "Salt-N-Pepa Rule in the Rap Galaxy," *St. Petersburg Times.* April 22, 1994, 22.

31 Cain, "The Growing Pains of Salt 'N' Pepa," 134.

32 Quoted in Dunn, "The Spice of Life," 21.

33 Quoted in Smith, "Straight Outta Queens," 34, 38.

34 Greg Kot, "Trying to Pose Some Questions," *Chicago Tribune.* April 29, 1994, 5.

35 Bill Stephney, "Funda-Mental Hip-Hop," *The Source*, January 1991, 38.

36 Quoted in Dunn, "The Spice of Life," 21.

37 Quoted in Smith, "Straight Outta Queens," 39.

38 For a quantitative analysis of tempos in hit singles, see Mark Bannister, "The Billboard Hot 100: Exploring Six Decades of Number One Singles." GitHub, April 2017, https://github.com/mspbannister/dand-p4-billboard/blob/master/Bill board_analysis__100417_.md#the-billboard-hot-100-exploring-six-decades-of-number-one-singles

39 Amy Coddington, "'Check Out the Hook While My DJ Revolves It': How the Music Industry Made Rap into Pop in the Late 1980s," in *The Oxford Handbook of Hip Hop Music*, ed. Justin D. Burton and Jason Lee Oakes (Oxford: Oxford University Press, 2018).

40 This line references the Prince song "Sexy MF," released a year earlier.

41 Quoted in Craig Rosen, "Rap on Radio: Don't Expect to Hear Much, If Any—But That's OK with Music's Creative Optimizers," *Billboard*, December 16, 1989, R-34.

42 Coddington, "'Check Out the Hook While My DJ Revolves It.'"

43 The lyric interpolates a line from Cole Porter's "You Do Something to Me," from the 1929 musical *Fifty Million Frenchmen*.

44 Clover Hope, *The Motherlode: 100+ Women Who Made Hip-Hop* (New York: Abrams Image, 2021), 50.

45 See Recording Industry Association of America, "Gold & Platinum," RIAA, accessed October 29, 2020, www.riaa.com/gold-platinum/

References

Amber, Jeannine. "Salt 'n' Pepa: Sisters Doin' for Themselves." *YSB*, March 31, 1994.

Bannister, Mark. "The Billboard Hot 100: Exploring Six Decades of Number One Singles." GitHub, April 2017. https://github.com/mspbannister/dand-p4-billboard/blob/master/Billboard_analysis__100417_.md#the-billboard-hot-100-exploring-six-decades-of-number-one-singles

Cain, Joy Duckett. "The Growing Pains of Salt 'N' Pepa." *Essence*, October 1994.

Carby, Hazel V. "It Jus Be's Dat Way Sometime: The Sexual Politics of Women's Blues." In *The Jazz Cadence of American Culture*, edited by Robert G. O'Meally, 470–83. New York: Columbia University Press, 1998.

Coddington, Amy. "'Check Out the Hook While My DJ Revolves It': How the Music Industry Made Rap into Pop in the Late 1980s." In *The Oxford Handbook of Hip Hop Music*, edited by Justin D. Burton and Jason Lee Oakes. Oxford University Press, 2018. doi: 10.1093/oxfordhb/9780190281090.013.35

Davis, Angela Y. *Blues Legacies and Black Feminism: Gertrude "Ma" Rainey, Bessie Smith, and Billie Holiday*. New York: Pantheon Books, 1998.

Douglas, Susan Jeanne. "Why the Shirelles Mattered." In *Where the Girls Are: Growing Up Female with the Mass Media*, 83–98. New York: Three Rivers Press, 1995.

Dunn, Jancee. "The Spice of Life." *Rolling Stone*, June 30, 1994.

Durham, Aisha, Brittney C. Cooper, and Susana M. Morris. "The Stage Hip-Hop Feminism Built: A New Directions Essay." *Signs* 38, no. 3 (2013): 721–37.

Eichenberger, Bill. "Salt-N-Pepa Deliver Sound Messages with Spunk." *Columbus Dispatch*. August 6, 1994.

Fletcher, Nanci. "Nanci Fletcher Interview Part 1: About Deathrow, Snoop Dogg, Nate Dogg, Dr. Dre, 2Pac & More." YouTube, uploaded by 2Pac Forum Channel June 16, 2013. https://youtu.be/VvXFzt4KrTU

Gaunt, Kyra D. "Translating Double-Dutch to Hip-Hop: The Musical Vernacular of Black Girls' Play." In *That's the Joint!: The Hip-Hop Studies Reader*, edited by Murray Forman and Mark Anthony Neal, 251–64. New York: Routledge, 2004.

Green, Tony. "Salt-N-Pepa Rule in the Rap Galaxy." *St. Petersburg Times*. April 22, 1994.

Greene, Leonard. "Weld Could Find Betta Role Models." *Boston Herald*. December 8, 1995.

Hope, Clover. *The Motherlode: 100+ Women Who Made Hip-Hop*. New York: Abrams Image, 2021.

Keyes, Cheryl L. "Empowering Self, Making Choices, Creating Spaces: Black Female Identity via Rap Music Performance." In *That's the Joint!: The Hip-Hop Studies Reader*, edited by Murray Forman and Mark Anthony Neal, 265–76. New York: Routledge, 2004.

Kot, Greg. "Trying to Pose Some Questions." *Chicago Tribune*. April 29, 1994.

Leland, John, and Marc Peyser. "Our Bodies, Our Sales." *Newsweek* 123, no. 5 (January 31, 1994): 56.

Maurstad, Tom. "Role Reversal." *San Antonio Express-News*. March 30, 1994.

Morgan, Joan. *When Chickenheads Come Home to Roost: A Hip-Hop Feminist Breaks It Down*. New York: Simon & Schuster, 1999.

Newman, Jason. "Martha Wash: The Most Famous Unknown Singer of the '90s Speaks Out." *Rolling Stone*, September 2, 2014. www.rollingstone.com/feature/martha-wash-the-most-famous-unknown-singer-of-the-90s-speaks-out-231182/

Pitts, Leonard, Jr. "Don't Ask Salt-N-Pepa to Act Like Sugar 'n' Spice." *Greensboro News Record*. June 3, 1994.

Recording Industry Association of America. "Gold & Platinum." RIAA. www.riaa.com/gold-platinum/

Rose, Tricia. "Never Trust a Big Butt and a Smile." *Camera Obscura* 8, no. 23 (May 1, 1990): 108–31.

Rosen, Craig. "Rap on Radio: Don't Expect to Hear Much, If Any—But That's OK with Music's Creative Optimizers." *Billboard*, December 16, 1989.

Saunders, Michael. "Salt-N-Pepa Is Now Seasoned and Slick: And Sometimes Rock Critics Are All Wet." *The Province*. June 10, 1994.

Siegmund, Heidi. "Parental Distraction Advised." *Los Angeles Times*. January 23, 1994.

Smith, Dinitia. "Straight Outta Queens: How Salt-N-Pepa Turned Rap on Its Head." *New York Magazine*, January 17, 1994.

Spillers, Hortense J. *Black, White, and in Color: Essays on American Literature and Culture*. Chicago: University of Chicago Press, 2003.

Stephney, Bill. "Funda-Mental Hip-Hop." *The Source*, January 1991.

Touré. "The Hips vs. the Head," *The New York Times*. January 16, 1994.

Warwick, Jacqueline. *Girl Groups, Girl Culture: Popular Music and Identity in the 1960s*. New York: Routledge, 2007.

Weingarten, Christopher R. "Salt-N-Pepa: Our Life in 15 Songs." *Rolling Stone*, September 5, 2017. www.rollingstone.com/music/music-lists/salt-n-pepa-our-life-in-15-songs-111537/

13 Hanson—"Mmmbop" (1997)

Louie Dean Valencia

"Mmmbop," the 1997 breakout hit song by the band Hanson remains a cultural curiosity of the late 1990s. Hanson was composed of three brothers with long, blond hair from Tulsa, Oklahoma, named Zachary, Taylor, and Isaac—who were ages 11, 13, and 16 at the time. The single, released March 24, 1997, debuted at #49 on the Billboard charts. Just six weeks later, the song was at number one and was Mercury Record's first number-one single in seven years.[1] With its quick rhythm, "Mmmbop" echoed both bubblegum pop and Motown, and is remembered (by non-Hanson fans) mostly as just another vacuous, one-hit-wonder pop song by a boy band.

However, despite the upbeat tone, the song's lyrics were surprisingly somber, describing how a person only has "so many relationships in this life" and how "only one or two [relationships] will last." Referencing "pain and strife," the chorus emphasizes that one can simply turn their back and the relationship can be "gone so fast"—urging the listener to "hold on the ones who really care," as they will be the only ones who will be there in the end. Humorously, but in all seriousness, the song continues: "When you get old and start losing your hair / Can you tell me who will still care?"[2]

The song claims that "in an mmmbop" a person can be "gone." Although Lea Wierød Borčak argues "mmmbop" is a "nonsense word," when read in context an "mmmbop" is a sort of fleeting temporality that acknowledges a future probability in which few relationships survive.[3] The song speaks of losing relationships, aging, and appreciating those who stay. Taylor Hanson, the middle brother, defined the term as only a fourteen-year-old can, "[A]n 'mmmbop' is a second ... appreciate the people you have around you, they could be gone in a second."[4]

Hanson was an early adopter of new internet and media technologies to communicate directly with their fan community. This early adoption helped them maintain a robust musical ecology in which they essentially operated outside of the mainstream corporate label system—cultivating a long-term relationship between the band and their fans. This approach engendered very dedicated and enduring forms of fandom—a kind of "safe space" for Hanson fans. As Mark Duffett argues, "In their role as celebrity followers, music fans frequently seek greater intimacy with their heroes."[5] The

DOI: 10.4324/9781003093206-14

internet allowed for Hanson fans to feel a greater sense of lasting intimacy with the brothers.

The Hanson brothers were a part of a generation of "digital natives"—a phrase coined by Marc Prensky in 2001 to describe " 'native speakers' of the digital language of computers, video games, and the Internet." Natives, for Prensky, were accustomed to receiving information quickly. He argued, "They like to parallel process and multi-task. They prefer their graphics *before* their text rather than the opposite. ... They function best when networked. They thrive on instant gratification and frequent rewards."[6] As one of the first to suggest this form of common generational identification, Prensky's ideas were echoed by other adults who to some degree essentialized and stereotyped an entire generation.[7] There was a sense that the generation that became known as "Millennials" was communicating differently than their predecessors. Those who did not grow up as natives, for Prensky, were "digital immigrants"— people who were socialized in an analogue world. For Prensky, immigrants held a "thicker accent"—they printed out emails and called people to confirm receipt of an email. While the modes had changed with access to new technology, the social functions were not drastically different. While many baby boomers eventually learned to correspond via emails without printing them out, Prensky was right to assert that many young people, those who had internet access, were more networked than before and were craving more information and interaction in part because of the access to knowledge and digital community spaces these new technologies provided.

By analyzing the different media used to distribute "Mmmbop" and how the song gained popularity, we can better understand the ways in which teenagers and pre-teenagers at the turn of the millennium interacted with both analogue and digital technologies. Moreover, we see many contemporary polemics and uses of the internet already present in 1997. The digital culture surrounding Hanson highlighted a wide array of issues ranging from a certain homogeneity in the media of the era to queerphobic online hate groups and the creation of digital communities and safe spaces. Citing *PC Magazine*'s 1997 year-end wrap-up, Hanson's large-format, print fan magazine, *MOE* (*Middle of Everywhere*), reported, "Hanson was noted for having the most dedicated fan pages on the internet, over 1,000 pages amazingly enough. ... In addition, 'Hanson' was the second most searched for word on the net." *MOE* also reported, "Hansonline was THE most attended music-related site on the net, beating out such giants as *MTV*, *Rolling Stone* and *Billboard*."[8] Hanson's online fan community formed an interconnected global community, what I call a "digital imagined community"—to borrow from Benedict Anderson—which was constructed through webpages, chats, and online forums.[9] By looking at this culture, we can better understand how Hanson survived because of their ability to navigate the digital world.

In 2017, Hanson celebrated their 25th anniversary as a band with a sold-out world tour accompanied by a greatest hits compilation album. They released a new full-length Christmas album, complemented by a line of ugly sweaters, Hanson snowflake ornaments, mugs, notecards, cookie cutters, scarves, beanies, and T-shirts—one of which proclaimed "Peace on Earth." It was their tenth album since the release of their 1997 breakout album, *Middle of Nowhere*, which featured "Mmmbop." The following year, Hanson launched their String Theory tour, recording and performing new music and new arrangements of popular songs from their oeuvre, like "Mmmbop," with renowned symphony orchestras in the United States and abroad. The band has not stopped producing new music since their childhood (sometimes recycling the hits)—with a total of two demo albums and eleven full-length studio albums by 2022, in addition to releasing a new EP yearly for subscription members of their fan club. The brothers—now 36, 39, and 41—even have their own brand of beer, "Mmmhops."

Their concerns as expressed in their music also changed over time. In a 2017 interview at the South by Southwest (SXSW) music festival in Austin, Texas, Isaac, the eldest, mentioned a fear of being killed in a car wreck and never getting the chance to play music again being instilled in them at a young age by their father. In response, Zac, the youngest, quipped, "So, our plan is…work hard; you might be dead." When asked how their conversation went from "Mmmbop" to death, Taylor, the middle brother, added in a matter-of-fact tone, "That's what 'Mmmbop' is about…it's about death." This motivation led the group to both "work hard" in the studio and also maintain their connection to fans, helping them to survive—along with emergent technology that allowed them to do their work independently of a major record label. What could have been a one-hit-wonder band, gone in an mmmbop, partially because of the technological innovations of the time, Hanson found, maintained, and has catered to a community of fans which has sustained their independent career. When capitalism failed the band (that is, when their record company was acquired and they lost executive support), Hanson broke out on their own, founded an independent record company, 3-Car Garage Records (3CG Records), and continued to produce their own music. The boy band singing about the ephemerality of relationships used digital technology to maintain their relationships with their fans—attempting to adapt to the digital era in real time.

Bubble Gum, Pop, and Cassette Tapes

While the band embraced digital media early, their origins were firmly in the analogue universe. The audio cassette tape was first developed in Belgium and released to the public in 1962 by the Dutch Philips corporation.[10] Later that decade, personal portable cassette recorders became popular, used primarily by journalists and the likes of Andy Warhol, but were still not known for having high-quality sound. It was not until the late 1970s that the cassette found popular success among DJs in the disco scene, and even more so once Sony's Walkman was introduced to the mass market in 1979.[11] While the audio cassette tape is by no means specific to Hanson's story, it was part of their foundational myth for their fans.

The cassette was central to the musical education of the band. Hanson's love of doo-wop and Motown came from the family's move to Ecuador, Venezuela, and later Trinidad in their younger years—yes, younger years—as their father worked in the oil industry. While abroad, the brothers listened to cassette tapes of music from the 1950s and '60s.[12] A prepubescent Zac explained in 1997:

> Our mom and dad got [the tapes] before we left [Oklahoma] since there would be no English radio we could listen to where we were going. They were these "Call now! Not available in stores!" type tapes. People often assume the tapes were our parents' music that we just happened to listen to. Actually, that music was before their time, too! The three of us saw the TV commercial and asked them to buy them.[13]

Time Life Records' 1958 tape,[14] for example, included rock and roll standards like "Johnny B. Goode," "Splish Splash," "Rockin' Robin," "Summertime Blues," and "Good Golly, Miss Molly."[15] Cassettes were portable, reliable, and universal in the late 1980s and early 1990s.

Not surprisingly, the cassette tape also played an important role in Hanson's process of finding an audience. The boys only started playing instruments about two years before *Middle of Nowhere* was released in 1997. However, they began performing for local audiences in 1992, mostly a cappella and rhythm and blues–style music. First discovered in 1994 after a SXSW softball tournament, the brothers represented a generational shift in both music taste and technological use between Generation X and the rising Millennials.[16] At SXSW, the boys busked, asking to sing a cappella to attendees and passing out demos.[17] As the "official" Hanson book, a *New York Times* bestseller, noted in 1997

> Here, at the very peak of grunge's popularity were three well-scrubbed, blond lads running about, singing a cappella pop songs to a bunch of record company people who were looking to discover the next Pearl Jam, not the next Jackson 5.[18]

Hanson was "discovered" by music attorney Christopher Sabec, who also discovered the Dave Matthews Band. Sabec sent copies of their demo cassette tape out to hundreds of scouts, and eventually got the attention of Steve Greenberg, a talent hunter at Mercury Records at the time.[19] "I got this tape and loved it," Greenberg said to the *New York Times* in 1997,

> but I was convinced it was fake…I was sure there was some adult pulling the strings or the vocals were manipulated and they weren't really playing

their instruments. I wasn't going to do it. But then I saw them at a county fair in Kansas, and they played and sang just as well as they did on the record. There wasn't an adult in sight—except their dad, who was loading up the equipment, and their mom, who was selling T-shirts.[20]

To be sure, Hanson was interested in building a fan base early on, but it was also a family-run enterprise.[21]

In many ways, the cassette brought a democratizing element to the consumption and reproduction of music. The cassette, unlike the vinyl record, allowed people to record and remix their own music. The cassette was portable, like the 8-track, but could hold more songs and was easier to record over—to say nothing about being more reliable. In contrast, the compact disc had high-quality sound but was not as portable—despite later anti-shake technology. Even though the CD eventually gained easier writing/rewriting capabilities, it did not initially replace the cassette tape because of prohibitive cost. One could cheaply buy a cassette tape player and recorder in the 1990s. In that decade, burning CDs was cost-prohibitive, requiring computers, external drives, and so forth. The CD was significant in that it brought to the forefront new possibilities for digital media. Although it wasn't obvious in the 1990s, the CD was a transitionary technology, like most, making digital files usable, if not wholly practical in the same way that a cassette recording could be. As Eric Rothenbuhler argues, "[The CD] was one of the first consumer products prominently labelled digital at a time well before home and office computers had become normal."[22] Mixed CDs were still in the future—at the turn of the millennium—and only appeared once digital MP3 files became widespread.[23] Only later did digital media formats such as wav files and MP3s completely usurp both the compact disc and the cassette's utility—primarily though Apple's iPod. Curiously, Sabec went on to cofound Digital Rights Inc. in 2009, now Rightscorp Inc., a publicly traded company that locates and threatens a fine, or legal action, against alleged copyright infringers who have illegally downloaded music. Within just 15 years Sabec moved from sending out cassettes to record companies to searching out digital copyright infringers.

In an Mmmbop, They're Gone

"Mmmbop" was originally self-released on a 15-song demo album by the same name in 1996.[24] That version featured a much slower tempo, as opposed to the upbeat variation released in March 1997 which found mainstream success and was even nominated in the Grammy Award categories of Best Pop Performance by a Duo or Group with Vocal and Record of the Year. With numerous remixes made for international markets, "Mmmbop" reached number one in the United States and 26 other countries, selling ten million copies of their first studio album, *Middle of Nowhere*.[25] As a band, Hanson was nominated for a Best New Artist Grammy. At 12, Zac Hanson still remains the youngest songwriter ever nominated for a Grammy. Robyn

J. Stilwell lauded "Mmmbop" in *Popular Music and Society* in her 1999 review, comparing Taylor Hanson's vocals to Michael Jackson and Steve Winwood, describing his voice as "a bigger voice than Jackson's and a more precise one than Winwood's ... at fourteen, he has far more control of that voice than either of them did at the same age." She continued, "He shifts from chest voice to throat or head with remarkable ease."[26] Of the chorus of "Mmmbop," she wrote,

> The rhythm is taken literally to another level in the chorus of "Mmmbop," where the half-bar "bounce" shifts to a whole bar, creating a greater sense of suspension through the longer rhythmic span and the syncopation springing the middle. Again, this core rhythm is accentuated by texture: the chorus is much more chordal, the beats three and four relatively "empty," thus emphasizing the fall to the downbeat and the ultimate "bounce" in the song, the title itself, "Mmmbop." It's a great record.[27]

The rise of "Mmmbop" benefitted from the song being streamed online using RealAudio Player (although, because of slow internet connections in the late 1990s, that was often the worst option). "Mmmbop" was pressed on vinyl for promotional purposes for DJs, and was available on both cassette and CD and played (what seemed like) at least once an hour on MTV according to *Girls' Life* magazine.[28] A blitz of publicity followed the meteoric rise of the band. MTV, VH1, and all the major broadcast networks featured Hanson—*The Today Show*, *Good Morning America*, *Fox after* Breakfast, Jay Leno's *Tonight Show*, David Letterman's *Late Show*, *Live with Regis and Kathie Lee*, *Rosie O'Donnell*, *Oprah*, *Howie Mandell*, *Jenny McCarthy*, *Total Request Live*—the list goes on and on. Within a year of the release of "Mmmbop," Hanson had the attention of the likes of Gus Van Sant, Oscar-winning director of *Good Will Hunting* (1997) and *My Own Private Idaho* (1991), and Weird Al Yankovic, parodier extraordinaire. Van Sant directed the video for "Weird" (1997), a melancholic song about feeling like an outsider, and Yankovic both appeared in and co-directed the music video for "River" (1998)—which parodied *Titanic*, even casting Gloria Stuart, who starred in the 1997 blockbuster film as the older version of Kate Winslet's character, Rose.

The boys probably garnered attention because of the ways they subverted expectations. The young brothers' aesthetic mixed a grunge-like flannel and a neo-mod style with Doc Martin boots, sporting bright colors that in many ways transgressed teenage masculinity of the era. The boys wore multiple leather bracelets and necklaces, sported long hair, and never were seen out and about not looking perfectly preened—golden locks abounded. In many ways, Hanson marked a decisive turn away from the grunge and punk music of the 1990s, from bands like Nirvana, Green Day, and Silverchair. While members of those bands certainly had long hair, too, the Hanson brothers were younger and played music that seemingly lacked edge—despite having songs on their album about death, suicide, being social outcasts, and missing lost loved ones. Top-40 music was more generally moving away from rock to a hybrid pop-rock. Emo, a genre that was also rising, borrowed from pop/rock and the melodramatic notes of early 1990s grunge music.

Music and media studies scholar Martin Scherzinger has pointed to the rise of the giant radio conglomerates, such as Clear Channel, Infinity, and Cox, to explain why music became more homogeneous—not just in the United States but internationally. In 2005, Scherzinger convincingly argued:

> FM radio ... remains America's most widely used medium for listening to music. Nothing in earlier history matches the scope and power of the cartel-like integration of corporate and governmental groups to permeate the social fabric of American society. With the technological capacity to surround most citizens with controlled images and sounds, the new state-corporatist oligarchy has the power to transform the cultural and political agendas of the United States and, increasingly, the world.[29]

Was Hanson just another band that was a part of this new state-corporatist oligarchy taking over popular culture? Hanson was indeed part of the hegemonic corporate power structure, but they also were able to maintain some sort of autonomy because they were not as easy to define as some of those that came after. Moreover, because of their use of technology, they were able to eventually assert even more agency, breaking off from their record company.

Despite their influences, drawn from the likes of Chuck Berry,[30] Aretha Franklin,[31] Otis Redding, the Supremes, the Temptations, the Four Tops, Buddy Holly, Elvis Presley,[32] and a long list of Motown sounds, the group was categorized as a boy band. In the popular press, comparisons were made to everyone from the Jackson 5 and the Beatles to New Kids on the Block—a wide swath—and perhaps this confusion was the result of the absence of a clear definition of what a Millennial boy band looked like just yet. Hanson rejected any comparison to the boys from Liverpool outright—although they did appear in a 1998 Ringo Starr music video.[33] Wedged between the arrival of the Spice Girls and Backstreet Boys, with "Mmmbop" Hanson's music mingled both bubblegum pop and a sort of Motown-sounding bop, pop, and rock—tambourines, bongos, harmonicas, pianos, and keyboards played by middle brother Taylor, electric and acoustic guitars played by eldest brother Isaac, and a full drum kit played by the youngest, eleven-year old Zac. Vocals and harmonies were shared among all, with Taylor taking the lead (see Figure 13.1). While there are numerous ways to define what constitutes a boy band, oft-cited characteristics usually include band members who do not play live instruments, a branded "look," and performing songs written by others.

Before the explosion of N'Sync, Backstreet Boys, and 98 Degrees in the late nineties, there was Hanson, who were, oddly, considerably younger than the boy bands who came up around them. In contrast to those groups, because Hanson always wrote their own music and took pride in playing their instruments, these factors might have played a part in why they did not fit into the new Island Def Jam Records conglomeration that had gobbled up Mercury Records in 1998. After the release of their second album, *This Time Around* (2000), the band faced challenges getting support for their next album because the music scene had shifted beneath them, both in the broader world and also at their record label. Zac exclaimed in a moment of frustration in 2001, "We're on a rap label, with the creator of Britney Spears and the Backstreet Boys."[34] Zac's referencing a "creator" of the Backstreet Boys and Britney Spears both implied a rejection of such a comparison and asserted a lack of artistic voice in both the Backstreet Boys and Britney Spears. In 2002, the band decided to leave their label and make a go of it on their own, canceling their contract and eventually independently releasing the album that Island Def Jam had refused to greenlight. That album, *Underneath*, was released in April 2004, debuted at #25 on the Billboard 200 album chart, and at number one on the Billboard Top Independent Albums chart. *Underneath* became one of the most successful self-released albums of all time.[35] While it enjoyed financial success, it was purchased, primarily, by die-hard fans, who were legion.

Hanson Love/Hate IRL and Online

Among the many critiques lobbed at Hanson—including comparisons to the Jackson 5 and Motown[36]—one that seems obvious, especially relative to three blond boys from Tulsa, might be cultural appropriation—or what Scott Poulson-Bryant contemporarily alluded to as the "co-opting" of black music. Many of the songs on *Middle of Nowhere* used record-scratching sounds, borrowing from hip-hop. Scott Poulson-Bryant, cofounder of *Vibe* magazine, who later wrote his PhD dissertation at Harvard on the intersections of race and popular culture, wrote of Hanson in June 1997 in the *Village Voice*:

> Are you there God? It's me, Scott.
>
> I have some requests. Save me from the nobler-than-thou antiheroes littering the alt-rock landscape. Save me from the hiphop ghetto fantasy passing itself off as a black-power worldview. But most of all, save me from *Pop*, in the U2 sense of the word. And give me Pop, in the Hanson sense.
>
> "Mmmbop." Mmm Mmm Good. Yummy to my tummy. Real chew bubblegum in an era of self-important Everlasting Gobstoppers, with a fun-loving video to rival anything Bazooka Joe or Archie ever dreamed up. They don't make 'em like this anymore.
>
> I am an old man when it comes to pop culture—30—so I should know.
>
> I was nobler than thou once; there was a time when I would have decried the Dust Brothers turntable scratching lurking beneath the infectious "Mmmbop" melody as nothing more than another white-boy attempt to co-opt my beloved hiphop flavor. Nobility be damned. I wanna sing

along, not be yelled at. I wanna love a single, not de-cypher it. I wanna hold its hand and tell it how much I want it back.[37]

Poulson-Bryant readily accepted the boys. He wasn't alone. David Cantwell of *MTV News* called *Middle of Nowhere* his pick for Album of the Year. Richard Harrington of the *Washington Post* wrote in May 1997:

> Hanson seems delightfully out of step with the brother's angst-ridden peers. Ebullient harmonies and joyful melodies don't always cover the trio's limited song structures or instrumental skills, and there will be a major hurdle when Taylor Hanson's voice changes, but the group's high spirits are as hard to criticize as they are to resist.[38]

In 1997, Taylor Hanson explained the shift away from angsty rock of the decade as such: "The alternative thing is fading. People don't hate their parents as much anymore."[39]

However, not everyone loved Hanson. In June 1997, Taylor described his email correspondence, "We get both sides—the 'Oh, I hate you guys, you stink' side and 'You guys are so awesome'. The positive outweighs the negative by far."[40] Because of the internet, the brothers were getting immediate feedback—for better or worse. Hanson hater Will Hines, in his article "Stop Hanson!: The Latest Overplayed Evil Song," described the boys as such:

> The backwoods metalhead haircuts. The lead singer whose voice has yet to change. The plague-like catchiness of the melody. A white Jackson 5 that dresses like Australian grungies Silverchair. It's Hanson, and their hit "Mmmbop" has firmly established itself as the latest Catchy Overplayed Song. They're the next, big, irritating thing in pop music.[41]

Published on the online magazine *Spite*, Hines' article was featured with a completely unscientific online "Mmmbop" meter to estimate how many times the song had been heard by Hines—estimating three times for every 19 hours since 8:00 p.m. on Friday, May 2, 1997. The internet fought back. A slew of comments left from angry Hanson fans certainly foretold the future of such open forums.[42]

Hanson took the hate in stride, and even embraced it. In December 1997, the satirical television show *Saturday Night Live* featured a skit highlighting the ubiquity of "Mmmbop" with a parody that featured a man and a woman (Will Ferrell and Helen Hunt) accosting the brothers in an elevator, asking them: "Are you aware that during the spring and summer of 1997 your song 'Mmmbop' was played over 7.8 million times worldwide?" In retaliation, Hunt and Ferrell lock the trio in the elevator, armed with a radio and machine gun, threatening them: "Now you will suffer like we did." Isaac, the eldest, retorts, "Look, we're just trying to make fun, catchy music." Hunt replies, "No, no, no! Don't try to pull that 'We're just trying to make people happy' crap!"

While Ferrell and Hunt insert earplugs, the band is forced to listen to their song on repeat. Isaac is the first to break, and starts to scream, falling into a catatonic state after just three hours. Zac, the youngest brother, also starts to crack: "Ooooh, God! It hurts! I can't take it!" After ten hours locked in this elevator, Taylor is unaffected, eventually convincing Ferrell to remove his earplugs and listen to the song, winning his captive over.[43] The boys escape, and Hunt shoots Ferrell to put him out of his misery.

While seemingly light hearted, the omnipresence of "Mmmbop" was hardly coincidental. Because of the consolidation of mass communication media, including radio and television, in the 1990s, once a song entered rotation, its hit status was all but guaranteed. The success of "Mmmbop" was unique in that even before the debut full-length album hit stores, the boys already had a growing legion of fans who were craving more information about them. In fact, from the start, the brothers were aware of this. Having just taped the *Rosie O'Donnell Show*, the brothers signed on to the subscription-based online platform America Online (AOL), which had come to dominate as an internet service provider in the US in the late 1990s, to search out their fans. There they entered a chat room dedicated to them.

For context, only about 20 million adults in the US had access to internet in 1996. In that year, Americans with internet spent fewer than 30 minutes a month "surfing the web." America Online had about five million subscribers and was by far the largest internet service provider in the US.[44] The interactions the boys had in what was an impromptu question and answer session not only excited users in the chat room but also foretold the future of online culture in many ways. Most of the questions in that chat room centered around verifying whether or not the user with the handle "Mmmbop" was actually the brothers, a fact later confirmed by their official fan-club magazine.[45] In the chatroom of about 20 to 30 people, the brothers informed the participants that the website they had been developing was "held up" for a couple of days—demonstrating that the brothers understood the need for an online presence already in 1997. Mmmbop also confirmed that they had received emails from one of the chat room participants. One user asked for the definition of "an Mmmbop"—a variation of a question that would plague the brothers for decades.

Another participant asked, "What happens when your voices change?" Another user, "TaylorHLvr," responded that Taylor's voice already sounded different, but that they liked it, to general agreement from the room. When another user asked why Taylor's voice was (comparatively) low, Mmmbop simply responded facetiously, "It's called puberty." Indeed, for the boys, puberty and questions around their sexuality were trending topics, foreshadowing privacy questions all teens in the digital age would soon face as social network platforms developed in the 2000s. One person in the chat mentioned they did not have the money to buy the album—what would young people do who did not have the financial resources to buy an album in the digital age?[46] Could the savvy tech users of the day have predicted social media, privacy settings, user verification, pirated music, and the importance of an online platform from this unplanned, chaotic 1997 chat room conversation? Could they have imagined fans and celebrities becoming a part of each other's lives digitally?

That chat room conversation, as banal as it might have been, pointed to some very real experiences of young people in the late 1990s. Because of new technologies, not only could young people communicate directly with celebrities, they also were tasked with identity verification—asking the brothers questions they thought only the brothers could answer. Financial constraints also seeped into the conversation: How could they get the album if they could not afford it? One option was "ripping" digital music files from their CDs. One webpage, published in early 1997, gave a link to an official Hanson streaming of "Mmmbop" hosted by Polygram, the parent company of Mercury Records, as well as a version of the song saved as an MP3 format, an open-sourced compressed audio file that was first invented in 1993 by the Moving Picture Experts Group and which was gaining popularity already in 1997.[47] The popularity of the MP3 would shape the music industry for over two decades until the rise of successful streaming services like Pandora, Spotify, and Apple Music.

While it's virtually impossible to track down the users in that original chat room, as one of those participants, I can confirm that at least one person was transformed into a longtime Hanson fan through such experiences. In fact, it was then that I asked the brothers, via private "instant message" using my new screen name, "KidMMMBop," if I could make a fan page dedicated to them. Not only did they give me permission, but they later featured that website in their fan magazine. If Yahoo's database is an indication, Hanson websites were numerous. On my own website I even developed a simple search database with more than four hundred websites listed with descriptions—though there was a large variation in quality.

Despite the presence of true believers like myself, Hanson hate was ubiquitous. It was common for a Hanson hater to enter a chatroom and spew hateful, mostly queerphobic vulgarities in a sort of hit-and-run fashion. In August 1997, Greg Baker wrote for the *Miami New Times*:

> The Internet is infested with hate pages aimed at [Hanson]. And media outlets such as VH1 found ways to simultaneously bitch-slap the boys of Hanson while playing their videos all the while...the omniconspicuous Hanson does deserve attention (as opposed to hype), fan reaction (good art provokes that), and critical consideration (the reviews have been shockingly positive). What the perky, Rollerblading brethren don't deserve is the smug dismissal and public slander being dished their way by the legions of cool. ... Much more baffling at this point is the unrestrained rage against the mmmpop sensations one encounters on that electronic repository of profound thought, the Internet. The recurrent (read: obsessive) theme of Hanson cyberbashers is that the three pubescent boys are, in fact, gay fag girls. (Personally, some of my favorite people are gay fag

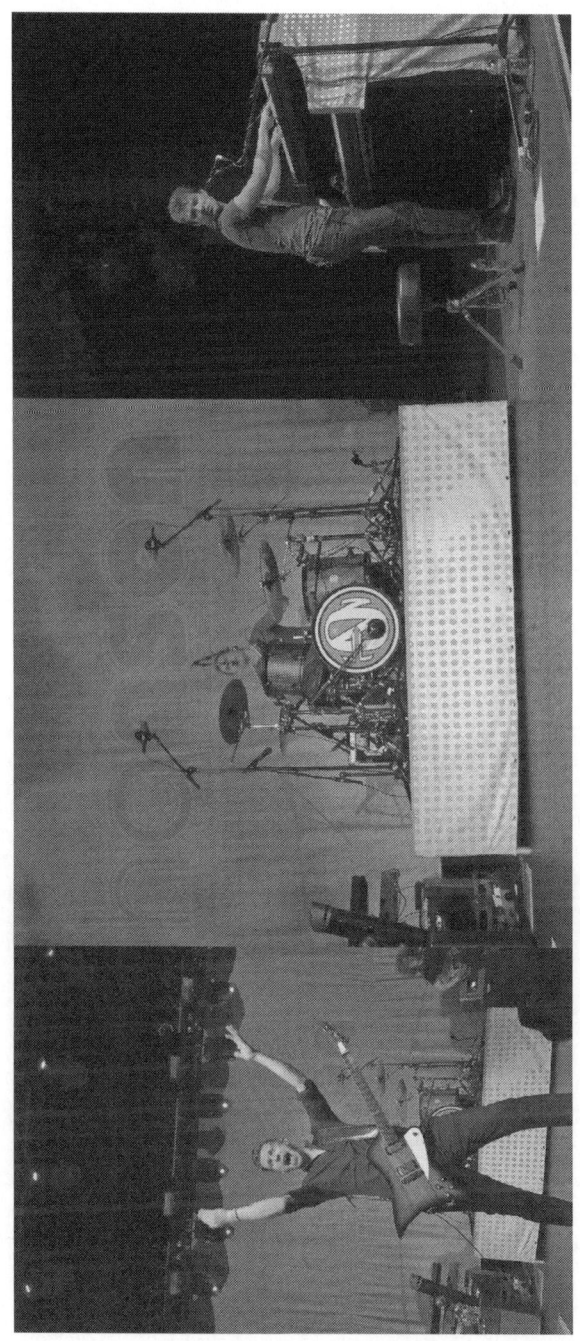

Figure 13.1 Isaac, Zac, and Taylor Hanson (L–R) performing in Austin, Texas, at Emo's during a tour celebrating the 25th anniversary of the band. Credit: Louie Valencia.

girls, and I'd be surprised if any red-blooded American male wouldn't want to fur the frog with Taylor, the middle and sexiest Hanson.) [sic][48]

Baker goes on to describe the "Hanson Sucks page," which dismissed Hanson because they "looked like girls." He cites another page—"We Hate Hanson Girls"—which incited Americans to "kill the virus that is Hanson." The page placed the boy's heads on women's bodies, adding makeup. These were early internet trolls, as it were. Another page mentioned in the article decried the size of the eldest brother's mouth. But for Baker, the "sickest" page was the "Hanson Ate My Balls" page. The boys' promo photos were imposed with thought bubbles reading, "God I wish I had balls" and "I'll never be a famous supermodel if I keep munching on these balls." The page's creator, Charles Whitman, claimed he was promoting "freedom of speech"—a common refrain of dubious, hate-spewing, radical right-wing cultures online today. As Baker points out, these attacks against the boys were led by radio provocateur Howard Stern, who claimed, " 'Mmmbop' is a fag song. It's for gays."[49]

On my own website, Kidmmmbop.com, as a prepubescent boy myself I created a directory where "Guy Hanson Fans" could proclaim their love of Hanson's music. Young boys, mostly in their teens, listed their names, ages, websites, email address, and screen names. Girls could also list themselves as "allies." In fact, many Hanson fan pages included "Guy Hanson Fan" banners that I designed to show support—digital safe spaces, as it were. Indeed, the vitriol of the internet was there at a very early time, and what the band endured certainly could have counted as a form of cyberbullying, to be sure. Very real cultural shifts were happening in the ways people related to celebrities, their ability to demonstrate frustration at gender nonconformity, and the ability for fan communities to come together despite a particularly nasty form of queerphobia and misogyny targeted at children—the brothers and their fans. At the same time, the fans were creating communities for themselves as much as for Hanson.

From the Middle of Nowhere to the Middle of Everywhere

In September 2017, speaking with a casual tone to thousands of fans, including myself, packed into the legendary Austin, Texas, music venue, Emo's, Taylor Hanson discussed the band's break with Island Def Jam: "We looked around and we realized we were sort of getting eaten alive by a huge corporate monster, and we wanted to get the hell out. So, most everyone we worked with thought we were crazy." Isaac, the eldest, interrupted, "Maybe we are just a little bit." To roars, Taylor continued:

> The difference is we had met you guys. So, we bet on you guys. Thanks for following through. Especially those of you who have seen us all along the way. So, for everybody who has ever had to stand up for this band,

and had to explain what the heck "Mmmbop" is about, or anything like that: screw those guys, you are head and shoulders above the rest.

At that same concert, Isaac Hanson called their online fan club the "backbone" which has allowed him and his brothers, Taylor and Zachary, the ability to continue to make music. Taylor continued:

> So, Hanson.net is a fan club, but it's not really that, it's a community which we started officially in 2000—we're all old, that was almost 17 years ago. But we, every year, we put out music just to that group, five songs, no matter what is going on. Sometimes we overshare. We stream ... and show videos. That's one of the things we know we needed to do. We even invite you guys once a year if you become a part of Hanson.net, you can come to our hometown, since we come to your hometown, and we throw a party, play a show, and even throw a beer festival ... We have a real badass job, and we would like to keep it. So, if you guys keep on coming on, we think it would be a party for you guys.

An evolution of Hanson's newsletter, *MOE*, Hanson.net was a venture undertaken with elder statesman of pop/rock David Bowie, who also had a taste for bright colorful clothes and transgressing norms of masculinity on occasion.

MOE in many ways looked like a luxuriously printed website, using layouts that mimicked online chats and pages. The first issue of *MOE*, in 1998, even included a non-Macintosh-compatible enhanced CD with exclusive music and photos. More importantly, the title of the print magazine had the intention of *being* everywhere. For this to happen, it was logical that *MOE* become a website. *MOE* even featured webpages made by Hanson fans—most of which were of a high quality by Web 1.0 standards. As previously mentioned, my own website was featured in the penultimate issue. That website had hundreds of thousands of visitors, many of whom came for the free Kidmmmbop. com email service, search engine, videos, photo galleries, fan fiction, concert reports, merchandise, and trading. The website was eventually sold to Big Shot Entertainment, a San Francisco startup that purchased fansites and then paid fans to continue to run their websites, placing advertising on those sites.

MOE did not disappear because of a lack of interest in the band but rather was a move by the band to transition into a digital-only space. In late March 2000, Hanson launched Hanson.net with Bowie shortly before the band's second album, *This Time Around*, was released. At first, Hanson.net was an internet service provider (ISP) and provided an official Hanson.net email address and exclusive content, including tour videos, interviews, special ticket offers, and contests. For those who already had internet, they could pay $6.95 per month for access to the site. When the band gave up their record contract, ending it in 2002, these were the fans with whom they first connected to fundraise, offering music exclusives and other incentives to join the subscription service. This shift, from being just a teenage band to an ISP, also reflected troubled waters ahead for AOL. By the early 2000s, there was a drastic shift in who was able to afford the internet and why they connected. This was very different from the internet of 1996, when America Online still charged by the hour for use.

In the 2000s the website remained quite dynamic, with periodic refreshes—animated images, videos, and exclusive material. Members also began to get added benefits, such as opportunities to attend meet-and-greet events and exclusive music. Throughout much of the 2010s the websites' design stagnated to the point where it became difficult to navigate the years' worth of comments, posts, and ephemera. Fans could often expect surprise responses from the brothers, responding to their comments and private messages. The website received its first major refresh in a decade in 2020. Today, a Hanson. net membership goes for $40 per year, and comes with an exclusive EP with at least five new songs, the ability to cut lines when going to Hanson concerts, advance and exclusive event access, and the chance to enter a lottery to meet the brothers.

You Have So Many Relationships in This Life, Only One or Two Will Last

Although the turn of the millennium was characterized by new developments in technology, their popularization came piecemeal. In 1998, the average person would have needed multiple apparatuses to convert analogue video to digital: one can imagine recording a broadcast TV program to VHS, then perhaps transferring that video to magnetic digital video minitapes, and from the video camera one might use the now defunct Firewire cable to save the video to a computer, at miserable quality, because a brand-new 1998 bondi blue iMac only had a four-gigabyte hard drive. The amount of effort to digitize something in the period was considerable—and it makes sense that it was young fans with some expendable money, imagination, time, and energy who took up the challenge.

What do "Mmmbop," Hanson, and early internet culture tell us? Generally, we find that many of the elements that we associate with internet fan culture today were already present in some form in 1997. In the popular imagination, people draw strong lines between Web 1.0, 2.0, and 3.0. However, while the form has changed and the user experience has become more aesthetically pleasing and accessible, the function has not changed drastically. As seen through "Mmmbop," young people were already trying to find their way into virtual communities that intersected with their "real life." While new technologies constantly appear, most of the time that technology overlaps with existing forms—message boards, instant messages, and chat rooms have become Reddit, SMS messages, GroupMe, Discord, and TikTok—which will eventually fall to the wayside, too. In fact, when Hanson released their 2017 collection of greatest hits, titled *Middle of Everywhere*, it was released on audio cassette, CD, digitally, and on vinyl. Indeed, the release of their first audio cassette in years was "on trend"—as any Brooklyn hipster would have told you that year—with indie and mainstream musicians selling cassette tapes at dive bars and online. The release in multiple formats demonstrates how the band adapts to new trends in technology, and sometimes even to old technology.

While the internet sustained the band for 20 years, it was also the internet that caused chaos for the fan community in 2020, the twentieth anniversary of Hanson.net—an event that has become known has "Hansongate." In the midst of the global COVID-19 pandemic, as the band prepared for the first major update to the website's infrastructure in years, the small but loyal Hanson fanbase was rocked in the aftermath of the death of George Floyd, a Black man killed in Minnesota by police officers in late May. While numerous celebrities posted messages of solidarity with the Black Lives Matter movement for social justice and racial equality, Hanson fans began to express frustration that the band had not expressed support. As described on one Reddit group, r/postHanson, "This was when things began to escalate: the main Hanson account was still silent, refusing to say black lives matter, and now we had Zac silencing black fans by deleting all comments on his post." Recounting the June discovery of seemingly right-wing posts on Zac's Pinterest account, one user on r/postHanson claimed:

> The Pinterest board has been particularly damaging as it was full of rightwing propaganda. Including but not limited to racism, homophobia, transphobia, xenophobia, and islamophobia. Worse still, several of the Pins included commentary from Zac…that reaffirm his stance on the media he shared. One of the worst things was a pin supporting George Zimmerman, the man who murdered Trayvon Martin, a black teenager."[50]

Some fans found a draft copy of a blog post on Hanson.net that was never published, presumably intended to be released around the time of the website revamp. The unpublished draft included an apology, stating, "Because of things I have said or liked many of you have been hurt. Please accept my sincere apology and admiration, and know I am truly sorry that I have hurt you."[51] The post was deleted shortly after its discovery, leaving many Hanson fans with a very serious question as to whether they wanted to continue their decades-long relationship with the band.

Curiously, in the aftermath, while many moved away from Hanson's official community, some fans have continued "calling out" Hanson on Facebook, Instagram, and Twitter. Although many condemned the band's actions, the community didn't fall apart. Instead, it reformulated itself into an active group of former fans who wished to hold their band accountable—showing the strength of the online community in continuing despite their inability to support the band.

Conclusion

While never again garnering the massive attention they did in 1997, when "Mmmbop" made its debut, Hanson has remained connected with their fans through both their music and the internet. Today, within the Hanson fan community, lovers of the band often refer to themselves as "fansons." In this way, a fan's very identity can become enmeshed with the band.

Initially, the internet helped to build the fanbase, but it also provided the naysayers a platform for hate. Escaping their record label allowed Hanson to maintain their fan base directly, promising new intimacy through their online platform—sustaining them for two decades. Just as the band was about to celebrate the twentieth anniversary of Hanson.net, the internet became the site of a controversy that caused many fans to question whether or not they wanted to continue their relationship with the band—falling out of love with their heroes.

But what happens when a fan falls out of love? Mark Duffett argues that

> fan passion often seems an exceptional form of love, collectively expressed but open to change and revision. It seems to be a love that is frequently unrequited; perhaps premised on loss; primarily serviced through the partial promises and piecemeal satisfactions of the commodity form. It is a love emergent without traditional intimacy and one that can be transformed by new awareness of the reality of its own object. Yet sometimes it is not really love for a person at all. It is a love for a performance and for the continued pleasure that each performance can bring to the life of the fan. In other words, a conditional love; enthusiasts, after all, can be displeased by their heroes.[52]

Despite feeling some sense of loss because of Hansongate, many fans created another online community out of that strife, a community ready to continue following Hanson, but ready also to simultaneously critique the band members for what these fans perceived as intolerance. The passion they felt did not simply go away; instead, it was redirected. In an mmmbop, the internet allowed for a new fan to emerge—the critical fan.

Notes

1 Bill Bennett, "Hanson,"*Contemporary Musicians* 20 (1997).
2 Hanson, *Middle of Nowhere*, CD (Mercury Records, 1997).
3 Lea Wierød Borčak, "The Sound of Nonsense: On the Function of Nonsense Words in Pop Songs," *SoundEffects: An Interdisciplinary Journal of Sound and Sound Experience* 7, no. 1 (2017): 35.
4 Girl's Life, "The True Story behind the Hanson Brothers—The Hottest Act since, Well, They'd Prefer We Don't Say It," *Girl's Life*, September 30, 1997.Hanson's 1998 tour documentary, *Hanson, Tulsa, Tokyo & the Middle of Nowhere*, also defined the word similarly. See: Ashley Greyson, *Hanson: Tulsa, Tokyo & the Middle of Nowhere* (New York: Polygram Video, 1997).

5 Mark Duffett, ed., *Popular Music Fandom: Identities, Roles and Practices*, Routledge Studies in Popular Music (New York: Routledge, 2014), 155.

6 Marc Prensky, "Digital Natives, Digital Immigrants Part 1," *On the Horizon* 9, no. 5 (September 2001): 1–6.

7 The concept of "generations" is a dubious nationalistic concept that has its origins in generationalism of the early twentieth century. See the second chapter of my book: Louie Dean Valencia-García, *Antiauthoritarian Youth Culture in Francoist Spain: Clashing with Fascism* (London: Bloomsbury Academic, 2018).

8 Hanson, "Net News," *MOE* 1, no. 1, (1997).

9 See Benedict Anderson, "Nationalism," *Imagined Communities: Reflections on the Origin and Spread of Nationalism* (London: Verso, 2006).

10 Mike Corder, "Tape That: Dutch Inventor of Audio Cassette Dies at Age 94," *Washington Post*, March 12, 2021.

11 Ueyama Shu, "The Selling of the 'Walkman,'" *Advertising Age*, March 22, 1982; Paul Du Gay, *Doing Cultural Studies: The Story of the Sony Walkman*, Second edn. (Los Angeles, CA: Sage Publications, 2013).

12 Regis Philbin and Kathie Lee Gifford. *Live with Regis and Kathie Lee*, episode aired May 8, 1997, on ABC.

13 Jarrod Gollihare, *Hanson: The Official Book* (New York: Billboard Books, 1997), 9.

14 Girl's Life, "The True Story behind the Hanson Brothers."

15 Ibid.

16 The term would not be popularized until 2000, by William Strauss and Neil Howe in their book *Millennials Rising: The Next Great Generation* (New York: Vintage, 2000).

17 Howie Mandel, *The Howie Mandel Show*, episode aired November 8, 1998, on NBC.

18 Gollihare, *Hanson*, 9.

19 Kyle Smith, "Boys in the Band," *People*, July 7, 1997.

20 Neil Strauss, "A Success Story with More Trimmings than Christmas," *The New York Times*, May 7, 1997.

21 In fact, there are seven Hanson siblings total—all younger brothers and sisters who traveled with them while touring. Today, Zac, Taylor, and Isaac and their wives each have five, seven, and three children, respectively, and still live in Tulsa.

22 Eric W. Rothenbuhler, "The Compact Disc and Its Culture: Notes on Melancholia," in *Cultural Technologies: The Shaping of Culture in Media and Society*, ed. Göran Bolin (New York: Routledge, 2012), 36–50.

23 For a contemporary account of the history of the MP3, see: Paul Théberge, "'Plugged in': Technology and Popular Music," in *The Cambridge Companion to Pop and Rock*, eds. Simon Frith, Will Straw, and John Street, Cambridge Companions to Music (Cambridge: Cambridge University Press, 2001), 21.

24 Many of the songs from the *MMMBop* album were later repackaged as part of the 1998 album *3-Car Garage*.

25 Geoff Edgers, "Is There Life after 'Mmmbop'? Hanson—Yes, That Hanson — Turns 25," *The Washington Post*, August 30, 2017.

26 Robyn J. Stilwell, "Hanson. 'Mmmbop.' CD SIngle Mercury 574 499-2. 1997," *Popular Music and Society* 23, no. 2 (Summer 1999): 113.

27 Stilwell, "Hanson. 'Mmmbop,'" 114.

28 Girl's Life, "The True Story behind the Hanson Brothers."

29 Martin Scherzinger, "Music, Corporate Power, and Unending War," *Cultural Critique*, no. 60 (2005), 63.
30 Rosie O'Donnell, *The Rosie O'Donnell Show*, episode aired May 14, 1998, on NBC.
31 Philbin and Gifford, *Live with Regis and Kathie Lee*.
32 Gollihare, *Hanson*, 9.
33 Mandel, *The Howie Mandel Show*.
34 Ashley Greyson, *Hanson: Strong Enough to Break*, DVD (Tulsa, OK: 3CG Recrods, 2006).
35 Independent Music Awards, "Hanson," *Independent Music Awards,* http://independentmusicawards.com/judges/hanson/
36 Caroline Sullivan, "The Little Brat Pack," *The Guardian*, May 30 1997.
37 Scott Poulson-Bryant, "The MMM and Bop Poll: Why Has the Fluffiest Single of the Year Inspired the Most Critical Chatter?" *Village Voice*, June 24, 1997.
38 Richard Harrington, "Let's Hear It for the Boys," *The Washington Post*, May 18, 1997.
39 Girl's Life, "The True Story behind the Hanson Brothers"
40 Jill Hamilton, "Hanson," *Rolling Stone*, June 12, 1997.
41 Will Hines, "Stop Hanson! The Latest Overplayed Evil Song,"*Spite*, May 1997, www.willhines.net/spitemag/tricks/hanson.html
42 Ibid.
43 Saturday Night Live, "December 13, 1997," *Saturday Night Live*, episode aired December 13, 1997, on NBC.
44 Farhad Manjoo, "Jurassic Web: The Internet of 1996 Is Almost Unrecognizable Compared with What We Have Today," *Slate*, February 24, 2009.
45 Hanson, "The Chat Room," *MOE* 1, no. 1 (1997).
46 Personal archive.
47 "Home Page," Hanson, www.oocities.org/sunsetstrip/towers/Towers/1682/?201728
48 Greg Baker, "Hanson Rules!," *Miami New Times*, August 28, 1997.
49 Ibid.
50 Reddit, "r/PostHanson—HANSONGATE Timeline: WHAT HAPPENED," *Reddit*, post uploaded by Hantifa Commander, June 9, 2020,
51 Ibid.
52 Mark Duffett, ed., *Popular Music Fandom: Identities, Roles and Practices*, Routledge Studies in Popular Music (New York: Routledge, 2014), 149.

References

Anderson, Benedict. "Nationalism." In *Imagined Communities: Reflections on the Origin and Spread of Nationalism*. London: Verso, 2006.
Baker, Greg. "Hanson Rules!" *Miami New Times*, August 28, 1997.
Bennett, Bill. "Hanson," *Contemporary Musicians* 20 (1997).
Borčak, Lea Wierød. "The Sound of Nonsense: On the Function of Nonsense Words in Pop Songs." *SoundEffects: An Interdisciplinary Journal of Sound and Sound Experience* 7, no. 1 (2017): 35.
Corder, Mike. "Tape That: Dutch Inventor of Audio Cassette Dies at Age 94." *Washington Post*, March 12, 2021.
Duffett, Mark, ed. *Popular Music Fandom: Identities, Roles and Practices*, Routledge Studies in Popular Music. New York: Routledge, 2014.

Du Gay, Paul. *Doing Cultural Studies: The Story of the Sony Walkman*, 2nd edn. Los Angeles, CA: Sage Publications, 2013.

Edgers, Geoff. "Is There Life after 'Mmmbop'? Hanson — Yes, That Hanson — Turns 25." *The Washington Post*, August 30, 2017.

Girl's Life. "The True Story behind the Hanson Brothers—The Hottest Act since, Well, They'd Prefer We Don't Say It." *Girl's Life*, September 30, 1997.

Gollihare, Jarrod. *Hanson: The Official Book*. New York: Billboard Books, 1997.

Greyson, Ashley. *Hanson: Strong Enough to Break*, DVD. Tulsa, OK: 3CG Records, 2006.

Greyson, Ashley. *Hanson: Tulsa, Tokyo & the Middle of Nowhere*. New York: Polygram Video, 1997.

Hamilton, Jill. "Hanson," *Rolling Stone*, 12 June 1997.

Hanson, "The Chat Room." *MOE* 1, no. 1 (1997).

Hanson. "Net News." *MOE* 1, no. 1 (1997).

Hanson, *Middle of Nowhere*, CD. Chicago: Mercury Records, 1997.

Harrington, Richard. "Let's Hear It for the Boys." *The Washington Post*, May 18, 1997.

Hines, Will. "Stop Hanson! The Latest Overplayed Evil Song." *Spite*, May 1997. www.willhines.net/spitemag/tricks/hanson.html

Independent Music Awards. "Hanson." *Independent Music Awards*. http://independentmusicawards.com/judges/hanson/

Mandel, Howie. *The Howie Mandel Show*, NBC, November 8, 1998.

Manjoo, Farhad. "Jurassic Web: The Internet of 1996 Is Almost Unrecognizable Compared with What We Have Today." *Slate*, February 24, 2009. www.slate.com/articles/technology/technology/2009/02/jurassic_web.html

O'Donnell, Rosie. *The Rosie O'Donnell Show*, NBC, May 14, 1998.

Philbin, Regis and Kathie Lee Gifford. *Live with Regis and Kathy Lee*, ABC, May 8, 1997.

Poulson-Bryant, Scott. "The MMM and Bop Poll: Why Has the Fluffiest Single of the Year Inspired the Most Critical Chatter?" *Village Voice*, June 24, 1997.

Prensky, Marc. "Digital Natives, Digital Immigrants Part 1." *On the Horizon* 9, no. 5 (September 2001): 1–6.

Reddit "r/PostHanson - HANSONGATE Timeline: WHAT HAPPENED." *Reddit*, post by Hantifa Commander, June 9, 2020. www.reddit.com/r/postHanson/comments/gzp5t0/hansongate_timeline_what_happened/

Rothenbuhler, Eric W. "The Compact Disc and Its Culture: Notes on Melancholia." In *Cultural Technologies: The Shaping of Culture in Media and Society*, edited by Göran Bolin. New York: Routledge, 2012, 36–50.

Saturday Night Live. "13 Decemberm, 1997." *Saturday Night Live*, NBC 13 December 1997.

Scherzinger, Martin. "Music, Corporate Power, and Unending War." *Cultural Critique*, no. 60 (2005): 63.

Shu, Ueyama. "The Selling of the 'Walkman.'" *Advertising Age*, March 22, 1982.

Smith, Kyle. "Boys in the Band." *People*, July 7, 1997. http://people.com/archive/boys-in-the-band-vol-48-no-1/

Stilwell, Robyn J. "Hanson. 'Mmmbop.' CD Single Mercury 574 499-2. 1997." *Popular Music and Society* 23, no. 2(Summer 1999): 113.

Strauss, Neil. "A Success Story with More Trimmings than Christmas." *The New York Times*, May 7, 1997.

Sullivan, Caroline. "The Little Brat Pack." *The Guardian*, May, 30 1997.

Théberge, Paul. "'Plugged in': Technology and Popular Music." In *The Cambridge Companion to Pop and Rock*, edited by Simon Frith, Will Straw, and John Street. Cambridge: Cambridge University Press, 2001.

Valencia-García, Louie Dean. *Antiauthoritarian Youth Culture in Francoist Spain: Clashing with Fascism*. London: Bloomsbury Academic, 2018.

14 Elton John—"Candle in the Wind 1997" (1997)

Christine Caccipuoti

Although "Candle in the Wind 1997" is regarded as the best-selling single in both the United Kingdom and United States since sales charts began in the 1950s, it was not written with the primary motivation of propelling its performer, Elton John, into the record books. While the majority of John's other songs (including the original version of "Candle in the Wind," released in 1973) were created with the intention of attaining commercial success, "Candle in the Wind 1997" is a commemoratory ballad with a charitable aim: it was written in response to the death of Diana, princess of Wales, to be performed at her funeral, and then released as a single benefitting the Diana, Princess of Wales Memorial Fund.

This chapter utilizes a narrative biographical approach to explore "Candle in the Wind 1997," including its original incarnation as a song dedicated to Hollywood actress Marilyn Monroe, its rebirth as a funeral elegy for Diana, princess of Wales, and the careful, intentional handling of it following its release as a single. In doing so, this chapter highlights the impact of the reputation of its subject, the timing of its release, private and public grief, celebrity, and media involvement in the creation and legacy of the most successful single in modern UK and US music history.

The Hollywood Star

In 1973, 24 years before the death of Diana, princess of Wales, prompted the writing of "Candle in the Wind 1997," Elton John released the double-album *Goodbye Yellow Brick Road*, containing the original "Candle in the Wind." At this point, John (born in Pinner, England, in 1947) was five years into a writing partnership that began at an audition for Liberty Records. Although John failed to get signed, Ray Williams, of Liberty's A&R department, had handed him an envelope containing lyrics submitted to the label and suggested that John attempt to write music for them. Aware that his forte was melody creation and not words, John discovered an immediate affinity for working with this stranger's lyrics. The stranger was Bernie Taupin, a man three years John's junior who was living on a Lincolnshire farm and who has been John's primary writing partner ever since that initial collaboration in

DOI: 10.4324/9781003093206-15

separation.[1] This experience created the foundation for their standard process, and by mid-1973 the duo had experienced significant success both in the United Kingdom and abroad with a series of increasingly popular albums, including *Elton John* (1970), *Honky Château* (1972), and *Don't Shoot Me, I'm Only the Piano Player* (1973).

For *Goodbye Yellow Brick Road*, John and Taupin spent several weeks holed up in the Château d'Hérouville in France (where they had previously created *Honky Château*) with their band members and producer Gus Dudgeon, but continued to work as they always had: apart. Taupin would have an idea, write lyrics, and present them to John, who then added the music. It could take as little as 30 minutes for a song to be completed, and several new songs might be recorded by the end of the night.[2]

"Candle in the Wind" was a product of this routine, initiated when Taupin was inspired by the life of American star Marilyn Monroe,[3] who had achieved fame for her roles in films like *Gentlemen Prefer Blondes* (1953) and *The Seven Year Itch* (1955). Monroe (born Norma Jeane Mortensen) had not been pleased with being perpetually typecast as a sexy, ditzy blonde, and her personal life's drama was regularly plastered on the front pages of newspapers whether she wanted it to be or not. She fought to be taken seriously by Hollywood executives, the press, and the public, but had little success. In August 1962, she died of a drug overdose in her California home at the age of 36.[4]

Shortly after writing "Candle in the Wind," Taupin called Monroe the "people's actress," a woman harmed by the Hollywood system but who transcended her reputation as a sex symbol and was someone that the public felt they could talk to.[5] He used his lyrics to expose the dual nature of Monroe's life, calling her "Norma Jean" when making a direct address, but referring to her as "Marilyn Monroe" in relation to the professional presentation of her life. Utilizing both forms of her name forced listeners to engage with Monroe on a deeper level, an acknowledgment that despite her public persona she was also Norma Jean, a woman whose life and image were not entirely in her own control and who, even in death, was the subject of tabloid discussions and salacious murder conspiracy theories. Through this, John subverted the narrative of the bubbly, empty-headed star and explicitly confronted the tragic aspects of her life and death: "All the papers had to say / Was that Marilyn was found in the nude."[6]

Despite the specificity of the language, in "Candle in the Wind," Marilyn Monroe was actually being utilized as a metaphor for fame.[7] In 2001, Taupin explained:

> I was enamored with … the idea of fame or youth or somebody being cut short in the prime of their life. I mean basically the song could have been about James Dean. It could've been about Montgomery Clift. It could've been about Jim Morrison. Anyone whose life is cut short at the prime point of their career, and how we glamorize death, how we immortalize people.[8]

The intention of its creators, then, was always for the song to be broadly applied, and such use of it was welcomed.

The UK received "Candle in the Wind" as the lead single off of *Goodbye Yellow Brick Road*, while the US market was (despite John's initial protests) treated to "Bennie and the Jets." "Candle in the Wind" reached number 11 in the UK charts but did not find success in the US market until the late 1980s when it appeared on a live album John recorded in Australia with the Melbourne Symphony Orchestra.[9] By then it was a staple in John's concert repertoire and, as Susan J. Hubert noted, its "vulnerability...made it an appropriate elegy for numerous people."[10] John himself contributed to broadening "Candle in the Wind's" application when he dedicated the song to Ryan White, a teenager with AIDS, at a Farm Aid benefit concert in 1990.[11] The song's function in the popular consciousness was to embody the loss of all those who were victims of painful or tragic situations, a development that helped lead to its eventual association with Diana, princess of Wales.

The Princess of Wales

The friendship between Elton John and Diana began shortly before her marriage to Prince Charles in 1981, when she was still known as Lady Diana Spencer. The pair met at a birthday party for Charles's brother, Prince Andrew, and became fast friends, with a bond that included a shared interest in helping those diagnosed with AIDS and funding AIDS research. Their friendship even survived one major, publicly-reported fracture. In February 1997, Diana withdrew a foreword she promised for *Rock and Royalty*, a photography book created to benefit the AIDS Foundation. Despite the charitable cause, Diana had concerns about associating the Royal Family with a book containing racy images. Her last-minute balk prompted a falling-out with John that did not mend until summer, when the death of their mutual friend, fashion designer Gianni Versace, prompted Diana to call John and reconcile. The two were then photographed sitting together at Versace's funeral on July 22nd.[12] This media-publicized reunion would likely have only strengthened the association of John with Diana in the minds of those who saw the photographs.

Just over a month later, on August 31st, Diana died in Paris, France, from injuries sustained in a car accident in the tunnel under the Pont de l'Alma.[13] As the news that the most popular (former) member of the British Royal Family was gone spread around the world, the outpouring of public grief was intense and immediate, with makeshift memorials popping up at places associated with the princess of Wales, such as Kensington Palace.

Meanwhile, officials representing the government and the Crown joined with members of her family to plan a proper farewell for her.[14] Quickly, they decided to ask Elton John to perform at the funeral, scheduled for September 6th at Westminster Abbey. John's inclusion ensured that the program reached beyond the traditional solemnity of a royal funeral to incorporate popular aspects that would resonate with the public who loved Diana so much. The specific choice of "Candle in the Wind" was influenced, too, by the public: radio stations around the UK experienced a significant surge in requests for John's original "Candle in the Wind"—it jumped from outside of the top-999 songs on airplay charts to the top 40 in the five days after Diana's death—and people were using the phrase when signing the condolence books at royal venues.[15] Although John briefly considered composing a completely new piece, "Candle in the Wind" was selected to honor the woman Tony Blair had recently dubbed "the people's princess" due to her ability to make the general public feel heard and understood.[16]

The parallels between Diana and Marilyn Monroe went beyond being the "people's princess" and the "people's actress" respectively. Like Monroe, Diana was an attractive blonde woman, hailed as a fashion icon, who lived a high-profile life, was hounded by the press and mistreated by those surrounding her (in this case, the Royal Family), and passed away at 36 years old in a shocking fashion. Even before her death added to their list of similarities, Diana was aware of the comparison. In the early 1990s she said the level of media attention she received was "like Marilyn Monroe publicity,"[17] further noting that, "Everyone said I was the Marilyn Monroe of the 1980s and I was adoring every minute of it. Actually I've never sat down and said: 'Hooray, how wonderful'. Never."[18]

While Monroe never truly broke free from the Hollywood system, Diana actively took control of her own narrative. In 1992 she covertly participated in the preparation of Andrew Morton's biography *Diana: Her True Story*, and in 1995, shortly before her divorce from Prince Charles, she gave a still-controversial interview on camera for the long-running British news program *Panorama*. In these actions, Diana purposely removed the veil of mystique that hid the imperfections of the Royal Family, undoubtedly humanizing her to the public and showing that, despite her exalted status, she was not immune to the struggles encountered by ordinary people, from an unhappy childhood and a failed marriage to bulimia and depression. Through media coverage, the public watched her leave the Royal Family and forge her own way as a single mother who traveled the world, leaned into her humanitarian work, and found love with a new man. This in-depth exposure to Diana's story allowed people who never met her to feel that they knew more about her than they did about some people in their real lives.[19] When she died while being chased by paparazzi[20] it seemed particularly cruel because, as Daniel T. Kline later elucidated, "the very mechanism that spurred on Diana's immense popularity seemed also to have been responsible for her death."[21] As a result, many turned to "Candle in the Wind," long established as an elegy for famous people who were victims of cruel treatment and tragic deaths.

Although the decision to use "Candle in the Wind" was directly related to the sentiments evoked by its original lyrics, the actual words proved inappropriate for the occasion. The explicit, even antagonistic nature of the original lyrics was problematic, as they could be interpreted as blows against the Royal Family for their role in Diana's unhappiness. In response, John asked Taupin to rewrite the lyrics for Diana, a task which had to be completed in less than a week's time.

What emerged from this request was the song now known as "Candle in the Wind 1997," sometimes colloquially called "Goodbye, England's Rose," in a nod to the lyric that replaced the original "Goodbye, Norma Jean." In order to honor Diana without stirring negative feelings toward the Royal Family, references to the loneliness and the pain of celebrity were removed. In their place were softer words, emphasizing her humanitarian work and compassion (Figure 14.1). The public's mood was also incorporated through lyrics alluding to the nation's tears over her death and gratitude for the joy she contributed to the peoples' lives. As for being a "candle in the wind"— the chorus for Diana alluded to her fortitude in difficult times, saying she "never faded with the sunset."[22] This newer, sentimental version of the song was approved by all concerned parties.

During the week following Diana's death, every detail of the approaching funeral was covered in the press, and the announcement of Elton John as a chosen performer figured heavily in the conversation, as did the use of "Candle in the Wind 1997." Luke Harding of the *Guardian* noted that it was a "symbolic concession by the palace to intense public pressure" to both include John and allow popular participation to be entwined with royal tradition.[23] *The Independent* published a pair of articles anticipating John's performance to be the highlight of the non-traditional aspect of the ceremony, and quoted the Dean of Westminster as saying that Diana would have wanted him to sing.[24] Perhaps the most effusive approval of the decision came from Christopher Howse of the *Daily Telegraph*, who called familiarity "a vital factor in ritual." He asserted that many of those unfamiliar with the prayers and hymns of the Church of England would know John's 1973 "Candle in the Wind." For Howse, even critiques of the lyrics (which he admitted "sound like the merest birthday-card doggerel") were unfounded, because simplicity is key for hymns used for such occasions as the princess of Wales' funeral. "Candle in the Wind 1997" would, he believed, make "the sternest traditionalist blub."[25]

However, not everyone received the news this well. Writing for the *Observer* after the funeral, Barbara Ellen revealed that although she eventually came around to the idea, her initial reaction was to think John's invitation to perform a pop song was "as appropriate as receiving holy communion in a nightclub toilet."[26] For some, though, it was the proposed lyrics that were the problem. Calling Diana only "England's rose" did not sit well with people in the other areas of the United Kingdom, and the *Daily Telegraph* reported a number of calls from Welsh readers who disliked that her title of princess of Wales was ignored.[27]

Nothing expressed in the newspapers appears to have diminished people's desire to view the funeral itself—reports estimate that in addition to the nearly two thousand people in Westminster Abbey and one million people lining the funeral route, over two billion people worldwide watched the service on television.[28] Elton John's performance of "Candle in the Wind 1997" occurred between a reading of 1 Corinthians 13 by prime minister Tony Blair and a tribute given by the princess's brother Charles, the earl Spencer. For the performance, John requested a teleprompter be placed near the piano, out of concern about mistakenly reverting to the Monroe lyrics in such a high-pressure, emotional situation.[29] Later, he would call this the biggest performance he had ever done, because "you're singing for your country. And you're singing for someone you've really loved and respected."[30] One of his biggest memories of the performance was the applause, which "seemed to start outside Westminster Abbey and sweep into the Church itself."[31] He was not alone in being taken in by its reception. *The Independent on Sunday* described the broken silence as sounding like "rain on a tin roof" that began outside the Abbey and eventually became "thunderous" even inside.[32] Despite the considerable debate about the inclusion of the song in advance of the funeral, it is evident that, in the moment, it served its purpose of giving voice to the feelings of many mourners who were not personally close enough to Diana to be in Westminster Abbey.

Immediately following the funeral, John met with producer Sir George Martin (known for his work with the Beatles) at Townhouse Studios to record "Candle in the Wind 1997" for release as a single. After John provided two takes of the song, Martin completed the process ahead of the single's release, which saw it paired with "Something about the Way You Look Tonight."[33] Significantly, all artist, composer, and record company profits would go directly to the Diana, Princess of Wales Memorial Fund to benefit the causes the Princess had championed in life.

Reactions to "Candle in the Wind 1997" from the press were as mixed as those to the original announcement that John was to perform the song at the event. Emma Forrest of the *Guardian* used the words "rude" and "crude" to describe what she felt was the inappropriate redevoting of a song about Marilyn Monroe to the princess of Wales, while John Mulvey of the *Observer* feared that the popularity of John's performance would throw Britain into another lengthy period of "schmaltz."[34] However, Anthony Payne of the *Independent* praised John's performance as "brave" and pointed out that many people interviewed by the BBC following the funeral called "Candle in the Wind 1997" a memorable moment in the ceremony, while Bryan Appleyard of the *Sunday Times* credited John with giving an understated performance that made the journalist cry.[35] In London, over a thousand members of the LGBT community gathered at popular night spot G-A-Y to remember Diana together and watch John's performance from earlier in the day, while the *New York Times* interviewed an attendee of a memorial for the princess in Central Park who said she eagerly anticipated the ability to purchase the single.[36]

Portions of the press and public were not alone in their appreciation for "Candle in the Wind 1997." In 2017, Prince Harry discussed his desire to remain outwardly stoic at his mother's funeral, but confessed that watching John sing "Candle in the Wind 1997" was the one time when the figurative

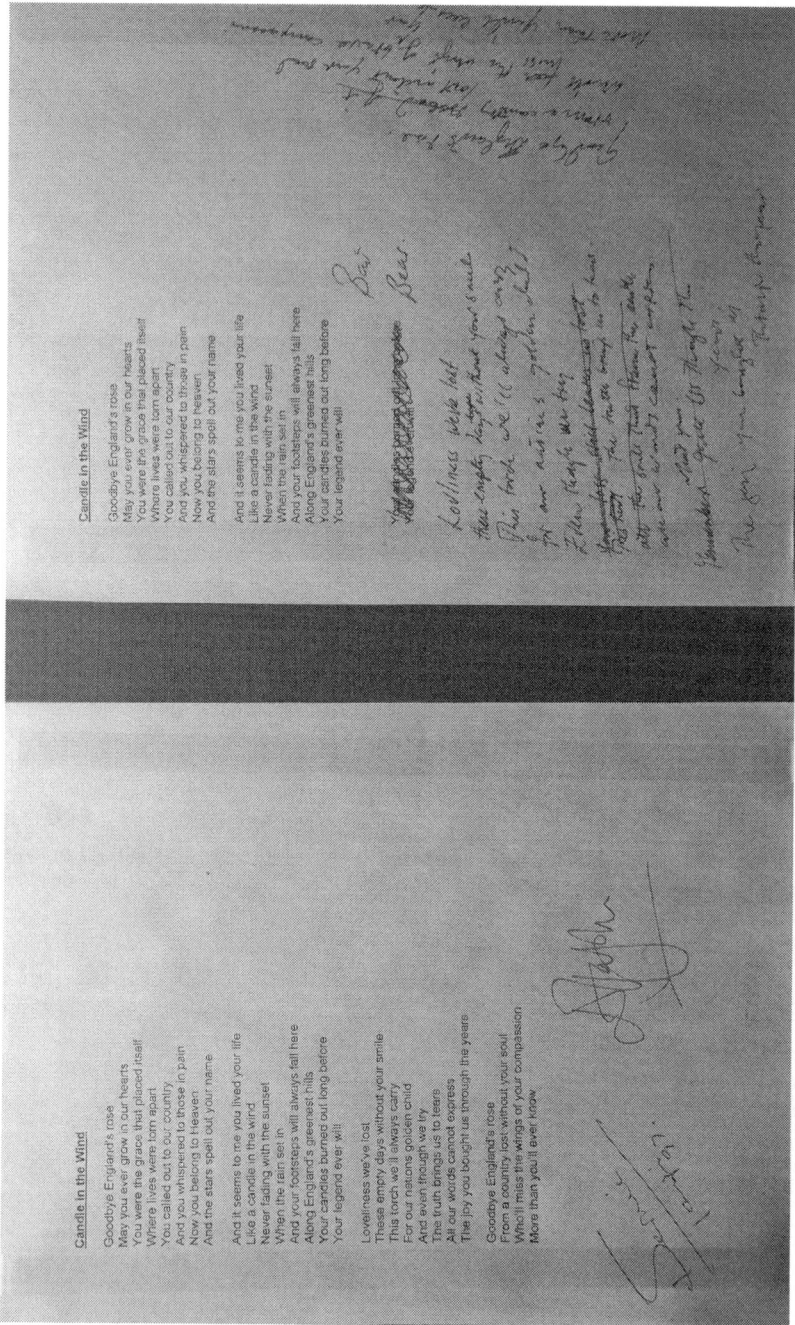

Figure 14.1 Lyrics for "Candle in the Wind 1997" as it was sung by Sir Elton John at Princess Diana's funeral in Westminster Abbey. Credit: ilpo musto/Alamy Stock Photo.

walls holding in his emotions were almost pierced enough to make him cry in public.[37]

The weekend of September 12–14, 1997, saw the initial release of the "Candle in the Wind 1997" single in Europe on both CD and cassette, with release in the United States and other world locations occurring either simultaneously or shortly after.[38] The Virgin Megastore in Paris, near to the site of Diana's death, was revealed by the *Daily Telegraph* as the first shop in the world to carry the single.[39] The store quickly sold out and had to order more by mid-day, with customers swiping up multiple copies at once. In London, lines of over three hundred people waited for the opportunity to buy the single at Tower Records. New York and New Jersey also saw people purchasing multiple copies. A variety of reasons for this were given by those interviewed, including the desire to contribute to charity and commemorate the event. A prime example of the latter is a pair of friends who cried while watching the funeral, then "bought this record so we can cry some more."[40] The song debuted on the charts at #1 in both the United Kingdom and United States, became the world's fastest-selling single within a day of its release, and performed better than any of John's past music in countries like Finland and Indonesia.[41] By October, the British Phonographic Industry had certified it nine-times platinum, while the Recording Industry Association of America certified it eleven-times platinum—eventually converting this to a diamond certification when the designation was created in 1999.[42]

The Legacy

The immediate success of "Candle in the Wind 1997" was "overwhelming" and "brilliant," John said in an interview for the *Oprah Winfrey Show* in late September 1997, but it also gave him pause. John explained that he chose to record the song to provide both a memory for those mourning Diana and to raise money for her favorite causes, but then decided he would not speak about it anymore for the time being to avoid people exploiting the tragedy.[43] He later also expressed that he thought people should not dwell on Diana's death, because she would not want it to continue, although Dr. Tony Carr, a clinical psychologist, estimated that it would take weeks to months for Diana's death to stop dominating people's thoughts and conversations.[44]

Carr's comments speak to the broader notion of collective mourning for the Princess that washed over Britain and other areas of the world like a tidal wave and encompassed a wide swath of people. There were those closest to her (Diana's sons, family, and friends like John), those who were touched by her charitable work (the LGBT community and victims of land mines, among others), those who identified with her personal struggles, and those who merely wanted to feel like they were participants in such a high-profile event.[45] In contrast to the release of the original "Candle in the Wind" over a decade after the death of Marilyn Monroe, "Candle in the Wind 1997" was issued when grief and media coverage of every variety was still at its peak. That grief aided sales was not a new phenomenon. Indeed, Diana's was not the only financially successful tribute song that year. A few months earlier Sean "P. Diddy" Combs (then known as Puff Daddy) and Faith Evans released "I'll Be Missing You," a tribute single for Christopher "Notorious B.I.G." Wallace, a popular rapper who was murdered in the spring. Notably, much like "Candle in the Wind 1997," "I'll Be Missing You" reimagined a pre-existing popular piece of music, in this case the Police's "Every Breath You Take." It also went to the top of the charts and remained ubiquitous for several months.[46] As a charity single, John's tribute to Princess Diana continued a long tradition in the British charts; in fact, when "Candle in the Wind 1997" took over the title of best-selling single in the country it unseated another benefit recording, 1984's "Do They Know It's Christmas?" from Band Aid, the Bob Geldof–helmed all-star collaboration to help provide relief from famine in Ethiopia.[47] The success of "Candle in the Wind 1997" came, then, from a perfect storm of Diana-related grief, timing, and a desire to help, aided by the known popularity of the singer and original song, and was further boosted by the media interest and its exposure to billions of people at its first performance.

As 1998 dawned, "Candle in the Wind 1997" continued to be a prominent part of the public consciousness. It won John a Grammy for Best Pop Vocalist (Male), remained in Britain's official singles charts for a total of 30 weeks, and spent 42 weeks on the US *Billboard* "Hot 100,"[48] while the Diana, Princess of Wales Memorial Fund received tens of millions of pounds.[49] The public, too, kept interest in the song brewing. In the UK it was the most-requested non-traditional song for funeral services, beating out other popular selections like Tina Turner's "Simply the Best."[50] As the still-nascent internet became a site for growing personal expression in the late 1990s, many chose to create memorial websites. According to Marguerite Helmers, seven major webrings (groups of websites choosing to be linked together due to a shared theme) sprung up, including hundreds of websites dedicated to the princess, and these mostly female-run sites[51] included many of the same features: photographs of Diana, writing about the host's personal grief, and the lyrics to "Candle in the Wind 1997."[52]

In stark contrast to how John and Taupin have encouraged widespread use of the original "Candle in the Wind," John has maintained a firm stance against the dissemination of "Candle in the Wind 1997" and regularly intervenes to prevent it from transitioning into generic, mainstream pop culture. He banned the inclusion of "Candle in the Wind 1997" in tribute documentaries about Diana's life by ITN and the BBC after they would not assure him that proceeds from its use would go to the Diana, Princess of Wales Memorial Fund, and refused to allow it to be included on a commemorative compilation CD.[53] He also declined to create an official video, causing the *New York Times* to report that the footage that went into the rotation on channels like VH1 and MTV (airing four to five times per day) was possibly the first time that a video contained no outside production to supplement the feed of a live performance.[54] Currently, while "Candle in the Wind 1997" is available through digital services like Apple Music and Spotify, John has chosen not to include it on any of his greatest hits collections or to reissue it.

After a brief period of not performing either version, he reinstated the 1973 "Candle in the Wind" in his concert set lists. In 2014, when a remastered edition of *Goodbye Yellow Brick Road* was released to celebrate the album's 40th anniversary, a cover of the Monroe "Candle in the Wind" was supplied by British singer Ed Sheeran, but to this date, no such officially promoted treatment has been given to "Candle in the Wind 1997."

The most effective means of attaching "Candle in the Wind 1997" to a specific moment in time, however, has been John's famous vow to never play the song again, which he made shortly after the funeral.[55] Initially, he implied that the only people who could convince him to revive it were Diana's sons, princes William and Harry, but that has proven untrue.[56] For the tenth anniversary of their mother's death in 2007, the princes organized Concert for Diana, a charity event in her honor. Despite speculation that John would perform "Candle in the Wind 1997," ultimately he chose an iconic song from his early career, "Your Song," as well as several others.[57] Yet the press could not resist reminding people about "Candle in the Wind 1997" in its coverage.[58]

Two decades after its release, interest in "Candle' in the Wind 1997" and its subject continue to animate both the public and the media. Each year, new articles inevitably surface in newspapers, magazines, and blogs covering "Candle in the Wind 1997's" inspiration, one and only performance, and financial success.[59]

The public, too, seems to embrace the idea that "Candle in the Wind 1997" is meant to stand as a testament to mourning for the princess of Wales and that its meaning is not to be diluted or extended to other moments of mourning. A search conducted on the popular public media host YouTube returns hundreds of covers of the 1973 "Candle in the Wind," including by singers like Sam Bailey on *The X Factor UK*—two videos of the same performance total over three million views—and Amir Haddad, whose performance on France's incarnation of *The Voice* collected 1.3 million views, as well as amateur recordings from users like scottmc127, who received 91,000 views.[60] "Candle in the Wind 1997" returns significantly less on both counts. One popular cover (with 99,000 views) shows Melanie Thornton from La Bouche performing the song in concert,[61] but the only cover filmed for television appears to be from Trayan Kostov, who performed it on *The X Factor Bulgaria*. It has 19,000 views, and the minimal user comments include the barbed "He should have sang the Marilyn Monroe version" and "Its [sic] a great cover but I disagree with the cover as a whole. Radios [sic] and Sir Elton John himself wont [sic] play this again and it should be kept this way!"[62] On the amateur front, the comparatively few covers that do exist have view counts significantly lower than those covering the original version; for example, YouTube users Lila and Liliana Tani hit approximately 14,000 views and 1500 views, respectively.[63]

This disparity in cover-song numbers suggests less that people are uninterested in hearing "Candle in the Wind 1997" than perhaps that they want to hear its original co-creator, Elton John. View numbers from YouTube strengthen this hypothesis: the top-three most viewed YouTube uploads of John's performance at Diana's funeral have a combined view count of over 43.4 million, and the most popular tribute video (in which photographs of Diana are shown while the audio recording of "Candle in the Wind 1997" plays) clocks in at 24.6 million views.[64] These numbers are particularly impressive when one considers that YouTube was created in 2005 and all the videos discussed above have been uploaded within the last decade.

Yet interest in Diana remains sustained in part due to her own popularity and, as David Cannadine predicted in 1998, because her sons William and Harry (and tangentially their wives and children) serve as constant living reminders of her.[65] Further, in 2020 a Broadway musical about her life was scheduled to open prior to the shutdown caused by the COVID-19 pandemic, and the popular Netflix series *The Crown* began tackling the story of Charles and Diana's tumultuous marriage.[66] These, by extension, power interest in "Candle in the Wind 1997," and proof that people still turn to it to commemorate the princess of Wales can be seen in more than just video views. Decades after the formal closing of the official condolence books, new comments from around the world appear daily on the YouTube videos expressing sentiments similar to those of users Teresina Cheung—"Hard to hold tears when watch Elton John played this song even after so many years. Your Royal Highness Princess Diana, as the song written 'Your candle's burned out long before, Your legend ever will'. Missed you very much! RIP!" and Khadija Love "Wish i didnt listen ☺☺☺ feels so fresh."[67] While UCLA's *Daily Bruin* pointed out that many successful pieces of tribute music have their meaning diluted due to an "abundance of publicity and mainstream influence," and that the "passage of time changes these songs from emotional statements to distant memories,"[68] these comments unintentionally show that "Candle in the Wind 1997" has avoided this pitfall.

Although its lyrics were revealed in advance, "Candle in the Wind 1997" entered the public consciousness in its entirety in a rare way: through a live performance before a historically large audience given by the artist at the funeral of its subject. But this in no way guaranteed the treatment of the song in perpetuity. Mass mourning for the princess of Wales, combined with media interest and the timing and location of its unveiling, provided a perfect catalyst for record-breaking singles sales. However, Elton John must receive credit for curating "Candle in the Wind 1997's" legacy. Because John identified dilution and commercialization as fates he wanted to prevent for "Candle in the Wind 1997," he was able to take action. He spoke directly to the press (and therefore, the people) about his desire to keep the song tied to a specific moment dedicated to Diana, and has relentlessly refused to allow it to be used anywhere, by anyone, since the funeral. While other songs (including the original "Candle in the Wind") might endure due to their continued application to new situations, the opposite is true here, where the elements surrounding the song have proven to exert more influence over its fate than the perceived beauty of its contents. John's proactive protection of "Candle in the Wind 1997" has solidified the best-selling single in chart history as an aural monument to Diana, princess of Wales, depositing the listener in the late summer of 1997 each time it is heard.

Notes

1 Elton John, *Me.* (New York: Henry Holt and Company, 2019), 6–7; Bryan Forbes, dir. "Elton John and Bernie Taupin Say Goodbye Norma Jean and Other Things (1973)," *Goodbye Yellow Brick Road (40ᵗʰ Anniversary Super Deluxe Box Set)*, DVD. (London: Mercury Records, 2014).
2 Forbes, "Elton John and Bernie Taupin."
3 Although many assume Taupin was a devoted fan, he has clarified that he was "not that enamored with Marilyn Monroe" and that she was "simply a metaphor." Bob Smeaton, dir., "Elton John – Goodbye Yellow Brick Road (Classic Album)," (UK: Eagle Rock Entertainment, 2001).
4 Margot A. Henricksen, "Monroe, Marilyn (1926-1962), film actress and sex symbol," *American National Biography*, 2000.
5 Forbes, "Elton John and Bernie Taupin."
6 Elton John, "Candle in the Wind 1997," *Something About the Way You Look Tonight/Candle in the Wind 1997* (London: Rocket, 1997).
7 Elton John, "Goodbye Yellow Brick Road Remastered & Revisited (Extended Interview)," YouTube, uploaded by Elton John, April 11, 2014. https://youtu.be/t4ODYfKrwqc.
8 Smeaton, "Goodbye Yellow Brick Road."
9 John Tobler, *Elton John – One Night Only*, (UK: Mercury Records, 2000),
10 Susan J. Hubert, "Two Women, Two Songs: The Subversive Iconography of 'Candle in the Wind,'" *NWSA Journal* 11, no. 2 (Summer 1999), 125.
11 John, *Me*, 217.
12 John Preston, "The Princess and the Showman," *Sunday Telegraph*, August 30, 1998; John, *Me*, 271–6.
13 Others killed in the crash included Diana's boyfriend (Dodi Al Fayed) and the car's driver (Henri Paul). Bodyguard Trevor Rees-Jones survived. K. D. Reynolds, "Diana [née Lady Diana Frances Spencer], princess of Wales (1961–1997)/" *Oxford Dictionary of National Biography*, 2004; Peter Childs, "Celebrity: Diana and Death." In *Texts: Contemporary Cultural Texts and Critical Approaches* (Edinburgh: Edinburgh University Press, 2006), 50.
14 According to Lt. Col. Sir Malcolm Ross, then comptroller of the Lord Chamberlain's Office, it was Queen Elizabeth II's decision to give Diana a royal funeral even though, due to her divorce, she was no longer guaranteed one. Henry Singer, dir. *Diana, 7 Days*, (UK: Sandpaper Films, 2017).
15 Luke Harding, "Elton John to Sing at Funeral Service: Tribute: Hit Rewritten to Hail 'Nation's Golden Child,'" *The Guardian*, September 5, 1997; Phillip Reay-Smith, "Elton's tribute to Diana will raise £10m for her charities." *The*

Pink Paper, September 12, 1997; Preston, "The Princess and the Showman"; Hubert, "Two Women, Two Songs," 126; John, *Me*, 276–9.

16 Preston, "The Princess and the Showman"; Singer, *Diana, 7 Days*; Andrew Morton, *Diana: Her True Story – In Her Own Words* (New York: Simon & Schuster, 2017), 409.

17 Morton, *Diana*, 88.

18 Ibid., 315–6.

19 Helen M. Hickey, "'And the stars spell out your name': The funeral music of Diana, Princess of Wales." In *Singing Death: Reflections on Music and Mortality*, edited by Helen Dell and Helen M. Hickey (New York: Routledge, 2017), 173.

20 Although blame was initially placed solely on the paparazzi, it was later discovered that her driver had been speeding and intoxicated. Reynolds, "Diana, princess of Wales."

21 Kline, "Princess Diana, Mother Teresa, and Medieval Women," 98.

22 John, "Candle in the Wind 1997."

23 Harding, "Elton John to Sing."

24 Michael Streeter, "More emotion, less ceremony," *Independent*, September 5, 1997; Steve Boggan, "A mixture of old and new: 'as she would have wanted,'" *Independent*, September 5, 1997.

25 Christopher Howse, "Familiarity breeds respect," *Daily Telegraph*, September 5, 1997.

26 Barbara Ellen. "The three minutes that define you," *The Observer*, September 7, 1997.

27 Fenton, "Song rewritten by Elton John."

28 Herwitz, "Candle in the Wind," 2; Lambert, "Lost Princess," 53; Wynne-Jones, "World bids a final farewell."

29 John, *Me*, 277-278.

30 Preston, "The Princess and the Showman."

31 John, *Me*, 280.

32 Wynne-Jones, "World bids a final farewell."

33 "Something About the Way You Look Tonight" was the lead single from John's album *The Big Picture*, released at the end of September 1997 and dedicated to Gianni Versace. John, *Me*, 280.

34 Forrest, "The singer, not the song"; John Mulvey, "Goodbye English Rock: Just as British Music had Recovered from Band Aid, Elton John's 'Candle in the Wind' Threatens to Lead Us into another Decade of Schmaltz," *The Observer*, September 21, 1997.

35 Payne, "Musical splendour on a day of mourning"; Bryan Appleyard, "The princess' final farewell," Sunday Times, September 7, 1997.

36 Pink Paper, "The gay world mourns Diana," *The Pink Paper*, September 12, 1997; Abby Goodnough, "In the Park, a Usually Tough Crowd Bares Hearts for Diana," *New York Times*, September 15, 1997.

37 Singer, *Diana, 7 Days*.

38 A full recording of the funeral service, which contained John's live performance and benefitted the Diana, Princess of Wales Memorial Fund, was also released. BBC, *Diana Princess Of Wales 1961-1997 - The BBC Recording Of The Funeral Service*, Decca 460 000-2, 1997, compact disc. London: BBC, 1997.

39 Daily Telegraph, "Parisians first to buy Elton John tribute," *Daily Telegraph*, September 13, 1997.

40   Halbfinger, "Musical Tribute to Diana Sells Briskly."

41   John, *Me*, 281; Sheffield, "Candle in the Wind becomes fastest-selling single in a day."

42   British Phonographic Industry. "BRIT Certified." *BPI*; Recording Industry Association of America, "Gold & Platinum." *RIAA*.

43   OWN, "Elton John Opens Up About Coping with Princess Diana's Death | The Oprah Winfrey Show | OWN," YouTube video, uploaded by OWN, May 16, 2019. https://youtu.be/gkvcpglSSSk.

44   Daily Mail, "It's time for the tears to stop, declares Elton," *Daily Mail*, September 12, 1997.

45   Childs, "Celebrity: Diana and Death," 53.

46   Combs, et al., *Tribute to The Notorious B.I.G.*; Billboard, "Chart History: Puff Daddy"; Official Charts, "Official Singles Chart: I'll Be Missing You."

47   Jordan Runtagh, "Heal the World: 20 Songs for a Good Cause," *Rolling Stone*, November 22, 2018.

48   New York Times, "The 1998 Grammy Award Winners: [List]," *New York Times*, February 26, 1998; Official Charts, "Official Singles Chart: Something About the Way You Look Tonight/Candle"; Billboard, "Chart History: Elton John."

49   When the Diana, Princess of Wales Memorial Fund was absorbed by the Royal Foundation of the Duke and Duchess of Cambridge and Prince Harry in 2012, an estimated 27 percent of its total income had resulted from sales of "Candle in the Wind 1997." George Arbuthnott, "Candle In The Wind raises £38 million for Diana's charities after Elton John's moving performance at Princess' funeral" *Daily Mail*, December 22, 2012.

50   Lyall, "Funeral Music with a Beat."

51   In-therapy women expressed stronger reactions to the death of the princess of Wales than men, so the more frequent desire of women than men to create websites dedicated to Diana is unsurprising. Jane Gross, "Diana's Death Resonates with Women in Therapy" *New York Times*, September 13, 1997.

52   Helmers, "Electronic Memorials to Diana, Princess of Wales," 439–40.

53   Barbie Dutter, "Elton John bans use of song on videos," *Daily Telegraph*, September 12, 1997; John, *Me*, 282.

54   Bill Carter, "Elton John's Revised 'Candle,' for a Princess and Charity," *New York Times*, September 9, 1997.

55   Pareles, "Elton John Steps Back."

56   Runtagh, "20 Songs for a Good Cause."

57   See, for example, Lucy Bannerman, "Our charity concert will be Diana's best ever birthday gift, say princes." *Times*, December 13, 2006.

58   Not so coincidentally, P. Diddy performed "I'll be Missing You" at the event and dedicated it to Diana. *BBC News,* "Diana concert a 'perfect tribute'."

59   See Joe Lynch, "17 Years Ago, Elton John's 'Candle In the Wind 1997' Started Its 14-Week No. 1 Run," *Billboard*, October 11, 2014; and Maureen Lee Lenker, "Princess Diana: Looking back on Elton John's 'Candle in the Wind' 20 years later." *Entertainment Weekly*, September 6, 2017.

60   X Factor UK. "Sam Bailey sings Candle In The Wind by Elton John - Live Week 9 - The X Factor 2013," YouTube video, uploaded by X Factor UK, December 7, 2013; Sam Bailey, "Sam Bailey Song 2 sings Candle In The Wind by Elton John Live Week 9 The X Factor 2013 Full," YouTube video, uploaded by Sam Bailey, December 8, 2013; The Voice: la plus belle voix, "Elton John – Candle in the

Wind | Amir Haddad | The Voice France 2014 | Blind Audition," YouTube video, uploaded by The Voice: la plus belle voix , May 27, 2016; Scottmc127, "Candle in the wind (cover) elton john," YouTube video, uploaded by Scottmc127, September 12. 2009.

61 FFFClub, "Melanie Thornton (LA BOUCHE) - Candle in the Wind (Gospel Version '97)," YouTube video, uploaded by FFFClub, March 12, 2012. Germany-based duo La Bouche included a cover of "Candle in the Wind 1997" on their album *A Moment of Love* in November 1997, stating that all profits and royalties from the song would go to the Mother Theresa [sic] Foundation. However, later versions of the album, including the version currently on services like Spotify and iTunes, do not include the track, which was likely not sanctioned by John.

62 MAR COS, "Candle In The Wind (Goodbye Englands Rose)-cover by TRAYAN KOSTOV," YouTube video, uploaded by MAR COS, May 18, 2015.

63 Lila, "Trauerlied "Candle in the wind" von Elton John - gesungen von Lila (Cover)." YouTube video, uploaded by Tani, August 31, 2018.; LilianaTani, "Elton John Candle in the Wind/Goodbye England's Rose cover by Liliana of One Voice Children's Choir," YouTube video, uploaded by Liliana Tani, August 31, 2019.

64 EltonJohnCollection, "Elton John - Lady Diana Funeral - Arrival + Candle in the wind," YouTube video, uploaded by EltonJohnCollection, June 30, 2010; EltonStuff, "Elton John - Candle in the Wind/Goodbye England's Rose - Princess Diana's Funeral 1997," YouTube video, uploaded by EltonStuff, December 5, 2013; and Phillip Anness, "Elton John - Candle in the Wind/Goodbye England's Rose (Live at Princess Diana's Funeral - 1997)." YouTube video, uploaded by Phillip Anness, December 1, 2014.

65 Cannadine, *History in Our Time,* 81.

66 Meyer, "*Diana* Begins March 2"; Sarah Lyall, " 'The Crown' Has Had Its Scandals, but There's Nothing Like Diana," *New York Times*, November 12, 2020.

67 EltonStuff, "Candle in the Wind/Goodbye England's Rose"; Missmariasiya, "Lady Diana - Candle in the wind (Goodbye Englands rose) - Elton John - Lyrics in text," YouTube video, uploaded by Missmariasiya, February 15, 2014.

68 Daily Bruin Staff, "Celebrity death cash-ins result in immoral profits," *The Daily Bruin*, October 6, 1997.

References

Anness, Phillip. "Elton John - Candle in the Wind/Goodbye England's Rose (Live at Princess Diana's Funeral - 1997)." YouTube video, uploaded by Phillip Anness, December 1, 2014. https://youtu.be/1o9rLDCfO6o.

Appleyard, Bryan. "The princess' final farewell." *Sunday Times*, September 7, 1997.

Arbuthnott, George. "Candle In The Wind raises £38 million for Diana's charities after Elton John's moving performance at Princess' funeral." *Daily Mail*, December 22, 2012.

Bailey, Sam. "Sam Bailey Song 2 sings Candle In The Wind by Elton John Live Week 9 The X Factor 2013 Full." YouTube video, uploaded by Sam Bailey, December 8, 2013. https://youtu.be/QU5G14D6haI.

Bannerman, Lucy. "Our charity concert will be Diana's best ever birthday gift, say princes." *Times*, December 13, 2006.

BBC. *Diana Princess Of Wales 1961-1997 - The BBC Recording Of The Funeral Service*. Decca 460 000-2, 1997, compact disc. London: BBC, 1997.

BBC News. "Diana concert a 'perfect tribute.'" *BBC News*, July 2, 2007.

Billboard. "Chart History: Elton John." *Billboard*.

Billboard. "Chart History: Puff Daddy." *Billboard*.

Boggan, Steve. "A mixture of old and new: 'as she would have wanted.'" *Independent*, September 5, 1997.

British Phonographic Industry. "BRIT Certified." *BPI*.

Cannadine, David. *History in Our Time*. New Haven: Yale University Press, 1998.

Carter, Bill. "Elton John's Revised 'Candle,' for a Princess and Charity." *New York Times*, September 9, 1997.

Childs, Peter. "Celebrity: Diana and Death." In *Texts: Contemporary Cultural Texts and Critical Approaches*, 49–59. Edinburgh: Edinburgh University Press, 2006.

Combs, Sean, Faith Evans, the Lox, and 112. *Tribute to The Notorious B.I.G.* Bad Boy 78612 79097 2, 1997, compact disc.

Daily Bruin Staff. "Celebrity death cash-ins result in immoral profits." *The Daily Bruin*, October 6, 1997.

Daily Mail. "It's time for the tears to stop, declares Elton." *Daily Mail*, September 12, 1997.

Daily Telegraph. "Parisians first to buy Elton John tribute." *Daily Telegraph*, September 13, 1997,

Diana, princess of Wales. "An Interview with H.R.H. the Princess of Wales." interview by Martin Bashir. *Panorama*, BBC1, November 20, 1995.

Dutter, Barbie. "Elton John bans use of song on videos." *Daily Telegraph*, September 12, 1997.

Ellen, Barbara. "The three minutes that define you." *The Observer*, September 7, 1997.

EltonJohnCollection. "Elton John - Lady Diana Funeral - Arrival + Candle in the wind." YouTube video, uploaded by EltonJohnCollection, June 30, 2010. https://youtu.be/7BrtCtv44Vg.

EltonStuff. "Elton John - Candle in the Wind/Goodbye England's Rose - Princess Diana's Funeral 1997." YouTube video, uploaded by EltonStuff, December 5, 2013. https://youtu.be/dg_MIysNGIU.

Fenton, Ben. "Song rewritten by Elton John for funeral." *Daily Telegraph*, September 5, 1997.

FFFClub. "Melanie Thornton (LA BOUCHE) - Candle in the Wind (Gospel Version '97)." YouTube video, uploaded by FFFClub, March 12, 2012. https://youtu.be/ponb5YY-DHY.

Forbes, Bryan, dir. "Elton John and Bernie Taupin Say Goodbye Norma Jean and Other Things (1973)." *Goodbye Yellow Brick Road (40th Anniversary Super Deluxe Box Set)*, DVD. London: Mercury Records, 2014.

Forrest, Emma. "The singer, not the song." *The Guardian*, September 10, 1997.

Goodnough, Abby. "In the Park, a Usually Tough Crowd Bares Hearts for Diana." *New York Times*, September 15, 1997.

Gross, Jane. "Diana's Death Resonates with Women in Therapy." *New York Times*, September 13, 1997.

Halbfinger, David M. "Musical Tribute to Diana Sells Briskly in U.S. Debut." *New York Times*, September 24, 1997.

Harding, Luke. "Elton John to Sing at Funeral Service: Tribute: Hit Rewritten to Hail 'Nation's Golden Child.'" *The Guardian*, September 5, 1997.

Helmers, Marguerite. "Media, Discourse, and the Public Sphere: Electronic Memorials to Diana, Princess of Wales." *College English* 63, no. 4 (March 2001): 437–56.

Henricksen, Margot A. "Monroe, Marilyn (1926-1962), film actress and sex symbol." *American National Biography*, 2000.

Herwitz, Daniel. "Candle in the Wind." In *The Star as Icon: Celebrity in the Age of Mass Consumption*, 1–22. New York: Columbia University Press, 2008.

Hickey, Helen M. " 'And the stars spell out your name': The funeral music of Diana, Princess of Wales." In *Singing Death: Reflections on Music and Mortality*, edited by Helen Dell and Helen M. Hickey, 166–79. New York: Routledge, 2017.

Howse, Christopher. "Familiarity breeds respect." *Daily Telegraph*, September 5, 1997.

Hubert, Susan J. "Two Women, Two Songs: The Subversive Iconography of 'Candle in the Wind.'" *NWSA Journal* 11, no. 2 (Summer 1999): 124–37.

John, Elton. "Candle in the Wind." *Goodbye Yellow Brick Road*. Universal City: MCA Records, 1973.

John, Elton. "Candle in the Wind 1997." *Something About the Way You Look Tonight/ Candle in the Wind 1997*. London: Rocket, 1997.

John, Elton. "Elton John - Goodbye Yellow Brick Road Remastered & Revisited (Extended Interview)." YouTube, uploaded by Elton John, April 11, 2014. https://youtu.be/t4ODYfKrwqc.

John, Elton. *Me*. New York: Henry Holt and Company, 2019.

Kline, Daniel T. "Digital Hagiography: Princess Diana, Mother Teresa, and Medieval Women in Cyberspace." *College Literature* 28, no. 2 (Spring 2001): 92–117.

La Bouche. *A Moment of Love*. New York: BMG, 1997.

Lambert, Pam. "Lost Princess." *People Weekly*, September 22, 1997.

Lenker, Maureen Lee. "Princess Diana: Looking back on Elton John's 'Candle in the Wind' 20 years later." *Entertainment Weekly*, September 6, 2017.

Lila. "Trauerlied "Candle in the wind" von Elton John - gesungen von Lila (Cover)." YouTube video, uploaded by Tani, August 31, 2018. https://youtu.be/G8R2 ozhqJm0.

Lyall Sarah. "Funeral Music With a Beat the Deceased Could Dance To." *New York Times*, February 8, 1998.

Lyall, Sarah. " 'The Crown' Has Had Its Scandals, but There's Nothing Like Diana." *New York Times*, November 12, 2020.

Lynch, Joe. "17 Years Ago, Elton John's 'Candle In the Wind 1997' Started Its 14-Week No. 1 Run." *Billboard*, October 11, 2014.

MAR COS. "Candle In The Wind (Goodbye Englands Rose)-cover by TRAYAN KOSTOV." YouTube video, uploaded by MAR COS, May 18, 2015. https://youtu. be/kEA8gtC9XRs.

Meyer, Dan. "*Diana* Begins March 2, Starring Jeanna de Waal and Roe Hartrampf." *Playbill*, March 2, 2020.

Missmariasiya. "Lady Diana - Candle in the wind (Goodbye Englands rose) - Elton John - Lyrics in text." YouTube video, uploaded by Missmariasiya, February 15, 2014. https://youtu.be/OefdqK3jKi0.

Morton, Andrew. *Diana: Her True Story – In Her Own Words*. New York: Simon & Schuster, 2017.

Mulvey, John. "Goodbye English Rock: Just as British Music had Recovered from Band Aid, Elton John's 'Candle in the Wind' Threatens to Lead Us into another Decade of Schmaltz." *The Observer*, September 21, 1997.

New York Times. "The 1998 Grammy Award Winners: [List]." *New York Times*, February 26, 1998.

Official Charts. "Official Singles Chart: I'll Be Missing You." *Official Charts*. www.off icialcharts.com/search/singles/i'll-be-missing-you/.

Official Charts. "Official Singles Chart: Something About the Way You Look Tonight/ Candle." *Official Charts*. www.officialcharts.com/search/singles/something-about-the-way-you-look_slash_candle/.

OWN. "Elton John Opens Up About Coping with Princess Diana's Death | The Oprah Winfrey Show | OWN." YouTube video, uploaded my OWN, May 16, 2019. https:// youtu.be/gkvcpglSSSk.

Pareles, Jon. "Elton John Steps Back from 'Candle in the Wind.'" *New York Times*, September 15, 1997.

Payne, Anthony. "Musical splendour on a day of mourning." *Independent*, September 8, 1997.

Pink Paper. "The gay world mourns Diana." *The Pink Paper*, September 12, 1997.

Preston, John. "The Princess and the Showman." *Sunday Telegraph*, August 30, 1998.

Reay-Smith, Phillip. "Elton's tribute to Diana will raise £10m for her charities." *The Pink Paper*, September 12, 1997.

Recording Industry Association of America. "Gold & Platinum." *RIAA*. www.riaa. com/gold-platinum/.

Reynolds, K. D. "Diana [née Lady Diana Frances Spencer], princess of Wales (1961–1997)." *Oxford Dictionary of National Biography*, 2004.

Runtagh, Jordan. "Heal the World: 20 Songs for a Good Cause." *Rolling Stone*, November 22, 2018.

Scottmc127. "Candle in the wind (cover) elton john." YouTube video, uploaded by Scottmc127, September 12. 2009, https://youtu.be/YyBmhM0hceA.

Sheeran, Ed. "Candle in the Wind." *Goodbye Yellow Brick Road 40th Anniversary Edition*. London: Mercury Records.

Sheffield, Emily. "Candle in the Wind becomes fastest-selling single in a day." *The Guardian*, September 15, 1997.

Singer, Henry, dir. *Diana, 7 Days*. UK: Sandpaper Films, 2017.

Smeaton, Bob, dir. "Elton John – Goodbye Yellow Brick Road (Classic Album)." UK: Eagle Rock Entertainment, 2001.

Streeter, Michael. "More emotion, less ceremony." *Independent*, September 5, 1997.

Tani, Liliana. "Elton John Candle in the Wind/Goodbye England's Rose cover by Liliana of One Voice Children's Choir." YouTube video, uploaded by Liliana Tani, August 31, 2019. https://youtu.be/sgtswEGag5o.

Tobler, John. *Elton John – One Night Only*. UK: Mercury Records, 2000,

The Voice: la plus belle voix. "Elton John – Candle in the Wind | Amir Haddad | The Voice France 2014 | Blind Audition." YouTube video, uploaded by The Voice: la plus belle voix, May 27, 2016. https://youtu.be/FS-g-YyuRq4.

Wynne-Jones, Ros. "With a heavy heart, the world bids a final farewell to the people's princess." *Independent on Sunday*, September 7, 1997.

X Factor UK. "Sam Bailey sings Candle In The Wind by Elton John - Live Week 9 - The X Factor 2013." YouTube video, uploaded by X Factor UK, December 7, 2013. https://youtu.be/-TD6yd5tXHg.

15 LCD Soundsystem—"All My Friends" (2007)

Gabrielle Cornish

If James Murphy is having fun, he sure doesn't show it. Backlit and dressed for a funeral, the mastermind behind the group LCD Soundsystem stands still, staring straight into the camera, and mouths along as a steady stream of open fifths and octaves on the piano underlines his announcement.

"That's how it starts."

Murphy's face, painted white with silver geometric patterns, shows no emotion (see Figure 15.1). He breaks with the camera only occasionally, and only then to stare down at his feet, as if unsure whether to continue. Yet the music hammers on, building through the addition of bass, drums, and synths. Four-on-the-floor, glittering keyboards, unshifting harmonies: these are all the markers of a fast-paced, upbeat dance track. But Murphy, even as rain falls on his head and pyrotechnics erupt, stands still as the world around him crumbles. It's as if he's saying, "Go ahead. Dance. Here I am, and here I'll stay."

That's how it starts.

So goes the music video for LCD Soundsystem's "All My Friends," the climactic track off the group's second album, *Sound of Silver* (2007). And so, too, goes Murphy's general aesthetic: he stands steady, constant, and stuck in time, as younger acts pass him by. Murphy was thirty-seven when the album was released—ancient compared to the denim-clad hipsters who danced to his music night after night in dirty Brooklyn clubs and dimly lit bars. Yet Murphy, with disheveled sand-colored hair and eternal five o'clock shadow, doesn't seem to mind. He's here to make music and make you dance. When the beat takes over, the man himself disappears.

This essay takes "All My Friends" as a starting point to explore the post-9/11 indie music scene in New York City. The September 11th terrorist attacks fractured a New York City that, already in recovery from the dot-com bubble crash at the end of the '90s, was swiftly changing. The New York City that arose from the rubble, defiant and in the spotlight, brought with it new challenges for young artists. In both lyrics and sound, "All My Friends" recreates the past to engage with the present. The track draws on musical styles that range from synth-driven new wave sounds of bands like New Order to the electric bass-heavy style of younger indie groups like the

DOI: 10.4324/9781003093206-16

Strokes. All the while, a steady four-on-the-floor drum pattern undergirds Murphy's lyrics, which, resisting and reiterating partying tropes, are both an elegy for lost youth and a panegyric to the wisdom that comes with age. *Sound of Silver* would go on to top several best-of-the-year and best-of-the-decade lists, with "All My Friends" as its centerpiece.[1] As the indie music scene aged into the new millennium, Murphy became the frontman for the transitional decade.

Murphy himself represents a microcosm of New York history: he arrived in the city at the end of the 1980s, established himself as a leading producer and sound engineer in the 1990s, and became an icon of a nostalgia-laden dance music scene in the 2000s. His rise to fame straddled the 2008 recession, which coupled the hope of an Obama presidency with massive economic upheaval and instability. The Millennial generation, born between roughly 1980 and 1996, graduated into the worst economy in recent history. Yet Murphy, a Gen-Xer at least ten years the senior of any Millennial, became something of a figurehead for this younger generation. All the way, he made no secret of his age—and his relative uncoolness—which only made him more engaging to a generation beset by an uncertain future.[2] Perhaps more than any other song on *Sound of Silver*—a title that referred to the aluminum foil coating the walls of the studio but perhaps just as applicable to aging men and changing hair colors—"All My Friends" centers this generational schism.[3]

In many ways, the music behind Murphy's resigned vocals in "All My Friends" defies analysis. The track is repetitive; it builds not through harmonic development or tension but through addition: instruments join in, the volume rises, Murphy's voices grows strained. And then, just as quickly as it begins, this additive structure evaporates. Or, perhaps, not quickly, but only after minutes of the beat pulsing forward: it's hard to tell with LCD Soundsystem, as repetition leads to timelessness. This phenomenon is, in many ways, key to understanding dance music. It is process—musical, lyrical, and visceral—that organizes the meaning and rhetoric of the genre.[4] In this essay, I take this process—the music's gradual "unfolding" over the course of the track—seriously as an organizing structure.

Ultimately, Murphy's song is as much a critique of coolness as it is an attempt to dance away reality—a tenuous balance the musician keeps throughout much of his work. A slippery category of social and aesthetic critique, "cool" is perhaps best defined tautologically: something's cool if, well, *it's cool*. You know it when you see it, hear it, feel it. Yet nebulous as it may be, ideas of "cool" and "uncool," of "hip" and "unhip," underscored much of the discourse around New York City's music scene in the 2000s. Your coolness could shift based on what you did, what you knew, who you didn't know, and who else was in the room. Fleeting and always in motion, cool might be better thought of as an assemblage—a gathering of networks, aesthetics, genres, discourses, and people—than as a single concept. But in late capitalism, "cool" and its more polished cousin, "interesting," have become key categories of aesthetic experience.[5] Positioned within the "retromania" of the first decade of the new millennium, "All My Friends" plays with notions of aging, fashion, and nostalgia to compelling—and very cool—ends.[6]

That's How It Starts

In 1988, Murphy came to New York City from a small town outside of Princeton, New Jersey, to attend college at NYU. (His time as a student was brief, but he settled in the city for good.) He'd played guitar in bands and sang throughout high school but quickly found himself outpaced by more skilled musicians. Instead, Murphy picked up the drums and found their dynamic potential enlightening and empowering. "I thought, '[The drums] are great'," he recalled. "You hit them harder and they get louder."[7] Murphy then cycled through a series of bands, all of them relatively short-lived and mostly unsuccessful. He soon established a presence, however, running live sound for concerts, and learned the ins and outs of sound engineering from Steve Albini and Bob Weston, both of whom had established themselves both as skilled musicians (in the band Shellac) and as successful engineers and producers in the recording field. It was at this point that Murphy began in earnest to explore and validate the sounds of disco and dance music. A self-described "obsessive audio nerd," Murphy had stayed away from the genre for years. As Luke Jenner, lead singer of the Rapture, recalled: "When I first met him, James Murphy didn't like two things: he didn't like Bob Dylan, and he didn't like disco."[8]

Murphy befriended David Holmes, an Irish DJ, and Tim Goldsworthy, a British producer, and the three would become fixtures in Manhattan's Lower East Side, where they would gather—either to DJ or to dance—at Plant Bar in the East Village and other hot spots for young music lovers in the late 1990s. Holmes and Murphy had a falling out at the end of the decade, and the former returned to the United Kingdom. Murphy, however, continued working with Goldsworthy, and by the beginning of the new millennium he had produced some of the most popular tracks in the scene, like the Rapture's "House of Jealous Lovers." Jonathan Galkin, a young producer, took notice of Murphy's production skills, and a fruitful partnership between the three was born.[9]

DFA Records (also known as Death from Above) took up residence in an unassuming office in the West Village in 2001. The label quickly became a vessel for some of the newest and coolest music and threw parties—often DJ'd by Murphy—that introduced the hipster scene to a wide array of new acts: the Rapture, Juan McClean, Shit Robot, and more. Even as their local fame grew, the studio kept things casual (Murphy even took up residence on the couch for a bit), and their parties helped build the burgeoning dance scene. Yet even with DFA's success, the record label maintained its penchant for Murphy's signature irony. The label's motto—even some two decades after its founding—is "Too old to be new, too new to be classic."

The new millennium ushered in a period of uncertainty and rapid change for New York City. The dot-com bubble, which had brought unchecked speculation and expansion to the stock market in the 1990s, burst in March 2000.[10] The financial boom had helped cement Manhattan as a global financial center, and the resulting influx of capital and young professionals had transformed the slow trickle of the displaced middle class to the outer boroughs into a flood.[11] Musicians and creatives who, like Murphy and his friends, had made a home in Manhattan were forced out to Brooklyn—and Williamsburg in particular—to cultivate a new artistic community. The 2000 Presidential Election and subsequent legal decision in *Bush v. Gore* contributed to a loss of faith in American institutions, which had already been shaken by the economic turbulence. That which seemed certain suddenly seemed fleeting, and many of the city's creative class felt jostled by the millennium's shaky start.

No event brought more change to the city, however, than the September 11th terrorist attacks. Beyond the death toll and physical destruction, the attacks transformed cultural hierarchies and modes of production.[12] Mayor Rudy Giuliani, who had before been distrusted and despised by most of the city's intelligentsia, became a symbol of renewal and survival.[13] Artists took to the stage and the canvas to try to work through the impossible trauma of the attacks.[14] And the reverberations of 9/11—itself a booming sonic event— were soon heard in music.[15] The September 11th attacks changed the cultural landscape of the entire country—and indeed, the entire world.

For musicians in New York City, the attacks upended their daily lives in drastic fashion. With death looming overhead—quite literally, for the city blanketed in soot and debris—simply "following the rules" seemed no longer an option. As Tunde Adebimpe, lead singer of TV on the Radio, recalled:

> After 9/11 we basically decided there [was] no reason for being here besides to make the things we like to make and share them or not share them, because who's keeping score now? Try to find some kind of joy or meaning in your own life, because it's suddenly really fucked up outside.[16]

Echoing Adebimpe's dispassion, the producer, critic, and DJ Sarah Lewitinn (Ultragrrrl) argued that in such an uncertain time, the best thing one could do was enjoy the moment: "Post-9/11 NYC had the energy that you were gonna die anyway—taking a subway, opening mail, walking down the street—so why die sober?"[17] Life had changed in a single morning, and an uncertain future gave way to a more engaged present for many.

Murphy, however, was largely unfazed by the terrorist attacks. It had already been a heartbreaking year for him, with his mother's death in April and father's death in August. By the time of the attacks, he had already experienced his fill of tragedy. "When the towers came down, I was pretty blasé about it. To me it felt really normal. 'Well, my dad's dead. The person who held the world together while I was a crazy person is gone'."[18] In the months following 9/11, Murphy slept at the DFA office and was broke. Yet in his ascetic existence, however, he found a renewed vigor for music-making that echoed Adebimpe's and Lewitinn's casual indifference. "That was kind of a lonely period," he recalled. "But something really radical happened. It broke me free, in a way. Every day I thought, 'I'm going to die.' 'Losing My Edge' and the next wave of energy and combat was really driven out of that."[19]

Released in 2002, "Losing My Edge" throws notions of aging, fashion, and "coolness" into sharp relief. Murphy speaks listlessly over a cartoon drum machine with the kind of sounds one would expect from a children's Casio keyboard; he used a boom box with a built-in synthesizer, a gift from Adam "Ad-Rock" Horovitz of the Beastie Boys.[20] Stumbling through on the back of the beat, he tells us how he is slowly being overtaken by the "kids [who] are coming up from behind," kids from France, London, Tokyo, Berlin, and— of course—Brooklyn who reeked of "borrowed nostalgia for the unremembered '80s." Part defiant, part resigned to his fate, Murphy rattles off a list of times when he "was there": the first Can show in Cologne in 1968, the Paradise Garage DJ booth, the first Suicide rehearsals. It's telling that at one point he shouts, unprompted, "Gil Scott-Heron," whose poetic composition "The Revolution Will Not Be Televised" (1970) is as immediate a precursor to "Losing My Edge" as anything. Murphy follows this list of firsts with a list of records he owns, bands he knows, instruments he's played, parties he's attended. "I had everything before anyone," he proclaims, half-heartedly planting his flag for all the hipsters to see. (Critic Sasha Frere-Jones said that the track was "closer to standup comedy than to pop music."[21] Meanwhile, Stephen Malkmus, the lead singer of Pavement, has called it a "dance-rock workout."[22]) Throughout it all, the lo-fi accompaniment hovers around a single pitch—G—and provides a steady foundation for Murphy's increasingly unsteady vocal flailings. Murphy *is* cool, and he can prove it with records and stories. And yet the loathing turns inward, and rather than boast of his imagined accomplishments and street cred, he mumbles them lethargically and admits that the kids are "better-looking people / with better ideas and more talent." Foregrounding quantity before quality, Murphy critiques his own collector instincts and wonders if he, like those "coming up behind" him, knows what he really wants.

The song was an almost immediate hit and achieved the rare feat of being "cool" without trying, with sincerity and a cheeky nod to indifference. As the writer and critic Andy Greenwald later reflected:

> The thing that makes pop music so great is the way it parallel parks on the bleeding edge of cool: nothing could be better at this moment than this beat, this feeling, this chorus. It takes something ephemeral and impossible and for three-to-four exhilarating minutes, it makes it accessible and real. "Losing My Edge" is a song that's already bled out. It sticks its nose in all the parts you're supposed to ignore: jealousy, resentment, sarcasm, age. But it's not obnoxious in the way that "funny" music often is. The real trick is that it's hitting you while it's heckling you—the song bangs, even if the vocalist is a crank. I still don't quite know how he did it. Most breakthrough singles are about first love. "Losing My Edge" is about first

Figure 15.1 Guitarist Al Doyle, keyboardist Nancy Whang, lead singer James
Murphy, bass guitarist Phil Skarich, and drummer Jaleel Bunton of LCD
Soundsystem at the Virgin Festival in Baltimore, Maryland, on August 4,
2007. Credit: ZUMA Press, Inc./Alamy Stock Photo.

loss. And the second. And the third. And etc. etc. until everyone is just
a jaded music critic in the bar right after the ugly light switches on. And
you're dancing too much to care.[23]

Journalist Marc Spitz similarly found the song's indictment of cool to be
both liberating and accusatory. "Once the elation wore off," he recalled, "you
realized that he was taking the piss. And there was no being a rock snob again
after that song … James Murphy reduced rock snobs like myself and himself to an utter cliché in eight minutes."[24] The track flourished among "rock
snobs" and hipsters alike, going on to be included amongst the top tracks of
the 2000s in lists compiled for *Pitchfork*, *Rolling Stone*, and *NME*.

Murphy, too, seemed to sense a danger in the nostalgia that permeated
New York City's culture in the early 2000s. Musicians increasingly turned to
the past for inspiration over the course of the decade, not only in their "little
jackets," as the song accuses, but in recycling sounds and beats, reissuing
albums and remastering box sets, and reuniting groups for world tours. As
Simon Reynolds writes:

The 2000s [had] been about every other previous decade happening
again all at once: a simultaneity of pop time that abolishes history while

nibbling away at the present's own sense of itself as an era with a distinct identity and feel.[25]

And the September 11th terrorist attacks were a turning point in this recirculation of the past in music, with the resurgence of musical experiences ranging from the sounds of the 1960s to cassette culture playing a pivotal role in the altered cultural landscape.[26]

It Comes Apart

The music of LCD Soundsystem was uniquely positioned within the post-9/11 music scene, when a desire to live with abandon and to experience the present contributed to a flourishing resurgence of dance music and synthpop.[27] Since the 1970s, dance was linked to self-actualization and agency through the body. Disco, the genre in which this was the most prominent, drew both applause and ire for this very reason; its association with Black and Brown queer bodies was a threat to white masculine supremacy.[28] Yet, despite the discursive battles being waged around the genre, disco's greatest power was in its ability to transcend words. "From the beginning," Tan Lin writes,

> it was *always better not to think*. As an operating system, disco is not, as is mistakenly thought, an explosion of sound onto the dance floor but an implosion of pre-programmed dance moves into a head. No one really listens to disco, not even the listener; it is passively absorbed by a brain connected to a dancing body.[29]

Raving has even been anecdotally trumpeted as a treatment for depression: dance cures all.[30] Tracks like "All My Friends," drawing on disco's characteristic four-on-the-floor kick drum and accented hi-hat strikes on the upbeat, enabled a dancer to get lost in the groove—to get caught up in the flow.[31] At the same time, however, the gritty percussive timbres and graininess of Murphy's voice clearly gesture to the post-punk dance music of the early 1980s. Murphy's taste in dance music, explored not through individual albums but rather through the experience of DJs and New York City clubs in the '90s, reflects a sort of nebulous imagined past in which Donna Summer and Gang of Four gyrated next to each other on the dance floor.

If, as the oft-cited platitude goes, "where words fail, music speaks," then one might irreligiously say that where music falls short, drugs make up the difference. For decades, popular music has been linked to drug use. Yet for many years, Murphy had avoided them (at least the harder ones) completely: the man was notoriously straightedge and, like many stridently indie rockers, found them uncool.[32] When he finally tried ecstasy at a party in the late 1990s, he had something of an epiphany:

> I was like, "Sure, I'll try [ecstasy]." I was just going to try it to try it, but then it was the greatest thing ever! It was fucking awesome and I was

dancing and I was happy and I had a revelation: this is actually me. I was fully me. I was dancing and I was fully conscious. I wasn't sloppy. I wasn't drunk. I was alert and I was aware that I really enjoyed dancing. "This is me dancing. This isn't the drugs dancing. This is the drugs stopping myself from stopping myself from dancing."[33]

The dance music of the past races into the present with "All My Friends." If in "Losing My Edge" Murphy had somewhat reluctantly accepted his age and maturity compared to the hip young Brooklynites, then in "All My Friends" he embraced it with both arms. More than any of the group's previous releases, *Sound of Silver* seemed to turn to earlier styles to illuminate the musical moment. "It's the album," argues critic Ryan Leas, "where LCD's retro behavior shifts from genres sitting next to each other in jarring and interesting ways into a blended monogenre."[34] In an early review in *Pitchfork*, Mark Pytlik went even further, saying the album was "as close to a perfect hybrid of dance and rock music's values as you're likely to ever hear."[35]

The track begins with a piano playing a pair of octaves and dyads (A and D) in both hands. The right hand beats a steady pulse, while the left stutters at moments. Rising in the mix, the bass jumps between octave As while sixteenth notes in the hi-hat begin to trace the beat measure by measure. Electric guitar comes in—once again reiterating the dichotomy between A and D—while reedy synths fill in the chords. The tonal center is somewhat ambiguous: A major seems the most likely culprit, but without any major cadential motion or resolutions, the D (a fourth above or fifth below, depending on your reading) casts uncertainty throughout.[36] The mix is heavy but agile: there are many moving parts joined in counterpoint, but the beat drives onward. The kick drum and initial piano pattern are all we need—everything else is ornamentation, welcome and evocative, but of ancillary importance to the visceral four-on-the-floor that Murphy manically pushes forward. This is music that combines the best of rhythm with the most fundamental of harmony: music that moves the body while standing still.

Murphy knows this. Falling on the backside of the beat, his words are both a call to action and a call to stasis. His lyrics seem to reinforce this lateness; he speaks of nights out and dancing until dawn, of parties with friends and strangers alike, yet at the same time showing his age through references to Pink Floyd ("Set controls for the heart of the sun") and reiterating his many years of experience.

This is music that you *feel* just as much as it makes you listen. Music for the body as much as it is for the mind. Murphy moves you, effortlessly, because he doesn't need to *try*. Whatever your drug of choice may be—controlled substances or the delirium that comes from being young, unafraid, and totally lost—there's a place for you in "All My Friends."

The dance floor is a purgatory, one, Murphy sings, that can knock you off your feet, lead you to stumble home, and destroy you in the most delightful and exhausting of ways.

"I wouldn't trade one stupid decision," he reflects, "for another five years of life."

Repetition is key to "All My Friends." Indeed, while some scholars have dismissed pop music's proclivity for repeating itself as a crutch for the uninspired, the process that unfolds over the track's seven-and-a-half minutes is a deeply pleasing one. The "process pleasure"—as the musicologist Luis-Manuel Garcia has called it—that comes from repetitive dance music is one that both prolongs and amplifies sensation.[37] For Murphy, repetitive rhythm, rather than melody or harmony, made a song powerful. "Lyrically and vocally," he told NPR's Terry Gross in a 2010 interview,

> I was never all that interested in melody or great voices, and musically, I was never that interested in chord changes. I always just liked to find something that kind of did one thing for a really long time and did it very well—or just had a physicalness to it that I really liked. … Just repetition and rhythm.[38]

He further elaborated on his austere compositional process in an interview with Red Bull Music Academy:

> I try not to put too much stuff in, and I try also to leave gaps. Like, usually in songs that's one of the reasons I like the intros and outros. My songs are not very short, typically. I don't get in and get out. I'm not nearly as obsessed with melodies and hooks and things that you're supposed to be thinking about. So a lot of times it'll be little elements in the beginning, or breakdowns where things can feature, so that I can feel satisfied that there's something to dig into and look at … So I try instead to let things [i.e., sounds] have their little lives, 'cause intimacy is what gets me. Physicality and intimacy is what gets me.[39]

Indeed, even at its most expansive, Murphy's music tends to develop gradually and additively. His song "45:33," which he wrote for the sportswear company Nike (despite not being a runner himself) in 2006, combines disco's repetitive rhythms with unending ambient drones reminiscent of Brian Eno.[40] The title, too, seems a not-so-subtle reference to John Cage's "4'33" (1952), a piece that requires the performer to remain totally silent for—you guessed it— four minutes and thirty-three seconds, leaving the listener to ponder only the sounds of his surroundings.[41] Nothing, perhaps, is as repetitive as the banal soundscape of everyday life.[42]

But everyday life tends to be loud, too. With the addition of each instrument into the mix, "All My Friends" grows increasingly louder; it's less a crescendo than it is a series of rising plateaus. But for Murphy, too, this process is crucial. Connecting sound with bodies, loudness is essential to his music. "I like to make sure we're not punishing anybody on those frequencies that hurt your ears," he recalled,

> but I do like the visceral, physical experience of bass when it's attached to the rest of the sounds. I think it's bodily. The first shows I saw were really bodily loud, and it was a really incredible experience for me. Like, your adrenaline goes up. You kind of have a fight or flight experience that can be maintained in a nice way by volume.[43]

For Murphy, this all comes back to the process he discovered with his first taste of ecstasy. "For me," he stated simply, "I need a certain amount of volume to turn the brain off."[44]

Throughout "All My Friends," loudness builds, steadily, jarringly. Chaotically. Eventually, volume succeeds and supersedes, trading repetition for decibels as the track's organizing principle. The song ends with a flurry of kick drums, hi-hats, brittle guitars, and soaring synths. The piano dyad, covered by noise, remains the only constant while Murphy, his voice increasingly hoarse, shouts his lamentations of friendship and aging. Then, as suddenly as the chaos began, it ends. The drums stop, the guitar rings, the synths take one last gasp. If the song's birth was slow—building from silence to order—then its death is fast. Chaos, the final screams of an aging man, cuts sharply to silence.

Reviews of the album capitalized on Murphy's age compared to his peers in the genre (lovingly called, by one reviewer, "disco-punk")[45]. One critic even went on to ask "how a chubby 'old' guy [Murphy] became king of the hipsters."[46] Yet the album was also universally praised for its ability to connect young Millennials with the previous generation. "By combining undeniably catchy beats with lyrics about regret, coolness and nostalgia," Gilbert Cruz remarked,

> Murphy has hit on a formula that appeals both to 20-somethings who just want to lose their bodies to the music and to their more dignified elders who are beginning to realize they won't be able to do the same for much longer.[47]

Perhaps even more abstractly, Murphy seems to have captured a particular moment of postmodern malaise.[48] The drugs are gone and the sun is coming up; morning gives the weary partier the chance to survey his destruction—to clean up the scraped knees and broken glass in between glasses of water and aspirin. Maybe he'll do it again tomorrow, maybe he won't. Today, though, friends or no friends, there's recognition of his mortality, tempered by a hangover.

Conclusion

Then, in 2008, everything changed. Not so much Murphy, of course; he still sits, dust-colored hair awry and with the general air of a wise elder. But as the nation reckoned with the financial crisis and subsequent recession, so too did the New York City music scene reckon with a new generation of indie groups. Vampire Weekend, a group formed by students at Columbia University, looked not to the past for musical inspiration as much as they did to places outside of New York: to rhythmic traditions from Latin America and the African continent, spurred on by drummer Chris Tomson's studies of world music and ethnomusicology. ("Cape Cod Kwassa Kwassa," from the group's 2008 debut, features a Congolese *kwassa kwassa* rhythm alongside lyrics about young, upper-middle-class white identity.)⁴⁹ Compared to its predecessors like LCD Soundsystem and the Strokes, Vampire Weekend's polished, erudite tunes about punctuation ("Oxford Comma") and French domestic architecture ("Mansard Roof") represented a pivot toward a hipsterdom that had an Ivy-League pedigree and wore Vineyard Vines polo shirts. "Vampire Weekend are a band of guys who went to college," observed music editor Jenny Eliscu, "and the Strokes are guys who didn't go to college."⁵⁰ It was a hipsterdom more Hamptons than Portland, more Upper East Side than Williamsburg.

Along with the new wave and disco rhythms, drug use—especially psychotropics—also fell out of fashion. "With millennials [as opposed to Generation X]," recalled Karen O of the Yeah Yeah Yeahs, "there's a big divide, a big divide. And I was right on the edge of that, but definitely falling into the 'angst-ridden, more sex in our entertainment' side of the divide."⁵¹ Vampire Weekend's frontman, Ezra Koenig, concurred: "When I picture people who consider getting fucked up on drugs or getting naked as some sort of rebellion, I picture people from my parents' generation, and it feels deeply boring and done."⁵²

Vampire Weekend were the kids Murphy feared were "coming up from behind." And while LCD Soundsystem would go on to release another album, *This Is Happening*, Murphy began to lose interest. The group announced that they were disbanding in February 2011. Two months later, at Madison Square Garden, they played their final show.

The kids, it seems, had finally caught up.

Except, much like his music, Murphy tends to ebb and flow with time. In December 2015, LCD Soundsystem released a deeply ironic Christmas single, and two years later their album *American Dream* dropped, swiftly becoming the number-one album in the United States.⁵³ With his typical self-loathing and introspection, Murphy anticipated a certain amount of discontent amongst his followers. He feared—perhaps rightfully so—that many would see the reunion as a sellout or way to cash in on indie nostalgia. "We're not just playing Coachella," he asserted.

> We're playing all over. We're not just having some reunion tour., We're releasing a record (sometime this year—still working on it, actually), so this isn't a victory lap or anything, which wouldn't be of much interest to us. This is just the bus full of substitute teachers back from their coffee break with new music and the same weird gear—or as much of it as we still have. … Thank fuck we were never skinny and young. Or at least

I wasn't. That always happens with bands. … They aren't fat when they come back, typically, just, I don't know, thicker. I was lucky to start this band kind of fat and old, so there's no, like, "look how YOUNG they were!" shit to even find on the internet.[54]

It's easy to picture Murphy, grey beard and sandy hair askew, smiling when he wrote the final sentence:

"I mean, we were younger and everything, but we weren't young, if you know what I mean."

Notes

1 "2007's Best Albums," *The Guardian*, December 7, 2007; The Wire, "Records of the Year," *The Wire*, December 2007, 37; Josh Tyrangiel, "Top 10 Albums of 2007," *Rolling Stone*, December 9, 2007.

2 Larissa Wodtke, "The Irony and the Ecstasy: The Queer Aging of Pet Shop Boys and LCD Soundsystem in Electronic Dance Music," *Dancecult* 11, no. 1 (2019), 30–52.

3 Note, for example, lyrics in the album's title track: "Sound of Silver, talk to me / Makes you want to feel like a teenager / Until you remember the feelings of / A real-life emotional teenager / Then you think again." For more on the tinfoil walls and inspiration behind the title, see Sophie Harris. "LCD Soundsystem's 'Sound of Silver': 10 Things You Didn't Know," *Rolling Stone*, March 12, 2007.

4 Stan Hawkins, "Feel the Beat Come Down: House Music as Rhetoric," in *Analyzing Popular Music*, ed. Allan F. Moore (Cambridge, UK: Cambridge University Press, 2003).

5 Sianne Ngai, *Our Aesthetic Categories: Zany, Cute, Interesting* (Cambridge, MA: Harvard University Press, 2012).

6 Simon Reynolds, *Retromania: Pop Culture's Addiction to Its Own Past* (New York, NY: Faber and Faber, 2011).

7 "James Murphy: The Man Behind LCD Soundsystem," *NPR*, June 21, 2010,

8 Lizzy Goodman, *Meet Me In the Bathroom: Rebirth and Rock and Roll in New York City, 2001-2011* (New York, NY: Harper Collins, 2017), 51.

9 Michaelangelo Matos, "Behind the Scenes at DFA: Jonathan Galkin," *Resident Advisor*, September 21, 2011.

10 Roger Lowenstein, *Origins of the Crash: The Great Bubble and Its Undoing* (New York, NY: Penguin, 2004).

11 Loretta Lees, "Super-Gentrification: The Case of Brooklyn Heights, New York City," *Urban Studies* 41, no. 12 (2003), 2487–509; Jason Hackworth, "Postrecession Gentrification in New York City," *Urban Affairs Review* 37, no. 2 (2002): 815–43.

12 Craig Calhoun, Paul Price, and Ashley Timmer, eds., *Understanding September 11* (New York, NY: The New Press, 2002).

13 Giuliani was even named *Time* magazine's "Person of the Year" in 2001. His revival was short lived, however. See Jack Newfield, "The Full Rudy: The Man, the Mayor, the Myth," *The Nation*, June 17, 2002.

14 John Bell, "Performance Studies in an Age of Terror," *The Drama Review* 47, no. 2 (2003).

15 Timothy Rice, Lorraine Hiromi Sakata, Nazir Jairazbhoy, and Ali Jihad Racy, "Musical Perspectives on Sept. 11: A Roundtable on Music, Community, Politics, and Violence," *Echo: A Music-Centered Journal* 3, no. 2 (2001); Gage Averill, "Soundly Organized Humanity," *Echo: A Music-Centered Journal* 3, no. 2 (2001); Jonathan Ritter and J. Martin Daughtry, eds., *Music in the Post-9/11 World* (New York, NY: Routledge, 2007).

16 Goodman, *Meet Me In the Bathroom*, 205.

17 Ibid., 206.

18 Ibid,, 282.

19 Ibid., 283.

20 Ibid., 287.

21 Sasha Frere-Jones, "Let's Dance," *The New Yorker*, May 3, 2010.

22 Josh Terry, "Stephen Malkmus Listens to LCD Soundsystem," *Noisey*, January 29, 2019.

23 Goodman, *Meet Me In the Bathroom*, 287.

24 Ibid., 289.

25 Reynolds, *Retromania*, x-xi.

26 See, for example, essays by Jeffrey Roessner, S. Todd Atchison, and Craig Eley in *The Politics of Post-9/11 Music: Sound, Trauma, and the Music Industry in the Time of Terror*, eds. Brian Flota, Joseph P. Fisher, Stan Hawkins, and Lori Burns (London: Taylor and Francis, 2011).

27 It's perhaps unsurprising that the rallying cry for many American teens in the late aughts was "YOLO": "You Only Live Once."

28 Steve Dahl, Dave Hockstra, and Paul Natkin, *Disco Demolition: The Night Disco Died* (Chicago, IL: Curbside Splendor, 2016). Although in his account Dahl downplays the racism and homophobia behind the event, both of these elements have been well documented in the intervening decades. See Tim Lawrence, *Love Saves the Day: A History of American Dance Culture, 1970-1979* (Durham, NC: Duke University Press, 2003); Alice Echols, *Hot Stuff: Disco and the Remaking of American Culture* (New York, NY: W.W. Norton, 2010); Peter Shapiro, *Turn the Beat Around,* 2nd edn. (New York, NY: Faber and Faber, 2007).

29 Tan Lin, "Disco as Operating System, Part One," *Criticism* 50, no. 1 (2008), 88.

30 Kieran Dahl, "How I'm Raving My Way Out of Depression," *Noisey*, April 10, 2017.

31 Mihaly Csikszentmihalyi, *Flow: The Psychology of Optimal Experience* (London: Harper Perennial Classics, 2008).

32 Goodman, *Meet Me In the Bathroom*, 65.

33 Ibid., 66.

34 Ryan Leas, *Sound of Silver* (New York, NY: Bloomsbury, 2018), 36.

35 Mark Pytlik, "LCD Soundsystem: Sound of Silver," *Pitchfork*, March 20, 2007.

36 Frere-Jones has pointed to this tension between A and D as elevating "All My Friends" to the top of Murphy's output. See Frere-Jones, "Let's Dance."

37 Luis-Manuel Garcia, "On and On: Repetition as Process and Pleasure in Electronic Dance Music," *Music Theory Online* 11, no. 4 (2005).

38 Terry Gross, "James Murphy: The Man Behind LCD Soundsystem," *Fresh Air*, June 21, 2010.

39 Todd L. Burns, "James Murphy Lecture for Red Bull Music Academy," *Red Bull Music Academy*, 2013.

40 John Burgess, "45'33"." *The Guardian*, November 15, 2007.
41 It's not surprising then that Murphy has sampled eminent minimalist composer Steve Reich in some of his remixes. See Martin Schneider, "LCD Soundsystem's James Murphy Folds Steve Reich into His Epic Bowie Remix," *Dangerous Minds*, November 12, 2013.
42 In an interview with Sasha Frere-Jones, Murphy recalled that "he wasn't necessarily thinking of [famed minimalist composer] Reich" while writing "All My Friends," but that "he doesn't mind the comparison." See Frere-Jones, "Let's Dance."
43 Gross, "James Murphy: The Man Behind LCD Soundsystem."
44 Ibid.
45 Nate Chinen, "Still Disco-Punk, Still Spoiling for a Fight," *The New York Times*, March 18, 2007.
46 Jody Rosen, "The End of LCD Soundsystem," *Slate*, April 4, 2011.
47 Gilbert Cruz, "All Yesterday's Parties," *Time*, May 24, 2010.
48 J. D. Connor, "Fiction in Review," *The Yale Review* 99, no. 1 (2011), 178–86.
49 Simon Reynolds has suggested that the world music genre-mixing characteristic of Vampire Weekend and similar groups also stems from the omnivorous listening practices of younger people who grew up with easy access to internet and song streaming. See Goodman, *Meet Me In the Bathroom*, 527.
50 Goodman, *Meet Me In the Bathroom*, 528–29.
51 Ibid., 548.
52 Ibid.
53 Sam Wolfson, "Why the Indie Band Never Dies: Fake Breakups, Permanent Adolescence, and Cash Comebacks." *The Guardian*, November 4, 2017.
54 James Murphy, "Let's Just Start This Thing Finally with Some Clarity," *LCD Soundsystem.com*, January 2016.

References

Averill, Gage. "Soundly Organized Humanity." *Echo: A Music-Centered Journal* 3, no. 2 (2001).
Bell, John. "Performance Studies In an Age of Terror." *The Drama Review* 47, no. 2 (2003).
Burgess, John. "45'33"." *The Guardian*, November 15, 2007.
Burns, Todd L. "James Murphy Lecture for Red Bull Music Academy." *Red Bull Music Academy*. 2013. www.redbullmusicacademy.com/lectures/james-murphy
Calhoun, Craig, Paul Price, and Ashley Timmer, eds. *Understanding September 11*. New York, NY: The New Press, 2002.
Chinen, Nate. "Still Disco-Punk, Still Spoiling for a Fight." *The New York Times*, March 18, 2007.
Connor, J.D. "Fiction in Review." *The Yale Review* 99, no. 1 (2011): 178–86.
Cruz, Gilbert. "All Yesterday's Parties." *Time*, May 24, 2010.
Csikszentmihalyi, Mihaly. *Flow: The Psychology of Optimal Experience*. London, United Kingdom: Harper Perennial Classics, 2008.
Dahl, Kieran. "How I'm Raving My Way Out of Depression." *Noisey*, April 10, 2017.
Dahl, Steve, Dave Hockstra, and Paul Natkin. *Disco Demolition: The Night Disco Died*. Chicago, IL: Curbside Splendor, 2016.

Echols, Alice. *Hot Stuff: Disco and the Remaking of American Culture*. New York, NY: W.W. Norton, 2010.

Flota, Brian, Joseph P. Fisher, Stan Hawkins, and Lori Burns, eds. *The Politics of Post-9/11 Music: Sound, Trauma, and the Music Industry in the Time of Terror*. London, United Kingdom: Taylor and Francis, 2011.

Frere-Jones, Sasha. "Let's Dance." *The New Yorker*, May 3, 2010.

Garcia, Luis-Manuel. "On and On: Repetition as Process and Pleasure in Electronic Dance Music." *Music Theory Online* 11, no.4 (2005).

Goodman, Lizzy. *Meet Me In the Bathroom: Rebirth and Rock and Roll in New York City, 2001-2011*. New York, NY: Harper Collins, 2017.

Gross, Terry. "James Murphy: The Man Behind LCD Soundsystem." *Fresh Air*, June 21, 2010.

Hackworth, Jason. "Postrecession Gentrification in New York City." *Urban Affairs Review* 37, no. 6 (2002): 815–43.

Harris, Sophie. "LCD Soundsystem's 'Sound of Silver': 10 Things You Didn't Know." *Rolling Stone*, March 12, 2017. www.rollingstone.com/feature/lcd-soundsystems-sound-of-silver-10-things-you-didnt-know-110495/

Hawkins, Stan. "Feel the Beat Come Down: House Music as Rhetoric." In *Analyzing Popular Music*, edited by Allan F. Moore. Cambridge, United Kingdom: Cambridge University Press, 2003.

Lawrence, Tim. *Love Saves the Day: A History of American Dance Culture, 1970-1979*. Durham, NC: Duke University Press, 2003.

Leas, Ryan. *Sound of Silver*. New York, NY: Bloomsbury, 2018.

Lees, Loretta. "Super-Gentrification: The Case of Brooklyn Heights, New York City." *Urban Studies* 41, no. 12 (2003):2487–509.

Lin, Tan. "Disco as Operating System, Part One." *Criticism* 50, no. 1 (2008).

Lowenstein, Roger. *Origins of the Crash: The Great Bubble and Its Undoing*. New York, NY: Penguin, 2004.

Matos, Michaelangelo. "Behind the Scenes at DFA: Jonathan Galkin." *Resident Advisor*, September 21, 2011. www.residentadvisor.net/features/1445

Murphy, James. "Let's Just Start This Thing Finally with Some Clarity." *LCD Soundsystem.com*, January 2016. https://lcdsoundsystem.com/2016/01/lets-just-start-this-thing-finally-with-some-clarity/

Newfield, Jack. "The Full Rudy: The Man, the Mayor, the Myth." *The Nation*, June 17, 2002. www.thenation.com/article/archive/full-rudy-man-mayor-myth/

Ngai, Sianne. *Our Aesthetic Categories: Zany, Cute, Interesting*. Cambridge, MA: Harvard University Press, 2012.

NPR. "James Murphy: The Man Behind LCD Soundsystem." *NPR*, June 21, 2010. www.npr.org/2010/06/21/127745800/james-murphy-the-man-behind-lcd-soundsystem

Pytlik, Mark. "LCD Soundsystem: Sound of Silver." *Pitchfork*, March 20, 2007. https://pitchfork.com/reviews/albums/10017-sound-of-silver/

Reynolds, Simon. *Retromania: Pop Culture's Addiction to Its Own Past*. New York, NY: Faber and Faber, 2011.

Rice, Timothy, Hiromi Sakata Lorraine, Nazir Jairazbhoy, and Ali Jihad Racy. "Musical Perspectives on Sept. 11: A Roundtable on Music, Community, Politics, and Violence." *Echo: A Music-Centered Journal* 3, no. 2 (2001). www.echo.ucla.edu/Volume3-issue2/sept11_roundtable/rice.html

Ritter, Jonathan and J. Martin Daughtry, eds.. *Music in the Post-9/11 World*. New York, NY: Routledge, 2007.

Rosen, Jody. "The End of LCD Soundsystem." *Slate*, April 4, 2011.

Schneider, Martin. "LCD Soundsystem's James Murphy Folds Steve Reich into His Epic Bowie Remix." *Dangerous Minds*, November 12, 2013. https://dangerousmi nds.net/comments/lcd_soundsystems_james_murphy_folds_steve_reich_into_his_ epic_bowie_remix

Shapiro, Peter. *Turn the Beat Around* (2nd ed.). New York, NY: Faber and Faber, 2007.

Terry, Josh. "Stephen Malkmus Listens to LCD Soundsystem." *Noisey*, January 29, 2019.

The Guardian. "2007's Best Albums." *The Guardian*, December 7, 2007.

The Wire. "Records of the Year." *The Wire*, December: 37, 2007.

Tyrangiel, Josh. "Top 10 Albums of 2007." *Rolling Stone*, December 9, 2007.

Wodtke, Larissa. "The Irony and the Ecstasy: The Queer Aging of Pet Shop Boys and LCD Soundsystem in Electronic Dance Music." *Dancecult* 11, no. 1 (2019):30–52.

Wolfson, Sam. "Why the Indie Band Never Dies: Fake Breakups, Permanent Adolescence, and Cash Comebacks." *The Guardian*, November 4, 2017. www. theguardian.com/music/2017/nov/04/why-indie-band-never-dies-fake-breakups- permanent-adolescence-cash-comebacks

16 MIA—"Paper Planes" (2007)

Asif Siddiqi

Introduction

A down-tempo hip-hop song sung with a world-weary wink about the travails of immigrant visas—both fake and real—MIA's "Paper Planes" distills a dizzying array of sensibilities and worldviews into three minutes and 24 seconds of chart-hopping (if not chart-topping) pop. "All I wanna do," she demands, "is to take your money," a sentiment that, combined with staccato gunshots in the chorus, told us that capital and coercion were part and parcel of the same package in the chaotic post-9/11 order. Alex Miller of the British weekly *New Musical Express* identified it as "the inheritor of the true rebel music in an era of corporate punks."[1] One of those songs that evoked a different meaning on each listen, it was a track, as many critics noted, of layers and layers, less a song than a musical mantra of the global dispossessed. *The Village Voice* opined about its "layers of implication," while Ann Powers in the *Los Angeles Times* highlighted its "multiple layers of meaning."[2] Reaching the top 20 in the UK and #4 in the *Billboard* "Hot 100," the song was rewarded with a triple-platinum certification by the Recording Industry Association of America (RIAA), and has to date sold over four million digital copies.[3]

The song also brought MIA—real name Maya Arulpragasam—firmly into the American popular imagination, where features in *People* magazine or guest stints in Super Bowl performances became *de rigueur*.[4] As the post-9/11 war on terror was peaking in the late-period Bush era, MIA seemed to be a cipher for something both glamorous and slightly discomfiting to white liberals who knew little if anything about the brutal decades-long civil war in Sri Lanka or her avowal of the Tamil Tigers, the violent separatist movement that had waged a brutal battle against the dominant majority in Sri Lanka. Her ethnicity (South Asian), her location (global), her politics (violent?), her nationality (British), and her look (glamorous) all played powerfully to the public. Like all modern celebrity stories, critical adulation and popular fandom were followed by a period of opprobrium. A *New York Times* piece by Lynn Hirschberg titled (ironically, no doubt) "MIA's Agitprop Pop" was, in many ways, an attempt to deflate her politics by revealing her as a shallow faux-revolutionary who married rich. Such media attention marked her slow

DOI: 10.4324/9781003093206-17

decline in the popular imagination from leading pop-star revolutionary to confused pretender, someone less attuned to the politics of refuge than the aesthetics of "refugee chic."[5]

In the past 15 years, MIA's work has been subjected to much critical analysis, spanning blog posts, think pieces, and exposés as well as academic meditations on the relation between aesthetics and radical politics.[6] Writers continue to chronicle her various skirmishes with record labels, the *New York Times* magazine, fellow pop stars, the National Football League, Julian Assange, the Grammys, Anderson Cooper, and a litany of actors spanning the liberal intelligentsia.[7] To a lesser extent, her musical legacy has also been revisited, partly as a result of her own self-fashioning spirit, through a recent documentary, *Matangi/Maya/M.I.A.*, which premiered at the Sundance Film Festival in 2018 and was directed by her colleague and friend Steve Loveridge.[8] As she claimed in interviews that all new music "sounds like what [her] and Kanye used to make," Stuart Berman at *Pitchfork* positioned her debut album *Arular* (2005) and the subsequent mix tape *Piracy Funds Terrorism* (2005) as both the connective tissue to a might-have-been era for feminist British pop and the future of a fully internet-grounded pop star of late 2010s. In framing MIA's early friendship with Justine Frischmann, guitarist for British '90s post-punkish rock band Elastica, Berman writes that "MIA's ascent mirrored that of Elastica's: an insurrectionary, feminist force shaking up the established pop order of the day."[9] If MIA has made her way back from cultural excommunication, her mark on the broader public imagination remains wedded to "Paper Planes," a song that, despite further controversies and public moments, remains her banner moment in the pop culture milieu.

But as much as "Paper Planes" seemed to point to a future—an incursion of pan-global pop into the American charts—it also reaches back into the past. The song's sonic palette was grounded in a repeated ten-second sample (four bars) lifted from the Clash's 1982 song "Straight to Hell," originally released as a single from their album *Combat Rock*. The fact that a major pop hit in the Americas and Europe was built around a pre-existing sample makes "Paper Planes" both unremarkable and part of a long lineage dating back to, for example, Vanilla Ice or MC Hammer. (Berman, in his article also explicitly locates the song in a lineage of sampling, but one connected to Elastica's Frischmann: "Both artists are, at heart, samplers: Elastica pillaged from the glam-rock and punk of their youth just as MIA did from her childhood soundtrack of '80s pop, hip-hop, and dancehall."[10]) What makes "Paper Planes" remarkable in the recent history of pop is that it stands at the confluence of three other currents: this was one of the first songs to showcase a woman of color whose ethnic identity was rooted in the global postcolonial South—"The sounds of third-world slums hammer at the gates of first-world pop," as a *Spin* writer noted[11]; it advanced, however obliquely, a kind of post-9/11 critique of the inextricable links between the neoliberal state and the war on terror; and it represented a kind of obverse of the type of sampling that had gotten many Euro-American artists in trouble over the unlicensed lifting of "global" sounds for Western pop music—practices often associated with a form of cultural appropriation. Here, MIA took the Clash from the West and into the world.

In *The Culture of the Copy* (1996), an extended meditation on the history of Western fascination with copies, simulacra, and facsimiles, cultural historian Hillel Schwartz touches briefly on digital sampling in pop music, suggesting that "sampling is what imperialists did when they colonized the 'underdeveloped' ... [but] sampling is [also] what ghettoized colonies do in revolt against property laws wired around them."[12] His placing of a technical artifact—the digital sampler—at the center of a contested terrain of creativity in pop music, and the foreshadowing of a "reverse sampling" embodied in "Paper Planes," raises some interesting questions about the always-moving relationship between creativity, authority, and sampling technology in modern pop. Schwartz's formulation suggests a kind of neutrality of the object itself, the sampler becoming political only as a function of the location of the user. But *à la* Langdon Winner and his oft-cited question "Do artifacts have politics?" can we probe deeper, beyond the obdurate reality of the sampler itself, to suggest that, regardless of social or cultural contexts, samplers *always* produce reordered cultural forms that are *political* in nature?[13] In other words, does the digital sampler always alter, reinforce, and/or subvert power relations?

In trying to explore this question, I unravel here several different narratives that focus on MIA's use of digital samplers. One story here, told through a dive into the history of digital sampling, looks at sampling and the ways in which we might conventionally imagine the sampler as a technical object that alters modes of creativity in pop music. There are a number of ways to approach this. First, we can imagine the inexpensive digital sampler (introduced in the 1980s) as a democratizing force in pop music, whereby creativity is brought to a much larger population, beyond elite white men in Europe or North America. Here, I am interested in how sampling reoriented conversations about creativity in Western pop music away from the heteronormative white male with traditional musical instruments—think the great classic rock icon with his guitar—to typically under-represented groups such as African Americans, women, and non-Westerners. Second, we can also think of the sampler in terms of its ability to produce "sonic quotations" of prior work. One oft-discussed form of political outcome of this has been, of course, how sampling, while democratizing the domain of pop music away from auteurs and virtuosos to the less formally trained, also creates modes of control rooted in racial and colonial inequalities. There are many, many examples of Western pop artists sampling sounds from the Global South, or white pop stars sampling beats from uncredited African American artists. Here, samplers are essentially instruments of cultural appropriation. Third, we can also think of the sampler as distributing authorship in the Western pop canon, essentially diluting the normative categories of author, performer, producer, and so forth into multiple overlapping registers. Finally, we can think of the sampler as a form of insurgent technology, one that is more obviously political because it destabilizes the economic relations of capitalism in terms of intellectual property. Essentially, the wide proliferation and use of digital samplers has forced massive multinational corporations to deploy tools to fight to defend what they see as their intellectual property.

In all of these ways, digital samplers have enabled disruptions to the normative order of pop. MIA's "Paper Planes" offers an interesting locus for all these claims, because the song represents a disruption of the normative order in pop: it is a megahit by a woman of color self-identified with a postcolonial context, a self-conscious nod to global rather than Western pop. Idioms collapse the song, even as idioms collapse *in* the song, all nailed to a backbeat and riff appropriated from the Clash song, one that itself (as I'll show later) was a direct critique of the left-behind violence of Western colonialism. The song, made on Apple computers and software, was issued into the world by Interscope Records, owned by Universal Music Group, which is part of Vivendi, the multinational and multi-billion-dollar corporation based in France. Was "Paper Planes" a classic case of a digital sampler allowing the subaltern to imagine empowerment while in fact reproducing the old social order of creativity wherein power, money, and credit continue to reside where they always have, in large corporations identified with elite white Europeans? Or was "Paper Planes" something else, perhaps a small gesture that literally made history?

Sampling History

So, first a short diversion into the history of sampling. Conceptually, what the sampler does is uncomplicated. In contrast to "real" musical instruments which generate new sounds, samplers record discrete pieces of sound into digital memory, which can then be reconstructed, altered, damaged, and saved as a new replicable clip, which itself can then, at the push of a button, be overlayed onto other musical pieces. In essence, the person using the sampler could record audio from one source and dub that segment onto completely different other ones, what the musicologist and composer R. Murray Schafer has called "schizophonia," that is, the splitting of sounds from their sources.[14] Placed within the long history of musical borrowing, musical sampling has a genealogy dating back centuries in the Western tradition, with composers quoting antecedent works freely. But electronic sampling was qualitatively different; as Mark Katz has pointed out, if "traditional musical quotations typically cite works ... samples cite *performances.*"[15]

In the modern era, we can trace sampling practices to the early twentieth century with electromagnetic recording techniques and photoelectric sampling (on optical discs). After World War II (and largely enabled by the availability of high-performance recording tape), sampling was pioneered by avant-garde musicians such as John Cage, who in the early 1950s used eight layers of extracts from a combination of 42 vinyl records to produce a new piece, *Imaginary Landscape No. 5.*[16] In the 1960s and '70s, a number of popular artists, such as Lee "Scratch" Perry, Gavin Bryer, and Holger Czukay (of the band Can), adopted similar tape-based practices, culminating, at least in the pop imagination, with Brian Eno and David Byrne's much-lauded *My Life in the Bush of Ghosts* from 1981. Eno and Byrne essentially took a suite of samples from field recordings by anthropologists made in the 1970s in North Africa and the Middle East and overlayed them on to often-live ensemble playing.[17] In doing so, the album generated a wealth of discussion about the location of authenticity in music, partly because sampling allowed musicians to "drop in" sounds (and voices) from postcolonial spaces removed from context, history, and global inequality.[18] Some argued that this was colonialism in a different form.

Digital sampling became common in Anglo and American charts by the late 1980s, wherein songs built entirely from the sounds of other records—such as "Pump Up the Volume" by M/A/R/R/S—would barely raise an eyebrow. These pop songs privileged collage over linear context, embodying what of-the-time thinkers such as Fredric Jameson and Jean Baudrillard were calling both pastiche and postmodern. We were left with a kind of "depthlessness" whereby the basic mooring codes of cultural production were dislodged from time and space and jumbled into new and unrecognizable forms.[19]

In terms of the artifact itself, the first commercially available samplers included Computer Music Inc.'s Melodian, developed in 1976 and first used by Stevie Wonder, and Fairlight's CMI, introduced in 1979. Their cost (roughly $18,000 in 1980 dollars) made them prohibitively expensive for most musicians, but by the mid-to-late 1980s, new models brought sampling out of professional studios and into households, particularly as digital sampling features were incorporated into standard home-use keyboards.[20] The SP-1200, produced by E-mu systems and introduced in 1987, had a massive influence on the soundscapes of the first generation of hip-hop and electronic dance music, but it also exemplified one of the striking features of the expansion of digital computing instruments into modern pop: "creative subversion," that is, the ability and agency of the user to subvert and repurpose the original intent of the machines.[21] Originally designed as a drum machine, hip-hop producers in the late 1980s, taking creative agency into their own hands, repurposed the SP-1200 as a sampler that could create aggressive breakbeats and loops—each sample 2.5 seconds long—that gave foundation to a generation of hip-hop.[22] And because the sampling rate was relatively low (about half of that of a regular compact disc), it transformed original sounds into unexpectedly "gritty" sonic bits.[23] Many hip-hop producers sampled 33½ records at 45 RPM to increase the length of the sample, and then lowered the pitch by using built-in functions. The SP-1200's portability and relatively low cost gave producers, DJs, and rap artists the ability to create an entire track on a single machine, which could then be taped to cassette (another cheap distribution mechanism) and shared among communities. Most critically, cheap samplers allowed hip-hop artists and then rave DJs to summon past sounds previously consigned to obscurity and position them in new contexts.

By the early '90s, with an explosion of sampled music circulating on semi-official mix tapes, at rave parties, and in the pop charts, digital samplers had, in theory at least, subverted conventional notions of a sole authorial voice in popular music. Instead, music made with disembodied samples highlighted a more communal experience wherein not only enjoyment but creativity itself would be distributed.[24] Anthropologist Georgina Born has described how the "the ontology of the [traditional] musical work envisions a hierarchical assemblage" of composer over performer and performer over listener; but, she argues, the advent of "electronic and digital technologies [such as samplers] afford and enhance a dispersed and collaborative creativity."[25] If some panicked that this was a "crisis of authorship," I would argue it was a less malevolent *social distribution of creative agency* which allocated creative agency to be spread through space and time, including, in the case of hip-hop artists, to those who were economically or racially disenfranchised, made possible due to the mass production (and concomitant cheapness) of samplers, keyboards, and drum machines.[26]

Missing in Action

So where does that leave "Paper Planes"? MIA's road to "Paper Planes" came through a number of technical artifacts, including Roland's MC-505 Groovebox, principally a drum machine but incorporating other cognate features such as the ability to sequence music and program specific patterns of sounds. Introduced into the market in 1998, the MC-505 was, in technical terms, not a sampler, but in its ability to repeat and reproduce pre-recorded beats (encoded into the system at the time of purchase) which then could be re- and de-assembled by the user into mesmerizing repeated patterns, it functioned as such. A cover story in a 1998 issue of *Future Music*, the British newsstand magazine devoted to sequencers, samplers, and beatboxes, asked "Is Roland's new MC-505 the answer to all your dance floor dreams?"[27] For MIA, apparently so: the MC-505 was the foundation for MIA's debut album *Arular*, which combined an ebullient mix of hip-hop, dancehall, and grime. Songs such as "Galang" and "Sunshowers" (built around a prominent sample from the 1976 song "Sunshower" by Dr. Buzzard's Original Savannah Band) suggested a minimalist DIY approach to authorship and songcraft, grounded in hip-hop but with a face turned towards the club world.

By the time MIA arrived at her second album, *Kala*, her early fame, given charge through the early 2000s world of blogs and Myspace, was evolving into a different beast, and her mark on the cultural zeitgeist expanded beyond the world of bellwethers such as *Pitchfork* and into the *New York Times* and NPR (see Figure 16.1). Her advent into Middle America was helped by "Paper Planes," which soundtracked the trailer for the movie *Pineapple Express* (2008, Dir: David Gordon Green) and then was actually featured in *Slumdog Millionaire* (2008, Dir: Danny Boyle), winner of a host of Academy Awards, including Best Picture. As the song surged into the pop imagination, the hook

Figure 16.1 MIA at the Connect Music Festival in Argyll, Scotland, on September 2, 2007. Credit: Ben Collins/Alamy Stock Photo.

here was a combination of glamour, politics, and the global, each defined in amorphous and slippery ways, but with just enough coagulation to appeal to the American middle.

If you heard the lyrics of "Paper Planes" when it came out, they tumbled out in disconnected bits, but the story seemed to speak of immigrants trafficking in fake visas ("I fly like paper / get high like planes / if you catch me at the border / I got visas in my name / If you come around here / I make 'em all day"). The Third World looms large here in the daily rituals of immigrants and refugees in America fleeing from unspecific war-torn areas. She explained the genesis of the song in an interview for *Fader* in 2007 before the arrival of the album:

I actually recorded that in Brooklyn, in Bed-Stuy. I was thinking about living there, waking up every morning—it's such an African neighborhood. I was going to get patties at my local and just thinking that really the worst thing that anyone can say is some shit like "What I wanna do is come and get your money." People don't really feel like immigrants or refugees contribute to culture in a way. That they're just leeches that such from whatever. So in the song I say "All I wanna do is [sound of gun shooting and reloading, cash register opening] and take your money." I did it in sound effects. It's up to you how you want to interpret [it]. America is so obsessed with money. I'm sure they'll get it.[28]

These themes are foregrounded much more explicitly in the video for the song, which undoubtedly helped to promote it more than any other media, despite, (amazingly) MTV's censorship of a reference to marijuana, and more strikingly, the blanking out the gunshot sounds that punctuate the chorus. The video—directed by Bernard Gourley and largely shot where MIA had recorded the track, in Brooklyn's largely African American Bedford-Stuyvesant (or Bed-Stuy) neighborhood—shows MIA selling food from vans. We see scenes of the commercial fabric of immigrant life—working in food trucks, selling chains, watches, pirate videos, and dealing in cash. Nigerian rapper Afrikan Boy makes an appearance. as do two of the Beastie Boys. There's an aspect of swindle—playing the game, skirting the law, making a life—hovering over the video that makes the song just laden enough with universality to transcend the particulars. It's a critique from a British-Sri Lankan rapper who had trouble getting visas to the visit the United States, but it's also about the wizened immigrant who understands that what America does best is trade bullets for dollars, in the warzone and in the urban zone. It's capitalism's inevitable end point in the age of the war on terror.

"Paper Planes," and the rest of the album *Kala*, was co-produced by MIA and Switch (real name David Taylor), a British house DJ who used as the principal technical artifact a software program, Logic Pro (about $250), designed by Apple and produced for use on its computers. Like all modern "digital audio workstations," Logic Pro essentially converts a conventional desktop or laptop computer into a recording studio, including the ability to play musical instruments, generate audio effects and instrumental loops, score musical notation, and, of course, sample sounds. Although MIA and Switch used Logic Pro on a MacBook Pro (along with more traditional drum machines such as the Roland TR-909) to create the entire album, as MIA and others have repeatedly pointed out, there was much real-world collaboration beyond the studio. Among other places, MIA and Switch traveled to and recorded with individuals, ensembles, and street musicians in India, Trinidad, Jamaica, St. Vincent, Liberia, Australia, and Japan. Lily Moayeri, in an account published in *Electronic Musician* during the recording of *Kala*, describes these adventures in real-world sounds as an engagement with the "authentic":

[MIA's] proximity to authentic indigenous sounds in India sparked her latent knowledge about her native temple drums. Accompanied by her brother, she started meeting people and developing a network of musicians. Not restricting herself to professionals, the enthusiastic [MIA] corralled any person off the street who had something to contribute sonically.[29]

Field recordings were then made into the finished product, as on the song "Jimmy," which features bits and pieces of live drummers recorded in Chennai, India:

> Once the raw drum sounds were recorded, [MIA] and Switch would go through each track individually to find roughly half a dozen loops to single out. Following that, the drums were layered on top of each other so they could interact in a different way than the way they were originally played, still keeping the live feel intact. From these raw tracks, [MIA] and Switch created their new rhythms, paying particular attention to the bottom end, which comes from drum sounds rather than bass instruments/synths … the duo used Apple Logic Audio 7.2's host plug-ins for processing, tuning, compressing and EQing the drums.[30]

These real-world "plug-ins" for *Kala* (including on "Paper Planes") suggest a search for authenticity on MIA's part, the kind of authenticity that had been reformulated and de-emphasized by samplers and audio software. I don't want to get into a lengthy discussion about authenticity in modern pop— it's a well-worn topic that has generated a deluge of scholarly and journalistic meditations[31]—but it's remarkable how the principal animating issue in accounts of MIA's "Paper Planes" is the fact that it is built on a sample of a Clash song, sampled and recorded through a technical artifact, an Apple computer using Logic Pro. Here, the technology produces conditions (fakery, dissimulation) that require a kind of pre-emptive correction by, in this case, the artist's physical presence at the source of the sound. In other words, MIA's music was built on a combination of samples (fakery) rendered by a technical object (the sampler). This was counterposed to her own travels and encounters with musicians in "authentic" milieus. Each required the other in how she crafted her identity.

Of course, not all pop stars who use samplers and digital audio workstations care about accessing the source or privileging some notion of authentic sound. Well-known artists such as Girl Talk (the Pittsburgh artist whose real name is Gregg Gillis) or the Australian band the Avalanches have built entire albums (and careers) on music made entirely from samples. For them, the logic is one that actively dissimulates and delinks from the source so that there is no foundation. But MIA's position, I think, is different. The fact that she is not coded white or Euro-American or male but rather represents a kind of "global"— or more precisely, postcolonial—politics at odds with most pop stars puts a higher burden on her to legitimize her work. That legitimacy can come from many sources, one of which is a claim to an "authentic" source for her identity as a musician and a global citizen.

Within the framework that I've outlined so far—digital samplers as desta-bilizing traditional forms of creativity and authorship—MIA's case seems to point to a different kind of politics. In the many interviews she gave after *Kala* and into her "backlash" years, she came equipped with a defensive-ness cultivated after years of ironic derision, particularly of her politics. A common dismissive charge often leveled by British journalists was that she represented a kind of "terrorist chic" for explicitly and vocally supporting the often-violent Tamil independence movement in Sri Lanka. She represented, it was said, the distillation and culmination of hipster activism.[32] Her defen-siveness was couched in claims to authenticity: she emphasized her father's involvement with the Tamil Tigers, her experience of violence as a child, and her rootedness in a postcolonial nowhere, all of which gave her a potent understanding, she implied, of the inequalities, exploitations, and violence that dog a postcolonial subject besieged by the twin attacks of neoliberal cap-ital and imperial violence. She was required to repeat claims of fealty to some ineffable "politics" in her interviews, but also in her music, her comportment, her life, her boyfriends, her husband, her location, all because we demand more from someone outside the pop norm. If the technologies of sampling freed a generation of hip-hop and electronic artists, they also hobbled others in "global" locations with a higher burden; in MIA's case, they destabilized her claims to authorship and creativity precisely because she was a woman of color from "another" context. If she had remained obscure, on the margins of global pop, perhaps these questions would not register, but they dogged her everywhere precisely because she had become a product of the global capit-alist marketing system of pop.

Her defensiveness was also played out in the relationship between gender and technology. During MIA's brief flash into the universe of media coverage, journalists and writers frequently paid attention to the production of "Paper Planes," imagining the studio as a space of creativity, and invariably attributed a passive role to MIA herself, giving credit instead to other *male* collaborators, particularly the Philadelphia-based DJ Diplo, who was so often given credit for the manipulation of studio technology that MIA repeatedly and in public had to counter these claims about the importance of her own authorial and creative agency.[33] In a contentious exchange with *Pitchfork*, she excoriated the interviewer when the questions veered to Diplo:

> And I just find it a bit upsetting and kind of insulting that I can't have any ideas on my own because I'm female or that people from under-developed countries can't have ideas of their own unless it's backed up by someone who's blond-haired and blue-eyed. After the first time, it's cool, the second time it's cool, but after the third, fourth, fifth time, maybe it's an issue that we need to talk about, maybe that's something important, you know.[34]

She added, "There is an issue especially with what male journalists write about me and say 'this MUST have come from a guy'."[35] This was a trend dating back to her earlier work with the Roland MC-505 on *Arular*. In descriptions of that bedroom-made album, the press were quick to distribute creative agency; one journalist wrote that "[a] large coterie of producers and engineers worked on her 2005 debut, *Arular*, but it still had the euphoric feel of a novice punching buttons."[36]

It's worth noting that Diplo claimed to have brought the original Clash riff from "Straight to Hell" to her attention—she never commented on this— thus ensuring an author credit on the song, although the lyrics, the production, the arrangement, and the video essentially belonged to MIA. Here, we should not be surprised to see the authorial role as one that is ordered not only along Western, racialized, and class lines but also along gender lines. When aesthetics are fused with the manipulation of technical artifacts, as with MIA.'s "Paper Planes," the domain of creativity becomes reflexively male.[37] In other words, the availability and use of inexpensive digital samplers here both empowered a voice previously marginalized while at the same time, through our unquestioned assumption that the technical is a fundamentally male domain, reinforcing prevailing and existing gendered social orders in the popular imagination. Here, the sampler acts as a political artifact, but one that reinforces the gender order instead of disrupting it.

A second point about the politics of "Paper Planes" bears on the issue of copying. Here, we might invoke Walter Benjamin's "The Work of Art in the Age of Mechanical Reproduction," wherein he argued that, as the increased ability to reproduce art became pervasive, we lost some ineffable "aura" of the original, even in the case of exact reproductions. This was both a point of lament for Benjamin and a vehicle for hope since the technology of copying could cultivate a kind of mass cultural literacy.[38]

As I have noted, the principal sample that MIA used is from a fairly well-known song, "Straight to Hell" by the British punk band the Clash, one of the leading lights of the original wave of punk but also a group that had taken increasing sonic risks in the late 1970s, moving quickly from Ramones-like guitar attacks to a frenetic voyage over a three-to-four year period into idioms such as dub, reggae, ska, dancehall, and rap. They positioned themselves as champions of an outsider and outlaw ethic; calling their 1980 triple-album *Sandinista!*, the Clash took on the contradictions of capitalism with little care for irony or accusations of hypocrisy—a kind of antecedent to MIA herself. "Straight to Hell" is a song, like "Paper Planes," about American empire, but its message is deeply ambivalent: it's a story of a child fathered and then abandoned by an American GI while in Vietnam. It pinpoints the vain hope of a young person, literally a child of American imperialism, whose home is nowhere, now part of a global migration displaced by the Cold War.

MIA's sampling of the Clash song works on two levels. First, there is the literal copying of the Clash riff into a new musical creation whereby creative agency is distributed among disparate actors—all the members of the Clash are, in fact, credited as authors of "Paper Planes" as per legal edicts coming down from a team of intellectual property lawyers representing CBS, the company that owns the Clash's canon. This is the politics of sampling that deploys the neoliberal capitalist order to stabilize what has been rendered unstable by the use of sampling technology.

The second level is the one that, I think, is more important, as it is about producing history for those without history. Let me explain. Copying the Clash's original meditation on the human cost of the Cold War in the Third World invokes what we might think of as "a sonic quotation" (a phrase originally used by musicologist Paul Harkins to describe one of the tools available to producers when they build songs piece by piece in a studio).[39] As with writers and historians who liberally quote from prior works, by analogy, hip-hop artists using the digital sampler invoke, echo, and cite earlier artists through mechanical reproduction. MIA's citation of the Clash serves both a musical purpose and a political one, for her message regarding the vagaries of disaffections caused by globalization is now situated in a longer *historical* genealogy of anti-colonial critique. Here, digital sampling allows artists to *create their own history*, to give context to struggles frequently defined by the powerful as ahistorical or irrational. Sampling, here, is thus not only a mode of copying but is also mode of world-building, a mode of history-writing for those who were never allowed a history.

History

More than a decade after "Paper Planes," MIA was again in the public eye, this time as the principal subject of the documentary *Matangi/Maya/M.I.A.*, directed by Steve Loveridge. The film, constructed from 700 hours of film shot over 22 years by MIA herself that she handed over to her longtime friend Loveridge, presents a kind of coherent narrative about the life of the artist. Contrary to expectations, Loveridge used most of the MIA-filmed footage to focus mostly on her early life outside of the music industry, including her upbringing, her family's emigration to the UK, and her stance on her father's political activism. The lack of substantial material on her career as a musician and performer was the source of some friction between MIA and Loveridge. She told *Billboard* that:

> He took all of my cool out. He took all the shows where I look good and tossed it in a bin. Eventually, if you squash all the music together from the film, it makes for about four minutes. I didn't know that my music wouldn't really be a part of this. I find that to be a little hard, because that is my life. It's not the film that I would have made.[40]

More to the point, as with "Paper Planes," hovering over the new documentary were issues of authorship. The film used MIA's own footage, but she received no directorial credit, a point raised by some reviewers.[41] The optics were hard to avoid: a white male taking credit for depicting and shaping the life of a highly accomplished woman of color in a cultural arena where women had to continually fight for attribution.

Yet, there was also some level of reassessment of MIA's legacy. In a 2018 feature on NPR on "the 200 Greatest Songs by 21st Century Women+," [sic] the standard bearers of the white liberal Starbucks set seemed to feel the need for some recalibration, putting MIA's "Paper Planes" at number one, ahead of Adele, Beyoncé, Janelle Monaé, Nicki Minaj, and Lana Del Rey.[42] MIA responded with a statement of gratitude, but also with the kind of surprise that many people of color will recognize: "I've never come first at anything." She added, "To me it's so layered. And it did represent a time where we had the financial crisis and also the immigrant stuff, and also it's about sort of mixing genres."[43]

Beyond mixing genres, MIA was also destabilizing them. And this is where the act of sampling goes beyond the mundane and prosaic. From its arrival into pop music, the digital sampler produced, shaped, reinforced, and subverted certain political formations of power. Readily available from the late '80s due to capitalist markets and the profit motive, the sampler enabled a kind of democratization of musical production which itself then destabilized established notions of the "original" and the "copy." The original destabilization worked on a number of levels: samplers democratized creativity for those who were outside of the world of virtuosos with guitars; it allowed Western pop artists to drop sounds from the Global South without visiting the site of their theft; it destabilized conventional notions of authorship; and it helped rear up an industry of lawyers to chase after violations of intellectual property.

But in a track like "Paper Planes," the destabilization is ambivalent, revealing dual and conflicting political formations. On the one hand, the original subversion of the sampler—as a democratizing force for the dispossessed—is itself thwarted: instead of freeing the artist, MIA is forced to make all sorts of claims to "authenticity" in the face of accusations of false politics or inept technical acumen. These were undoubtedly gender-coded and color-coded in tone. Add in the neoliberal capacity to commodify resistance to empire, and we see the sampler, through "Paper Planes," reifying the very male imperial order of America in the post-9/11 world of George W. Bush. But there is another side, and this is a hopeful one: the cheap digital sampler allows those from disenfranchised, marginalized, and exploited global communities to fight against capitalism's power to negate history; the digital sampler here is not simply a musical instrument, a technical artifact, it also becomes, as MIA shows in "Paper Planes," a tool for writing and rewriting history for those for whom history has always been written by others. Now we write our own history.

Notes

1 Alex Miller, "Mia: Kala," *NME*, September 6, 2007.
2 Tom Breihan, "M.I.A. and the Double Standard of MTV Censorship," *The Village Voice*, December 18, 2007;Ann Powers, "Third World Beats,"*Los Angeles Times*, August 20, 2007. www.latimes.com/archives/la-xpm-2007-aug-20-et-mia20-story.html
3 RIAA, "Gold & Platinum – RIAA,"www.riaa.com/gold-platinum/?tab_active= default-award&ar=M.I.A.&ti=Paper+Planes#search_section
4 People, "Rapper M.I.A. Says Pregnancy Makes Her 'Less Angry'," *People*, December 2, 2008. https://people.com/celebrity/rapper-m-i-a-says-pregnancy-makes-her-less-angry/
5 Lynn Hirschberg, "M.I.A.'s Agitprop Pop," *The New York Times Magazine*, May 25, 2010. www.nytimes.com/2010/05/30/magazine/30mia-t.html.
6 Anamik Saha, "Locating MIA: 'Race', commodification and the politics of production," *European Journal of Cultural Studies* 15, no. 6 (2012): 736–52; Lisa Weems, "Refuting 'Refugee Chic': Transnational Girl(hood)s and the Guerilla Pedagogy of M.I.A.," *Feminist Transformations* 26, no. 1 (Spring 2014): 115–42.
7 A useful summation here: Marc Hogan, "M.I.A. vs. the System: A Complete Timeline of Her Controversies," *Pitchfork*, May 26, 2016. https://pitchfork.com/thepitch/1165-mia-vs-the-system-a-complete-timeline-of-her-controversies/
8 Steve Loveridge, dir. Matangi/Maya/M.I.A. New York: Cinereach, 2018.
9 Stuart Berman, "The Connection is Made: Elastica Goes M.I.A." *Pitchfork*, February 26, 2015. https://pitchfork.com/features/article/9602-the-connection-is-made-elastica-goes-mia/
10 Berman, "The Connection is Made."
11 Jon Dolan, "Deconstructing M.I.A." *Spin*, February 6, 2012. www.spin.com/2012/02/deconstructing-mia/
12 Hillel Schwartz, *The Culture of the Copy: Striking Likenesses, Unreasonable Facsimiles* (New York: Zone Books, 1996), 310.
13 Langdon Winner, *The Whale and the Reactor: A Search for Limits in an Age of High Technology* (Chicago, IL: University of Chicago Press, 1986), 19–39
14 The ethnomusicologist Steven Feld has invoked this term in some of his work to refer to how sound recordings can move in circuits and networks of actors and become recontextualized and resignified into different meanings. For the original, see R. Murray Schafer, *The Tuning of the World* (New York: A. A. Knopf, 1977).
15 Mark Katz, *Capturing Sound: How Technology Has Changed Music* (Berkeley: University of California Press, 2004), 141. Emphasis mine.
16 Hugh Davies, "A history of sampling," *Organised Sound* 1, no. 1 (April 1966): 3–11.
17 Asif Siddiqi, "Technology, Transcultural Idioms, and the Question of Authenticity: Brian Eno and David Byrne in the Studio" in *Creativity: Technology and Music*, eds. Hans-Joachim Braun and Susan Schmidt Horning, 187–207 (New York: Peter Lang, 2012).
18 Steven Feld and Annemette Kirkegaard, "Entangled Complicities in the Prehistory of 'World Music'; Poul Rovsing Olsen and Jean Jenkins Encounter Brian Eno and David Byrne in the Bush of Ghosts," *Popular Musicology Online*, 2010. www.popular-musicology-online.com/issues/04/feld.html
19 Fredric Jameson, *Postmodernism, or the Cultural Logic of Late Capitalism* (Durham, NC: Duke University Press, 1991); Jean Baudrillard, *Simulacra and Simulation* (Ann Arbor, MI: University of Michigan Press, 1994).

20 See for example, Paul Gilby, "The Sound on Sound guide to samplers," *Sound on Sound* (November 1987): 34–40. The magazine *Keyboard* devoted special issues solely to sampling in March 1989 and August 1994.

21 Bill Brewster and Frank Broughton, *Last Night a DJ Saved My Life* (New York: Grove Press, 2000), 315; Jon Pareles, "Digital Technology Changing Music," *New York Times*, October 16, 1986.

22 Rosie Swash, "The SP-1200 sampler changes everything," *The Guardian*, June 12, 2011. www.theguardian.com/music/2011/jun/13/music-sampler-sp-1200; Primus Luta, "The Blue Notes of Sampling," *Sound Studies* (blog), (n.d.). https://sound studiesblog.com/2014/04/07/the-blue-notes-of-sampling/; David McNamee, "Hey, what's that sound: Sampler," *The Guardian*, September 28, 2009. www.theguard ian.com/music/2009/sep/28/whats-that-sound-sampler

23 Ben Detrick, "The Dirty Heartbeat of the Golden Age," *The Village Voice*, November 6, 2007. www.villagevoice.com/2007/11/06/the-dirty-heartbeat-of-the-golden-age/

24 For a useful summary of a theoretical approach to distributed creativity, see R. Keith Sawyer and Stacy DeZutter, "Distributed creativity: How collective creations emerge from collaboration," *Psychology of Aesthetics, Creativity and the Arts* 3, no. 2 (2009): 81–92.

25 Georgina Born, "On musical Mediation: Ontology, Technology and Creativity," *Twentieth-Century Music* 2, no. 1 (2005): 7–36 (see especially, 25–6).

26 "Crisis of authorship" is from Andrew Goodwin, "Sample and hold: pop music in the digital age of reproduction," *Critical Quarterly* 30, no. 3 (1988): 34–49.

27 Matt Overton, "Groove is in the art," *Future Music* 68 (April 1998): 20–4.

28 FADER, "Video+Interview: MIA, 'Jimmy'," *FADER*, August 7, 2007. www.thefa der.com/2007/08/07/video-interview-mia-jimmy

29 Lily Moayeri, "Out on a Whim," *EM*, September 1, 2007.

30 Moayeri, "Out on a Whim."

31 R. A. Peterson, *Creating Country Music: Fabricating authenticity* (Chicago: University of Chicago Press, 1997); H. Barker & Y. Taylor, *Faking It: The quest for authenticity in popular music* (New York: W. W. Norton, 2007).

32 J. Griffith Rollefson, *Flip the Script: European Hip Hop and the Politics of Postcoloniality* (Chicago: University Of Chicago Press, 2017), 93–138.

33 Candice Haddad, "Immigration, Authorship, Censorship and Terrorism: The Politics of M.I.A.'s US Crossover" in *In the Limelight and Under the Microscope: Forms and Functions of Female Celebrity*, eds. Su Holmes and Diane Negra (New York: Continuum Books, 2011), 280–302.

34 Paul Thomson, "M.I.A. Confronts the Haters," *Pitchfork*, August 3, 2007. https:// pitchfork.com/news/27349-mia-confronts-the-haters/

35 Thomson, "M.I.A. Confronts the Haters."

36 Jon Dolan, "Deconstructing M.I.A."

37 B. D. Herman, "Scratching out Authorship: Representations of the Electronic Music DJ at the Turn of the 21st Century," *Popular Communication* 4, no. 1 (2006): 21–38.

38 Walter Benjamin, "The Work of Art in the Age of Mechanical Reproduction" in *Illuminations*, ed. Hannah Arendt (London: Fontana, 1968), 217–252.

39 Paul Harkins, "Microsampling: From Akufen's Microhouse to Todd Edwards and the Sound of UK Garage" in M*usical Rhythm in the Age of Digital Reproduction*, ed. Anne Danielsen (London: Routledge, 2010), 177–94.

40 Andreas Hale, "M.I.A. Wrestles with Sundance Doc 'MATANGI / MAYA / M.I.A.': 'It's not the Film That I Would Have Made," *Billboard*, January 25, 2018. www.billboard.com/articles/news/8096118/matangi-maya-mia-interview-sunda nce-documentary
41 Charlie Phillips, "Matangi/Maya/MIA review—combative musician shows she is director of own life," *The Guardian*, January 24, 2018. www.theguardian.com/film/ 2018/jan/24/matangi-maya-mia-review-musician-film-tamil-sri-lanka-sundance
42 NPR, "The 200 Greatest Songs by 21st Century Women+," *National Public Radio*, July 30, 2018. www.npr.org/2018/07/30/627400055/turning-the-tables-the-200- greatest-songs-by-21st-century-women-part-10
43 Kristy Guilbault, "'It's Amazing How It Stood The Test of Time': M.I.A. On 'Paper Planes' 11 Years Later," *National Public Radio*, October 4, 2018. www.npr. org/2018/10/04/652687578/it-s-amazing-how-it-stood-the-test-of-time-m-i-a-on- paper-planes-11-years-later

Bibliography

Barker, H. & Y.Taylor. *Faking it: The quest for authenticity in popular music*. New York: W. W. Norton, 2007.
Baudrillard, Jean. *Simulacra and Simulation*. Ann Arbor, MI: University of Michigan Press, 1994.
Benjamin, Walter. "The Work of Art in the Age of Mechanical Reproduction" in *Illuminations*, edited by Hannah Arendt. London: Fontana, 1968, 216–252.
Berman, Stuart. "The Connection is Made: Elastica Goes M.I.A." *Pitchfork*, February 26, 2015. https://pitchfork.com/features/article/9602-the-connection-is-made-elast ica-goes-mia/
Breihan, Tom. "M.I.A. and the Double Standard of MTV Censorship," *The Village Voice*, December 18, 2007.
Brewster, Bill and Frank Broughton, *Last Night a DJ Saved My Life*. New York: Grove Press, 2000.
Born, Georgina. "On musical Mediation: Ontology, Technology and Creativity." *Twentieth-Century Music* 2, no. 1 (2005): 7–36.
Davies, Hugh. "A history of sampling." *Organised sound* 1, no. 1 (April 1966): 3–11.
Detrick, Ben. "The Dirty Heartbeat of the Golden Age," *The Village Voice*, November 6, 2007. www.villagevoice.com/2007/11/06/the-dirty-heartbeat-of-the-golden-age/
Dolan, Jon. "Deconstructing M.I.A." *Spin*, February 6, 2012. www.spin.com/2012/02/ deconstructing-mia/
FADER. "Video+Interview: MIA, 'Jimmy.'" *FADER*, August 7, 2007. www.thefader. com/2007/08/07/video-interview-mia-jimmy
Feld, Steven and Annemette Kirkegaard. "Entangled Complicities in the Prehistory of 'World Music'; Poul Rovsing Olsen and Jean Jenkins Encounter Brian Eno and David Byrne in the Bush of Ghosts." *Popular Musicology Online*, 2010, www.popu lar-musicology-online.com/issues/04/feld.html
Gilby, Paul. "The Sound on Sound guide to samplers." *Sound on Sound* (November 1987): 34–40.
Goodwin, Andrew. "Sample and hold: pop music in the digital age of reproduction." *Critical Quarterly* 30, no. 3 (1988): 34–49.

Guilbault, Kristy. "'It's Amazing How It Stood The Test of Time': M.I.A. On 'Paper Planes' 11 Years Later." *National Public Radio*, October 4, 2018. www.npr.org/2018/10/04/652687578/it-s-amazing-how-it-stood-the-test-of-time-m-i-a-on-paper-planes-11-years-later

Haddad, Candice. "Immigration, Authorship, Censorship and Terrorism: The Politics of M.I.A.'s US Crossover." In *In the Limelight and Under the Microscope: Forms and Functions of Female Celebrity*, edited by .Su Holmes and Diane Negra. New York: Continuum Books, 2011, 280–302.

Hale, Andreas. "M.I.A. Wrestles with Sundance Doc 'MATANGI / MAYA / M.I.A.': 'It's not the Film That I Would Have Made," *Billboard*, January 25, 2018. www.billboard.com/articles/news/8096118/matangi-maya-mia-interview-sundance-documentary

Harkins, Paul. "Microsampling: From Akufen's Microhouse to Todd Edwards and the Sound of UK Garage." In M*usical Rhythm in the Age of Digital Reproduction*, edited by Anne Danielsen, 177–94. London: Routledge, 2010,

Herman, B. D. "Scratching out Authorship: Representations of the Electronic Music DJ at the Turn of the 21st Century." *Popular Communication* 4, no. 1 (2006): 21–38.

Hirschberg, Lynn. "M.I.A.'s Agitprop Pop." *The New York Times Magazine*, May 25, 2010. www.nytimes.com/2010/05/30/magazine/30mia-t.html

Hogan, Marc. "M.I.A. vs. the System: A Complete Timeline of Her Controversies." *Pitchfork*, May 26, 2016. https://pitchfork.com/thepitch/1165-mia-vs-the-system-a-complete-timeline-of-her-controversies/

Jameson, Fredric. *Postmodernism, or the Cultural Logic of Late Capitalism*. Durham, NC: Duke University Press, 1991.

Katz, Mark. *Capturing Sound: How Technology Has Changed Music*. Berkeley: University of California Press, 2004.

Loveridge, Steve, dir. *Matangi/Maya/M.I.A.* New York: Cinereach, 2018.

Luta, Primus. "The Blue Notes of Sampling." *SoundStudies* (blog), (n.d.). https://soundstudiesblog.com/2014/04/07/the-blue-notes-of-sampling/

McNamee, David. "Hey, what's that sound: Sampler." *The Guardian*, September 28, 2009. www.theguardian.com/music/2009/sep/28/whats-that-sound-sampler

Miller, Alex. "Mia: Kala." *NME*, September 6, 2007.

Moayeri, Lily. "Out on a Whim." *EM*, September 1, 2007.

NPR. "The 200 Greatest Songs by 21st Century Women+."*National Public Radio*, July 30, 2018. www.npr.org/2018/07/30/627400055/turning-the-tables-the-200-greatest-songs-by-21st-century-women-part-10

Overton, Matt. "Groove is in the art." *Future Music* 68 (April 1998): 20–24.

Pareles, Jon. "Digital Technology Changing Music." *New York Times*, October 16, 1986.

People. "Rapper M.I.A. Says Pregnancy Makes Her 'Less Angry'." *People*, December 2, 2008. https://people.com/celebrity/rapper-m-i-a-says-pregnancy-makes-her-less-angry/

Peterson, R. A. *Creating Country Music: Fabricating authenticity*. Chicago: University of Chicago Press, 1997.

Phillips, Charlie. "Matangi/Maya/MIA review—combative musician shows she is director of own life." *The Guardian*, January 24, 2018. www.theguardian.com/film/2018/jan/24/matangi-maya-mia-review-musician-film-tamil-sri-lanka-sundance

Powers, Ann. "Third World Beats." *Los Angeles Times*, August 20, 2007. www.latimes. com/archives/la-xpm-2007-aug-20-et-mia20-story.html

RIAA. "Gold & Platinum – RIAA." *RIAA*. www.riaa.com/gold-platinum/?tab_act ive=default-award&ar=M.I.A.&ti=Paper+Planes#search_section

Rollefson, J. Griffith. *Flip the Script: European Hip Hop and the Politics of Postcoloniality*. Chicago: University Of Chicago Press, 2017.

Saha, Anamik. "Locating MIA: 'Race', commodification and the politics of production." *European Journal of Cultural Studies* 15, no. 6 (2012): 736–52.

Sawyer, R. Keith and Stacy DeZutter. "Distributed creativity: How collective creations emerge from collaboration." *Psychology of Aesthetics, Creativity and the Arts* 3, no. 2 (2009): 81–92.

Schafer, R. Murray. *The Tuning of the World*. New York: A. A. Knopf, 1977.

Schwartz, Hillel. *The Culture of the Copy: Striking Likenesses, Unreasonable Facsimiles*. New York: Zone Books, 1996.

Siddiqi, Asif. "Technology, Transcultural Idioms, and the Question of Authenticity: Brian Eno and David Byrne in the Studio." In *Creativity: Technology and Music*, edited by Hans-Joachim Braun and Susan Schmidt Horning,187–207. New York: Peter Lang, 2012.

Swash, Rosie. "The SP-1200 sampler changes everything." *The Guardian*, June 12, 2011. www.theguardian.com/music/2011/jun/13/music-sampler-sp-1200

Thomson, Paul. "M.I.A. Confronts the Haters," *Pitchfork*, August 3, 2007, https:// pitchfork.com/news/27349-mia-confronts-the-haters/.

Weems, Lisa. "Refuting 'Refugee Chic': Transnational Girl(hood)s and the Guerilla Pedagogy of M.I.A." *Feminist Transformations* 26, no. 1 (Spring 2014): 115–142.

Winner, Langdon. *The Whale and the Reactor: A Search for Limits in an Age of High Technology*. Chicago, IL: University of Chicago Press, 1986.

Index

Printed in Great Britain
by Amazon

51420253R10172